BUTLER'S
LIVES OF THE SAINTS

NEW

FULL EDITION

MARCH

BUTLER'S
LIVES OF THE SAINTS

NEW FULL EDITION

Patron
H. E. CARDINAL BASIL HUME, O.S.B.
Archbishop of Westminster

BUTLER'S LIVES OF THE SAINTS

NEW
FULL EDITION

MARCH

Revised by
TERESA RODRIGUES, O.S.B.

BURNS & OATES

THE LITURGICAL PRESS
Collegeville, Minnesota

First published 1999 in Great Britain by
BURNS & OATES
Wellwood, North Farm Road,
Tunbridge Wells, Kent TN2 3DR

First published 1999 in North America by
THE LITURGICAL PRESS
St John's Abbey, Collegeville,
Minnesota 56321

ISBN 0 86012 252 2   Burns & Oates
ISBN 0-8146-2379-4   The Liturgical Press

The emblems appearing at the foot of some pages are taken from W. Ellwood Post,
Saints, Signs and Symbols: A Concise Dictionary. © Copyright 1962, 1974 by
Morehouse Publishing, with the permission of the publishers.

Library of Congress Catalog Card Number: 95-81671

Typeset by Search Press Limited
Printed in the United States of America

CONTENTS

(Entries in capital letters indicate that the feast or saint is commemorated throughout the Roman Catholic Church with the rank of Solemnity, Feast, Memorial, or Optional Memorial, according to the 1969 revised Calendar of the Latin [Roman] Rite of the Catholic Church, published in the Roman Missal of 1970, or that the saint is of particular importance for the English-speaking world. These entries are placed first on their dates. All others are in chronological order. The paragraph at the end of each day headed "*R.M.*" lists those saints and blessed who appear in the new Roman Martyrology but are not given an entry in this volume.)

Contents

PREFACE

At the close of his biography of St Margaret Clitherow, John Mush, her spiritual director, addressed a series of rhetorical questions to those who had condemned her: "You chose [for the day of her death] the 25th of March, wherein all true Christians celebrate with great solemnity the most gracious Annunciation of our blessed Lady, the Mother of God. Was not this the first day of the creation of the world, as most of yourselves hold opinion? Was not this day man formed and endued with life, as many think . . . ? Was not man's redemption finished by Christ upon the Cross this same day, as many judge? Was not this day, as it were, the midst of the time called in Christ's Church *Tempus Passionis?* Nay, was it not Friday also wherein all Christendom celebrateth the memory of Christ's death and piteously lamenteth his pains suffered this day for our offences?"

John Mush highlights here the unique character of the month of March. The official spring equinox on the 25th was thought to be the day the earth was created, but it was also the day, according to Tertullian, Hippolytus, Augustine, and some ancient calendars, when Christ was believed both to have begun his earthly existence and to have ended it on the cross. Unscientific as they may be, these assumptions were still current in the sixteenth century. However, John Mush's rhetoric takes its cue from the concrete fact that Margaret's martyrdom took place on 25 March, Friday in Passion Week according to the old-style calendar then in use in England, Good Friday in those places where the Gregorian calendar was followed. Beyond that, in this impressive conflation of events from the creation of the world to its re-creation, he is signalling to those who would hear that Margaret's martyrdom—and it may be added, every Christian martyrdom, indeed, the life of every Christian who has stayed the course—is caught up into an infinitely greater movement far transcending the particularities of the situation that occasioned it. God foresaw the irruption of sin within creation and countered its power by the promise of redemption. The arms of Christ's cross—in the words of Pseudo-Hippolytus, "the foundation of the world, binding-force of the cosmos"[1]—have ceaselessly supported creation. When the Son accepted our humanity and the Virgin pronounced her *fiat* at the Annunciation, their consent entailed, however distantly, the cross and its culmination on Calvary. To suffer evil with love, and so to overcome it, is the divine response to sin. Christ's lovers cannot do other than he did; it is thus they come to share in his resurrection.

This volume does not include entries on the liturgical celebration of Christ's passion and resurrection, which sometimes falls in March. This work is devoted rather to the lives of saints, whose holiness his redemption made possible. As will be seen in the entry on the feast of the Annunciation, the Church had been reluctant at first to introduce even this celebration, fearing that it would detract from the Lenten liturgy. The Calendar of 1969 is marked by the same reluctance; there are only nine celebrations listed, the Annunciation (25th), the feast of St Joseph (19th), and memorials of seven outstanding saints: St Casimir of Poland (4th), the martyrs Perpetua and Felicity (7th), St John of God (8th), St Frances of Rome (9th), St Patrick, apostle of Ireland (17th), St Cyril of Jerusalem (18th), and the apostle of Peru, St Turibius of Mogrovejo (23rd). They come from countries the whole world over and span the centuries from New Testament times to the opening years of the seventeenth. To these must be added the monk-bishops SS Chad of Lichfield (2nd) and Cuthbert of Lindisfarne (20th) as of special interest to the English-speaking world. Cuthbert's Lives are generally too stereotyped to be convincing, but his popularity as northern England's most famous saint endures. Like the cult of St Patrick, his persists although we have so little contemporary information on either of them.

These and the other saints who appear in this volume are listed in the Roman Martyrology for March on the day of their death. They vary in importance, whether because of their influence, their holiness, or merely because their lives are more fully recorded than others. Considerable space is allotted to St Eulogius and the many martyrs of Córdoba (11th), who are dealt with as a homogeneous group. They are concentrated in a short span of time, react to the same exterior circumstances, and are strongly influenced by their immediate martyr-predecessors. As in some instances of persecution—here, a mild but persistent religious oppression—there are those who opt for a *modus vivendi* with the oppressors and those who see their loyalty to Christ as requiring an attitude of confrontation, even to the point of martyrdom. How far such an attitude is a matter of temperament is difficult to judge. The English martyrs were more circumspect, if one may so speak, not seeking martyrdom, yet bearing it bravely when it had to be suffered—but the persecution they endured was active, invasive, and pursued to the death. For them martyrdom was not an option to be taken up or set aside but an ever-present possibility.

Two outstanding martyrs of the Protestant Reformation occurring in the month of March, the already mentioned St Margaret Clitherow (25th) and the Jesuit St John Ogilvie (10th), seem to require ample treatment, the one because justice could not be done to her in a general account of the Forty Martyrs, the other because he is Scotland's own hero. Ogilvie's trials are generously quoted to give a direct impression of his invincible faith, keen mind, wit, and humour.

March is not wanting in mystics: Bd Joanna-Maria Bonomo from Bassano in Italy (1st); St Colette of Corbie (6th); the little-known St Teresa Margaret Redi, so like St Thérèse of Lisieux (7th); St Catherine of Bologna (9th); St Catherine of Vadstena, daughter of St Bridget of Sweden (24th); the two attractive Eastern saints, Symeon the New Theologian (12th) and Stephen of

Mar Saba (31st), who introduce into this constellation of Western saints the Orthodox sensitivity to the transforming presence and action of the Holy Spirit; and the Lebanese Bd Rebecca Al Rayes (23rd). Precocious signs of sanctity make their appearance in some of these lives. The sixteen-year-old Catherine of Bologna resolves to forgive her enemies and to honour those who persecute her—one wonders who these might possibly be, but over the years she would come to grips with the demand for total generosity: "If you would have all, you must give all." Within her community, divided on the question of their religious identity, there would be hostility if not enmity. What is impressive in saints called by God at a very early age is their fidelity to a youthful vision, however imperfectly grasped at the outset. Symeon the New Theologian practically vaults from the status of novice to that of abbot, so that when he is addressing the community he seems sometimes to be rehearsing the resolutions taken in his novitiate, and indeed to have remained locked within his understanding of an individual spiritual experience, but the end of his life is bathed in the light of a universal charity. He himself explains that the difference between the saints and those who regard the programme he advocated as impossible is that the saints keep their will fixed on God.

March has a fair share of founders and foundresses of religious Congregations: Bd Angela Guerrero (Sisters of the Cross; 2nd); Bd Teresa Verzeri (Daughters of the Sacred Heart; 3rd); Bd Katharine Drexel (Sisters of the Blessed Sacrament; 3rd); St John of God (Brothers Hospitallers; 8th); St Frances of Rome (Oblates of Tor de' Specchi; 9th); Bd Marie-Eugènie Milleret (Religious of the Assumption; 10th); Bd Aloysius Orione (Little Work of Divine Providence; 12th); Bd James Cusmano (Missionary Servants of the Poor; 14th); St Louise de Marillac (Sisters of Charity; 15th); Bd Francis Palau y Quer (Missionary Carmelites; 20th); Bd Benedicta Frassinello (Benedictine Sisters of Providence; 21st); and St Leonard Murialdo (Congregation of St Joseph; 30th). They range over three centuries of the Church's existence, come from four countries and from every class of society. Their foundations are as diverse as the needs they strove to meet, and their inspired work is carried on to this day.

Marcel Callo (19th), a twenty-four-year-old victim of Hitler's concentration camps, is representative of the many who perished in them rather than abandon their religious principles and practice. His youth makes his case particularly poignant and is a reminder that every age is capable, under grace, of heroism.

Nivard Kinsella, of the abbey of Roscrea in Ireland, wrote for his Cistercian brethren a short reflection on the absence of recall in present-day liturgy of the lives of the heroes of our faith:

It is in its way an astonishing fact that we are no longer telling the stories of the saints in the liturgy. The Roman Breviary is the most widely used prayer book in the Christian world and it is totally lacking in any account of the saints, other than the few lines at the beginning of the office of the saint's day, which we are told should NOT be read in the liturgy. Never before in history have we had such good historical scholarship in the Church; never before have we been less in danger from the legendary and the imaginary. The psychology of the saints has been studied extensively in this century, the philosophy of religion has been written about at length, and the sociology of religion and holiness and of canonization itself have been discussed and explained at length. But we have now reached a state of things in the liturgy where the one thing that is never done is to tell the stories of the saints. I am convinced that in this way we are producing a spiritual wasteland, full of ideas about God and nothing about people. This is not Christianity. Cardinal Newman (himself a saint) said, "The saints are the proper and true evidence of the God of Christianity."

If we do not tell their stories we cannot know them. If we do not know them we cannot hear them speak to us and give us the prophetic word of judgment about our own lives. And if they do not speak to us there is little point in saying in the preface [of the Mass] that God gives us their friendship and inspires us by their lives. How can we be inspired by something we do not know?[2]

We may not be able to re-design the official liturgy of the Church in order to redress the situation Prior Nivard so tellingly describes, but we may hope that these revised volumes of the *Lives of the Saints* will cause the wasteland to rejoice once more and bloom.[3]

Unless otherwise noted, translations of extracts from Passions and Lives are my own, made from texts printed in standard reference works. My thanks are due in the first place to my own community for allowing me the time to work on this book, and to those who read the MS and gave me their advice and suggestions. My thanks are due also to Paul Burns, the managing editor of the series, for his attentiveness and help; to consultants David Farmer, Henry Wansborough, O.S.B., and Gerard McGinty, O.S.B., for reading through some of my texts; and, last but not least, to our present chaplain, Fr Geoffrey Scott, O.S.B., for patiently ferrying back and forth from the Douai library the volumes I could not find in our own.

Feast of the Transfiguration, 1997
Dame Teresa Rodrigues, O.S.B.

1. P. Nautin, *Une homélie inspirée du Traité sur le Pâque d'Hippolyte*, S.C., 27 (1950). Cf also St Irenaeus, *Adversus Haereses* 5, 18, 3, where he speaks of the Word already invisibly stamped on the created universe in the form of a cross since he sustains it by his power and rules it by his providence, from which it follows that he must necessarily be displayed visibly on the wood of the cross. A. Rousseau *et al.*, *Irenée de Lyon: Contre les Hérésies*, S.C., 152, 153 (1969).
2. Nivard Kinsella, O.C.S.O, "A Spiritual Wasteland," *Hallel*, 21, 2 (1996), pp. 120-6.
3. Isa. 35:1

Abbreviations and Short Forms

A.A.S.	*Acta Apostolicae Sedis, Commentarium officiale.* Rome, 1908-.
AA.SS.	*Acta Sanctorum.* 64 vols. Antwerp, also Rome and Paris, 1643- (* after a page reference refers to appendices; page and volume numbers vary in different editions.).
AA.SS.O.S.B.	L. d'Achéry and J. Mabillon (eds.). *Acta Sanctorum Ordinis Sancti Benedicti,* 9 vols. Paris, 1668-1701.
A.C.M.	H. Musurillo, S.J. *Acts of the Christian Martyrs.* Oxford, 1972.
Anal.Boll.	*Analecta Bollandiana* (1882-).
Anstruther	G. Anstruther, O. P. *The Seminary Priests.* 4 vols. Ware, Ushaw, and Great Wakering, 1968-77.
Bede, *H.E.*	The Venerable Bede. *Historia Ecclesiastica.* Various editions.
Bibl.SS.	*Biblioteca Sanctorum.* 12 vols. Rome, 1960-70; Suppl. 1, Rome, 1987.
C.F.S.	*Capuchin Franciscan Sacramentary.*
C.W.S.	Classics of Western Spirituality, New York, 1977-.
D.A.C.	*Dictionnaire d'Archéologie chrétienne et de Liturgie.* 15 vols. F. Cabrol and H. Leclerq (eds.) (1907-50).
Dan-Marrou	J. Daniélou and H. Marrou. *The Christian Centuries.* 3 vols. (1964, 1969, 1978).
D.C.B.	W. Smith and H. Wace (eds.). *Dictionary of Christian Biography.* 4 vols. London 1877-87.
D.H.G.E.	A. Baudrilliart (ed.). *Dictionnaire d'Histoire et de Géographie Ecclésiastique.* Paris, 1912-.
Dict.Sp.	M. Viller *et al. Dictionnaire de spiritualité.* Paris, 1937.
D.T.C.	A. Vacant, A. Mangenot, and E. Amann (eds.). *Dictionnaire de Théologie Catholique.* 15 vols. Paris, 1903-50.
Euseb., *H.E.*	Eusebius of Caesarea. *Historia Ecclesiastica.* Various editions.
Fl-Martin	Fliche and Martin (eds.). *Histoire de l'Eglise.* 24 vols. 1946-.
Healy	J. Healy. *Ireland's Ancient Schools and Scholars* (1893).
H.S.S.C.	F. Chiovaro (ed.). *Histoire des Saints et de la Sainteté Chrétienne.* 12 vols. Paris 1972-.

Jedin–Dolan	H. Jedin and J. Dolan (eds.). *History of the Church.* Eng. trans., 10 vols. London and New York, 1968-81. The full translation of *Handbuch der Kirchengeschichte,* with ample bibliographies up to mid-1960s.
J.T.S.	*Journal of Theological Studies.* 1900-.
K.S.S.	A. P. Forbes (ed.). *Kalendars of Scottish Saints* (1872).
Léon	*Lives of the Saints and Blessed of the Three Orders of St Francis* (1885).
L.E.M.	E. H. Burton and J. H. Pollen (eds.). *Lives of the English Martyrs.* Second series, on the martyrs declared Venerable 1583-8. London, 1915.
M.G.H.	G. H. Pertz *et al.* (eds.). *Monumenta Germaniae Historiae, Scriptores.* 64 vols. Hanover, 1839-1921. Sub-series include *Auctores Antiquissimi, Epistolae Selectae,* and *Scriptores Rerum Merovingicarum.*
M.M.P.	R. Challoner. *Memoirs of Missionary Priests.* New ed. by J. H. Pollen. London, 1924.
M.S.K.	Committee for Bicentennial Commemorative Projects of the Catholic Church in Korea. *Lives of 103 Martyr Saints of Korea.*
N.C.E.	*New Catholic Encyclopedia.* 14 vols. New York, 1967.
N.S.B. 1	T. Lelièvre. *100 Nouveaux Saints et Bienheureux, de 1963 à 1984.* Paris, 1985.
N.S.B. 2	T. Lelièvre. *Nouveaux Saints et Bienheureux, de 1985 à 1988.* Paris, 1990.
O.D.C.C.	F. L. Cross and E. A. Livingstone (eds.). *The Oxford Dictionary of the Christian Church.* 2d ed. Oxford, 1974; 3d ed. 1997.
O.D.S.	D. H. Farmer. *The Oxford Dictionary of Saints.* 3d ed. Oxford, 1992; 4th ed. 1997.
P.G.	J. P. Migne (ed.). *Patrologia Graeca.* 112 vols. Paris, 1857-66.
P.L.	J. P. Migne (ed.). *Patrologia Latina.* 221 vols. Paris, 1844-64.
S.C.	*Sources Chrétiennes.* Paris, 1940-.

IRELAND: Places associated with St Patrick (17th)

ST DAVID OF WALES
A white dove is said to have perched on his shoulder at a synod
of the bishops of Wales, enabling him to be heard.
White dove, gold nimbus, blue pile, green mount, on silver field.

1

ST DAVID OF WALES, *Bishop* (? 589)

St David, the patron of Wales, is one of the most celebrated of British saints. Unfortunately, there is no contemporary account of his life. All the extant accounts are based on a single biography, that of Rhygyfarch (Ricemarch), son of Bishop Julien of St David's, written about 1090. Rhygyfarch claims to have drawn on old written sources, and that may well be so, but he has also included purely fictional elements.

According to the legend, David (or Dewi in Welsh) was the son of Sant, of a princely family in Ceredigion, and of St Non (3 Mar.), granddaughter of Brychan of Brecknock. He was born perhaps about the year 520. "The place where holy David was educated," says Rhygyfarch, "was called Vetus Rubus [Henfynyw in Cardigan] and he grew up full of grace and lovely to behold. There it was that holy David learnt the alphabet, the psalms, the lessons for the whole year and the divine office, and there his fellow-disciples saw a golden-beaked dove playing at his lips and teaching him to sing the praise of God."

David was ordained priest and afterwards spent several years studying under the Welsh St Paulinus. His biographer describes him founding twelve monasteries in different places, among them Menevia and, less likely, Glastonbury. He himself settled finally in Menevia, where he established the most important of his abbeys. There the community lived a life of extreme austerity, modelled on that of the hermits of the Thebaid. Hard manual labour was obligatory for all. They might not speak without necessity. They lived on bread, vegetables, and salt, and drank only water, sometimes mingled with a little milk—which won for the saint the nickname of *Aquaticus*, or man of water, the inspiration of those Welsh monks whom Gildas criticized as being sometimes more abstemious than Christian. Candidates had to wait at the gate for ten days and be subjected to harsh treatment before admission. A strict vigil was kept from Friday evening to dawn on Sunday, with continuous prayer except for an hour's rest after Saturday Matins.

Gerald of Wales (Giraldus Cambrensis), who wrote a paraphrase of Rhygyfarch, says that St David was the great ornament and example of his age and that he continued to rule his diocese until he was a very old man. He died, according to Geoffrey of Monmouth, in his monastery at Menevia. His last recorded words were, "Be joyful, brothers and sisters. Keep the faith and do the little things you have heard and seen me do."

The cult of St David was approved by Callistus II in 1120, but he is already

1

mentioned in the *Catalogue of Saints of Ireland* (?c. 730) and appears in the Irish martyrology of Tallaght, which must be dated before the year 800. There he is inscribed on 1 March, the traditional day of his death. He also appears written into the Leofric calendar, compiled at Glastonbury about the year 970. Subsequent calendars witness to the spread of his cult to other regions of the south outside Wales. St David is found also in a litany of saints in the tenth-century Salisbury Psalter. By the Middle Ages, devotion to him was well established in the south of England and in the Midlands. In his own country he was certainly a highly popular saint. More than fifty pre-Reformation churches in south Wales are known to have been dedicated to him.

In art St David is represented standing on a mound with a dove on his shoulder—an allusion to the legend that when he was speaking at a synod at Brevi a white dove descended on his shoulder while at the same time the earth on which he stood rose up to form a mound from which his voice could be heard by the whole assembly. In Shakespeare's *Henry V* there is a reference to the practice of Welshmen wearing leeks on St David's day: "an ancient tradition begun upon an honourable respect," but there is no adequate explanation of this tradition.

A. W. Wade-Evans edited the text of Rhygyfarch's Life in *Y Cyrmmrodor*, 24, and published an English translation together with some other relevant documents in *The Life of St David* (1923). The Latin text appears in his *Vitae Sanctorum Britanniae* (1944). The adaptation by Gerald of Wales of Rhygyfarch's Life may be found in vol. 3 of his works in the Rolls Series. See J. Ryan, *Irish Monasticism* (1931) for the connection with St David; S. M. Harris, *St David in the Liturgy* (1940), E. Rhys, *The Life of St David* (1927), and D. Latham, "St David," in *They Built on Rock* (1948) and *The Story of St David* (1952); *O.D.S.* pp. 127-8.

St Felix III (II), *Pope* (492)

Pope St Felix is identified by the Roman Martyrology as Felix III, since it regards the administrator Felix, who merely ruled the Church during the exile of Pope Liberius, as Felix II. He was an ancestor of Pope St Gregory the Great (3 Sept.), who spoke of him appearing to his dying aunt, St Tharsilla (24 Dec.), to summon her to heaven.

He succeeded Pope Simplicius in the year 473 at a time when the East was in turmoil in the aftermath of the Council of Chalcedon. By and large the council was not accepted by the Monophysite East nor even by the Catholic bishops, who had reservations concerning its supposed repudiation of St Cyril of Alexandria (27 June). The disunity that resulted prompted the emperors to intervene to settle the matter by force or coerce the bishops to sign documents emanating from themselves or from one side or the other.

Acacius, patriarch of Constantinople, seemed at first the very bastion of loyalty to Chalcedon, even sending a legate, Talaia, to the court to ensure that the Monophysite Peter the Stammerer should not be appointed to the see of

Alexandria. The court agreed on condition that Talaia should not become personally involved in the dispute. However, when the Catholic patriarch of Alexandria died, Talaia was elected, accepted the election, and was subsequently repudiated by the emperor. He fled to Rome, where he found Pope Simplicius on his death-bed.

Acacius had by then changed tack and was attempting to bring all the sides together by means of a document called the *Henoticon*, composed by him but issued in the name of Emperor Zeno. It was addressed to the bishops, whom the emperor reassured as to his personal orthodoxy, claiming loyalty to the councils of Nicaea, Constantinople, and Ephesus. It condemned Eutyches, as Chalcedon had done, accepted St Cyril's twelve propositions against Nestorius, but deliberately avoided even a mention of Chalcedon. This was tantamount to a repudiation of the council, and of the Tome of Leo, regarded as the official condemnation of the heresiarch Eutyches.

In Rome Talaia laid formal charges against Acacius, to which Felix III responded by sending an embassy to Constantinople requiring Acacius to answer them. The ambassadors were arrested, their papers confiscated, and they themselves finally won over to the patriarch's side. They not only signed the *Henoticon* but took part in the liturgy at which Acacius pontificated, thus giving the impression that he had won the approval of Rome. A synod of seventy bishops tried and condemned the legates on their return. It also explicitly condemned Acacius and all his supporters. The resulting schism endured for thirty-five uneasy years and was brought to an end only with the accession of Emperor Justin.

Nothing is known of the personal life of St Felix III, but it is clear that he was cast in the mould of his predecessor, St Leo the Great (10 Nov.). Clear-sighted, energetic and practical, he held to the priority of conciliar decisions over against the manipulations of emperor and patriarch. If Chalcedon remains a milestone in the history of christology, due credit must be given to Felix III, who would not permit its decisions to be discounted or dismissed even at the price of a schismatic East.

In the West Felix helped restore the African Church after its long persecution by the Arian Vandals. He died in 492, after a pontificate of almost nine years.

Duchesne, *Liber pontificalis*, 1, pp. 252-3; P. Hughes, *A History of the Church*; Dan-Marrou, 1, pp. 353-8.

St Senan, *Abbot* (Sixth Century)

St Senan of Scattery Island (Inis Cathaigh), Ireland, was the most celebrated of the twenty-two saints who, according to the hagiographer Colgan, bore the name of Senan. The Life preserved for us by this compiler seems to have been written some five or six centuries after the saint's death and follows a formalized pattern of hagiography. Though it may contain some historical elements, the events and miracles recorded read as more legendary than real, but his importance as a monk and founder of monasteries abides in a country where monasticism was highly esteemed from the earliest days of its conversion to Christianity.

Senan was born near Kilrush in County Clare and as a young man looked after his father's cattle. He became a monk under Cassidan and later studied under Notal, abbot of Kilmanagh in Ossory. When Notal decided that it was time for Senan to take over the direction of others he suggested that he set out, relying on God to tell him where he should go.

Senan founded the monasteries of Iniscarra, near Cork; Inis Mor on Canon Island; Mutton Island in Co. Clare; but especially Scattery Island close to his birthplace. This piece of land in the estuary of the river Shannon contains a round tower attributed to him and also a church dedicated to him, part of which is very ancient.

According to the legend, Senan had laid down that no woman should be allowed to land on the island. Cannera, knowing she was about to die and wanting to receive *viaticum* and be buried there, arrived on the shore. Senan met her and would not allow her to proceed further. "If you believe that Christ will receive my soul, why do you reject my body?" she asked. "I do indeed believe," replied the saint, "nevertheless, we do not allow women to come here. Go back to the world and do not bother us. You may be pure in soul, but you are still a woman!" The Irish life of Senan allows Cannera more scope for some display of feminine assertiveness: "God did not become incarnate for men more than for women," she argued. "He did not suffer for men more than he did for women. Heaven is open to both sexes equally. In fact, Christ did not in the least refuse the companionship of holy women who ministered to him and his disciples." Finally, she concluded, all she wanted was to be given the Sacrament while she was still alive and when dead a portion of earth on the shore to bury her body. Senan had to agree. She died, and the biographer remarks that for the brethren it was a rather unusual funeral.

The St Senan venerated in Cornwall seems to have been a different person.

The life of St Senan is to be found in Colgan's *Acta Sanctorum Hiberniae*, reproduced and re-edited by the Bollandists, *AA.SS.*, Mar., 1, pp. 759-78. There is an Irish life preserved in the *Book of Lismore* (ed. Whitley Stokes), in the *Anecdota Oxoniensia* (1890). See also Gleeson in the *North Munster Antiquarian Journal* (1940), pp. 14-30; *Anal.Boll.* 66 (1948), pp. 199-230; Kathleen Hughes, *Early Christian Ireland: Introduction to the Sources* (1972); Kathleen Hughes & Ann Hamlin, *Celtic Monasticism* (1981); G. H. Doble, *Saint Senan, Patron of Sennen* (1928); N. Orme (ed.), *Nicholas Roscarrock's Lives of the Saints: Cornwall and Devon* (1992).

St Swithbert, *Bishop* (713)

St Swithbert was one of a band of twelve missionaries who, under the leadership of St Willibrord (7 Nov.), set out in the year 690 to evangelize the German tribes of Friesland—part of present-day Holland.

A Northumbrian by birth, he had gone over to Ireland, like many other Englishmen of his time, in search of a more fervent monastic life. There he had come under the influence of St Egbert (24 Apr.), another Englishman, who dreamed of travelling to the Continent to convert the Saxons, as St Wilfrid (12 Oct.) had attempted previously with some success. Egbert had indeed once assembled a group of missionaries and prepared ship in order to set out but was prevented by what he interpreted as a divine command to desist. In his place he sent Wigbert, who, however, returned home after two years. The country had completely reverted to heathenism under its leader, Radbod, and he was unable to make any headway.

Undaunted, Egbert planned a second expedition. This stood a much better chance of success, as Pepin II had by then ousted Radbod from part of Frisia. The missionaries landed at the mouth of the Rhine and, according to Alcuin, made their way as far as Utrecht. Swithbert worked mainly in the southern part of Holland, the northern portion of Brabant, and the provinces of Guelderland and Cleves. In the meantime Willibrord had left for Rome to obtain the pope's sanction for opening this new mission field. The group of missionaries left behind, seeing that Swithbert's efforts had met with success, chose him to be consecrated bishop, for he was "a modest and sober man outwardly and, inwardly, humble in spirit."

Swithbert returned to England seeking consecration. Theodore of Canterbury had died, and his successor, Bertwald, was out of the country for his own consecration. Wilfrid, then in exile in Mercia, consecrated his fellow-countryman, thus providing the region, where he himself had initiated the work, with its first bishop. On his return Swithbert planned to push further into the country, so he settled the churches he had founded and left them in the care of his companions. He travelled up the right bank of the Rhine and converted a considerable number of the Bructeri in southern Westphalia. However, the Saxons subsequently overran the territory and occupied it. The converts were dispersed. Swithbert, finding his work undone, withdrew into Frankish territory, where he resolved to retire from directly pastoral work and prepare for death. Pepin, at the request of Plectrudis, his wife, gave him a small island on the Rhine, where he built a monastery that flourished for many years. The town of Kaiserswerth (six miles north of Düsseldorf) grew up around the monastery. (It is now joined to the mainland, as a channel of the Rhine has changed its course.) Swithbert died in his abbey around 713, and has ever since been held in great veneration in Holland and the other places where he worked.

The movement in which St Swithbert took part initiated a century of English influence on the Continent. It contributed to the forging or re-forging of a relationship between the Frankish or Germanic Churches and the Roman See that was to have tremendous spiritual, administrative, and political repercussions in the centuries to come. The English contribution, through the migration of monks and ecclesiastics to the Continent, is seen at its most gracious in the collaboration with Charlemagne in the work of education throughout the empire.

St Swithbert is joint patron of St Peter's, Kaiserswerth, where his relics, which were found in 1626, are still preserved and honoured. Many miracles were ascribed to him, and he is invoked in cases of angina. He is sometimes spoken of as St Swithbert the Elder to distinguish him from St Swithbert the Younger, bishop of Werden.

Bede, *H.E.*, 5, 9-11; Alcuin, *De Sanctis Ebor.* 5, p. 1073 in Jaffé's edition. A panegyric and hymn by Radbod, bishop of Utrecht, may be found in *P.L.*, 122, 547-59. Cf also *AA.SS.*, Mar., 1, pp. 67-87; and Bouterwek, *Der Apostel des Bergischen Landes*; *Bibliotheca Hagiographica Latina*, 2, 7939-42; Van der Essen, *Etude sur les saints mérovingiens*, pp. 428ff; and W. Levison, *England and the Continent in the Eighth Century* (1946). This author ascribes to Bishop Theutbert of Dorostat the famous fifth-century manuscript of Livy preserved in Vienna and once thought to have belonged to Swithbert.

Bd Christopher of Milan (1484)

Christopher, called the apostle of Liguria because of his great success in evangelizing that part of Italy, received the Dominican habit in Milan early in the fifteenth century. Soon after his ordination he became known as an outstanding preacher. His biographers' record that his sermons, which brought about numerous conversions wherever he went, were always based on the Bible, St Thomas, and the Fathers and that he denounced those preachers who set out to be popular and up-to-date. He travelled untiringly over difficult country in order to preach the gospel. At Taggia, where he was particularly successful, the inhabitants built him a church and monastery, of which he became prior.

One day, as he was watching the people of Castellano dancing in the square, he exclaimed, "Now you are having fun dancing, but trouble will soon be here, and your joy will be changed into sorrow." A few years later the plague carried off most of the inhabitants. He also foresaw the destruction of Triora by the French, and he warned the population of Taggia that they would flee from their city even though no one was pursuing them, and that their river would burst its banks, destroying their property—all of which happened as predicted. He was preaching the Lenten sermons at Pigna when his last illness came on him. He had himself carried to Taggia, where he died. His cult was confirmed in 1875.

Mortier, *Histoire des Maîtres Généraux O.P.*, 4, pp. 371-72, 648; Procter, *Lives of Dominican Saints*, p. 56; Taurisano, *Catalogus Hagiographicus O.P.*, pp. 44-5.

Bd Joanna Maria Bonomo, *abbess* (1606-70)

Maria Bonomo was born on 15 August 1606 in the town of Asiago, capital of *La Reggenza dei Sette Communi* in the region of Lombardy in northern Italy. Her parents, Giovanni Bonomo and Virginia Ceschi di Valsugana, both belonged to the nobility. When she was four years old her father killed a man he suspected of comitting adultery with his wife and was only prevented by Maria from killing Virginia also. He served a short term in prison, and in 1612, when Maria herself was not quite six years old, her mother died.

Three years later Maria was sent to the Poor Clares of Trent for her education. When she was twelve she asked her father's leave to enter the community. This was immediately and emphatically refused, and Giovanni took his daughter away from the convent without further ado. She returned home to face a round of parties and distractions which her father hoped would turn her mind toward marriage. While she had been away at school he had married Luisa Paurinfaint, with whom Maria felt at ease, but their mutual understanding was no match for Giovanni's determination. Two years later a crowd outside the local church propelled Giovanni inside. A Capuchin friar was preaching, publicly reproaching those parents who prevented their children from entering the religious life. The charge went home, and Giovanni told his daughter she might enter if that was still her wish. He begged her only not to go as far as Trent but to remain nearer home. It was finally agreed that she should enter the Benedictine monastery of Saint Jerome in the town of Bassano, where the observance was known to be strict. She was fourteen and a half years old.

A century after the Council of Trent, most monasteries were reformed according to its directives. Very few of the women's monasteries enjoyed the exempt status of the monks, and that only when they belonged to Congregations that embraced both monks and nuns. Monasteries of nuns outside such Congregations found themselves for the most part under the bishops, whose hand might lie heavy on the internal life of the monastery especially when wide-ranging powers were given to a chaplain or a confessor who was the bishop's nominee and rarely a Benedictine monk. Moreover, the office of abbess had little in common with the Rule of St Benedict. To facilitate reform Pope Gregory XIII had laid down that the abbess' term of office should extend for only three years, a period too short to be beneficial and recurring so frequently that the sense of upheaval became endemic. These factors had a preponderant role to play in the new postulant's life.

Maria was clothed as a novice on her fifteenth birthday and given the name of Joanna Maria. A year later, in 1622, she was received for profession by the unanimous vote of the community. She was sixteen, the minimum age allowed by Trent. Parents and friends filled the church for the ceremony on the feast of the Birthday of Our Lady (8 Sept.). To the dismay of the congregation the novice stopped abruptly while reading her chart of profession. She had gone into an ecstasy during which, she was to relate, Our Lord had appeared to her in the company of Our Lady and St Benedict and many other saints and angels.

There followed a period of abundant spiritual consolation, followed in 1623 by one of searing aridity. Beginning in 1631 she began to re-live Christ's passion, often going into and remaining in ecstasy from Thursday until Friday or Saturday. Six years later she is said to have received the stigmata and the grace of mystical marriage. Her ecstasies had so far been kept private, but as they multiplied they would come over her at any time or place and were now known to all. Inevitably, Sr Joanna Maria became a source of division both inside and outside the community. Many thought her the victim of diabolic deception if not possession; in addition the abbess was concerned about the Inquisition. The young nun prayed earnestly to Our Lady that the stigmata might become invisible and her ecstasies manageable. Her prayers were granted. The marks of the stigmata remained but the wounds were no longer open, while her Friday ecstasies were confined to the night hours. She was thus able to take her place in choir and refectory, unnoticed, though no longer unknown. Often she was called to the parlour to see the many people who sought her prayers and advice. For her own guidance she had Don Alviso Salviano as confessor. Initially sceptical himself, he asked her to write an account of all her spiritual experiences. The manuscript was submitted to other theologians, who approved them. Once convinced of the authenticity of her mystical life, Don Alviso became her staunch friend, guide, and father.

For about ten years she was pursued by fear: fear of damnation, fear of mocking devils, evil thoughts, aridity, and obscurity. Unable to eat or sleep, her health began to deteriorate. Eventually she felt herself delivered through the intercession of St Cajetan (7 Aug.), the founder of the Theatines. Don Alviso died soon after. She was able to recover her manuscript, which she promptly burned.

Appointed novice-mistress, a charge that embraced not only the novitiate but also the pupils, Sr Joanna Maria drew more applicants to the monastery than could be accommodated. She was particularly fond of Catherine Miozzi, whom she had helped when she was attacked by doubts concerning her vocation and who eventually entered and became her confidante. Sr Catherine is the chief source of information about Sr Joanna Maria's interior life; having been given access to some of the saint's autobiographical writings, she took notes which have survived. These indicate that the novice-mistress' gift of seeing into the souls of others enabled her to exercise a sure discernment and that her teaching focussed on the virtue of humility as the foremost condition for holiness of life.

Sr Joanna Maria was now well known, and she was besieged by visitors and letters. So great was her longing for solitude that she begged her confessor to let her transfer to the Capuchins, but this was discouraged. A more anguished solitude became her lot as the opposition within the community—restricted to four nuns—hardened into a hostility that went so far as to solicit support among the clergy, including the bishop and his vicar general. In 1643 the vicar general arrived to conduct a canonical visit and to preside over the election of an abbess. Sr Joanna Maria was elected, but the vote was quashed by the vicar general on the grounds that she was not canonically eligible, being under the required age. The community succeeded in getting her elected as assistant to the abbess, but the vicar general then proceeded to tie her hands: she was not to write to people outside except her father, and that but rarely; she could go to the parlour only to see her relatives; she could help the abbess with correspondence on condition that she always state that she was writing in the name of the abbess and never add a personal postscript.

At this point a new confessor was appointed, Dominico de Veglia, an upright, exemplary, self-opinionated, and perhaps unwittingly cruel man, who entered fully into the spirit of the vicar general in his opposition to the visionary. He refused to listen to her if she spoke of herself, snubbed her in private and in public, withheld permission to perform any penance, and chased her out of the confessional. Sr Joanna Maria maintained a respectful attitude toward him. She wrote to her father that she was privileged to suffer and felt no resentment: "The greatest affliction I could undergo is to be without affliction." Communion was now allowed her only twice a year. She wrote again to her father, "I live as it were dying. But I am happy. Resignation to God's will brings me peace. I let everything flow over me like water flowing into the sea." Her father was now one of her most trusted confidants. Under her influence he had gradually turned to God. She was now forbidden to write to him, the prohibition persisting for seven years.

The next election for an abbess became due in 1652, and Sr Joanna Maria was again elected. This time the vicar general could not raise any objections, but the abbess-elect was overwhelmed and wished to refuse. Only after several hours of prayer did she come to see it as the will of God. Her tenure of the abbacy showed that there could be no incompatibility between the highest mystical union with God and practical administration. She proved herself a great reforming abbess in the spirit of the Council of Trent. Persuasion and compassion were her preferred approach in dealing with the community, but her own example counted for more. She was firm in insisting on monastic observance, in encouraging her Sisters in the ways of prayer; she suppressed the worldliness that had found its way into the cloister but knew how to be gentle and compassionate toward every need. Her open-handedness toward the poor moved the cellarer to accuse her of squandering the property of the monastery. This reached the ears of the bishop, who asked for the books to be submitted to him. They showed that the monastery had been renovated, the church restored, all debts paid, the nuns well looked after, and there was money still in reserve.

Her term as abbess came to an end in 1655. As she could not be re-elected for an immediate second term, she was elected to the post of prioress. The vicar general withheld the results of the vote and took the file to the bishop in the expectation that he would quash it, but it was allowed to stand. A new bishop was appointed in 1660, but this changed nothing, as he too was deeply mistrustful of mystics. In 1661 he came to Saint Jerome's to preside over the election of the abbess. The votes were in favour of Abbess Joanna Maria for a second term. The bishop called for another scrutiny, but the result was the same. He then declared the vote null and void. To resolve the impasse, Sr Joanna Maria withdrew her candidacy, opening the way for another candidate, and returned to her life of isolation—she considered that she was still bound by the curia's strictures against visits to the parlour until they should be specifically lifted. A sympathetic abbess may have prevailed on the curia to cancel the prohibitions against Sr Joanna Maria's visits to the parlour, and she resumed her fruitful apostolate.

Elections for the abbess were again due in 1664, and this time there was no interference with the manifest wish of the majority in favour of Sr Joanna Maria. It was to be her second and last term. Under her, Saint Jerome's became a house of fervent prayer and a model of regular observance. Her paean to the virtue of faith was the fruit of a hard fight against every conceivable obstacle: "Without faith, everything is in vain. Faith is the remedy for all evils and trials. Through faith we can surmount every difficulty; without faith, nothing will succeed." Her faith was to be put to the test further still. The diocesan curia had appointed as cellarer one of the nuns still opposed to her, Sr Teresa Fava, to act as a counterweight to the abbess' supposedly imprudent charity. But there was famine in Lombardy; in addition the rich had been drained by the wars against the Turks. The poor came to the monastery to ask for food, and the abbess would not send them away. The last vegetables were to be used to make soup for them. The cellarer was furious, but the next day a carriage drew up to the monastery gate with a plentiful gift of vegetables. Sr Teresa Fava's brother was wounded, and the abbess spared no pains to do what could be done for the victim, but nothing seemed to mollify Sr Teresa.

A new confessor, Don Giovanni Batista Freschi, was appointed in 1667 and proved to be no more accommodating than his predecessors. The abbess had decided to put up an enclosure wall to ensure greater privacy for the community, but the priest thought that pertained to his authority, not hers, and promptly ordered it to be pulled down. He used the confessional to hurl abuse at her so that all the waiting nuns could hear his voice raised in anger. The abbess kept her composure. 1667 saw another election and Abbess Joanna Maria took up the post of prioress once more. In 1670 she became seriously ill, and she died on 1 March. Sr Teresa Fava was the last of the opposition to admit her errors of judgment. She prayed to the saint daily for pardon.

Most of Joanna Maria's writings have been lost, but two treatises on the passion were printed in the seventeenth and eighteenth centuries. Her correspondence with her father has been preserved. Joanna Maria Bonomo was beatified on 9 June 1783. When the monastery was suppressed in 1810, her relics were placed in the parish church of Bassano.

L. Bracco, *Vita della B. Giovanna Maria Bonomo*, 2 vols. (1883; English version, 1886). A shortened version of this by A. du Bourg exists in French, *Une extatique au XVII siècle. La Bienheureuse Jeanne-Marie Bonomo, 1606-1670* (1910); P. Schmidt, *Histoire de l'Ordre de Saint Benoît*, 7, *Les Moniales* (1956); More recent Life by D. M. Giovanna, (1937); *Bibl.SS.*, 3, 346-8.

R.M.
SS Nestor and Tribimaeus, martyrs at Perga, Pamphylia (third century)
St Simplicius, bishop of Bourges, Aquitaine (*c.* 480)
St Albinus, bishop of Angers (550)
St Siviard, abbot of St Cales, region of Le Mans (*c.* 680)
St Leo, apostle of the Baionenses, Gascoigne (ninth century)
St Rudesind, bishop of Cella Nueva, Galicia (977)
St Leo Luke, abbot of Mount Mula, Calabria (*c.* 1000)

ST CHAD
Red and silver sections

2

ST CHAD, *Abbot and Bishop* (672)

Chad came from a close-knit Northumbrian family, of whom four brothers were to become outstanding priests, two of them bishops. A disciple of Aidan (31 Aug.), he presumably spent some time or was educated at Lindisfarne. While still a youth he crossed to Ireland, where he lived as a monk, praying, fasting, and meditating on scripture with the young Egbert as a companion.

At some point, probably on his return to England, Chad was ordained priest. A veil descends on his life until the death in 664 of his brother Cedd (26 Oct.). Historically the two brothers are in many ways inseparable. Preacher of the gospel to the Middle Angles, bishop and apostle of the East Saxons, Cedd founded and ruled the monastery of Lastingham, which he bequeathed to Chad. The new abbot swiftly found himself a political focus. Lastingham had been established because King Aethelwald of Deira wanted a place in southern Northumbria where he could pray during his lifetime and be buried at the end of it. A later king of Deira, Ahlfrith, founded a monastery at Ripon, where Roman customs were introduced. Wishing to have a bishop of his own for his people, he turned to Ripon's abbot, Wilfrid (12 Oct.), and in 664, with the consent of Ahlfrith's father and overlord, Oswiu of Northumbria, sent him to be consecrated bishop in Gaul.

Wilfrid, however, delayed overseas. Perhaps forced by events, notably the death of Tuda, bishop of the Northumbrian people, Oswiu intervened and sent Chad to Kent to be consecrated bishop of the church of York. Did Oswiu intend to rebuff Ahlfrith or was the abbot from Deira's other royal monastery the only obvious alternative in Wilfrid's continuing absence? Whatever the truth, no one disputed Chad's sanctity and qualities of leadership. If Bede's (25 May) praise of "a holy man . . . learned in the Scriptures and zealous in carrying out their teachings" carries weight, the testimony of Wilfrid's biographer, Eddius, that his hero's rival was "a very devout servant of God and remarkable teacher," is compelling.

On his arrival in Kent, Chad found that Archbishop Deusdedit had died. As there was a bishop in the kingdom of the West Saxons, Chad continued his journey and was consecrated by Wine with the assistance of two British bishops of dubious orthodoxy. Chad was probably not yet thirty if Bede is right in stating that he and Egbert, who was to die in 729 at the age of ninety, were both youths together in Ireland. Returning to his native Northumbria, he modelled himself on Aidan and Cedd. He preached the gospel everywhere, making a point of travelling on foot rather than horseback.

Wilfrid meanwhile had returned to Northumbria, found Chad acting as bishop, and retired to his monastery of Ripon. In 669 Theodore of Tarsus (19 Sept.), appointed archbishop of Canterbury in succession to Deusdedit, arrived in England. One of his first actions was to visit every part of the country and to consecrate bishops where they were needed. In Northumbria he upheld Wilfrid's claim to the see of York and told Chad that his consecration had been irregular. Chad replied, "If you consider that I have not been properly ordained, I gladly resign. I never thought myself worthy of the office and agreed to undertake it, though unworthy, only under obedience." Moved by his humility, Theodore supplied what was defective in his episcopal consecration, and Chad retired to Lastingham.

Once again it was not to be for long. Mercia had been without a bishop since the death of Jaruman in 667, and King Wulfhere requested Theodore to appoint a successor. Rather than consecrate a new bishop, the archbishop asked King Oswiu for Chad, who was duly appointed to a diocese extending from Mercia to Lindsey. He ordered the new bishop to ride on horseback whenever he was undertaking a long journey in the service of the gospel. As Chad was inclined to protest, the archbishop, at the age of nearly seventy, settled the matter by lifting him on to a horse himself. Presumably Chad was small and light in build.

The new bishop established his see at Lichfield and near the church built a place where, when free from other duties, he could retire to pray and read with seven or eight other monks. Wulfhere also gave Chad land to found a monastery at Ad Baruae, probably Barrow, in Lindsey. For two and a half years he was an outstanding leader of his flock.

One day in 672, according to Bede, one of his monks, Owini, was outside working when he heard sweet and joyful singing. The sound came nearer, filled the oratory where Chad was at prayer, and after about half an hour returned heavenward. Chad opened the oratory window to summon Owini and told him to fetch the other brothers. He urged them to live in peace with all and to remain faithful to the monastic discipline they had learned from him and his predecessors. Then he announced that his death was drawing near: "The beloved guest who has made it his custom to visit our brothers came to me today, too, and summoned me from this world. Return to the church then and ask the brothers to commend my passing to the Lord."

Seven days later, on 2 March, after receiving the body and blood of the Lord, Chad died of the plague that had already taken many of his people. His old friend Egbert declared that the soul of Cedd was seen descending with a host of angels to escort his brother from this life into heaven. Chad had always borne the day of reckoning in mind. Whenever a high wind arose he would stop what he was doing and invoke God's mercy on the human race. If the wind grew stronger, he would lie prostrate in prayer. If the storm proved violent, or if thunder and lightning broke out, he would go to church and devote himself to prayers and the psalms until the sky cleared. "For," he used to say, "it is God who stirs the air and raises the winds, who makes lightning flash and thunders from heaven, to remind the inhabitants of the earth of that awful day when heaven and earth will flame as he comes on the clouds with great power and majesty to judge the living and the dead. Whenever he raises his hand through the trembling sky as if to strike, but does not yet allow it to fall, these are times when we should beg his mercy and search the depths of our hearts."

Chad was buried near the church of St Mary. Before long his bones were translated to the church of St Peter, on the site of the present Lichfield Cathedral. Miracles were reported in both places, and his cult spread. Above his grave in Bede's time was a wooden coffin in the form of a little house, with an opening in one side through which pilgrims could insert their hands and remove a little dust. It was believed that this dust, added to water, had the power of healing the sick. Chad's name appears in Anglo-Saxon calendars and litanies. Many medieval churches in the Midlands were dedicated to him, as also several wells. Later legend attributes Wulfhere's foundation of monasteries and endowment of Peterborough to an act of penance laid on him by Chad. The eighth-century manuscript known as the Gospels of St Chad or the Lichfield Gospels (now in Lichfield Cathedral library) was probably associated with the shrine of St Chad only later in its history.

The relics were translated several times after the Norman Conquest. At the Reformation some were saved from destruction. Divided and transferred from one place of custody to another, they were thought to be lost by the early nineteenth century. In 1839, on the site of a chapel dedicated to St Chad, the building of Birmingham's Catholic cathedral began. At the same time six of the bones were discovered in a chest at Aston Hall, near Stone in Staffordshire. When the cathedral was consecrated in 1841 these were placed in a casket above the high altar; in 1931 one, the tibia, was removed to a reliquary in the chapel of St Edward. Archbishop Couve de Murville permitted the relics to undergo osteological analysis and radiocarbon dating. The results of the tests were announced in 1996: the tibia was assigned to the eighth century and the five other bones, those of at least two individuals, to the seventh century. These, now restored to their casket in St Chad's Cathedral, may very well be connected with the seventh-century saint and include relics of St Chad himself, patron of the archdiocese of Birmingham.

The main source is Bede, who obtained his information from the monks of Lastingham, one of whom, Trumberht, was Bede's scripture tutor. See Bede, *H.E.*, 3, 28; 4, 3; J. M. Wallace-Hadrill, *Bede's Ecclesiastical History of the English People, a Historical Commentary* (1988, 1991); B. Colgrave (ed.), *Life of Bishop Wilfrid by Eddius Stephanus* (1927, 1985); C. E. Whiting, *St Chad* (1939); N. Brooks, *The Early History of the Church of Canterbury* (1984); *The History of St Chad's Cathedral, Birmingham* (1904); M. W. Greenslade, *Saint Chad of Lichfield and Birmingham* (1996), gives the carbon-dating report.

St Pontius of Carthage (*c.* 260)

Pontius is known only as the biographer of St Cyprian of Carthage (16 Sept.), whose deacon he was. His *Vita et Passio Cypriani* was both admired by Jerome and prized by Augustine and his community at Hippo. In one of the two references to himself he reveals that he chose to accompany his bishop into exile. Since the edict of Valerian against the Christians was directed at bishops, priests, and deacons, it is noteworthy that Pontius was in a position actually to make a choice. It may be that the proconsul aimed to liquidate the bishops only in the hope that the whole Church of North Africa would thus be too weakened to survive. The narrative suggests that Pontius remained with St Cyprian until the end, actually witnessing his passion.

There is no reason to doubt the basic facts he records concerning the bishop: his vow of chastity prior to Baptism, his concern for the poor, his zeal in forming his flock to the standards of the gospel, for these are mostly substantiated by those writings of Cyprian's that have come down to us. Pontius' aim was to preserve for posterity the glorious memory of a man of God and a martyr to Christ. His work is a panegyric rather than a biography in our sense.

It is also revealing of the writer. Pontius himself aspired to the holiness he found in his model. The cry of anguish at missing martyrdom himself rings true: "From the very first day he allowed me to live with his household as a voluntary exile. O, why was I not thought worthy to share his sufferings as well?" And at the end of his description of the martyrdom he speaks of how he is torn between joy at Cyprian's victory and disappointment at his own exclusion. "I am so happy, so exceedingly happy for the glory he has gained, yet I am more aggrieved than glad because I am left behind." There is, however, no trace of Pontius suffering martyrdom himself in this or in any subsequent persecution.

This Pontius must not be identified with the martyred Pontius whose feast is observed on 14 May.

Harnack (ed.), *Das Leben Cyprianus von Pontius*, in the series Texte und Untetsuchungen, vol. 39.

Bd Charles the Good, *Martyr* (1081-1127)

Charles, count of Flanders and Amiens, was the son of St Canute, king of Denmark (10 July), who was slain in 1086. Charles, but five years old at the time, was then taken by his mother, Adèle, to the court of her father, Count Robert of Flanders. There he learned to read and write, and he is known to have owned a Psalter, which he used.

When Robert joined the Crusade in Palestine, his nephew accompanied him and covered himself with glory and scars. Charles also helped his uncle fight against the English. Robert was succeeded by his son Baldwin VII, who, having no children, designated his cousin Charles as his heir and also arranged his marriage with Margaret, daughter of Count Renault of Clermont. Finally, he associated him with himself in the government of Flanders, so that when he died the populace, who had learned to know Charles and esteem him, were ready to accept his rule.

There were, however, several feudal lords who thought they could increase their own power by taking advantage of the newcomer, and for several years Charles had to face turbulent resistance to his authority. Once these lords had been finally vanquished or brought to sue for peace, he set himself to improve both the material and moral standards of his people. Such was his dedication to them that he refused to accept the position of emperor on the death of Henry V, nor would he accept the kingdom of Jerusalem. He showed deference toward the authorities of the Church and was especially concerned to set them free from the sort of exactions other princes used to impose. He had such a horror of blasphemy that any member of his household who swore by God's name was punished by a fast of forty days on bread and water. One of his humane regulations forbade the taking away of a child without the consent of its parents.

Charles' overriding concern was for the poor. Reproached for unfairly espousing their cause against the rich, he replied, "It is because I know the needs of the poor and I know the pride of the rich." There was widespread famine following the terribly severe winter of 1125 and the resulting poor harvests of 1126. The count fed a hundred poor men every day at Bruges in each of his castles and, at Ypres, distributed 7,800 two-pound loaves in one day. He gave away clothes and shoes daily and reprimanded the inhabitants of Ghent for allowing men to die at their gates. He forbade the brewing of beer in order to conserve grain for the poor and fixed the price of wine. While famine remained likely, he ordered the land to be sown two thirds with grain and one third with fast-growing peas or beans to ensure a supply of vegetables.

His concern lest the poor be exploited by the rich led eventually to his death at the hands of a Saxon family that had gained power and wealth by criminal means. Erembald was a serf who fought for Baudrand, magistrate of Bruges. On a dark night he threw his master into the river Escaut and subsequently married the widow, accomplice to the crime. With money he obtained from her, he bought the post of governor of Bruges. Charles discovered that Erembald's sons had bought up grain and were hoarding it in order to resell it at higher prices, and he and his almoner Tancmar obliged them to yield up their stores, thus providing them with cause for resentment. On the feast of the Epiphany, 1126, Charles had invited a few friends to celebrate the feast. The presence of the abbot of Saint-Bertin surprised the count, who asked him how he could abandon his community on such a solemn feast. The abbot explained that he had come to lodge a complaint against Lambert, son of Erembald, who was withholding the tithes due to the monastery. Charles promptly threatened Lambert and his brothers with confiscation of all their goods if the abbot's grievances were not met that very evening. This added fuel to the fire.

The profiteers carried out their revenge, targeting Charles' almoner. Lambert's son, Borchard, took Tancmar's château and killed his uncle and his daughter. Charles, who had been away, learned of the disorders on his return and called the barons in Ypres to pass judgment on Borchard. Since blood had been shed on both sides, it was decreed that only Borchard's dwelling should be burnt to the ground. Some Flemings then came to Charles to ask for clemency for the rest of the family. Seeing that they could not move him, they retired to lay their plans to assassinate the count the following day.

Charles used to go barefoot every morning to pray before Mass in the church of St Donatian, in the gallery adjoining his palace. On this Lenten morning, 2 March 1127, his servants had dispersed in the nave while he prayed before the altar of Our Lady, and there he was set upon by the conspirators: his arm was cut off at a first blow and his head split open by Borchard.

The cult of the saint was approved in 1883. Representations of Charles the Good usually contain baskets of bread to recall his generosity to the poor and an axe, the instrument used in his martyrdom. His body still rests in the church of St Donatian at Bruges.

AA.SS., Mar., 1, pp. 152-218, gives contemporary biographies by Walter, archdeacon of Thérouanne, and Galbert, a notary at Bruges. Further materials are also contributed by other chroniclers, *e.g.,* Abbot Suger. See also F. L. Ganshof, *La Flandre sous ses premiers comtes* (1943) for the background of politics; J. B. Ross, "Rise and Fall of a twelfth-century clan," *Speculum* 34 (1959), pp. 367-90; S. M. de Smet in *D.H.G.E.,* 12, pp. 483-6; *Bibl.SS.,* 3, 794-7.

Bd Angela of the Cross, *Foundress* (1846-1932)

Angela (Angelita, "little angel") Guerrero Gonzalez was born on 30 January 1846 in Seville, Spain. She was one of fourteen children, of whom only six survived infancy. Her mother had a special devotion to Our Lady of Sorrows, to the mystery of the Assumption, and like every good native of Seville, to the *Virgen de los Reyes.* Angelita's father died when she was still very young.

She had a happy and normal childhood, though without much schooling. Later, the intensity of her spiritual experience would burst the constraints of this lack of schooling, as is shown by the fact that more than four thousand of her letters are extant as well as other writings. She had to learn a trade in order to help support the family. In 1862 her mother placed her with a cobbler in whose workshop a group of young people sewed expensive shoes for the high-society ladies of Seville and for the clergy. Antonia Maldonado, who was in charge, relates that "every Friday Angelita would give away her meal to the poor; at midday she would beg of her companions, for charity's sake, to give her a morsel of bread to add to her own alms." Her penances were already known. Antonia Maldonado also relates that one day they heard a sort of cry upstairs and were stupefied to see Angelita, her face quite serene, in a state of ecstasy, her body remaining suspended above floor level. She told the young girls to go back to the workroom and not to talk about it. An hour later Angelita arrived with an innocent "You let me go on sleeping!" Antonia Maldonado later spoke to Fr Torres Padilla, asking him to interview the young woman. After thinking it over, Angelita decided to talk to him frankly about her religious experiences.

Torres, a native of the Canary Islands, had settled some years previously in the Guadalquivir region and was known in Seville as a holy man and spiritual director. The encounter was important as he was to accompany Angelita on her entire interior journey and advise her on the foundation of her Institute, of which he was appointed director for life. A cultured man and trained theologian who had been an adviser at the First Vatican Council, he respected the personal itinerary of those who sought his direction. On his recommendation Angela tried her vocation as a discalced Carmelite and then with the Sisters of Charity, where her continual sickness put an end to a short-lived attempt. She finally returned home, and it was at this time that she wrote down her interior experiences at some length.

One evening some friends of hers were discussing the good works of a lady of Seville. She gave medicines and money to the poor while counselling resignation and patience; the population in the *barrios* was not appreciative. One of those present remarked, "If this woman were of no use to anybody, of no account, poor, lacking the necessities of life, and at the same time content with her lot and not given to grumbling, then I would regard such a person as a saint." This was the inspiration for Angelita: she would be poor among the poor. The foundation of the Sisters of the Cross followed in due course.

The Company of the Cross was born on 2 August 1875. Four shabbily-dressed women set out on the adventure. Without the ringing of bells or any fuss whatever, they consecrated themselves to God in a nearby convent for the love and service of the poor. Torres designated Sr Angela the "eldest Sister." From then on they were to look after the sick. A small room with right of access to a kitchen was to be their convent. Many young women came to join them, so they had to look for larger accommodation, but Angela stipulated that it had to be poor and, as she had envisaged it even before they had begun, "a house where total silence reigns, its walls white and everything very clean; no furniture in the corridors, only at intervals some small cheap pictures of the Stations of the Cross with a small crucifix above." And so it was, and is. From then on there was a steady expansion and during the lifetime of the foundress; foundations were made in Huelva, Jaén, Málaga, and Cadiz. There was no form of need that the Sisters would not address: the working class with all its problems particular to the nineteenth century, rural workers adrift in the city or in slums outside it, homeless families, the sick, orphans, illiterate children or adults. The poorest of the poor were to be their special sphere of work. Their only means were to be the work of their own hands and the alms they might obtain from others.

There are many specific allusions to poverty in Sr Angela's writings, reflecting her day-to-day life: "The Sister of the Cross ought to go to extremes in the matter of poverty. And she ought to humble herself all the more when she sees the poor who practise poverty not by choice but by necessity. She ought to say: 'I who have been called by God, who has shown me that in this virtue is the source of all wealth, I work not only for God, but also for myself and I do not succeed in practising total poverty. I hardly notice I need something but I find a way of meeting that need. I have no more than the merest vestige of poverty in comparison with the poor.'"

Sr Angela of the Cross saw the whole of the spiritual life centred on the cross. She wrote to her Sisters, "Imagine on Calvary another cross, close to that of our Lord and at the same height, neither to the right nor to the left but directly in front of his." She and her Sisters were to take possession of that empty cross so as to be crucified before the Lord by their poverty, detachment, and humility. United thus with him, they could reach out with his love and compassion to the poor and the needy. It was said of Sr Angela that she seemed "immersed in Easter joy," a spiritual trait she bequeathed to her company.

Sr Angela died on 2 March 1932 after a long and full life of eighty-six years, bringing consolation to the poor and marginalized. She was beatified by Pope John Paul II in Seville on 5 November 1982.

Ecclesia, 13 Nov. 1982. There is a biography by J. M. Javierre.

R.M.
St Quintius, martyr, Lipari (*c.* 284)
St Joavan, bishop of Léon, Brittany (sixth century)

19

3

BD KATHARINE DREXEL, *Foundress* (1858-1955)

Katharine Mary Drexel was born in Philadelphia, Pennsylvania, U.S.A., on 26 November 1858, the second of three children raised in an affluent but pious home. Katharine's father, Francis Drexel, owned an international banking empire, and the Drexels, powerful and wealthy, moved in the highest circles of society. However, their social position did not shield them from knowledge of the poverty existing in such a large metropolis. To ensure that their children should know the poor as individuals, Emma, Katharine's stepmother (Hannah, her own mother, having died only five weeks after Katharine's birth), opened their city home to Philadelphia's poor three days a week. Emma herself distributed vast amounts of money to the needy and even ran a dispensary from the house for the sick, while Francis contributed to his own charities. The example of her parents sharing their wealth with others in this way marked Katharine for life.

Francis Drexel supervised the upbringing of his three children. The entire family attended Mass and practised one half-hour of mental prayer every day. Their education was thorough; the three children were trained in classical and modern languages, art, music, philosophy, and mathematics and groomed to take their place in society.

Although attractive and lively, "Kate" was not drawn to elaborate social gatherings. She seemed quite unenthusiastic about her "coming out" party, referring to it in an offhand manner as "a little party the other night where I made my debut." Several young suitors approached her; marriage was proposed. However, her deeply religious outlook kept all her experiences of travel and society in perspective, giving her a certain detachment. Tragically, Emma Drexel, Kate's stepmother, died in 1883, and Francis died within two years of his wife. Francis Drexel left one-tenth of his estate to charity and divided the rest among his three daughters.

Bishop Martin Marty, a Benedictine monk, first alerted Katharine to the plight of the American Indians. Worried that the U.S. government would undo all progress made by the Catholic missions since their inception in 1884, Bishop Marty had approached the Drexels for financial assistance. Katharine, who since childhood had been particularly interested in the American Indians, gave a sympathetic ear to the bishop, and the sisters even discussed the matter with Pope Leo XIII. The pope granted the young women two private audiences in which Katharine pleaded with him to send more missionaries to the

Indians. Though she did not grasp it at the time, it was Pope Leo who first encouraged her to be a missionary. From the age of fourteen she had always thought of embracing the religious life but leaned rather to the contemplative, cloistered life. Her stepmother was not in favour of this, and Katharine abandoned the idea until after her death. Even Bishop O'Connor, a friend of the family, encouraged Katharine to retain her place in society. He feared that her background had not been such as to prepare her for life in a cloister, whereas in her position and with the wealth at her disposal she could do much good for the causes she had espoused.

Fr Joseph Stephen, the director of the Bureau of Catholic Indian Missions, escorted Katharine to Bishop Marty's territory in the American Dakotas, where many of the Indians lived. The dire poverty of these Indians, as well as their leader, the great chief Red Cloud, made a deep impression on her and her sisters. There and then, Katharine vowed to assist the Indians with her own portion of the inheritance.

Despite the reservations of Bishop O'Connor, Katharine remained steadfast in her desire to become a religious. The bishop eventually capitulated, encouraging her to combine her two interests: instead of joining an existing religious community, he suggested she begin a new Congregation that would have as its apostolate missionary work among peoples of colour. To obtain the requisite formation, he directed her to the Sisters of Mercy. She entered their novitiate at the age of thirty-one, only too conscious of her own insufficiency. After a year, on 12 February 1891, she pronounced her vows, along with thirteen companions, as the first Sister of the Blessed Sacrament.

Mother Drexel began her missionary work by transforming the old Drexel summer house at Torresdale, Pennsylvania, into a convent and then opening boarding schools for African American children and Pueblo Indians. So influential was she in her work with the American Indians that she earned the respect of their great chief Red Cloud. When the United States government cut financial aid to the natives and restricted their land even further, the Indians rioted. They burned schools and lodges built with government funds and killed white Americans around the Indian reservations. It was due to Mother Drexel's close and influential relationship with Chief Red Cloud that the Sisters, convents, and schools for the Indians were spared.

It is interesting to note that her Institute received no grants from her estate—she felt that the Sisters should be self-supporting—so that her aid went directly to the missions. In 1915 she opened a teachers' college in Louisiana, which was eventually chartered as Xavier University of New Orleans, one of the first schools in the U.S.A. to admit people of colour. This was an important move, as discrimination against African Americans existed even among Catholics. While Mother Katharine took exception to some aspects of segregation as practised in church, she had, nevertheless, to work within the existing laws and customs of the country. By the time her active missionary life was brought to an end, Mother Katharine had herself established 145 Catholic missions and twelve schools for Indians and fifty for African Americans, but she had brought a whole generation of Catholic Americans to an awareness of the needs of these minorities. She was to die within the very decade marked by the campaigns for civil rights led by Martin Luther King, Jr. It may be said that Katharine Drexel, while not uninterested in the civil rights aspect of the life of these minorities, had her sights fixed elsewhere. What she wanted passionately to bring to them was the life of grace and the food of the Eucharist.

Mother Drexel's desire for the contemplative life was fulfilled when, in 1935, she suffered a severe heart attack and spent the next twenty years in prayerful retirement. She died on 3 March 1955 and was beatified by Pope John Paul II on 20 November 1988.

K. Burton, *The Golden Door: The Life of Katharine Drexel* (1957); K. Woodward, *Making Saints* (1991); *Bibl. SS.*, Suppl. 1 (1987), 431-2; Sr Consuela M. Duffy, S.B.S., *Katherine Drexel: A Biography* (1996).

SS Marinus and Asterius, *Martyrs (c. 260)*

Eusebius relates the story of St Marinus in his *Ecclesiastical History*. He belonged to a noble and well-to-do family of Caesarea in Palestine. Able and conscientious, he had held many posts in the army and was about to be offered the vine branch—a sign of honour—and a pledge of promotion to the position of centurion. This post was indeed vacant at the time, and it was coveted by another officer. Seeing Marinus' preferment, his rival approached the magistrate, Achaeus, pointing out that, as a Christian, Marinus could not be trusted to offer sacrifice to the emperor and therefore forfeited the honours of State.

Achaeus took the point and questioned Marinus about his beliefs. The latter acknowledged without flinching that he was a Christian, and Achaeus gave him three hours to reconsider his position. Marinus left the court and just then met Theotecnus, the bishop of Caesarea, who led him into the church and there before the altar put before him the two emblems, the sword and the scriptures, emphasizing the choice he must make. Marinus did not hesitate; he chose the scriptures. "Hold fast, hold fast to God," said Theotecnus, "so that, strengthened by him, you may obtain the fruit of your choice. Go in peace." Marinus returned to the judge and showed even greater firmness than before. He was immediately led away to execution.

Rufinus adds that a Roman senator, Asterius, a patrician of outstanding qualities and a highly-placed politician, was present at the martyrdom. He himself wrapped the martyr's body in his own cloak. For this act of reverence he was himself subsequently martyred.

Euseb., *H.E.*, 7, 15, is the sole source for the story of Marinus. The martyrdom of Asterius is mentioned only by Rufinus and repeated in some ancient martyrologies.

St Non (*c.* 540)

Non (Nonna, Nonnita) was the mother of Saint David of Wales (1 Mar.). Most of the information about her comes from the biography of her son written by Rhygyfarch (Ricemarch) in the late eleventh century.

According to his story there was in the sixth century a religious community of women at Ty Gwyn (Dyfed), north-east of the village-city now called St David's and close to the Whitesand bay (Porth Mawr). There was a young woman of noble birth and great beauty named Non in the community. She came to the notice of Sant, a local chieftain, who violated her; in due course Non gave birth to David. He is supposed to have been born during a storm at the spot on the coast where the ruins of the medieval St Non's chapel still stand.

Another tradition holds that she was the daughter or granddaughter of Brechan, a chieftain of Pembrokeshire, and was married to Sant, but the truth of either story is now impossible to establish. According to some Irish writers she had other children later, and it may well be that, before or after David's birth, she was Sant's wife. Her name, Non, may have given rise to the legend of Ty Gwyn, as the Latin form of her name, *Nonna*, means *nun*.

Place names in Cornwall and Brittany show that there was considerable devotion to her in Celtic lands. She was often called "Non, the blessed," and the bards refer to her beauty. Lewis Glyn Cothi (fifteenth century) in one of his poems swears "by the hand of Non," perhaps a reference to the legend that while in labour with David she left the impression of her hand on a stone that was by her side. In the West Country during the Middle Ages she was thought to have been buried at Altarnun in Cornwall, but the grave shown in the church of Dirinon in the department of Finisterre in Brittany seems to have a greater claim to authenticity. It is covered by a striking medieval table-tomb on which there is a recumbent effigy of the saint. She is still the patron saint of Dirinon.

There are holy wells of St Non at Dirinon, in several places in Cornwall, and at St David's. This last has been rebuilt and re-dedicated, and close by is a new chapel of Our Lady and St Non.

See bibliographical note to St David (1 Mar.). There is an interesting reference to St David's birth in *Blackfriars* 29 (1948), pp. 123-5. G. H. Doble in *St Nonna* (1928) suggests that the Cornish St Non was a man.

St Winwaloe, *Abbot* (Sixth Century)

The Life of St Winwaloe (Guénolé, Winnol, or Onolaus) was not written until the ninth century. Its legendary character is evident from the extravagant miracles with which it is freely embroidered, but it probably retains some authentic elements.

Winwaloe was entrusted to the Irish monk Budoc, who lived on the island of

Laurea. When his training was completed he became a hermit on the island of Tibidy, off the coast. Later he settled with a group of monks on an island at the mouth of the river Aulne. The place was very exposed, and after three years they migrated to the mainland. In a sheltered valley on the opposite side of Brest harbour, they founded the monastery of Landévennec, in which they continued the Celtic monastic tradition taught by Budoc. There Winwaloe ruled over a large number of monks for many years. When he learned that he was about to die, he called the brethren together and instructed them to elect a successor who should be "sweet as honey and bitter as absinth. Seek not for peace here," he exhorted them, "so that you may enjoy peace and tranquillity in heaven." He died while standing at the altar at the end of Mass, in the company of all the Brothers.

His popularity is otherwise attested by the number of dedications made to him throughout Brittany and by the many variations of his name. This appears in two or three late-medieval English calendars, but his cult was restricted to the area of Celtic influence; there are churches dedicated to him in Cornwall, at Gunwalloe, and Landewednack, while some of his relics were claimed by Exeter, Glastonbury, Abingdon, and Waltham. A church in Norwich was dedicated to him; the church has gone but the street retains his name.

The Norsemen burned the monastery in 914. A portion of his relics was taken to Mont Blandin in Ghent—from where they may have found their way to England—and another to Château-du-Loir, later translated to the abbey of Saint-Sauve in Montreuil-sur-Mer but destroyed at the French Revolution.

St Winwaloe is shown in art with a goose beside him. This may be a reference to the incident in which his sister is said to have had one of her eyes plucked out by a goose she was chasing. Called to her side, Winwaloe ordered the goose to disgorge the eye, which it did. The saint put it back and all was well. He is also depicted with a bell, by means of which he is said to have summoned the fish.

The longest biographical text, *Anal. Boll.* 7 (1888), pp. 167-264, seems to have been the composition of Wrdisten, abbot of Landévennec, who lived more than 300 years after the saint. In Baring-Gould and Fisher's *Lives of the British Saints*, 4, pp. 353-62, there is a discussion of the various texts. See also G. H. Doble, *St Winwaloe* (1940); J. Le Jollec, *Winwaloe, le saint de Landévennec* (1952), gives an account of the cult and of the abbey of Landévennec, which was restored in the 1950s by the Benedictines of Kerbéneat and inaugurated in 1958.

St Cunegund (1039)

Cunegund was brought up by her parents, Sigfried, first earl of Luxembourg, and his wife, Hedwig, in a profoundly religious environment. She married St Henry, duke of Bavaria (15 July). Although she is commemorated as a virgin in the liturgy of the Church, there is no evidence to support the assertion by some writers that the couple took a vow of chastity on their wedding day.

On the death of Emperor Otto III, who had no children, Henry, scion of the house of Saxony, successfully pressed his claim to the throne of Germany. He was crowned by Archbishop Willigis at Mainz, and two months later Cunegund was crowned at Paderborn. In becoming king of Germany and heir to the Ottonian emperors, Henry was destined also to become emperor of a Holy Roman Empire drawing its inspiration from Charles the Great. According to an anointing formula found in a Mainz *ordo*, the king was raised to a superior status whereby he shared in some way in the episcopal office and enjoyed the position of intermediary between clergy and people. Such a conception of office had already led the Ottonian emperors to exercise a certain hegemony over the papacy and, indeed, over the whole episcopate of the empire. The emperors were thus in a position to dictate policy to the Church in every essential. This was not, at the time, necessarily a bad thing, as these men were motivated by a desire to reform the Church, which could not always be said of the bishops or even of the popes.

With the death of Otto III the factions in Rome had come to the fore, and the two parties, that of Crescentius, an old player on the scene, and the Tusculan counts just emerging as a political power, each produced its own pope to succeed Sergius IV, who had died in 1012. Since the emperors held the right of veto, there were those who looked to Germany to decide between Gregory, the candidate of Crescentius, and Benedict, the candidate put forward by the Tusculan count. Gregory himself came to Germany to put his case to Henry. The latter merely promised to come to Rome to review the situation when he was free. When Henry did go to Rome he had already opted for Benedict VIII, who had in the meantime taken up office. There was hardly any question but that the pope would agree to the coronation of Henry II and Cunegund as emperor and empress. This took place on 14 February 1014.

It was at the instigation of Cunegund that the emperor founded the monastery and cathedral of Bamberg, which always remained dear to them both. Sergius IV, though in some measure under the thumb of Crescentius, had granted privileges to the church of Bamberg; these were confirmed by Benedict VIII even before Henry's first visit to Rome. When the cathedral was consecrated, Pope Benedict was present.

Cunegund was also responsible for the foundation of the Benedictine monastery at Kaufungen, following a vow she had taken during a grave illness. The building was nearing completion when St Henry died. On the anniversary of his death she invited a number of prelates to the dedication of the monastic church. After the Gospel, she offered a relic of the true cross on the altar, and then, putting off her imperial robes, she was clothed in a religious habit. Once consecrated to God, she seemed to forget entirely that she had ever been empress. She gave herself to prayer and reading and made a point of visiting and comforting the sick. She spent fifteen years in the monastery, never permitting the least favour or preference to be shown her.

As she lay dying on a coarse hair cloth, she noticed that a cloth fringed with gold was being readied to cover her remains. She asked that it be taken away and would not rest until she had been promised that she would be buried in her religious habit. She died on 3 March 1033, and her body was taken to Bamberg to be buried near that of her husband. Pope Innocent III canonized her in 1200.

SS Henry and Cunegund are usually represented together, wearing imperial robes and a crown and holding a lily or a model of a church between them. This was no mere artistic device, for the Ottonian dynasty ranked the empresses as co-regents of the empire. When depicted alone, St Cunegund sometimes holds a church, representing that of Kaufungen, or walks on red-hot ploughshares, a reference to the legend that she had undergone this ordeal by fire when her chastity had been impugned. The tomb in Bamberg Cathedral where their remains are preserved was designed and executed by Hans Thielmann (*c.* 1500). Scenes in bas-relief on the sides of the sarcophagus represent St Cunegund distributing alms to the poor, paying the architects and masons who built the cathedral, and undergoing the ordeal by fire. The death of St Henry is depicted, as also the supposed rescue of his soul by St Lawrence. Bamberg cathedral, built by Henry and Cunegund and containing the tombs of both, is their most striking memorial.

An edited version of a late biography of the saint together with the Bull of canonization appears in *AA.SS.*, Mar., 1, pp. 265–80. It was edited also by G. Waitz for *M.G.H.*, 7; see P. Corbet, *Les Saints Ottoniens* (1986), for a survey of the Ottonian dynasty and the characteristics of its saintly women; also R. Klauser, *Der Heinrichs und konigundenkult in mittelalterlichen Bistum Bamberg* (1957) and *Bibl. SS.*, 4, 393–9.

St Gervinus, *Abbot* (1075)

Gervinus was born in the district of Reims in France. He was related to Bruno, bishop of Toul, who later became Pope Leo IX. He received his own education in the episcopal school of Reims. Afraid that classical Latin poetry might lead him into sin, he abandoned secular studies.

He was a canon of Reims when his parents died, leaving him to care for his two sisters. One of these he gave in marriage to Haymo, a soldier, to whom he also handed over the greater part of his estate, while the other, who was set against marriage, became a nun. Gervinus then sought out Richard, the holy abbot of Saint-Vannes at Verdun, and asked to be received as a monk. He was given the monastic habit by Bishop Vitonus. He seemed to be an exemplary novice, but to put this apparent virtue to the test he was placed in charge of the young boys and acquitted himself well. Abbot Richard soon appointed him his chaplain. He took him to visit the Holy Places and again to visit the court on business. It was on this second occasion that King Henry I of France asked the abbot to release Gervinus for the post of abbot of Saint-Riquier. Reluctantly, Abbot Richard told his chaplain to accede to the royal request. Gervinus objected that he could not take on such a task without the consent of the community concerned. This consent given, Gervinus was blessed on the feast of the Annunciation.

His term of office was marked by the building of several chapels and sanctuaries and the acquisition of innumerable relics, by his careful management of the affairs of the abbey, and by his enrichment of the library with Greek and Latin manuscripts. His personal life was extremely austere; he fasted cheerfully and added extra hours of prayer to the canonical offices, which meant that he often had no sleep at all. Even on journeys he held to his rigorous schedule. He travelled through Picardy, Normandy, Aquitaine, and as far as Thuringia, preaching and hearing Confessions. He was a man of action as well as a man of prayer. When action threatened to engulf him or knotty problems weighed on his mind, he would withdraw to a kind of cell in the woods, where he could give himself up entirely to prayer.

The abbey held property in England, and Gervinus visited Britain several times. He was held in great esteem by St Edward the Confessor (13 Oct.). However, a curious story is told of his first meeting with Edward's queen, Edith. She came forward to welcome the abbot with a kiss, but thinking this unseemly, Gervinus declined the salute. She was so furious that her husband had some difficulty in placating her, but she seems to have come to terms with the cultural differences and subsequently made the abbot a handsome present of a cloak embroidered with gold and silver. When William the Conqueror invaded England, Gervinus prudently obtained from him a royal charter protecting his abbey lands.

So great was the veneration in which he was held that he was called "the holy abbot" during his lifetime. He seemed at the pinnacle of achievement both as a man of action and a man of God when he contracted leprosy. When he understood the nature of the disease he thanked God for it and prayed that it would redound to his salvation. As long as he could, he kept to his usual routine of prayer and penance. Four years of increasing suffering passed; then, on the feast of the Presentation of the Lord (then the Purification of Our Lady), he offered Mass for the last time in the crypt he had built. Taken back to his cell, he told his monks who stood round him in consternation, "Beloved sons, today I have been given leave to go by Our Lady, holy Mary." On Ash Wednesday he insisted on making a public confession of his sins and on Tuesday of the second week of Lent, according to his wish, he was taken to church and laid before the altar of St John the Baptist, where he died as the monks chanted the *Suscipiat te*. When his body was washed and laid out, it was remarked that no trace of leprosy remained.

The main source of our knowledge of the life of St Gervinus is the Chronicle of Saint-Riquier compiled by Hariulf. See *P.L.*, 174, 1322-60. A commemorative volume of Saint-Riquier was published there in 1962; see also *Bibl.SS.*, 6, 365-6.

Bd Peter Geremia (1399-1452)

Peter was born in Palermo in Sicily, the son of Arduin, a jurist and fiscal agent to King Alfonso I. At the age of eighteen he was sent to the university of Bologna to study law and eventually follow in his father's footsteps. He was such a brilliant student that in the professor's absence he would be asked to take his place. One night he was disturbed by what he interpreted as a divine message to abandon law and enter the religious life. Peter lost no time in acting upon the warning. Then and there he took a vow of perpetual chastity. The next morning he bought an iron chain which he wound three times round his body. Fifty-one years later, when his corpse was being prepared for burial, the chain was found embedded in his flesh and could not be removed.

Peter entered the Dominican convent at Bologna. News of this infuriated Arduin, who journeyed to Bologna with the intention of forcing the young man back to his studies. Peter refused to see his father but assured him that he was well and in no need of anything but the prayers of the family. While his father fretted and fumed, Peter prayed for perseverance in his vocation and for the resolution of the crisis. When an interview was at last arranged, and Arduin saw the quiet dignity and love of God shining in Peter's face, he broke down and wept. Returning to Sicily, he no longer tried to deter his son but even encouraged him to carry on.

Once professed and ordained, Peter began to preach and hear Confessions, bringing many back to the practice of their faith. St Vincent Ferrer (5 Apr.), who came to Bologna regularly to visit the shrine of St Dominic, greatly encouraged him, and soon all Italy knew about this young friar. He was sent in 1427 to Sicily to restore discipline in the Dominican friaries and convents and then in 1430 to Oxford to teach. A few years later he was summoned to the Council of Florence. Pope Eugenius IV was so impressed by his holiness and eloquence, especially when disputing with the Greeks, that he would have showered favours on him, but Peter could not be brought to accept them. However, he did accept the pope's commission to reform the regular and secular clergy in Sicily. After the council he returned there as apostolic visitator, taking up residence in the monastery of St Zita, which had been recently founded by some Spanish friars. He became prior of St Zita's, but without abandoning his dedication to preaching, prayer, and study. He was never seen to give way to anger; rather, he was kind to all without exception. Gentle of speech, mild in administering correction, he upset no one but encouraged all to the love of God. He was revered as prior and loved as a father, inspiring many young men with a love of the Dominican life. Several times he refused to accept a bishopric. However, he worked for three years in Catania setting up a university there, the *Siculorum Gymnasium*. The reform of Dominican life on the island is attributed to him. He formed Bd John Licco (14 Nov.), who entered in 1441 and was the inspiration of Bd Bernard of Scammaca, of the reformed friary of Catania. After his term as prior he was made novice-master, but he requested the provincial chapter for leave to give all his time to preaching. The same success attended his preaching on the island as on the mainland, so much so that no church could hold the crowds who came to hear him. He brought to his preaching an immense culture as well as respect for contemporary thought. He could quote from contemporary authors, even from popular songs, and was cognizant of current affairs. His presentation was always characterized by clarity, and when occasion required he would not mince his words.

He suffered from several complaints at the end of his life, but especially from pain in his legs, all of which he bore without murmuring. He was heard to pray, "Burn here, amputate there, spare no part of me now so as to spare me eternally."

AA.SS., Mar., 1, pp. 291-5; Taurisiano, *Catalogus Hagiographicus O.P.*; Mortier, *Maîtres Généraux O.P.*, 4, pp. 152-212; M. A. Coniglione, *Pietro Geremia* (1952); *Dict.Sp.*, 5, 1443; 12, 1601. See also *Bibl.SS.*, 6, 212-4.

BB Liberatus Weiss, Samuel Marzorati, and Michael Fasoli, *Martyrs* (1716)

The first missionary to Ethiopia was possibly Queen Candace's chief treasurer, baptized by the deacon Philip just after Pentecost. By the fourth century Ethiopia was reckoned to be Christian and has remained impressively faithful, with a Christian majority of the population over the centuries despite Egyptian domination and Muslim invasions. However, the end of the fifth century saw the arrival of the "nine monks" from Syria who brought with them the Monophysite heresy (belief that there is only one nature in Christ), which took root in Ethiopia and has never since been eradicated.

The first attempts we know of to bring the Ethiopian Church into the unity of Catholic orthodoxy were made in the thirteenth century by Dominicans; these suffered martyrdom. In the sixteenth century, when Ethiopia needed the help of the Portuguese to fight off the Muslims, missionaries from Portugal were admitted. Pope Julius III appointed as patriarch of Ethiopia a Jesuit, João Nunes Barreto, who died before reaching the country. Pedro Páez, also a Jesuit, succeeded in winning the confidence and respect of the autocratic ruler, Malak Sagad III, also known as Susenyos. The king was persuaded to accept the Chalcedonian formula concerning the two natures in Christ, and he set about the task of imposing it on the national Church. In 1622 he ordered obedience to Rome, installing Alfonso Mendes as patriarch. His high-handedness merely produced civil war.

He was succeeded in 1632, some say forcibly, by his son Fasilidas, who restored allegiance to the Monophysite Ethiopian Orthodox Church. Mendes was expelled in 1636, and a ban on Catholic priests remained in force for the next two hundred years. It is against this background that the attempt by Liberatus Weiss and his companions to reconcile the Monophysite Ethiopians must be situated.

29

John Laurence Weiss was born in Konnersreuth in Bavaria, the second of the six children of John and Regina Weiss. He was educated by the Cistercians but attracted to the Franciscans, who had often preached in Konnersreuth and fired him with zeal for the Franciscan ideal. He was clothed in the friary of Graz on 13 October 1693, receiving the name of Liberatus. After ordination in 1698 he engaged in pastoral work in Langenlois until 1703, when he became city preacher in Graz. While there he received a letter from the minister general, Fr Antony of Palermo, asking him to go to Ethiopia as a missionary, at the request of Jasu, ruler of Ethiopia. The Franciscan Fr Joseph of Jerusalem, the apostolic prefect of Ethiopia, had won over Jasu and some of the senior clergy to the cause of Rome, and these were requesting Pope Clement XI to send more Franciscans in order to prepare the way for reunion.

Michael Pius Fasoli was born on 3 May 1676 in Zerbo in the diocese of Pavia in Italy. He belonged to the Franciscan province of San Diego, while Samuel Marzorati, who was born at Biumo, belonged to the Franciscan province of Milan.

Fr Liberatus agreed to head the mission and in 1704 was accepted by the Congregation for the Propagation of the Faith as a missionary to Ethiopia. Shortly before he died, Fr Joseph nominated him vice prefect also. After a short period of preparation Liberatus set out with seven priests and three lay brothers in September of that same year. After enduring unbelievable hardships they reached Sennan (present-day Khartoum), where the regional ruler, Bade, refused to allow them to proceed and robbed them of all their possessions. Most of the group died of starvation so that only two were left, Fr Liberatus and Fr Michael Pius, who then returned to Egypt. In a letter of 29 December 1710 to the Congregation for the Propagation of the Faith Fr Liberatus reported the death of Fr Joseph and gave an account of the situation, requesting at the same time that he be relieved of his position as vice prefect, a post of which he was unworthy, adding, "however, as a subject, I am ready to shed the last drop of my blood for Christ, for his Bride, Holy Mother Church, and for the salvation of souls in Ethiopia." The reply from Rome, dated 20 April 1711, appointed him apostolic prefect for Ethiopia and instructed him to return there with two companions. Fr Liberatus replied, describing his past experiences and suggesting measures that should be taken for the success of the mission. By autumn 1711, not having heard anything further, he set out again with Fr Michael Pius and Fr Samuel Marzorati.

The trio landed at Massawa on 18 April 1712 after a difficult journey and proceeded to Gonder, then the capital, where they arrived in July 1712. They were well received by Justos, second in succession to Jasu, but because of his precarious hold on power he would not permit them to preach publicly. The missionaries learned the language and opened a hospice where they treated the sick free of charge. Three years later it seemed as if they might eventually be able to start work on the task for which they were sent. However, the emperor's opponents, who did not look with favour on the Roman mission and feared the friars' influence at court, began to spread malicious gossip about them. The emperor sent them to Tigre for safety, but then the populace turned on the emperor himself, who was forced to abdicate.

Justos was succeeded by the young and inexperienced David III, who at the instigation of the courtiers sent for the missionaries and brought them to trial. This turned on their mission. Questioned about this and about their attitude to circumcision, a practice the Ethiopian Church had inherited from Judaism, the friars declared that they would die uncircumcised, confessing to their last drop of blood the two natures in Christ. They were condemned to be stoned to death. The martyrs spent the last night of their life singing songs of praise to God.

They were taken in chains to Abbo, the place of execution, on 3 March 1716 and were there stoned by a mob incited to the deed. Pope John Paul II beatified Fr Liberatus and his two companions on 20 November 1988.

F. Holböck, *Die Neuen Heiliger der Katholischen Kirche*, 3 (1994), pp 96-102.

Bd Peter Rogue, *Martyr* (1758-96)

Pierre-René Rogue was born on 11 June 1758 in the town of Vannes in Brittany. His father died when he was only three, and he was brought up by his mother, who worked to support the family and to care for her son's precarious health. Peter entered the seminary in 1776 and was ordained in 1782. After four years as a chaplain he applied to become a member of the Congregation of the Mission of St Vincent de Paul, which admitted him in October 1786. His novitiate in Paris was cut short by a recall to the seminary of Vannes to take up the appointments of director and professor of theology.

The beginnings of the French Revolution hardly impinged on life in the seminary, but from 1791 every priest was called on to take the oath of fidelity to the State, required by the Civil Constitution on the Clergy (see "Martyrs of the French Revolution," 2 Jan.). Most of the clergy refused to take the oath. A year later the directors of the seminary were expelled and all left the town except Peter, who remained to minister to the parishioners of Méné. In August 1792 all those priests who had not taken the oath had to leave the country or go into hiding. Peter preferred the latter course, well knowing what his clandestine ministry might entail.

After the fall of Robespierre an amnesty was declared. Peter came out of hiding, presented himself to the authorities in June 1795, and pledged to keep the peace. For some months he was able to carry on his ministry openly, but in October of that same year the legislation was once more applied in its full rigour.

On Christmas Eve 1795 Peter was taking the Sacrament to the dying when he noticed that he was being followed by two well-known revolutionaries. He

31

asked his guide to leave him and he himself kept on walking. The men seized him and led him to the place where the district assembly was in continual session. The capture was not greeted with enthusiasm—Peter was too well known and esteemed by the townsfolk. The members of the assembly declared that they were not competent to arrest him, and while the two pursuers went off to the police the members advised him to make good his escape. Afraid that they would suffer for it after, Peter refused. He consumed the Sacrament and made no resistance as he was led away. His friends tried to get him released, but he believed that if he were freed further investigations would be set in hand and more arrests would follow.

At his trial, at which his mother was present, he replied briefly and concisely to the questions put to him: he had indeed refused the oath, he had never left Vannes, but he would not divulge the names of those who had harboured him. As he was plainly in contravention of the law, the judge had no choice but to condemn him to death. He spent the night writing to his friends and encouraging his companion priest, who shrank from the horror of the violent death in store. The two were guillotined at Morbihan the following day, 3 March 1796.

His tomb, prepared by his mother, became a place of pilgrimage where many miracles were said to have taken place. Peter Rogue was beatified on 10 May 1934, and his relics now rest in the cathedral of Vannes.

Bénédictins de Paris, Vie des Saints, 13, Suppl. (1959); J. Gontier, *Un martyr de la fidelité, Pierre-René Rogue, prêtre de la Mission* (1979). For a general treatment of the martyrs of the French Revolution, see the entry for 2 Jan. in the present work.

Bd Teresa Verzeri, *Foundress* (1801-52)

Teresa Verzeri, foundress of the Daughters of the Sacred Heart of Jesus, was born at Bergamo in Lombardy on 31 July 1801, the eldest of the six children of Antonio Verzeri and his wife, Helena, of the family of the counts of Pedrocca-Grumelli. She is said to have first thought of becoming a nun at the age of ten, at the time of her First Communion. By the time of her Confirmation she was sure that this was what she must do. Canon Giuseppe Benaglio, of the cathedral chapter of Bergamo, had meanwhile become the trusted adviser to the whole family on the death of Antonio Verzeri. It fell to him, therefore, to guide the young Teresa in responding to her vocation.

She entered the Benedictine monastery of Grata at the age of sixteen. As the laws of Joseph II forbidding the clothing of candidates before the age of twenty-four were in force, she could not receive the habit. Canon Benaglio suggested that she return home. In August 1821 she returned to Grata but came up against the same prohibition, which affected the community no less than it did the candidates. Political interference, before which the nuns were powerless, had disoriented the community, undermining its observance. Once laxity had become entrenched, opposition to reform built up. Teresa supported those who desired reform, but this did not endear her to all. However, she won the trust of her superiors, who gave her charge over the young entrants. The disunity of the community and the opposition to change created a situation that Canon Benaglio found too unpromising to allow her to continue. Moreover, he was planning to set up a community that would undertake the teaching of young women while retaining a contemplative orientation. Teresa was attracted by his project, and he suggested that she should leave Grata. She did so in a spirit of obedience. Later, she asked him if she might return once again, as she felt that enclosure corresponded best to her spiritual needs. He agreed, and she entered a third time in 1828. Her third entry was not viewed favourably by some in the community, and although she had held responsible jobs in the past, she was now assigned the humblest and hardest. Since she was now over twenty-four she was given the habit, but her doubts, coupled with great dryness of spirit and no doubt exacerbated by the problems of the community, brought on a period of intense suffering. Canon Benaglio consulted Bd Magdalen of Canossa (14 May), whose response encouraged him to suggest that Teresa leave Grata for good.

She joined Virginia Simoni, Canon Benaglio's other candidate, and began courses of religious instruction for young girls in a country house in Gromo. This proved to be the beginning of the new Congregation she was to establish. Her sister Antonia and Catharine Manghenoni also joined them, and the four made simple vows before Canon Benaglio, who proposed the formation of the young as the goal of the new Institute. They adopted a stern way of life, with long periods of fasting and silence. Teresa herself knew many spiritual difficulties, doubts, and temptations, but recruits arrived to swell their ranks, among them three more of her own sisters, Mary, Judith, and Catharine, and her widowed mother. The group lived under the general direction of Canon Benaglio and with his help drew up a Rule and Constitutions, which were approved by the bishop of Bergamo in 1842. The rule envisaged schools for poor children, visits to sick women, recreational and religious centres for girls in moral danger, and especially, retreats for laywomen, to be conducted according to the Spiritual Exercises.

The bishop, Mgr Charles Gritti-Morlacchi, who had initially been favourable, now began to raise obstacles, which compounded the internal difficulties resulting from Teresa's self-questioning and apparent indecisiveness. She visited Turin, where St Madeleine-Sophie Barat (25 May) had already begun her retreats for laywomen; struck by the similarity of the two Institutes, she thought of merging her group with that of the Society of the Sacred Heart. However, it became clear to her eventually that there was room and need for two separate Congregations. Many more difficulties had to be overcome before the Congregation could be solidly established, but at length, in May 1841, Mother Teresa and her companions made their final vows before Cardinal Constantine Patrizi, prefect of the Congregation of Bishops and Regulars. The approbation of the

Holy See followed a few days later and was confirmed in September 1847, when the Institute was authorized to open a house in Rome.

Among those who had helped Teresa was Bd Ludovic Pavoni of Brescia (1 Apr.). He printed the Constitutions of her Congregation at his Institute at a time when it might have been imprudent to do so, given the anti-religious and antipapal struggles of the time. When Mother Teresa acquired an old monastery at Brescia, Canon Pavoni was the architect and contractor for the alterations, which he supervised personally. He went several times to Bergamo and Trent on her behalf and provided a priest for daily Mass at the motherhouse. He and Teresa had a very high regard for each other, and this mutual esteem has lasted in their respective Congregations for the century and a half since the death of the founders.

For four more years after opening the house in Rome, Teresa grew in grace and holiness, and her foundation grew with her. Her deep experience of God and her intuitive understanding of character combined with her concern and respect for her spiritual daughters, each of whom she saw as destined to be a saint, gave her an authority and a humanity that won the respect and affection of all.

In a cholera epidemic that swept northern Italy she contracted the disease, and she died in Brescia on 3 March 1852. She was beatified by Pope Pius XII in 1946. Her Congregation works in Italy, Argentina, Brazil, India, and the Central African Republic.

From the Brief of beatification, *A.A.S.* 29, no. 1 (1947); *Dict.Sp.*, 15, 671. Biographies of Teresa Verzeri have appeared only in Italian. Several volumes of her letters have been published. Cf. *Un Apostolo della Gioventù Derelitta* [Bd Ludovic Pavoni] (1928), pp. 209-11.

Bd Innocent of Berzo (1844-90)

Giovanni Scalvinoni was born on 19 March 1844 at Niardo in Valcamonica, a region of Brescia in Italy. His father, Pietro Scalvinoni, a widower with one son, had taken a second wife, Francesca Poli, who left her native Niardo to live with him in Berzo. However, for the birth of her first child she had returned to her mother in Niardo. There the child was baptized and given the name of Giovanni.

Pietro died three months after Giovanni's birth, and his maternal grandmother, who was looking after him, died three years later. His uncle on his mother's side, Francesco, subsequently became a father to him. Life was hard for this rural population high up in the hills, but the natives of Niardo were decent, upright, and warm, if reserved.

Giovanni received his secondary education in Lovere. As he grew he showed an unlimited capacity for work. His reverence for the Eucharist showed an equally developed religious sense. One trait that became more and more marked throughout his life was his willingness to serve others without acknowledgement or recognition.

He entered the diocesan seminary of Brescia in the autumn of 1861. There he began to keep a journal of his spiritual journey and prayer life, adopting a régime of austerity that allowed for long hours of prayer. Ordained in June 1867, he was first assigned to Cevo in Valsaviore, where he remained for two years. He was then promoted to the post of vice rector of the seminary at Brescia, which he held for one year only, having been judged unable to exercise authority. This was the first of many failures on his part to hold responsible posts. He was then appointed assistant priest at Berzo, where he remained for four years, happily fulfilling his duties of preaching, hearing Confessions, and giving spiritual direction. However, his life still seemed to lack something, and in 1874 he decided to leave parish work and become a Capuchin at the Annunziata friary in Berzo.

At his clothing as a novice he was given the name of Innocent and from then on undertook to lead a life of continual penance. His first vows were taken on 29 April 1875, after which he was sent to the friary at Albino for a year; he then returned to the friary in Berzo. Two years later he made his final profession and was named assistant novice-master. The novitiate was moved to Lovere a little over a year later, but he remained at the Annunziata in Berzo. He was then given responsibility for the *Annali Franciscani* and sent to Milano-Monforte but was relieved of the job a few months later. He returned to the friary of the Annunziata in June 1881.

In 1889 the provincial asked Innocent to conduct the provincial retreats in the principal friaries of Milano-Monforte, Albino, Bergamo, and Brescia. While preaching at Albino he fell ill and was taken to the infirmary at Bergamo. There he died on 3 March 1890.

His writings, as much as his penances, reveal a preoccupation with the presence and weight of sin. Often consulted by priests on problems of moral theology, he had a gift for the simple and direct answer, for which he was much esteemed. Outwardly he was quiet and unassuming, intelligent but reserved, someone always ready to help but who then faded into the background. His superiors tried several times to entrust him with responsible posts but were soon forced to relieve him of them. It seemed not so much a case of responsibility shirked as an inability, born of a profound humility, to be set above anyone else. Innocent was happiest in a position of service in which his own decrease facilitated the increase of the grace of Christ within.

He was beatified by Pope John XXIII on 12 November 1961.

C.F.S., p. 73. G. M. da Spirano, *Beato Innocenzo da Berzo* (1961); see also the study by A. de Casorete in *L' Italia Francescana* 36 (1961), pp. 365-80, and *Bibl.SS.*, 7, 834-6.

R.M.

SS Emeterius and Chelidonius, martyrs in Calahorra (*c.* 304)

SS. Cleonicus and Eutropius, martyrs in Pontus (fourth century)

St Arthellais of Benevento (*c.* 570)

St Calupannus, hermit in the Auvergne (576)

St Anselm, abbot of Nonandola (803)

Bd Frederick, abbot of Mariegarde, Halle, Frisia (1175)

Bd Jacobinus, O.Carm., lay brother at Vercelli (1508)

4

ST CASIMIR (1458-84)

Casimir, whom his countrymen called *The Peacemaker,* was the third of the thirteen children of Casimir IV, king of Poland, and Elizabeth of Austria, daughter of Emperor Albert II of Germany, king of Bohemia and Hungary. John Dlugosz, historian and canon of Cracow, a retiring cleric of outstanding learning and holiness, formed part of the embassy sent to arrange the marriage, which proved both happy and fruitful.

Casimir was born on 3 October 1458. From the age of nine, together with his two brothers, Ladislaus and John, he was educated by the same John Dlugosz. Having agreed to accede to the royal wishes, John proved a fine but strict teacher, indeed another father, inspiring such reverence that his pupils required no coercion to concentrate on their studies.

When not yet fifteen years of age Casimir was sent by his father, at the request of the Hungarian nobles, to lead an army into Hungary against Matthias Corvinus, king of Hungary. Hearing that Matthias had assembled a large number of troops and realizing that not only had he been abandoned by the very nobles who had requested Polish intervention in the first place but also that he could not depend on his own troops, who were deserting, he took the advice of his officers and called off the expedition. In the meantime Pope Sixtus IV had appealed to the king of Poland to desist, fearing perhaps that the war could only help the Turkish cause. The king agreed to a discussion of the peace and sent a messenger to his son, who, however, had already retreated, much to his father's shame. As a punishment, Prince Casimir was not allowed to return to Cracow but told to retire to the castle of Dobzki, where he was confined for three months. Casimir could never again be persuaded to take up arms, though urged to do so by his father and invited once more by the disaffected Hungarian magnates.

According to his biographer, he had no ambition to rule, but he was not inactive, especially on behalf of the poor and oppressed, pilgrims, and captives. He would raise with his father any injustice or any needs of the poor that he thought had been overlooked. He experienced great satisfaction in giving away everything he had to the needy, who called him the *Defender of the Poor.* His own personal life was more monastic than princely. Meek and modest in appearance, his life was focussed more on the Church than on the court. Much of his day was spent in church, assisting at Mass and at the offices. Sometimes he was so rapt in prayer that he would miss meals. At night, he would return to the church to worship outside its locked doors. Friendly with all, he could be harsh with schismatics. At his insistence, his father forbade the restoration of churches where they assembled. He had an immense love for Our Lady. At his wish, a copy of the hymn he frequently recited in her honour was buried with him: *Omni die dic Mariae*, known to us as *Daily, daily, sing to Mary*.

No one, parents or friends, could ever persuade him to marry, even though there was a bride-in-waiting. To these he said that he knew no other salvation, no other life than Christ. He would be dissolved in order to be with him, and he predicted that that would not long be delayed. He died of tuberculosis in 1484, at the age of twenty-three, and was buried at Vilna (now Vilnius, capital of Lithuania), where his relics still rest in the church of SS Peter and Paul. So many miracles were reported at his tomb and on the battlefield that King Sigismund petitioned Leo X for his canonization. He is the patron saint of Poland and Lithuania. A famous representation of the saint is that by Carlo Docci. He is usually portrayed with a lily, a scroll on which his favourite hymn to the Virgin is partially inscribed, and a crown at his feet. His cult was approved by Pope Clement VIII in 1602; it has remained strong among Polish and Lithuanian immigrants in Canada and the U.S.A. His feast was extended to the whole Church in 1621.

AA.SS., Mar., 1, pp. 334-55, reproduces a Latin Life by Zachary Ferreri, printed in 1521. See also *H.S.S.C.*, 7, pp. 91-5.

St Peter of Cava, *Abbot and Bishop* (1123)

Peter Pappacarbone was a native of Salerno in Italy and the nephew of St Alferius, founder and first abbot of the monastery of Cava. He entered Cava in the time of Leo, Alferius' successor, and soon became outstanding for his fervour, asceticism, and love of solitude. It was said that he lived on only a few loaves of bread throughout all Lent, which he spent moreover in complete solitude on a hill just overlooking the monastery.

The fame of the abbey of Cluny had by this time spread all over Europe, and the young Peter was so attracted that he set out for Cluny with a few other monks. He was warmly welcomed by the abbot, St Hugh (29 Apr.). The seniors thought Peter should first be put into the school, but Hugh considered that the fervour and determination that had brought him from so far away to the gates of Cluny was a sign of maturity. He allowed him to enter the community without further ado. His trust was not misplaced, for Peter proved to be both observant and reliable.

He stayed at Cluny for some years; then, at the insistence of the archdeacon of Rome, Hildebrand, who later became Pope St Gregory VII (25 May), Abbot Hugh sent him back to Cava, where he was immediately elected to the see of Policastro. However, unable to bear the turmoil of a life in the world, Peter left Policastro after a short time and returned to Cava. Abbot Leo then conceived a plan whereby he might both keep Peter at Cava and ensure his own retirement. He called the community together and in their presence nominated Peter his successor.

The new abbot tried to introduce a Cluniac observance but met with opposition. The malcontents took their complaints to Abbot Leo, whom they worked up against the new abbot. Seeing all this and concerned to preserve the peace and harmony of the community, Peter departed to another monastery. Abbot Leo and the monks in opposition subsequently asked him to return to Cava, which he did, and this time his rule was accepted by all.

From then on Cava experienced a remarkable renewal. Young men of all classes flocked to the monastery. Money and lands were also generously donated by seculars, so that the monks in their turn could dispense charity to the sick and the poor. The abbey was enlarged to house the influx of vocations, and a new church was built. Pope Urban II, who had known Peter at Cluny, was present at the dedication and afterwards joined the community in the cloister. He spoke to them affectionately, begging them to share his burden by their prayers and lighten his lot by their sympathy and affection. Peter nominated his successor in 1118 and died in 1123.

The monastery of Cava, founded in 1011, continued without interruption until 1861, when it was officially suppressed by the Italian government. However, there were always resident monks who kept up the divine office and led the monastic life, ensuring its continuity. It exists to this day.

In 1912 the community published the Lives of their early abbots, thought to be written by Hugh of Venosa, a younger contemporary of St Peter. It is to this biography, which had already appeared in *AA.SS.*, Mar., 1, pp. 326-34, that we owe all our knowledge of St Peter of Cava.

BB Christopher Bales, Alexander Blake, and Nicholas Horner, *Martyrs* (1590)

Christopher Bales (or Bayles, Mallett, or Evers), the son of John and Catherine Bales, was born (or perhaps baptized) on 12 March 1564 at Coniscliffe in the diocese of Durham. He went first to Reims in 1581 and was subsequently enrolled as a student at the English College in Rome in October 1583. After a year in Rome he left on account of ill health and then returned to Douai. He was ordained at Laon in March 1587 and sent on the English mission in November 1588.

After a short ministry he was arrested on 15 August 1589 and imprisoned in the Bridewell in London, where he was tortured by Topcliffe, who tried to get him to reveal the names of those who had received him into their homes and the places where he had said Mass. Despite being racked and suspended by his feet for an unbroken period of twenty-four hours, he revealed nothing. He was condemned for having been ordained abroad and returning to England to exercise his priesthood. When, according to custom, he was given the opportunity to speak on his own behalf, he asked the court whether in its opinion St Augustine (of Canterbury; 27 May), who had been sent from Rome by the pope to preach the gospel in England, was guilty of treason in so doing. They thought not, and he countered: "Why then do you arraign and condemn me for a traitor, who do the same thing as he did, and to whom nothing could be objected but what might equally be objected to him?" They replied that the difference lay in the fact that such evangelization was now an act of treason according to the law of the land. He was hanged, drawn, and quartered on 4 March 1590.

Nicholas Horner, a tailor, had been imprisoned once before for helping Catholic priests. One of his legs had to be amputated, and he was allowed out of prison on compassionate grounds, but having committed the same crime by providing Fr Bales with a jerkin, he was finally condemned to death and hanged on the same day. Alexander Blake, an ostler, is said also to have rendered service to Fr Bales and was hanged outside his own door on the same day.

These martyrs were beatified in 1929 and 1987.

M.M.P., pp. 160-1; Anstruther, 1, pp. 18-9.

Bd Placide Viel (1815-77)

Victoire Eulalie Jacqueline Viel, who was to become second superior general of the Sisters of the Christian Schools, was born in the village of Val-Vacher in Normandy, France, in 1815. She was the eighth child of a family of eleven. The family had once been prosperous townsfolk of Quettehou but were by then reduced to the status of small landowners. Victoire attended a sort of dame's school in Quettehou for seven years from the age of five and then took sewing lessons for a year. Her education was therefore minimal, but her devotion led her to take up catechism classes in the parish. At eighteen she was a tall and warm-hearted girl but plagued with shyness.

Her father's cousin, Sr Marie Viel, loosely referred to always as her aunt, had been a pupil and later one of St Marie-Madeleine Postel's (16 July) first companions. She was the bursar of Postel's small community. Perhaps with a view to recruiting her young cousin, she invited her to visit the group, which had recently been installed at Saint-Sauveur-le-Vicomte. Victoire was immediately and profoundly attracted to the foundress and conceived the desire to share the very poor but obviously happy life of the community. The suddenness of this development created some havoc in her relationship with her eldest brother, Michel, with whom she had already agreed to set up house, but she left home in May 1833, feeling the parting with her father more than anything else.

A fine Benedictine abbey in its day, Saint-Sauveur-le-Vicomte was progressively diminished by the régime of *in commendam* abbots, the majority of whom despoiled its assets, which served primarily to support the monastic community. The French Revolution completed the decline of a house that had been in existence since the tenth century. The abbey lands were sold, and the ruins of the abbey church were treated as a possible source of revenue if and when stone could be sold at a profit.

After some years of moving uncertainly about the region, Marie-Madeleine Postel bought the ruins in 1832 to house her young community, with the intention of restoring the abbey church to its former splendour. On her arrival in 1833 Victoire found a community of fourteen professed religious and nine novices, living in conditions of dire poverty. She also found a saint, by then nearly eighty, whose religious qualities, ideas, aspirations, and entire spirit she was to absorb as a sponge absorbs water.

The postulant embarked on her new life with enthusiasm, even going beyond what was reasonable. Judging that her correspondence with her father was a source of distraction, she asked him not to write to her any more save in an emergency, to which he agreed. She was clothed as a novice in the ruined abbey church in 1835 with ten others and was given the name of Placide. She then worked as an aide to the cook. Her profession took place in 1838, and there followed a dizzying sequence of appointments to new jobs. First, the foundress sent her back to school to catch up on her education. The two-year course was completed in three months, after which she taught in the boarding school and was made novice-mistress and a counsellor. Sr Marie realized that the foundress had deliberately set out to form this young woman to the highest responsibilities, and her own efforts to groom the young girl in the ways of religious observance turned into a palpable hostility expressed in continual fault-finding but more specifically in an attempt to get her transferred to another convent. The foundress stood firm, appointing Sr Placide as assistant general and entrusting her with the task of establishing a new foundation. While Sr Marie's jealousy is easily understood, the rationale that lay behind the foundress' decisions is less obvious, but on one occasion the ecclesiastical superior of the Congregation was speaking to the foundress about his concern for the future. She did not answer immediately, but presently Sr Placide passed and Mother Mary Magdelen said to him, "It is that twenty-year-old Sister who will succeed me. God will tell her what to do." She then commissioned the young Sr Placide to go to Paris and there beg the funds needed to restore the church. She was to go to the queen and the relevant government ministries to ask for grants and, for the rest, to beg from door to door. It was a task she carried out during the next four years, day in and day out, in a spirit of obedience, accepting rebuffs, weariness, and unmitigated loneliness. In May 1846 she was recalled to Saint-Sauveur-le-Vicomte, as the foundress was failing. St Marie-Madeleine Postel died on 16 July 1846. The general chapter for the election of her successor took place in September of the same year, and all but two of the votes were cast in favour of Sr Placide. She was utterly overcome and begged on her knees to be excused, but the ecclesiastical superior was firm. Sr Marie, on the contrary, felt that she herself should have been elected, an opinion held also by the chaplain. A strange period followed: Sr Placide put to the chapter the need for her to complete the task laid on her by the foundress to collect funds for the restoration of the abbey church. She therefore proposed that her election be waived for a year while she continued fund-raising, though she reserved some functions to herself in the interim. The chapter agreed, appointing Sr Marie to take charge of the daily running of the house. This situation endured for ten years. The superior general extended her begging tours to the provinces, which she traversed on foot, often sleeping in the open or wherever she was when darkness fell. However, the Paris house she had inaugurated in 1844 was her favourite refuge when she was not in the provinces. She kept up a correspondence with the members of the community and arranged for the assignment of jobs. Her short stays in the motherhouse were particularly painful. Sr Marie had appropriated the superior's rooms, while Mother Placide was relegated to a leaky attic; she humiliated the young superior in front of the community, gave her orders, opened her mail, and made decisions together with the chaplain and then informed the superior as to what she should do. Why was this allowed to happen? Was it an abdication of authority on the part of Mother Placide? Should she not have acted somewhat more forcefully toward Sr Marie? In the end her long-suffering yielded its dividend. To have forced Sr Marie into a reluctant submission would have resulted in a polarization of the still fragile Congregation, which Mother Placide instinctively knew had to be avoided at all costs. Instead, the community remained united around her. Shortly after the dedication of the abbey church, as Marie-Madeleine Postel had predicted, Sr Marie died.

Mother Placide directed the Institute for thirty years, a period of great expansion during which orphanages, nursery-schools, workrooms, and free elementary schools were built. Thirty-six schools were opened in Normandy alone. Her ambition was to do for girls what St John Baptist de la Salle (7 Apr.) had done for boys. She saw the Congregation expand to meet these many needs, from thirty-seven to 105 convents, some of them beyond the borders of France, and from 150 nuns to over a thousand. This expansion had been foreseen by the foundress, but her choice of Sr Placide had not been made on the strength of her organizational abilities. What she saw in the young Sr Placide was total fidelity to the aims of the Congregation, inspired by a love of God and neighbour that was to reach heroic proportions. Bd Placide's life was of the simplest from every point of view, with no great spiritual trials or mystical graces. She consistently attributed the expansion and consolidation of the Congregation to the intercession of St Marie-Madeleine Postel, whose beatification process she initiated. She herself died on 4 March 1877, at the age of sixty-two, and was beatified in 1951.

L. Canuet, *Bonne Mère Placide* (1925); Pierre de Crisenoy, *La Vénérable Placide Viel* (1943); D. Meunier, *Une gerbe de Merveilles* (? date); S[ister] C[allista], *Blessed Placide Viel* (1951). See also Bd Martha Le Bouteiller (18 Mar.). The Sisters of the Christian Schools, now known as The Sisters of St Marie-Madeleine Postel, have three houses in England: in Birmingham, Worcester, and Reading.

R.M.
St Photius and Companions, martyrs in Nicomedia (third century)
SS Paul and Juliana, martyrs at Ptolemais (third century)
St Hesychius, martyr at Antioch in Syria (*c.* 303)
St Basinus, bishop of Trèves (705)
St Appianus, monk of Comachio (eighth century)
St Adrian and Companions, martyrs in Scotland (875)
Bd Humbert of Savoy (1189)
Bd Romeo, Carmelite friar at Lucca (1380)

5

St Mark the Hermit (*c.* 400)

Mark was a great lover of the scriptures and is said to have learned both Old and New Testaments by heart. When he was about forty years old he retired to the Egyptian desert and lived a solitary life. In the Greek *Menaion* he is called Mark the Wonder-worker, although no record of his miracles has been preserved. We are told only of the hyena which came to his cell and deposited at his feet her blind whelp in the expectation of a miracle. Mark rubbed the animal's eyes with his own saliva and prayed over it, and its sight was restored. The next day the hyena returned with a sheepskin as a thank-offering, but Mark was none too pleased and warned the hyena against robbing the flocks of the poor. He gave the sheepskin to St Athanasius (2 May), who in turn gave it to Melania the Elder.

Palladius relates that he once visited Mark's cell when the latter was a very old man. As can happen to elderly people, he was given to muttering his thoughts aloud, and Palladius felt no inhibitions about eavesdropping. What obsessed the old man was that in his increasing frailty he was obliged to drink some wine and use oil. He berated himself and Satan for his descent into gluttony and longed only to be free of his excesses. He lived to be 100, and beyond that according to some.

The Lausiac History of Palladius attributes the healing of the animal to St Macarius, but the Greek *Menaion* is thought to be more trustworthy. *AA.SS.*, Mar., 1, pp. 365-6.

St Gerasimus, *Hermit* (475)

St Gerasimus was a native of Lycia in Asia Minor, where he had lived the eremitical life for some time before coming to Palestine. He pursued his calling in the Jordanian desert with single-mindedness but subsequently fell prey to the Nestorian heresies being propagated in Palestine by the monk Theodosius. St Euthymius (20 Jan.), the founder of Judaean monasticism, whom he was moved to visit around 453 on account of the universal veneration in which he was held, brought him to accept the Council of Chalcedon. From then on Gerasimus practised greater penances than ever to repair his lapse.

So many disciples came to Gerasimus in the Jordan that he built for them a *laura* of seventy hermit cells around a monastery for aspirants. The Rule of life for the monastery was less severe than the one he drew up for the hermits. These observed complete silence, had only a reed mat for a bed, and were not

44

permitted a fire in their rooms. Their cells had to be left open in their absence so that anyone who chose to do so might avail himself of their chattels, which in principle were the property of all, after the example of the early Church. They were permitted only bread, dates, and water during the week; coming together in the monastery over the weekend for the liturgy, they were allowed cooked food and a little wine. Should anyone have been so rash as to request Gerasimus to permit him a light to read by, or cooked food, or the possibility of heating some water in his room, he would have been given short shrift: such things were not done by hermits; whoever wanted that sort of thing would be better off living in the monastery. Gerasimus himself ate nothing for the whole of Lent, subsisting only on the Holy Eucharist. Manual work consisted in basket-weaving or rope-making. Palm fronds were distributed on Sunday evening and finished work returned on Saturday morning.

St Euthymius had such a high regard for Gerasimus that he sent him Cyriacus, a young boy from Corinth, whom he would not accept in his own *laura* on account of his extreme youth. Gerasimus put him in the monastery and, finding him given to prayer during the nights after a long day's work cutting wood, carrying water, and working in the monastic kitchen, took him as his own companion.

It had been an Armenian custom, which Euthymius had brought with him to Palestine, to go into strict solitude from the Octave of the Epiphany, feast of the Baptism of the Lord, to Palm Sunday. A group of ascetics, whom Gerasimus joined, used then to go further into the desert with Euthymius for this period. They followed the established pattern of complete solitude from Sunday evening to Friday evening, coming together for a liturgical assembly on Saturdays and Sundays. It was in anticipation of such an exodus that Gerasimus, with Cyriacus as his companion, joined St Euthymius in 473. The latter however, anticipating his own death, asked that their departure be put off for a week. Some days later, seeing in a vision the soul of Euthymius going up to heaven, Gerasimus set out with Cyriacus to prepare the body of the saint.

The *laura* of St Gerasimus long survived its founder and was still flourishing a hundred years after his death, which took place in 475, under Emperor Zeno.

John Moschus in his *Spiritual Meadow* relates a charming story of St Gerasimus. One day a lion came up to him, evidently in great pain, with one of his paws held up in the air. Gerasimus examined it, extracted a sharp thorn embedded in it, and washed and bound the paw. After this, the lion would not leave him. Now, the monastery had a donkey that was used for fetching water, and after a time, the lion was sent to take care of the donkey while it was out to pasture. One day, Arab traders stole the donkey, and the lion returned home, alone and out of sorts. All it could do was to look over its shoulder. The abbot accused the lion of eating the donkey and ordered him henceforth to take on the task of carrying the water, which it did. Not long after the thief came again, with the stolen donkey and three camels. The lion chased the man off, seized the donkey's bridle in his mouth and led him and the camels back to the monastery in triumph. Gerasimus admitted his mistake.

When the old abbot died, the poor beast was disconsolate. The new abbot said to him, "Our friend has gone to the Master and left us orphans, but take your food and eat." The lion only moaned the more. Finally, the abbot led him to Gerasimus' grave. He stretched himself over the grave and beat his head upon the ground and could not be prevailed upon to leave. He was found dead there a few days later.

It is possible that the lion associated with St Jerome is really the lion of St Gerasimus. The confusion may have arisen because of the Latin form of St Jerome's name, Hieronimus or Geronimus, which is very like that of today's saint.

AA.SS., Mar., 1, pp. 384-7, gives extracts from the Life of St Euthymius by Cyril of Scythopolis, which mention Gerasimus, and a quotation from John Moschus' *Spiritual Meadow*. The Life of Gerasimus attributed to Cyril of Scythopolis has been published by K. Koikylides (1902); see also A. Grégoire, "La vie anonyme de S. Gérasime," in *Byzantinische Zeitschrift* (1914); D. J. Chitty, *The Desert a City* (1966).

St Ciaran of Saighir, *Abbot and Bishop* (? fifth century)

Linguistic traces and archaeological finds in the south and south-east of Ireland point to commercial exchange with Roman Britain or Gaul as well as to Christian influences brought by early traders and/or missionaries. This and the persistent legends of saintly personages in the region indicate that there was a fervent Christian life taking shape from earliest times. St Ciaran was one of several saints who flourished in the region before the arrival either of Palladius (7 July) or Patrick (17 Mar.). He is traditionally a contemporary of St Ailbhe (12 Sept.).

Ciaran is thought to have been a native of Ossory. We read that he made himself a cell in a lovely spot surrounded by woods near a famous spring and for some time lived as a hermit. His first disciples, according to the delightful legends recorded in his *Lives,* were animals: Brother Boar, Brother Badger, Brother Fox, Brother Wolf, and Brother Deer. The stories of their doings are intended to make some moral or ascetic point, as when Brother Fox, feeling a bit peckish, pulls off Ciaran's sandals to eat them. Brother Badger is quickly sent to bring him to a better frame of mind. When Brother Fox returns, he has to do penance by fasting for three days. Ciaran's *Lives* inaugurate a special genre of hagiographical literature, reflected elsewhere in this volume.

Disciples gathered round him, and he constructed a monastery or collection of huts, round which there sprang up a town, called after him Sier-Ciaran and Saighir, or Saigher, three or four miles from Burr in Offaly. He is thought to have been consecrated a bishop as well; if so, he is one of the first in a long line of the abbot-bishops characteristic of the Irish Church. The kings of Ossory were buried in the monastery, remains of which can still be seen. His hermitage, thought to be on the island of Cape Clear (Cork) may also survive in the ruins of a church and an ancient well found there. He is the patron of Ossory.

The Latin Life is reproduced in *AA.SS.*, Mar., 1, pp. 387-97. The Latin Life in MS Gotha I. 81, is printed in *Anal.Boll.* 59 (1941), pp. 217-71. See J. Ryan, *Irish Monasticism* (1931); C. Thomas, *Christianity in Roman Britain to A.D. 500* (1981); *D.H.G.E.*, 12, 822. There is a short account in D. Pochin-Mould, *The Irish Saints* (1964), pp. 76-9: "The early *Lives* tell little of the real Ciaran, being in fact an amalgam of animal stories, multiplication of food miracles and tales of the saint getting the better of various magnates and kings." See also *O.D.S.*, p. 100. The topography of Ossory and Saighir is interesting.

Bd Jeremy of Valacchia (1556-1625)

John Kostistik was the eldest son of Margherita Barbato and Stoika Kostistik, a farmer. He was born on 29 June 1556 at Zazo in Valacchia, Rumania. In this region there were Orthodox Christians, Protestants, Muslim Turks, and some Roman Catholics living together, and this diversity contributed to his tolerance of and respect for others, whatever their origin or background. At home John imbibed his great love of the poor. Not wealthy themselves, the family still gave all they reasonably could to those who were poorer than themselves, for whom John and his grandfather would chop wood. Surplus grain from the farm was set aside for his mother to bake bread for the poor.

At the age of eighteen John left Rumania, at his mother's prompting, to go to southern Italy to carve out a new life there. Her name suggests that she herself was Italian by origin, although it is not clear what sort of future she envisaged for her son and whether she counted on Italian relatives to befriend the young man and set him on a career. However, his first four years in Italy were precarious, and he planned to return home. As someone had suggested that he try his luck in Naples, he agreed to go there first, asking the Capuchins, whom he had got to know in Bari, to be received into the Order. He was accepted, given the habit and the name of Jeremy in 1578, and in 1579 he made his profession.

The rest of his life was spent in looking after the sick. He nursed them in several friaries, but he worked for forty years consecutively in Sant' Eframo Nuovo, where there were 160 beds but more than 160 sick, since he often gave up his own room to a sick person. He brought to their service a generous heart and heroic self-denial. The meanest, the most tiring jobs, the most difficult and demanding patients he would keep for himself, regarding such service as a special privilege granted to him.

Despite his heavy workload he spent many hours of the night in prayer and advised others to do the same. Intimacy with Our Lord in the Blessed Sacrament, devotion to the Mother of God, meditation on the passion—these were the support of his spiritual life and the source of his moral strength. So great a charity could not be concealed within the cloister, and people of all walks would ask Brother Jeremy to visit them when they were ill. It was such a request from a local priest, to visit the grand chamberlain of Naples, John Avales, who was gravely ill, that was the immediate cause of Brother Jeremy's death. The seven-mile walk on a wet winter's night brought on an attack of double pneumonia, from which he never recovered. He died on 5 March 1625, at the age of sixty-nine. Devotion to him remained constant over 350 years. He was beatified on 30 October 1983 by Pope John Paul II, the first Rumanian to be so recognized.

N.S.B. 1, pp. 218-9; *C.F.S.*, p. 49.

St John Joseph of the Cross (1654-1734)

Carlo Gaetano was born on the feast of the Assumption 1654 on the island of Ischia off the west coast of Italy opposite the town of Naples. Joseph Calosirto and Laura Garguilo, his parents, were a devout couple, five of whose seven sons were later to become religious. Laura herself prepared food and medicines for the poor, who were always welcome guests to the house.

Carlo's precocious piety was allowed free rein. His fasts and penance surpassed anything that one would expect of a child, and no one was surprised when he announced that he wished to become a Franciscan of the strictest sort. He himself had been uncertain of where his vocation lay, but after he had made a novena to obtain guidance, two friars of the Alcantarine observance of the province of Granada came to the house; their poverty and bearing convinced him that his future lay with them. He went to their friary in Naples, Santa Lucia del Monte, where he was put through a gruelling postulancy by Fr Carlo, who discerned in the young man the signs of being called to an outstanding holiness in the tradition of St Peter of Alcántara (19 Oct.). Charles was not more than sixteen when he received the habit, which we are told he never laid aside night or day for the sixty-four years of his religious life. He took the name of John Joseph of the Cross.

He was held in such esteem by the community of Santa Lucia del Monte that he was chosen to head a foundation in Piedimonte di Alife, although he was not yet twenty-one and not yet a priest. The young friar did not in fact wish to be a priest, preferring to remain a deacon like St Francis, but his superiors decided otherwise, and on the feast of St Michael in 1677 he said his first Mass. He took up the ministry of the confessional the following month and proved to be an exceptional confessor. In spite of, or because of, the innocence of his life, he seemed to be endowed with rare wisdom and insight into the spiritual needs of others.

For his own community he added to the friary he had built little hermitages to which the friars could retire for periods of prayer and austerity. From this ideal setting he was called to take up the position of novice-master at Santa Lucia del Monte, returning to Piedimonte after two years to be its guardian. As superior he was foremost in humility, the first to take up the most menial jobs in the house and garden, but he was not at ease in a position of authority and begged to be released. This was granted by the chapter of 1681. He was authorized to dedicate himself wholly to the ministry of the confessional and spiritual direction, especially for the benefit of the nuns of the diocese. He was nominated guardian once more in 1684.

1702 saw the withdrawal of the Spanish friars who had brought the Alcantarine observance to Italy. There had been some friction between Spaniards and Italians, but the more serious impediment to good relations was the papal Brief that had laid down that all the important charges should be confided to the Spaniards. As these dwindled, the choice of personnel became more restricted and therefore more controversial. With the decision to secede, the Spaniards left the Italians insufficiently organized, and in addition they retained the two most developed houses in Naples, one of which was Santa Lucia del Monte. The small group of Italian friars turned to John Joseph. He appealed to Rome to give its consent to an Italian province, which was granted—surprisingly, given the precarious state of the group. At the first provincial chapter in 1703, John Joseph of the Cross was elected the minister provincial. There followed a difficult period of consolidation. He used his influence to pour oil on the troubled waters, and he set about strengthening regular discipline, reorganizing studies, and even making other foundations. When he saw that the province was well established, and he himself having come to the end of his term as first minister provincial, he obtained from the pope a Brief which exempted him for the future from the exercise of voting rights.

In 1722 the two Neapolitan houses under Spanish jurisdiction were ceded to the Italian province, and John Joseph returned to the house where he had entered. His last years were devoted to the direction and salvation of others, for which he had once more to sacrifice his desire for a life of obscurity. He could not appear in the streets, hobbling along with the help of his stick, without being followed by crowds who begged his advice or blessing and even cut away bits of his tattered habit. On 1 March 1739 he had a violent stroke but lingered for a few days, dying on 5 March 1739. He was beatified in 1789 and canonized in 1839. His relics lie in the friary church of Santa Lucia del Monte in Naples. In 1790 the Neapolitans declared him patron of the city.

St John Joseph left little written material. Only forty of his letters are extant, but these show him to be an admirable director of souls.

D. dell' Assunta, *Saggio istorico* (1789) and *Compendium vitae, virtutum et miraculorum B. Joannis Josephi a Cruce* (1839). For a résumé of this last in English, see Léon, 1, pp. 349-68; *Dict.Sp.*, 8, 835-7; A. Salvatore, *S. Giovan Giuseppe della Croce nel Centenario della nascita, 1654-1954* (1954); *Bibl.SS.*, 6, 1009-12.

R.M.

St Conon, martyr at Magydos in Pamphylia (*c.* 250)

St Lucius, pope (254)

St Eulogius, martyr in Palestine (? third century)

St Phocas, martyr at Sinope in Pontus (? fourth century)

St Adrian, martyr at Caesarea in Palestine (309)

St Virgil of Arles, bishop in Provence (*c.* 618)

St Drausius of Soissons, bishop (*c.* 680)

St George, afterwards Gregory, bishop in Cyprus (eighth century)

Bd Christopher Macassoli of Vigevano (1485)

6

St Julian of Toledo, *Bishop* (*c.* 642-90)

When he died in 690 Julian, archbishop of Toledo, was the most influential person in Spain. The Visigothic king Wamba was not altogether weak, but the monarchy was too fragile to function without the support of the hierarchy and, in particular, without the archbishop of Toledo, in whose see the all-important councils of Toledo, touching both Church and State, were held periodically.

Julian was born there around 642. He is said to have been of Jewish extraction, though his parents were Christian. According to Felix, his successor and biographer, he was baptized in the chief church of Toledo and educated by Eugenius II, another prelate of the town. As a young man, in company with a like-minded friend, Gudila Levita, he tried a quasi-monastic life of withdrawal and study. However, conscious of the urgent need for pastors, they both abandoned their retreat, but Gudila, then only a deacon, died almost immediately.

Wamba appointed Julian successor to Bishop Quiricus of Toledo, and he was consecrated in 680. Felix describes him as a prudent and prayerful man, well-informed, generous, approachable, and concerned for the weaker members of society. His kindness was such that no one in trouble who appealed to him was left without help. He presided over four councils between the years 681 and 686 and succeeded in obtaining primatial rights for his see. The fourteenth Council of Toledo issued a condemnation of the heresy of Monotheletism (the belief that there is only one will in Christ), which Pope Benedict II queried and which initiated a protracted correspondence between the Spanish hierarchy and the Holy See. Later writers have censured Julian for encouraging the kings to revive the persecution of the Jews, but it was not until five years after his death that the really scandalous and cruel law was enacted whereby all adult Jews were to be sold as slaves and all Jewish children taken from their parents at the age of seven and reared in Christian families.

Julian was a prolific writer. He must have been just thirty when he accompanied Wamba on his expedition into Narbonne against the traitor Duke Paul. He included an account of it in his subsequent Life of the king, one of his best works. Among his other literary works was a revision of the Mozarabic liturgy in use in Spain at that period, a book against the Jews, and the three books of the *Prognostics,* which treat of death, the state of the soul after death, the resurrection of the body, hell, and heaven. It is a sober work, logically arranged and heavily dependent on scripture and the Fathers. It eschews all speculation, keeping strictly within the limits imposed by these authorities, but it is shot through with a personal faith and a conviction that make it rewarding reading even now. "Death," says St Julian, "is not a good in itself, but it is a good to those who are good, for it is the gateway to life." Love and the desire to be united to God are sufficient to extinguish in us the natural fear of death: "However great the horror of death, it can be overcome by the power of love in imitation of that love by which he, who is our life, willed to suffer death for our sakes." These books were much esteemed in the Middle Ages.

Julian was buried at Toledo; Oviedo also claims some of his relics. Mozarabic calendars from the tenth century record his feast.

The brief memoir written by Felix, Julian's successor in the see of Toledo, is our principal source of information. See *AA.SS.*, Mar., 1, pp. 780-3; further information may be gleaned from the chroniclers and the acts of the councils over which he presided. See H. Leclercq, *L'Espagne chrétienne* (1906) for the historical background; *P.L.*, 96, 427-807, for his writings. Life by J. F. Rivera Recio (1944); *Bibl.SS.*, 6, 1216-8.

St Chrodegang of Metz, *Bishop* (*c.* 712-66)

St Chrodegang was born near Liège, in present-day Belgium, probably at the beginning of the eighth century. His parents were noble Franks who had him educated at the abbey of Saint-Trond. He was an excellent linguist besides being attractive and well-mannered. Charles Martel recognized his exceptional qualities and appointed him head of the diplomatic and legal corps of secretaries in his service. After the death of Charles, Chrodegang was nominated by Carloman to the bishopric of Metz although still a layman (742). He retained his secular post and, through the double prestige gained from his worldly and ecclesiastical careers, was able to wield an enormous influence for good. As Pepin's ambassador to Pope Stephen III, Chrodegang was closely concerned with the defeat of the Lombards in Italy, the handing over of the exarchate of Ravenna and other territory to the Holy See, and Pepin's own coronation as king in 754.

However, it is as a reformer of the clergy that Chrodegang is remembered. There was a general decline of morality among the secular clergy, encouraged by the laxity and lawlessness of the times. Chrodegang determined to put his own house in order, beginning with the priests of his city and cathedral of Metz. He brought together in clergy houses all the ecclesiastics, higher and lower, and obliged them to attend the offices in choir and to live a common life according to a Rule he had drawn up, based on that of St. Benedict. The code in use at Metz consisted of thirty-four chapters. At the prescribed daily meetings, one of the chapters had to be read, and from this reading the meeting came to be called the *chapter*. Soon the name was attached to those who were present at the readings, whilst those who were bound by these canons (rules) were called *canonici*, or canons, the conventual communities governed by their own regulations becoming known as regulars. Other directives concerning enclosure, residence, study, liturgy, dress, and meals were all designed to establish a form of community life, quasi-monastic in character, to ensure mutual support for the stricter observance of chastity and other virtues proper to the clerical state. Canons differed from monks specifically in one respect: they were able to hold private property and possess their own funds, a custom that would later be challenged. Chrodegang's Rule was applied to other dioceses and in an expanded form was eventually made obligatory by Charlemagne, who enacted that all bodies of clerics should live either as canons or as monks. The rule was adopted in other countries also, including the British Isles. The conception of such a life for the urban secular clergy, though it did not endure for various reasons in the form given it by Chrodegang, remains valid. The Church has seen it decline and revive under different guises at different periods of its history.

Metz under Chrodegang also became a centre of liturgy where Roman customs were observed and Roman chant performed. In time, Gallican compositions were added to the Roman collections, and the repertoire found its way back to Rome to be disseminated again throughout all Europe. The choir school of Metz was renowned, and its reputation lasted for several centuries. In 805 Charlemagne ordered that all choirmasters should be drawn from the school there.

After the death of St Boniface in 754, Chrodegang was the most effective leader of church reform in the Carolingian dominions. Another of his activities was the building and restoration of churches, monasteries, and charitable institutions. The abbey of Gorze, which he loved above all others, was one of his foundations; he was laid to rest there after his death on 6 March 766. The church of Saint-Symphorien of Metz also claims some relics.

AA.SS., Mar., 1., pp. 451-5; *Dict.Sp.*, 2, 463-6, 877-8; Dan-Marrou, 2, pp. 148-51, 191; J. Dickinson, *The Origin of the Austin Canons* (1950); *H.S.S.C.*, 4, pp. 99-102.

St Ollegarius, *Bishop* (1137)

Ollegarius (or Oldegar) was descended on both sides from noble Visigothic families. During his childhood Catalonia was suffering severely from the ravages of the Saracens. Ollegarius was offered by his parents to God and to St Eulalia in the church of Barcelona dedicated to this celebrated though misidentified martyr, apparently as a votive offering for protection from Saracen incursions.

At the age of fifteen the boy was made over to the canons attached to this church, together with an endowment of vineyards, buildings, and other property. He was appointed provost, and although it did not at all follow that he would adopt a celibate life and be ordained, it seems that he made a definite decision to do so and to live according to the Rule of St Augustine. For some years he was prior of Saint-Adrien in France, in which the bishop of Barcelona had recently installed canons regular, and he was later elected abbot of Rufus, also in France.

Ollegarius was in Barcelona by chance when he heard that Count Raymond was planning that he, Ollegarius, should be the next bishop of the then vacant see. At cock-crow he boarded a boat for France and took refuge in his monastery of St Rufus. Raymond then appealed to the pope, who ordered Ollegarius to accept the post. Although a reluctant bishop, he immediately showed that he could be an energetic one. Not long after, Count Raymond handed over to him the archiepiscopal see of Tarragona, a move confirmed by Pope Gelasius II, who sent him the *pallium*. In 1123 Ollegarius went to Rome to attend the First Council of the Lateran. He asked Pope Callistus II and the Fathers of the council to extend to those who would fight against the Moors in Spain the privileges then accorded the Crusaders. With reinforcements from abroad Count Raymond was able subsequently to dislodge and drive the Moors from some of their strongholds. Ollegarius also encouraged the spread of the Order of Knights Templars in his diocese.

The metropolitan city of Tarragona had been almost destroyed by the Moors, and the archbishop set to work to rebuild it and repair the churches. He was especially concerned for the sick poor, above all the mentally afflicted, and laid down that the possessions of defunct clergy should go to them.

At a diocesan synod in November 1136, the archbishop, old and in failing health, nevertheless spoke earnestly during the three days of meetings of the state of the Church and its pastoral needs, of the priesthood, of faith, and of works of charity. He also begged the synod to pray for him as he was close to death. He lived until the Lenten synod in the following year, 1137.

Two separate Lives of Ollegarius were printed by Florez in his *España Sagrada*, 29, pp. 472-99, together with a collection of the saint's miracles. J. Rebullosa, *Vida y milagros del d. Olaguer* (1609); *AA.SS.*, Mar., 1, pp. 480-97.

St Agnes of Bohemia, *Abbess (c. 1280)*

Agnes of Bohemia, or "of Prague," whom St Clare called her "half-self" and who founded the first convent of Poor Clares north of the Alps, was a descendant of St Wenceslaus (28 Sept.). Her father was Ottokar I, who succeeded to the throne of Bohemia in 1197, and her mother was a sister of Andreas II, king of Hungary. St Elizabeth of Hungary (17 Nov.) was her first cousin and two years her junior.

Agnes was born some time after 1200. For the first twenty-eight years of her life she was the object of dynastic schemes, which crumbled about her one after the other until she was free to do what she really wanted with her life. At the age of three she was engaged to Boleslaus, the son of Duke Henry of Silesia and St Hedwig (16 Oct). She was sent away from home immediately the arrangement was made, in the care of her nurse and with her retinue, to live in the Cistercian monastery of Trebnitz in Silesia, which St Hedwig had founded. According to a fourteenth-century document in the Bamberg library, "she was taught the rudiments of faith and morals by a daughter of St Hedwig," who must have been the abbess Gertrude. Boleslaus died when she was six, so she returned to Bohemia where she was placed in the Premonstratensian convent of Doxan.

Two years later she was recalled to her father's court. At the age of nine she was engaged to Henry, son of the emperor Frederick II. She was sent away again, this time to the Austrian court to learn the German language and customs, and placed in the care of Duke Leopold of Austria. He was all the while plotting to marry his own daughter to the prince and, having got what he wanted, he sent Agnes back home, to her great joy. By this time she was convinced that she must consecrate herself to a life of virginity.

However, there were two more suitors for her hand, Henry III of England and the widowed emperor himself, father of the Henry to whom she had been previously engaged. Her brother, King Wenceslaus, agreed to the engagement with the emperor despite her objections. Agnes increased her prayers and penances. She was twenty-eight years old and a beautiful woman when, in 1235, the emperor sent an ambassador to Prague to escort her back to Germany where the marriage was to take place. Her brother would listen to no remonstrances. Agnes succeeded in delaying her departure and wrote to Pope Gregory IX, asking him to prevent the marriage because she had not consented to it and indeed had long desired to be consecrated to Christ. Gregory sent his legate to Prague and corresponded directly with Agnes, who showed the letters to her brother. Wenceslaus found himself in a dilemma: he did not want to alienate the pope but neither did he want to incur the emperor's displeasure. He decided to tell Frederick the truth and let him deal with the matter. Surprisingly, Frederick offered to cancel the arrangement. "If she had left me for a mortal man," he said, "I should have made my vengeance felt, but I cannot take offence if she prefers the King of Heaven to me."

Agnes now set about consecrating herself and her possessions wholly to God, even winning her brother's co-operation. Her father had brought the Friars Minor to Prague, and she now built or completed a friary for them. With Wenceslaus' help she endowed a great hospital for the poor and entrusted it to the Knights Hospitallers. The two then built a convent for Poor Clares. It is said that the workmen, determined to donate their labour, would often slip away unperceived in order to avoid being paid. St Clare (11 August) sent five of her religious from San Damiano to begin the foundation, and on Whitsunday 1236 Agnes herself received the veil. Not only did over a hundred young girls in Bohemia follow her example, but all over Europe high-ranking ladies built and often entered the Poor Clare convents they had established.

Agnes embraced Lady Poverty with as much zeal as any of the early Franciscans. She refused the income with which her brother wished to endow the monastery, even obtaining from the pope the same concession as that accorded to St Clare at San Damiano, namely that the community be allowed to resign all revenues and property. She performed the humblest tasks in the monastery, sweeping, cleaning, cooking, mending the clothes of the lepers. Her nights were given to prayer. It was with difficulty that she was persuaded, when nominated by Pope Gregory IX, to accept the dignity of abbess. St Clare was overjoyed to hear of the progress of the young nun and wrote her affectionate letters of encouragement: "Love with your whole heart the One who offered himself with his whole heart for you, before whose infinite perfections sun and moon are lost in wonder and whose greatness is measureless. . . . There is nothing greater than a person who is faithful. She is greater than the heavens, for no creature is capable of containing the creator whereas she is his dwelling-place, his seat and his throne." Agnes indeed seemed to be her best-loved daughter: "As your own mother loved you with all her being, so do I love you. . . . Absorbed in your contemplation, remember me your poor mother, knowing that I have inscribed you on the tablets of my heart, for I hold you more than any other in the greatest affection."

Agnes spent some forty-four years as a Poor Clare, always thanking God for the grace of her vocation. She died on 6 March, some time after 1280. She was canonized by Pope John Paul II in 1989, about seven hundred years after her death and just as the Czechs were throwing off the yoke of Communism.

AA.SS., Mar., 1, pp. 501-29; Léon, 1, pp. 339-48.

St Colette of Corbie, *Abbess* (1381-1447)

St Colette is venerated as the reformer of one of the most austere of the religious Orders, the Poor Clares. The impression she made on the Franciscan Order was very great, and one branch still bears the name of Colettines.

Her father, Robert Boellet, was a carpenter at the abbey of Corbie in Picardy, in France. He and his wife, Marguerite, were a devout couple, who late in life had an only child, whom they called Nicolette in honour of St Nicholas (6 Dec.), to whose intercession they attributed her birth. Colette, as she was called, received a primary education and later lived at home almost as a solitary, busying herself with prayer, manual work, and catechism classes.

By the time Colette was seventeen both her parents had died, leaving her in the care of the abbot of Corbie. She was now free to choose what she wanted to do—subject to the approval of the abbot—but she did not quite know what she wanted, except to love and serve God with all her heart and strength. She consulted a holy Celestine monk in Amiens, who advised her to make a vow of virginity and gave her a few instructions on prayer. He judged that her will to serve God so totally was a sign of a religious vocation. Colette first tried a group of Béguines who served the local hospital, then a community of Urbanist Poor Clares (who observed the Rule of St Clare as revised by Pope Urban IV), and lastly the Benedictines. In none of these did she find the austerity and strictness of life that she craved. She returned to Corbie and to a further period of uncertainty about her future.

56

3688888888888888888

Not long after, Fr Pinet, a Franciscan, had occasion to pass through Corbie, and Colette sought his advice. After prayer and careful deliberation he suggested that she join the Franciscan Third Order and take up the life of a recluse. Colette did not hesitate. The abbot of Corbie presided over the ceremony in which she pledged herself, at the age of twenty-two, to the life of an anchoress. He himself conducted her to the anchorhold adjoining the church, which he had assigned to her and which he then sealed. There Colette remained immured from 1402 to 1406. A window of her oratory opened on to the church; one part of her dwelling served as a parlour where she could receive visitors behind a grille, but in time the visitors became so numerous and also so belligerent when they were told their time was up that all visits were halted for three years. Two faithful friends saw to all her needs; Colette for her part looked after the church linen, mended the clothes of the poor and, for the rest, gave herself wholly to prayer and penance. As with many another recluse, her days alternated between abundant grace and what she regarded as diabolic assaults.

To Colette, whose difficult itinerary had led her at last to the hermitage, to which she was bound by a vow of enclosure, nothing could be more inconceivable than a call to leave it. Any intimation of a new vocation could only come from the devil, who was tempting her to abandon her real vocation. The last few months spent in her cell were months of anguish as she struggled against demands made on her, the uncertainty as to their true source, and the awareness of her own incompetence. The struggle was initiated by a vision she was given of St Francis (4 Oct.), prostrate before the feet of Christ, begging to be given Colette for the reform of the nuns and friars of his Order. The Virgin added her supplications to those of St Francis. Colette's immediate reaction was one of recoil, but even in the cold light of reason it still remained unthinkable. Finally, she accepted what she saw to be God's will unconditionally and was told that she would be sent a companion and guide for the work she was to do.

Henri de Baume was a Franciscan of the strict observance, belonging to a friary in Savoy, who suffered deep anguish at the state of the Order and of the Church. By a series of extraordinary events he was led to visit the recluse of Corbie, with whom he agreed to cooperate to further the work of reform. With his help Colette set out for Nice to visit the antipope, Peter de Luna (Benedict XIII) regarded by the French as the legitimate pope. He received her with great kindness and in his presence she pronounced her vows according to the first Rule of St Clare. Deeply impressed by her, he appointed her superior of all the convents she should found or reform, with a mission to the friars and tertiaries as well. Henri de Baume was appointed her assistant.

The reform, which consisted in a return to the first Rule of St Clare supplemented by new Constitutions (approved in 1434), could hardly be imposed from the outside on existing Poor Clare convents. That of Besançon did indeed accept the reform, but there were only two nuns resident, one of whom chose to go the Bernardines, the other to adopt the reform. The other convents established by Colette were generally new foundations, which sprang up and flourished with remarkable rapidity under her direction. Altogether she founded seventeen, besides those that accepted her reform. A convent closely connected with Colette is Le Puy-en-Velay, which has had an unbroken life to this day. Twelve friaries accepted her reform but were eventually reabsorbed into the main branches of the Franciscan family.

Colette was convinced that if prodigies were necessary to sustain the work they would be granted. In fact, the story of the foundations reads like that of an itinerant wonder-worker, so that the duchess of Bourbon could write, "I am longing to see that wonderful Colette who raises people from the dead." She did see her, and no family was more deeply influenced by her. This woman of humble origin exercised an extraordinary sway over people of high rank in the world, such as Blanche of Geneva, the duchess of Nevers, Amadeus II of Savoy, the princess of Orange, and Philip the Good, duke of Burgundy. Colette had left her hermitage, but she seemed to take with her into the world inviolable depths of interior silence where she remained in continual union with Christ. It was this that sustained her throughout her career. There were times when activity had to yield to the imperious action of grace as she remained in ecstasy for many hours after Holy Communion or during Holy Week when meditating on the passion. She had seen Our Lord in a vision suffering and dying on the cross, and always on Fridays, from six in the morning until six in the evening, she meditated and prayed, neither eating nor drinking. Once she had a vision of men and women falling from grace in appalling numbers, like flakes in a snowstorm, and ever after she would pray with great fervour for the conversion of sinners and for the souls in purgatory. She was sometimes subject to attacks of depression but knew great joys also. On the feast of SS Peter and Paul in 1446 she learned something of the devastation that the Reformation would bring in its train, especially to religious houses, while on Corpus Christi she was assured that her reform would weather the storms. During this year she experienced the grace of spiritual marriage.

Toward the end of 1446, after forty years of activity, Colette began to feel ill. She retired from active life for the six months that remained to her. In July 1447 she had to be put to bed, and she died in her convent in Ghent in her sixty-seventh year.

Many kings and princes petitioned the Holy See for her canonization, among them Charles the Bold in 1478 and Henry VIII in 1513. Owing to the divisions in the Franciscan Order, the Reformation, and then the French Revolution, her canonization, by Pius VII, did not take place until 1807. Her relics were frequently moved to ensure their safety. They were finally taken to Poligny, the convent that made three foundations in England. St Colette is generally represented with birds about her, for she is said to have understood their communications, as well as with a pet lamb which always accompanied her to church. Her breviary survives at Besançon, but Ghent is the principal centre of her cult.

A good number of Colette's letters and the copious but disjointed recollections of Fr Peter de Vaux, her confessor in her last years, survive. The Lives by Sister Perrine and Peter de Vaux, which were published in Latin by the Bollandists, *AA.SS.*, Mar., 1, pp. 531-626, have been edited in their original language by Ubald d'Alençon (1911). The biography by Sainte-Marie Perrin has been translated into English with some useful additions (1923), as has the Life by Fr Sellier (1864). See also Léon, 1, pp. 369-94; J. Goulven, *Rayonnement de sainte Colette* (1952); *H.S.S.C.*, 7, 117-25; *Bibl.SS.*, 4, 76-81.

R.M.

St Marcian, martyr at Tortona (second century)

St Victorinus, martyr at Nicomedia in Bythinia (? third century)

St Quiriacus, priest of Trèves, (fourth century)

SS Cyneburga, Cyneswide and Tibba, religious at Peterborough (seventh century)

St Fridolin, abbot of Sackingen, (eighth century)

Forty-two martyrs of Syria (848)

St Cadroe, abbot of Waulsort in the Ardennes (975)

St Rose, religious at Viterbo (1253)

ST PERPETUA
Gold dragon, silver ladder, on red field

7

SS PERPETUA and FELICITY and Companions,
Martyrs (203)

The record of the passion of St Perpetua, St Felicity, and others who died with them is one of the great treasures of hagiological literature that have come down to us.

In the year 203 five catechumens were arrested in Carthage, North Africa, during the persecution initiated by Severus: the two slaves Revocatus and Felicity, who was nearing the end of her pregnancy, Saturninus, Secundulus, and Vivia Perpetua, aged twenty-two, the wife of a high-ranking man and mother of an infant at the breast. Perpetua's parents were still alive. Her father was a pagan, she his favourite child. One brother was already a Christian, another a catechumen like herself, while a third had died at the age of seven. These five prisoners were joined by Saturus of his own accord. He seems to have instructed them in the Faith and to have been unwilling to leave them alone to their fate. The five were arrested and kept under guard in a private house. Perpetua relates:

While we were still under arrest and my father in his affection for me was trying to subvert and weaken my faith by his arguments, I said to him, "Father, do you see this vase here—or waterpot, or whatever it is?"

"Yes," he said.

"Could it be called by any other name?"

"No," he replied.

"Neither can I be called other than what I am, a Christian."

My father was so angered by the use of this word that he lunged at me as if to tear out my eyes but he only shook me and then, himself overcome, made off with his diabolical arguments. I gave thanks to the Lord during the few days that I was free of my father, in whose absence I regained my composure. During those few days we were baptized. The Spirit inspired me to ask for nothing at my baptism but bodily endurance. A few days later we were lodged in the prison. I had never known such darkness and was terrified. It was a day of horror, what with the overpowering heat due to the crush of people and the manhandling on the part of the soldiers. To crown it all, I was tormented with worry for my child in such a place. Tertius and Pomponius, those blessed deacons who looked after us, bribed the soldiers to let us go to a better part of the prison, where we might obtain some relief for a few hours. Quitting the prison, we were all left to ourselves. I nursed my baby who was faint with hunger. Worried about him, I spoke to my mother on his behalf and I comforted my brother, confiding my son to their care. I felt myself flagging as I saw their fears for me. For several days I lived with these problems. Then I obtained leave for my baby to remain in prison with me. At once, relieved of my worry and concern for the child, I recovered my spirits. The prison suddenly became a palace where I would have chosen to be rather than anywhere else. . . .

A few days later there was a rumour that we would be given a hearing. My father came from the city, stricken with grief. He came up to me hoping to shake my resolution, saying, "Daughter, pity my white hairs! Pity your father, if indeed you regard me as a father worthy of the name. Have I not with these very hands brought you to this, your prime of life? Have I not preferred you to all your brothers? Do not bring this disgrace upon me then. Think of your brothers, think of your mother and your aunt, think of your child who will not survive without you! Give up this resolve of yours, or you will kill us all. If anything happens to you, we shall no longer be able even to speak of you." He said all this out of his father's love, kissing my hands and throwing himself sobbing at my feet, no longer calling me "daughter" but "lady." I grieved for my father because he alone of all my family would find no joy in my martyrdom. I comforted him, "Whatever happens when I stand in the dock will be what God wills. We are in his hands not our own." He went away, grieving.

One day while we were having a meal we were suddenly taken away for the hearing. We arrived at the forum and immediately the news spread to the neighbourhood and an enormous crowd gathered. We went up into the dock. The others were questioned and confessed their faith. Then it was my turn. And there was my father, with my child. He drew me down, saying, "Perform the sacrifice, have pity on your child."

Hilarian, procurator of the province, who had by then succeeded the deceased proconsul, Minutius Timinianus, said the same thing:

"Spare your father's white hairs, spare your infant son. Offer the sacrifice for the emperor's welfare."

I replied, "I will not."

"Are you a Christian?" Hilarian asked.

"Yes, I am," I replied.

As my father, still trying to make me give in, would not budge, Hilarian ordered him to be thrown out, and he was struck with a rod. I felt for my father as if I had myself received the blow and grieved for such unhappiness in his old age. Judgment was then passed: we were all condemned to the beasts. We returned to prison in a state of exultation.

As my baby was used to being nursed and to being in prison with me, I sent Pomponius the deacon without delay to my father to ask for the baby. Father refused to give him up. But as God had disposed things, the child no longer needed to be fed at the breast and I myself suffered no discomfort so that I was relieved on both counts.

Before Hilarian had pronounced sentence he had had Saturus, Saturninus, and Revocatus scourged, and Perpetua and Felicity struck about the face.

61

Secundulus died in prison before the examination; the others were reserved for the shows planned to entertain the soldiers at the military camp on the festival of Geta, whom the emperor Severus had made Caesar some four years before.

Perpetua continues:

The adjutant Pudens, who was warder of the prison, now began to make much of us seeing that some great power was at work in us. He allowed many visitors to come and see us so that we might console each other. As the day fixed for the games approached, my father, overwhelmed with grief, came to see me. He began to tear out his beard and throw it on the ground, to fling himself on his face and curse his old age, uttering things that no one could listen to unmoved. I ached for the pain he was suffering in his old age. . . .

Perpetua concludes:

I have written this up to the day before the games. Let whoever has a mind to do so write down what will take place at the actual games.

The rest of the acts were indeed added by another person, apparently an eyewitness:

As for Felicity, she too was favoured by the Lord. When arrested she was already eight months into her pregnancy. As the day of the games drew near, she was concerned that her martyrdom would be postponed—it is unlawful for pregnant women to be exposed to punishment—and she would have to shed her holy and innocent blood afterwards in the company of common criminals. Her fellow-martyrs were also very upset to leave such a fine companion behind to travel on the same road of hope by herself. Two days before the contest they prayed together for her to the Lord. Immediately the pains of childbirth came upon her. Her labour was naturally intense, it being only the eighth month. One of the assistants to the prison guards said to her, "You suffer now like that, what will you do when you are thrown to the beasts? How is it that you thought so little of them when you refused to sacrifice?" She replied, "I suffer now, but then another within me will suffer for me, for I shall be suffering for him."

She gave birth to a girl whom a certain sister brought up as her own. . . .

The tribune had been warned by some stupid fellows that the prisoners might be spirited out of the prison by magic, so he treated them with greater severity. Perpetua was the one to confront him, "Why do you not allow us, Caesar's most distinguished prisoners, some nourishment? Are we not to fight on his birthday? Would it not do you credit if we were to appear well-cared for on the day?" The point went home and the tribune flushed. He gave orders that they were to be treated more humanely and allowed to receive their relatives and others visitors and eat with them. Prudens, the jailer was by now a believer.

The day before the games they had a last meal, known as the "free feast" which they transformed as far as possible into an agape. To the people who surrounded them they spoke with composure of the judgments of God and of the joy of their sufferings. Saturus even mocked their curiosity, "Will tomorrow not satisfy you? Why do you crave to see people you hate? Friends today, enemies tomorrow. But take good note of our faces so that you may recognize us on the day." They all left the prison in a state of amazement, and many of them believed.

The day of their triumph dawned and the martyrs set out for the amphitheatre rejoicing, as if on their way to heaven. Their faces were serene and, if they trembled, it was with joy rather than fear. Perpetua, the beloved of God and matron of Christ, followed the rest with unhurried gait, her face radiant, her flashing eyes challenging the gaping onlookers. Felicity, too, was there, pleased that she had been safely delivered so that now she could fight the beasts, pleased to exchange the blood shed at delivery for the blood of martyrdom, the midwife for the gladiator, post-natal washing for a second baptism.

When they arrived at the gates and were being forced to change their clothes, the men to put on the robes of the priests of Saturn and the women those of the priestesses of Ceres, the noble Perpetua opposed them to the last, "We came here without resistance so that in return you should respect our liberty; we pledged our own lives so as to avoid this, and you too pledged your agreement." Injustice recognized the justice of the claim and the tribune yielded. They were led into the arena just as they were. Perpetua was singing a psalm. Revocatus, Saturninus, and Saturus threatened the spectators with judgment; arriving within sight of Hilarian they suggested by their gestures, "You have condemned us, but God will condemn you." The crowd became angry and demanded that they be scourged by the band of wardens keeping the beasts. The martyrs for their part were delighted to win a share in the Lord's passion.

He who said, "Ask and you shall receive" accorded the martyrs the death each one had requested. Whenever they had talked among themselves about their desire for martyrdom, Saturninus for one used to say that he wanted to be exposed to all the different beasts so as to win a more glorious crown. As the contest opened therefore he and Revocatus had a brush with a leopard and on the platform were also set upon by a bear. However there was nothing Saturus dreaded more than a bear; he hoped to be dispatched by the bite of a leopard. When he was exposed to a wild boar, the keeper who had lashed him to the animal was himself gored and died a few days after the games. Saturus was merely dragged. He was then bound in the stocks, but the bear would not leave its den, so Saturus was recalled once again unhurt. The devil had prepared for the young women a most savage heifer, not usually used for this purpose but selected so that its sex might match theirs. They were stripped and led out into the arena. There was a movement of revulsion in the crowd as they saw that one was a delicate young girl, the other fresh from childbirth with milk issuing from her breasts, so they were recalled and dressed in loose tunics.

Perpetua was the first to be thrown, falling on her back. Sitting up she pulled the tunic which was torn open at the side over her thighs, concerned more for her modesty than her pain. Then she asked for a clasp and fastened her hair which had come loose—for a martyr should not suffer with dishevelled hair and give the impression that she was mourning in the hour of her glory. Seeing that Felicity had been winded, she went and helped her up and both of them stood together. The crowd by then had had their lust for cruelty appeased, so the martyrs were led to the Porta Sanavivaria. There Perpetua was supported by the then catechumen Rusticus, who stayed with her. As if awaking from sleep (so lost in the Spirit and rapt in ecstasy was she), she began to look around and to the amazement of all said, "When are we going to be thrown to that heifer, or whatever it is?" When told that it had already been done she did not at first believe it until she saw the marks of the ill treatment on her body and dress. She then sent for her brother and said to him and the catechumen, "Stand fast in the Faith, love one another and don't let our sufferings upset you."

At another gate Saturus was encouraging the officer Pudens: "So there, it is exactly as I anticipated and predicted. So far I have felt no animal touching me. Now, so that you may believe with your whole heart, I shall enter the arena and be brought to an end with one bite of the leopard." The spectacle was nearing its close as he was exposed to a leopard. He was so covered with blood from its one bite that as he came back the crowd shouted in witness of his second baptism, "Well washed! Well washed!" And indeed he was truly washed who had been washed in this manner. Then to the officer Pudens he said, "Good-bye. Keep the Faith and remember me. Don't let these things distress but rather strengthen you." So saying, he asked Pudens for the ring from his finger, dipped it into his wound and returned it to him as a legacy, leaving him a token and souvenir of his martyrdom. Then, half-conscious, he was thrown with the rest in the usual place to have his throat cut. However, the crowd demanded that they be brought into the open so that, seeing the sword go through their bodies, their eyes too might be the accomplices of the crime. The martyrs rose up and, after having embraced each other and sealed their martyrdom by the solemn kiss of peace, they went of their own accord where the mob wanted them to go. Some remained erect, receiving the blow in silence, especially Saturus, who was the first to mount the gangway and so the first to yield his soul. Once again he was waiting for Perpetua. She, however, had some pain to endure still. Inadvertently struck on the bone, she screamed, then herself guided the inexperienced gladiator's unsure hand to her throat. Perhaps such a woman, feared as she was by the unclean spirit, could not die unless she herself had willed it.

These saints were honoured in all the early calendars and martyrologies. They appear in the Philocalian calendar at Rome and the Syriac calendar in the latter half of the fourth century. For some time their feast on 7 March was displaced by that of St Thomas Aquinas (now 28 Jan.), but it has now been restored to its original date. In 1907 an ancient inscription was found in the Basilica Majorum at Carthage where the bodies of these martyrs were buried. SS Perpetua and Felicity figure in the mosaic Procession of Martyrs in the church of San Apollinare Nuovo in Ravenna.

The extracts from the Passion above are trans. from the Latin version published in *A.C.M.*, pp. 106-31; E. Owen, *Some Authentic Acts of the Early Christian Martyrs*, pp. 74-92 (1927); H. Delehaye, *Les Passions des Martyrs et les Genres Littéraires* (1921); P. Monceaux, *Histoire Littéraire de l'Afrique Chrétienne* (1901-). See also M. R. Miles, *Carnal Knowing: Female Nakedness and Religious Meaning in the Christian West* (1989; Brit. ed., 1992); J. Amat (ed.), *Passion de Perpétue et de Félicité* 1996).

BB John Larke, John Ireland, and German Gardiner,
Martyrs (1544)

Nothing is known of John Larke's background or early life, but it is assumed that he was well on in years at the time of his martyrdom. In 1504 he was appointed rector of St Ethelburga, Bishopsgate, and held the post until a few years before his death. In 1526 he became rector of Woodford in Essex but resigned the living four years later, when Sir Thomas More (22 June) nominated him to Chelsea.

Cresacre More in his *Life of More* said that "[More's] death so wrought on the mind of Dr Larke, his own parish priest, that he following the example of his own sheep, afterwards suffered a most famous martyrdom, for the same cause of the Supremacy," although this did not in fact happen until 1544.

German (or Jermyn) Gardiner was a layman, secretary to Stephen Gardiner, to whom he may have been related. He engaged in controversy with the Reformers, which was to tell against him later, but his heroes were those martyrs especially who suffered for the defence of the papacy. Cresacre More speaks also of Gardiner in his *Life of More*: "German Gardiner, an excellent, learned and holy layman, coming to suffer death some eight years after, avouched at his end before all the people that the holy simplicity of the blessed Carthusians, the wonderful learning of the Bishop of Rochester and the singular wisdom of Sir Thomas More had stirred him up to that courage."

Four Catholics were brought before the Westminster sessions on 15 February 1544: John Larke; John Ireland, a secular priest of whom little is known; and German Gardiner and John Heywood, laymen. They were charged with "attempting treason against the King in the matter of his dignity, title and name of Supreme Head of the Church of England and Ireland, by words, writing and acts" and convicted. John Heywood recanted and was pardoned. The others were hanged, drawn, and quartered on 7 March 1544 and were beatified in 1929.

L.E.M., 1, pp. 541-7.

St Teresa Margaret Redi (1747-70)

Anna Maria Redi was born in Arezzo in Tuscany, Italy, on 15 July 1747. Her parents, Ignatius Redi and Camilla Balatti, were a noble and devout couple whose well-regulated home nurtured three vocations to the religious life, that of Anna Maria herself and those of her two sisters.

At nine years of age she was sent for her education to the Benedictine nuns of Sant' Apollonia in Florence. She was allowed to make her First Communion at ten. Her intuitive understanding of the demands of divine love led her to follow the path of self-denial with remarkable determination. One of her early decisions, which she would maintain during her career as a religious, was to avoid any manifestation of her inner spiritual life so as not to stand out from her companions in any way. She knew that she was being called to a religious life but was uncertain of the Order to which she should commit herself. One of the rare preternatural experiences related of her steered her irrevocably toward the Carmelites.

When she was sixteen, she was brought home from Sant' Apollonia and at home lived as if already in Carmel. She slept on a palliasse and practised the penances current in any convent of the time. Strangely, her father failed to see the direction in which his daughter was moving. On the advice of her confessor she told her parents that she wished to enter Carmel. Both were devastated by the news. Her father consulted eminent churchmen who, after speaking with Anna Maria, concluded that she did indeed have a vocation to the religious life. Ignatius Redi bowed to the inevitable and agreed to his daughter writing to the Carmel of Florence to seek admission. All was arranged, yet he could not bring himself to talk to her about it until one evening when he broke down and reproached her for wanting to abandon him. Quietly she left the room.

She entered the Carmel of Florence on 16 August 1764 at the age of seventeen. Her postulancy was uneventful save for an infection on the knee. Although it was exceedingly painful, she continued to kneel and carry out all her other duties and so exacerbated the condition that a high fever caused her to collapse. The infected area was lanced, but the cure was long and slow. However, she had by now shown her mettle and was accepted for her clothing, which took place on 11 March 1765. She took the name of Teresa Margaret Marianna of the Sacred Heart. She once wrote to another religious, "Love does not want a divided heart; he wants all or nothing." This meant entering fully and without concession to human frailty into the ascetic practices of Carmel while responding totally to the inner demands of its contemplative spirit. As she was the recipient of measureless love, she would go well beyond what was required so as to give love for love: "Nothing will seem difficult when we realize that the loved one wants only love for love. He has given himself completely to us; let us give him our whole heart and we shall live in joy."

The novice-mistress, Teresa Maria of Jesus, was severe. She knew that the new novice was well advanced in the ways of the spirit, but such precocious perfection needed to be put to the test. Reprimands were not spared even when uncalled for and unjustified. After her clothing, Sr Teresa Margaret's other knee became infected, and the same long-drawn out procedure seemed likely. As the novice saw that her time for profession was approaching and began to fear that it would be either put off or even refused, she prayed earnestly to Our Lady and was cured. Her admission to profession was carried without a single dissenting voice, and her profession subsequently took place on 12 March 1766.

Sr Teresa Margaret held two jobs during her short professed life; she was appointed sacristan and later infirmarian. In both occupations there was plenty of opportunity to suffer and to serve others. No one even gave a thought to what she might be suffering, so successfully did she camouflage her feelings. She wrote, "The best way to love God is to do so in silence, remembering the words, 'but Jesus said not a word.'"

She was remarkably free from complexities of any kind. A clear conception of what holiness entailed, a courageous acceptance of the realities of our human existence, an untroubled faith, a pure conscience, and a childlike confidence in God enabled her to sustain a life of unremitting penance as well as the burdens of her office. As infirmarian, she had to look after a mentally-deranged nun who as often as not repaid her with physical violence. She seemed always to know when she was needed by an epileptic patient or indeed by anyone in distress. A deaf nun could hear no one but always seemed to understand the infirmarian, who, nevertheless, spoke in an ordinary tone of voice. There were some extraordinary occurrences—the novice with agonizing toothache who was cured by a kiss on her cheek, the sick eased by the touch of her hand.

At Terce of Pentecost 1767, Sr Teresa Margaret heard as if for the first time the words, "God is love." Thereafter, she seemed to live in love, but it was a sort of martyrdom. Every action, every aspiration toward God spoke of her love of God, but it was a love barely felt emotionally, so that she believed that she was bereft of the ability to love. The more love dilated her being, the greater her anguish at her inability to respond. She prayed daily to the Holy Spirit, casting upon him her own needs and those of the whole Church. Although always outwardly composed, she lived again the great St Teresa's (15 Oct.) "I die because I do not die." She went so far as to ask her deaf patient, who was on the point of death, to obtain from God for her the grace of an early death. This prayer was heard. After two days of great pain Sr Teresa Margaret died of what seems to have been peritonitis in her twenty-third year, on 7 March 1770. Her body lay exposed for fifteen days without a sign of decomposition, and it has remained incorrupt until the present time.

Sr Teresa Margaret Redi was beatified on 9 June 1929 and canonized on 13 March 1934. Her spirituality and the age at which she died have made many see her as an eighteenth-century Thérèse of Lisieux.

A copy of the *summarium de virtutibus* printed for the process of beatification is in the library of the British Museum. The biography, written by Albergotti, bishop of Arezzo, was used for the English biography, *Sr Teresa Margaret Redi*, by L. Hartwell, rev. by J. Donovan (1848). Ildefonso di San Luigi Gonzaga, *Relatione sulla vita e le virtù di S[uor] Teresa Margherita Redi*, (1773); G. Bardi, *S. Teresa Margherita Redi, una precorritrice di S. Teresa de Lisieux* (1957); *Dict.Sp.* 15, 674-8. *Ephemerides Carmeliticae* 10 (1959) is consecrated to the saint, her family, and religious community.

St John Baptist Nam Chong-Sam, *Martyr* (1812-66)

John Baptist Nam Chong-Sam was born in Ch'ungju, Korea, in 1812. He entered the civil service and, at the age of thirty-nine, became a regional governor. Finding it difficult to reconcile his duties with his Christian faith, he resigned his post and took up teaching Korean to foreign missionaries. Later he went to Seoul, where he taught Chinese literature to the children of higher civil servants.

In 1866 a Russian vessel attacked Hamgyong province. It was thought that the European powers in Beijing might be in a position to give the Russians chase. John was known to the regent's wife as a Catholic, and she suggested that he might act as an emissary to those French missionaries already in Korea, notably Bishop Berneux. John was asked to bring the bishop to the royal palace where he would be officially requested to intervene with his compatriots in Beijing. Unfortunately, the bishop was away in Pyongyang. When he finally arrived in Seoul, the Russians had already left.

Government officials, angry that a Catholic had been thus used where they were impotent, determined that the Catholics must be suppressed. John was arrested, tortured, and finally beheaded on 7 March 1866. He died calling on the names of Jesus and Mary.

M.S.K., pp. 138-9; see 20 Sept. for a general treatment of the martyrs of Korea.

R.M.

St Basil and companions, bishops and martyrs in the Crimea, (fourth century)

St Esterwine, abbot of Wearmouth (*c.* 686)

St Gaudiosus, bishop of Brescia (fifth century)

St Ardo (Smaragdus), abbot of Aniane (843)

St Paul, bishop of Prusa in Bythinia (850)

St John, abbot of Gorzes (976)

St Siméon and companions, martyrs of Korea (1866)—see 21 Sept.

8

ST JOHN OF GOD, *Founder* (1495-1550)

It took St John of God forty-three years to discover his vocation and thirteen to arrive at the highest degree of sanctity in pursuance of the call to serve Our Lord Jesus Christ in the persons of the sick poor.

His parents lived in the town of Montemor-o-Novo in the diocese of Evora in Portugal, where John was born on 8 March 1495. He was lured away to Spain at the age of eight by a visiting priest whose motives remain unclear. About a fortnight later his mother died—of grief, it was said—and his father subsequently became a Franciscan.

Meanwhile he found another family at Oropeza in Castile, on the frontier between Portugal and Spain, where the priest had left him. The boy was taken in by the count of Oropeza's bailiff and given a basic education and instruction in the Faith. He was a good and reliable boy and at the age of fourteen was put in charge of the flock. Later he was entrusted with the management of the entire estate. At twenty-two he was such a fine figure of a man that he might have been thought better fitted for the army. His biographer considers that it was the desire for freedom and the longing to see the world that led John to choose just that profession, without realizing how much of an occasion of sin it might prove to be. Charles V was at war with Francis I of France and had sent out an appeal to the local nobility to raise an army. The count of Oropeza solicited recruits, and John enlisted in 1522. One day he went out to forage for food on a horse taken from the French. Unused to the animal, he let it take the direction it wished and found himself being taken toward the French camp. An attempt to turn the horse back resulted in his being thrown. Stunned and hurt, he implored the help of the Virgin to whom he had always been devoted and eventually found his way back to the Spanish camp. He was then put in charge of the booty taken by the army. When some of it was found to be missing, he was accused and condemned to hang. An officer, convinced that he was innocent, suggested that in return for his life he should renounce the profession of arms. John was freed and is said to have spent two days in prayer before a wayside crucifix and to have been unable to go on for weakness. Bread and wine appeared, and strengthened by them he returned to Oropeza, where he spent four years. Hearing that the count was about to leave for Hungary to fight the Turks and forgetting his past unhappy experiences, he decided to join him and acquitted himself well this time.

When the army was disbanded, John, feeling some nostalgia for the village where he was born, decided to return there. An old uncle told him what had happened to his parents and offered to adopt him as his own son. This may have been the moment of John's total conversion. He told his uncle that he would emulate his father and go far away to serve God and thus make reparation for his sins. He moved on to Andalusia, where he was employed by a rich woman to look after her flock. But he was very unhappy, remembering how even when he was working for the count of Oropeza he used to think that the animals he groomed with such care were better treated than the poor who came to beg for alms. He then decided to go to Africa, where the Christians were being persecuted by the Moors. He might try to rescue them and, he hoped, become a martyr himself. In Gibraltar, the port of embarkation, he met a Portuguese family under sentence of exile to the Portuguese enclave of Ceuta in Africa, and, with this family, John began his life's work of serving others. The husband fell ill in Ceuta, and John hired himself out to work as a labourer to feed the family, doing the chores for them at night. However, a Christian fellow-labourer shook him to the core by throwing in his lot with the Moors and denying his faith. He begged a Franciscan to advise him: should he go after the apostate? His counsellor was in no doubt: John would needlessly expose himself and in any case his hopes of martyrdom were a bit romantic. He advised him to go back to Spain.

There he hit upon the idea of peddling religious books and images as a way of combining an apostolate with earning his living and took to travelling from town to town with his goods. It is related that on one such trip he met a barefoot child to whom he offered his own shoes, which were obviously far too large to be of any use. He then offered to carry the child on his back. Tired and perspiring, he stopped for water at a stream and found himself before the child Jesus, who held in his hand a half-open pomegranate surmounted by a cross and said, "John of God, Granada will be your cross." The pomegranate is at once an emblem of charity and of the town of Granada. He understood that there he would find his field of work, arrived in Granada in 1536 at the age of forty-two, and gamely continued to peddle his books, still not knowing what he should do. In January of the following year Bd John of Avila (10 May) came to Granada to preach on the feast of St Sebastian (20 Jan.), and John went to hear him. The preacher spoke of the joy experienced by those who suffer for Christ and the rewards laid up for them. John began to fill the church with his cries, beating his breast and imploring mercy. Then, as though demented, he ran about the streets, tearing his hair and behaving so wildly that he was pelted with sticks and stones and returned home a pitiable object. There he gave away his stock and again took to roaming the streets distractedly until some kind persons took him to John of Avila, who promised he would be his spiritual director. John was quiet for a time but soon returned to his extravagances and was carried off to a lunatic asylum, where, according to the practice of the times, he was subjected for months to flogging and spells of solitary confinement. John of Avila heard of this and went to see him. He told him there had been enough of his outlandish penance and he must now do something more useful. To the astonishment of his keepers John was instantly restored, but he stayed in the hospital to tend the other patients, learning at least how not to treat the insane, and going to other hospitals to help the sick.

John of Avila suggested that his penitent make a pilgrimage to Our Lady of Guadalupe for direction. He saw her with the child Jesus, holding out some clothing to him, which he was to use to dress the child. He understood: he must clothe the naked Christ, feed the hungry Christ, and succour the needy Christ. One day, as he was praying before a crucifix in a church, he felt the presence of Our Lady again. She presented him with Christ's crown of thorns, saying, "It is by thorns, labours, and sufferings that you must earn the crown my Son has prepared for you." On leaving the church he saw a sign outside a building, "House to let for lodging the poor." He took it, not knowing how he would pay the rent. So in 1538, when he was in his forty-third year, John took possession of his first hospital. He was to surprise many by the way he ran it.

Somehow or other he obtained sufficient money to buy forty-six beds, mattresses, and bolsters. In no time the beds were all occupied. Perfect order reigned: each person had his own bed—which was rare enough at the time. Cases of contagious diseases were kept separate, wards were aired regularly, all was spotlessly clean, and meals were served punctually at fixed times. Material wellbeing was vital but not the priority. John urged each newcomer to put his conscience in order and brought in priests to hear Confessions and to administer the Last Sacraments as required. He woke the residents to say morning prayers together. After Mass, he would himself wash the sick and renew their dressings. When his patients were settled for the night he would set off for the town with his empty hampers to beg of the citizens standing at their doors or in the *plazas* in the cool of the evening. They told him he would never maintain the hospital with such resources as could be obtained through begging, but the logic of the situation asserted itself: if John could not do it merely by begging, as they pointed out, then they must do something themselves. They came with money, bread, or other provisions; doctors, chemists, and nurses offered their services free. When John came home, he prepared the vegetables for the following day. The rest of the night he spent in prayer, snatching only an hour's sleep for himself on a mat spread on the hard ground with a stone for his pillow.

The house became too small and John was obliged to find another. He moved all the sick himself. With more space he could organize things even more efficiently, allocating different needs to different wards: the serious cases to one, the lighter cases to another, cripples in their own ward, the contagious cases apart; but this time he was able to add a new ward, a night shelter for the homeless. John did not forget the prostitutes. He opened a home to which they too could go and entrusted them to the care of ladies in the town.

71

The bishop of Túy, who was also the president of the Royal Chamber of Granada, hearing about John, wished to see him. Just before the interview John had given his own clothes to a beggar and appeared before the prelate in the beggar's. The bishop questioned him at length and, eliciting from him the story of the vision of the Christ Child directing him to Granada, suggested that he should take the name given to him then, "John of God," and that as a token of his life of dedication should wear a religious habit, which he himself provided and blessed. John kept the habit all his life.

Meanwhile the work was always expanding. John handled it alone until gradually others, inspired by his heroism, offered to help. His first two helpers, Antonio Martín and Pedro Velasco, were sworn enemies, each out to destroy the other. John reconciled them, and they joined him in his work. So was the Congregation of the Brothers of St John of God begun. The citizens of Granada made it possible for John to run his hospital, but not all were well disposed toward him. One Simón de Avila calumniated the saint endlessly and once followed him into a widow's house hoping to incriminate him. He peeped through a crack in the door, but what he saw was a list of his own sins written up on the wall and a flaming sword above him. He fainted and fell over backwards down the stairs, lying unconscious at the foot. John revived him and so won a new recruit. Piola, a rich Italian to whose generosity John appealed for a loan of thirty ducats at a moment when he was out of funds and desperately in need, declined to help him, pretending that John could not offer him any security. John pulled out his crucifix and declared, "Here is your security!" The crucifix emitted such blinding rays of light that Piola handed John the required sum instantly and six months later, after his wife's death, committed himself and his whole fortune to the work of the hospital.

A fire that swept through the royal hospital and John's heroic intervention may have secured for him once and for all the affection and admiration of the whole town. The fire-fighters dared not enter the building because of the raging fire, but John, hearing that the sick were trapped inside, went in and brought them out. In an attempt to save as much as he could he threw the bedding and furniture out of the windows. An adjacent building was likely to catch fire and preparations were being made to detach it from the burning building by the use of cannon shot. John halted these preparations and himself went up with an axe, hacking the roof and beams with a frenzied and superhuman strength until the building stood free. Then he seemed to disappear into the flames. The crowd groaned but a few minutes later he stood among them, his eyebrows only having been singed. They never grew back.

By now John had won the approval of the archbishop of Granada, who supported his hospital both morally and materially. The second building had become too small. The archbishop himself summoned the leading citizens to decide what should be done. An unused monastery was bought, and there John set up his hospital for the third time, always on the same principles, only now the civil authorities decided to pay the expenses of doctors' visits and medicines. John did not confine his charity to his own hospital; he helped all in need, much to the disapproval of some who thought his charity indiscriminate. Perhaps because his charity was overextended, he found himself increasingly in debt. He decided to go begging in Andalusia. This journey brought in much-needed aid, but he had to try again. This time it was suggested that he go to the court at Valladolid. His reputation had preceded him, and he was received with honour. Many gifts were poured into his lap, but as there were as many poor in Valladolid as in Granada, they were all given away. He returned with letters of credit to pay his debts in Granada.

For thirteen years John had worked, prayed, and done penance. He had fed the hungry, clothed the naked, sheltered the homeless, converted sinners, without a thought for his overworked and exhausted body. It could do no more, and yet there was another superhuman effort to be made. One night he heard that the river Xenil had overflowed and was carrying away much of the wood that would normally serve the poor. He went out with another brother and with a youth working in the hospital. They gathered what they could, but suddenly John saw that the young man was being carried off by the fast-flowing river. He swam to his rescue, but the boy was out of reach and he himself was being overwhelmed. He was hardly able to return, overcome by grief, fatigue, and cold.

One last criticism had to be met before the book was closed. The archbishop sent for him to investigate a complaint that he harboured tramps and women of bad character. John fell to his knees at the prelate's feet, saying, "The Son of Man came for sinners, and we are bound to seek their conversion. I am unfaithful to my vocation because I neglect this, but I confess that I know of no bad person in my hospital except myself alone. I am indeed unworthy to eat the bread of the poor." The archbishop dismissed him.

Conscious of the fact that he was now very ill, John went over the inventories of the hospital and inspected the accounts. He revised the rules of administration, the timetables, and the devotional exercises to be observed. As he grew weaker, news of his illness spread through the city. Ana Ossorio, who had helped him in his many good works, obtained from the archbishop an order requiring him to go to her house and be cared for there. She found him on his mat with his begging basket under his head and an old cloak for a blanket. He would have preferred to die among his patients but he would not now disobey: "The Son of God obeyed his Father unto death, even death on a cross, and his most unworthy servant, John of God, shall to the last moment of his life by his blind obedience adore and honour that of his redeemer." He put Antonio Martín in charge of the brothers and before leaving visited the Blessed Sacrament, staying there so long that the masterful Ana caused him to be taken forcibly into her coach and driven to her home.

Knowing the hour he was to die, he asked to be left alone. He rose from his bed, put on his habit and, kneeling before the altar which had been erected in his room and at which the archbishop had recently said Mass, he died on his knees on 8 March 1550, his fifty-fifth birthday. The whole of Granada accompanied his body to the church of the Minims where he was buried. In 1586, Pope Sixtus V established the Congregation of the Brothers of St John of God, which has spread to every continent. John of God was canonized in 1690 and made patron of hospitals and the sick, and of booksellers.

The biography by Francis de Castro, rector of St John's own hospital at Granada, is reproduced in Latin by the Bollandists, *AA.SS.*, Mar., 1, pp. 813-32, and is the basis of all subsequent biographies. That by A. De Govea uses both Castro and the reports for the Beatification process and it too is reproduced by the Bollandists, pp. 834-57. A translation of the life by G. de Villethierry was included in the Oratorian Series in 1847, and there are lives by E. Baillon (1884), by M. and F. Leonard and by N. McMahon (1952). An English translation of A. Magnin's *St John of God* appeared in 1936. See also *H.S.S.C.*, 8, p. 293, and *Bibl.SS.*, 6, 741-8.

Murillo's painting of the saint carrying a sick man on his back is in the Caridad of Seville. The saint is sometimes depicted with a pomegranate surmounted by a cross or an alms bowl hung round his neck, or with a crown of thorns on his head.

St Felix of Dunwich, *Bishop* (648)

Sigebert, ruler of the East Angles, when earlier in exile in Gaul, had accepted the Christian faith and been baptized; on becoming king in 631, he obtained from St Honorius of Canterbury (30 Sept.) the services of the Burgundian bishop Felix, whom he designated as apostle of the East Anglians.

Dunwich in Suffolk was appointed the episcopal see by the king, and for seventeen years Felix preached the gospel in what are now the counties of Norfolk, Suffolk, and Cambridge. A school was set up, for which Felix secured teachers to run it on the Kentish model. The Church in East Anglia was further strengthened at this time by the arrival from Ireland of St Fursey (16 Jan.), who founded a monastery, probably at Burghcastle near Yarmouth.

Although once a considerable town, Dunwich, where St Felix died and was buried in 648, has been entirely swallowed up by the sea. His relics were translated first to Soham, near Ely, a monastery he had founded, and then to Ramsey Abbey, where they still were in the twelfth century. St Felix (whose name appears in Felixstowe) appears in a number of English medieval calendars.

Bede, *H.E.*, 2, 15; 3, 18-20. J. M. Wallace-Hadrill, in "Rome and the Early English Church," *Settimano di Studio sull'alto medioevo* 8 (1960), 514-49, sees him as a notable example of Frankish participation in England's conversion.

St Theophylact of Nicomedia, *Bishop* (845)

St Theophylact came as a boy from Asia to Constantinople. St Tarasius (25 Feb.) took a liking to him and gave him a good education. When his benefactor was raised to the patriarchate of Constantinople, Theophylact and Michael the

Confessor became monks. The two were sent by the patriarch to a monastery beside the Bosphorus, and when Tarasius judged them ready, he ordained them bishops, Michael to the see of Synnada and Theophylact to that of Nicomedia.

Nicephorus succeeded Tarasius in the see of Constantinople in 806. In 813 Leo the Armenian became emperor and gradually showed himself an Iconoclast. Calling together a few bishops, among whom were Theophylact and Michael, Nicephorus went with them to see the emperor, with whom they argued their case. Leo remained obdurate. When they all fell silent, Theophylact, moved by the spirit of prophecy, said to the emperor, "I know that you care nothing for the patience and forbearance of God, but a terrible death will overtake you like a storm and there will be no one to deliver you." Leo was infuriated and ordered them all into banishment. Theophylact was imprisoned in a fortress in Caria where he remained for thirty years until his death in 845. His prophecy was fulfilled when, on Christmas Day 820, Leo was attacked in his chapel by conspirators. Although he seized the cross from the altar and fought desperately with it against his assailants, he was cut down and killed before assistance could arrive.

Theophylact excelled in works of charity, being especially concerned for widows and orphans. He built hospitals and houses of refuge and gave alms generously. It is said that he even took water around with him to wash the wounds of the sick he might encounter.

AA.SS., Mar., 1, pp. 786-7.

St Humphrey of Thérouanne, *Bishop* (871)

In 855 the emperor Lothair arrived at the monastery of Prüm in the diocese of Trèves, a dying man, hoping to atone for his crimes by taking the monastic habit at his eleventh hour. He survived only six days and, as an ancient chronicle notes, "The Brothers reverently buried the emperor in the church of the Holy Saviour." One of these Brothers was Humphrey.

Within a year another important personage, the saintly Folkwin, bishop of Thérouanne, died, and Humphrey was chosen by Lothair II to take his place. Such a constellation of events must have dismayed the young Frankish monk, but the reality that awaited him was appalling. The second Council of Toul, held in the town of Tusey in 860, to which he appended his signature, describes the state of Gaul at the time: "With the help of God we begin by describing conditions as they are at present and the dangers that face the people under our care: how our sins have contributed to the contempt in which both divine and human laws are held, how every religious Order is in turmoil, how a flood of curses, lies, adultery and murder surges over us, and blood touches blood; how the land is eaten up and all its inhabitants are sick." Canon 5, concerning the clergy and monks on the loose, reads, "Our sins have brought it about that many places dedicated to God have been burnt and destroyed by renegade Christians as well as by the cruel Northmen and, taking advantage of this, several licentious priests and monks have gone back on their commitment; without any canonical leave and without shame, they appear as vagabonds, straying from God's sheepfold."

The diocese of Thérouanne was particularly hard hit by the invading Northmen. They had penetrated as far as they could in their ships and then descended on the country, laying waste the fields and burning towns and villages. At Whitsuntide 861 they seized the great monastery of Saint-Bertin at Saint-Omer and set it on fire after looting it and killing four monks left in charge. The town of Thérouanne was also attacked, and the bishop was obliged to flee. Overcome with grief, Humphrey appealed to Pope St Nicholas I (13 Nov.) for permission to retire to a monastery. The pope replied kindly but firmly, "Do you not realize, dearest brother, that if it is dangerous for the pilot to abandon ship when the sea is calm, it is far worse to do so in troubled waters?" He made it clear that Humphrey was justified in escaping from the marauders, but he urged him to be ready to return as soon as the storm blew over and gather together his scattered flock. The barbarians soon withdrew, and Humphrey went back to his devastated see and played a noble part in encouraging the people to return to their homes and restore their sanctuaries.

Adelard, abbot of Saint-Bertin, died in 844. All were unanimous in wanting Humphrey to be his successor. In his ninth year as bishop of Thérouanne he accepted the further charge and held it until 868, when he was ousted by Charles the Bald, who replaced him with a favourite of his own, a secular canon named Hildwin. Humphrey continued to rule the diocese for another three years and died in 871. By his order the feast of the Assumption, only fitfully observed until then in certain churches, was universally kept in the diocese.

AA.SS., Mar., 1, pp. 789-92; Destouches, *Vie des Saints de Cambrai et Arras*, 1, pp. 310-14; Duchesne, *Fastes*, 3; P. Smet, *Saints et Grands Hommes du Catholicisme en Belgique et dans le Nord de la France* (1867).

St Veremund, *Abbot* (1092)

The Benedictine abbey of Hyrache was the most important of the religious houses in the kingdom of Navarre during the eleventh century. It was revered for its antiquity, its fidelity to the true faith during the combats with the Arians, its careful observance of the Rule of St Benedict, its fine community, the excellence of its liturgy, and the high standard of its school.

Veremund entered the monastery as a mere boy under his uncle Munius, from whom he later received the habit. He grew up an exemplary monk, much given to penance and prayer. When his uncle died he was elected abbot and did not disappoint the expectations of the community. The chronicler regards the election as particularly pleasing to God because the abbot-elect in no way relaxed or altered his penitential way of life. Veremund gave a wonderful example in word and deed, not only to his subjects but to all the inhabitants of the region, of a man wholly given to the Lord in the work of the liturgy and the exercise of charity.

Already when quite a young monk he was remarkable for his love of the poor; as abbot, his munificence was multiplied and enhanced. He was reputed to have healed the sick, rescued a drowning man, given sight to the blind, expelled demons, and obtained the cessation of rain. The chronicler attributes to his love of Our Lady the building of the city of Estrella. Once when some shepherds were out at night watching their flocks they saw a shower of stars fall on a hill, afterwards known in the local dialect as "Yricarra" (starry). A subsequent examination of the meteorites was rewarded by the find of a re- markable statue of Our Lady. So impressed was King Sancho Ramírez that he built Estrella on the spot and ceded all its proprietary rights to the monastery.

Veremund died after an abbacy of over forty years. Over the tomb where his relics are kept are three angels, still to be seen, about to crown him for his threefold role as monk, celibate, and abbot.

AA SS., Mar., 1, pp. 793-8; Mabillon, *AA.SS.O.S.B.*, 9 (1733), p. 763.

St Stephen of Obazine, *Abbot* (1159)

Stephen was born in the Limousin district of France. After completing his education he took over responsibility for the family but, judging that the claims of the poor were more urgent than his parents' needs, gave himself completely to works of mercy. However, he did not like others to know of his good works, so he posed as something of a dandy.

After being ordained he felt called to a stricter life and, renouncing all pleas- ures, began to subject himself to very severe mortification. So on fire was he with divine love that he seemed to communicate it to his hearers, who seemed never to have enough of his preaching. He thought he must go even further and, poor and naked, follow Christ in his poverty. He first consulted a saintly priest, who told him that he should not delay in following the inspiration of grace. Stephen took this as coming from God and, together with his friend Peter, also recently ordained, determined to forsake the world. They called their families and friends together the week before Lent, probably in the year 1130, distributed their goods, and bade a final farewell. The next day at dawn they set out, barefoot, for the forest of Obazine, a wild district about two miles from Tulle. They arrived at their destination on Good Friday and built them- selves a rough shelter. As they were joined by others, Bishop Eustace gave them leave to build a monastery and celebrate Mass. When the first buildings became too small, another monastery was built. The question then arose as to who should be the superior. Stephen and Peter fell out over the matter, each thinking the other better fitted for the task. The matter was settled by the apostolic legate, Gaufrid, who chose Stephen.

The austerities practised by the small community were extreme, and Stephen, though he had a gentle and kindly nature, was rigid in enforcing them. All their time was spent in prayer, reading, and manual labour, and they never ate until evening. St Stephen cooked and carried water like the rest, doing the work of two. All things were shared in common, but their life was regulated by no written Rule—Stephen was their living rule. This must have troubled the prior, as we find him consulting the Carthusians in 1135 on the possibility of affiliation with them. These were not keen to accept the new foundation as they were already numerous and limited in their resources; they suggested the Cistercians.

A monastery of nuns was established by the prior in that same year of 1135, not far from that of the men and subject to the strictest enclosure, all its members' needs being supplied by the Brothers. Two other communities of men were established by Stephen, one in the Limousin and the other in the Auvergne.

On Palm Sunday in 1142 the members of the community of Obazine made their profession in the presence of an unnamed abbot and their own bishop, and Stephen himself was blessed as abbot. They were subsequently instructed by the monks of Dalon in the ways of the Cistercians, but it was not until the Cistercian pope, Eugenius III, was in Reims and present at the chapter of Cistercian abbots in 1147 that Stephen submitted a formal request to be received into the Cistercian Order. Both his Congregation and that of Savigny were accepted at this same chapter. There were already two monasteries of Cistercian nuns, Jully and Tart. To these were now added those of Obazine and Savigny, although it was not until 1188 that the general chapter undertook to regulate the observance of the nuns.

Stephen founded two more communities, one in 1148 in the Alps, another in 1150 in Aquitaine. He died on 8 March 1159.

See *AA.SS.*, Mar., 1, pp. 799-808; J. Bouton, *Histoire de l'Ordre de Cîteaux* (1959).

R.M.

St Cyril, bishop and martyr at Beroea in Thrace (third century)
St Provinus, bishop of Como (*c.* 420)
St Duthac, bishop of Ross in Scotland (*c.* 1065)
Bd Vincent Kadlubek, bishop of Cracow (1223)
SS Simeon, Simon, Peter, and Bernard, martyrs of Korea (1866)—see 20 Sept.

9

ST FRANCES OF ROME, *Foundress* (1384-1440)

The gentle saint who was known first to her fellow-citizens and then to the Church at large as Santa Francesca Romana, St Frances of Rome, possessed an extraordinary ability to attract the love and admiration of those who came in contact with her. She was born in the Trastevere district of Rome in 1384 at the beginning of the Great Schism of the West, which was to cause her much grief and almost ruin the family into which she had married. Her parents, Paul Busso and Jacobella dei Roffredeschi, belonged to the most illustrious and wealthy families of Rome. The child was, then, brought up in easy circumstances but in a profoundly religious household also. Jacobella frequented the church of Santa Maria Nuova, which was served by Benedictine monks of Monte Oliveto, and to one of these, Dom Antonio di Monte Savello, she entrusted the instruction and spiritual direction of her daughter. He was to remain Frances' director for thirty-five years.

Very early in her life Frances conceived the desire to become a nun and discussed it with Dom Antonio, who drew up for her a rule for an ascetic way of life. At the age of eleven she asked her parents' permission to follow her vocation but was met with a point-blank refusal. Her father had already arranged for her to marry Lorenzo Ponziano, a young man of equally illustrious birth and status, and no entreaty would move him to renege on his promise. Dom Antonio advised her to accept the situation as willed by God, and at the age of thirteen she became Lorenzo's wife. She did her generous best to please her husband and her parents-in-law, but her heart was heavy. Her sister-in-law, Vanozza, wife of Lorenzo's elder brother, Paluzzo, found her sobbing one day. Frances was disarmed by the older girl's sympathy, and soon they were exchanging confidences. Vanozza too would have preferred to give herself wholly to God. Discovering a kindred spirit so unexpectedly among her husband's family, Frances regained her courage. Together they plotted the best course for them both: they would live their married lives with the utmost generosity and guard their interior sanctuary by the practice of prayer, almsgiving, and penance. The friendship thus begun was to endure for thirty-eight years.

The two were seen regularly visiting the hospital of Santo Spiritu, where they helped to nurse the sick and distributed alms. Frances kept up her weekly Confession to Dom Antonio and her weekly Communion. At home, they prepared an oratory where they could pray quietly once their duties were discharged. Their mother-in-law thought such behaviour odd, urged them to devote more time to recreation, and even solicited the support of her sons in the matter. However, both Paluzzo and Lorenzo were disinclined to impose their mother's ideas on their wives, whom they had come to love and revere.

Frances gave birth to her first child, Giovanni Battista, in 1400. A year later her mother-in-law died. By common consent the family decided that Frances should be the mistress of the household. To her perfectly justified remonstrations that this position belonged by right to Vanozza, the wife of the elder son, her father-in-law argued that their decision was unanimous. Vanozza herself pleaded with Frances to accept it; before such a united front Frances had to accept the charge. Their trust was not misplaced. She was gentle but firm, courteous and methodical, watchful of the servants' needs, especially their spiritual needs, and she was loved by all. She allowed nothing, not even her devotions, to come between her and her duty. In all the forty years that she lived with her husband there was never the slightest dispute or misunderstanding between them.

Her first and perhaps her only disagreement with her father-in-law arose in the year 1402 when Rome was struck by famine and pestilence due to the wars between the duke of Anjou and Ladislaus Durazzo, each out to secure the kingdom of Naples for himself. The family of the Colonnas, enemies of the pope, taking advantage of the situation, attacked Rome, depriving the population of provisions. The Ponziano household being well supplied, Frances gave orders that no poor person applying to the palace for sustenance should be turned away. Andreazzo Ponziano was aghast at his daughter-in-law's liberality and thought he would restrain it by leaving within the cellars just enough for the family. Frances and Vanozza went out into the streets to beg on behalf of the poor, whom they could no longer help from their own resources.

Frances was twenty years old when her second son, Giovanni Evangelista, was born and twenty-three when she gave birth to her daughter, Agnes. She allowed no one else to look after the children, so eager was she to instill into them from the earliest age habits of devotion and discipline. They were still infants when in 1408 the troops of Ladislaus, a supporter of the antipope, gained control of Rome. The brutal Count Troja was appointed governor. Louis of Anjou, supporter of Pope Alexander V, also entered Rome, which became a battleground. The Ponziani had always supported Pope Alexander, and in one of the frequent skirmishes Lorenzo was stabbed. He was carried home to Frances and owed his life to her devoted nursing. Troja resolved to leave the city after having wreaked his vengeance on the principal papal supporters. Amongst these were the Ponziani. He not only arrested Paluzzo but also demanded little Giovanni Battista as a hostage, threatening to kill the uncle if the nephew were not delivered into his hands. Frances, almost demented, sought out Dom Antonio, who counselled compliance. Like Abraham placing Isaac on the pile, Frances herself gave up her son to Troja and then fled into the church of Ara Coeli, where she prostrated herself before the statue of the Virgin. Troja handed the child to one of his officers, who mounted his horse, which would not move. He changed horse, with the same result. Finally, the child was sent back to his mother, but not for long.

Alexander V died in 1410, and John XXIII was elected pope. With the help of Louis of Anjou he drove Ladislaus out of Rome; Louis withdrew too soon, Ladislaus pretended peace, and the city was again given over to pillage. Lorenzo fled into hiding. The Ponziano palace was ruined, and Giovanni Battista again taken, though later father and son were reunited in exile. Vanozza, Frances, and the other children lived in a corner of the palace, but famine and pestilence raged once more. The Ponziano farms and vineyards had been despoiled and the workers killed, so that provisions ran low. In spite of her own anguish over the fate of her elder son, Frances opened a hospital in the palace and brought in the victims of the pestilence, whom she and Vanozza nursed. Her second son caught the infection and died. Frances carried on, bearing the burden of these intimate sorrows as well as a life of severe penance. She and Vanozza personally went to the family vineyards and collected bundles of wood for fuel, which they distributed to the poor. It was then that Frances began to exercise a remarkable gift of healing, some sixty cases of which were recorded for her canonization process. She attributed her special gifts to the presence—visible to her—of a guardian angel ever at her side.

Frances herself fell victim to the plague in 1414 and was ill for several months, during which she was granted visions of hell, which later she could not recall without sobbing. She predicted the end of the schism, which did indeed come to pass. Ladislaus died in August of that year, the pope called the Council of Constance, at which all the popes, legitimate or otherwise, were deposed, and one sole pope, Martin V, was elected. Peace obtained, Lorenzo and Battista returned. Frances continued the hospital in her home and her daily forage for firewood. She had now a greater authority, a greater influence over her fellow-Romans. Her mere presence brought a blessing, and many conversions were ascribed to her. The one that touched her most closely was that of her daughter-in-law. At the age of eighteen, Battista had married Mobilia, an inexperienced and hot-tempered young woman who had been brought up very strictly but who considered marriage a form of emancipation. She despised her mother-in-law for her shabby clothes and good works among the poor, openly rejected her advice when proffered, and made fun of her in public. When Mobilia fell gravely ill, Frances nursed her with such tenderness that the young woman was completely changed and became one of her most devoted followers.

Lorenzo's health was now broken, and he became completely dependent on his wife, while seeing that her life was so completely possessed by God that his own claims on her faded into insignificance. He released her from her marital obligations, begging her only not to leave the palace but to continue to live there. This she agreed to do, even though a plan to set up a religious company of like-minded women had already begun to take shape.

The plan was approved by her director, Dom Antonio, who obtained the affiliation of the projected society to the Benedictines of Monte Oliveto. Known at first as the Oblates of Mary, they were afterwards called the Oblates of Tor de Specchi, where the group was housed from 1433. As their name implies, they were not religious. They did not take vows and were not subject to enclosure but were held to the common life. They were to be wholly committed to the works of mercy, supported always by prayer and reading. Frances spent whatever time she could spare from her home duties with the oblates. She never allowed them to refer to her as the foundress but insisted that all should be subject to Agnes de Lellis, who had been chosen as the first superior. When Lorenzo died, Frances entered her own foundation on the feast of St Benedict. Agnes de Lellis immediately insisted on resigning office, and Frances had to take her place in spite of her protestations.

Her life was now lived closer than ever to God. She could hardly increase her austerities, as she had long subsisted on dry bread and occasional vegetables. Visions and ecstasies became more frequent, and she sometimes spent whole nights in prayer. One evening in the spring of 1440 she was called to Mobilia, who was ill. Feeling very unwell herself, she tried to get back to the convent afterwards. On the way she met Dom Matteoti, who had succeeded Dom Antonio as her director some years before. Seeing her condition, he suggested that she return immediately to her son's house. It was soon evident that she was dying, but she lingered on for seven days. On the evening of 9 March 1440, her face shone with an unearthly light and she spoke her last words, "The angel has finished his work. He is beckoning me to follow." Her body was exposed in Santa Maria Nuova, later to be known as the church of Santa Francesa Romana, and became the focus of innumerable cures. It was buried in the chapel of the oblates. Frances was canonized by Pope Paul V on 29 May 1608.

AA.SS., Mar., 2, pp. 89-219, contains the collection of visions, miracles, and biographical details compiled by Dom Matteotti and the biography of Mary Magdalen Anguillaria. There are Lives in French by Rabory (1884), Rambuteau (1900), Berthem-Bontoux (1931), in English by Georgiana Fullerton, *St Frances of Rome* (1855) and in Italian by C. Albergotti (1940). See also *H.S.S.C.*, 7, p. 276; *Bibl.SS.*, 5, 1011-28.

On her tomb in the church in Rome named after her there is a recumbent statue by Bernini. In the frescoes at Grotta Ferrata by Domenichino she is seated on clouds with her angel beside her. A painting by Guercino shows her holding her book, with a basket of bread beside her and her guardian angel watching over her.

St Pacian of Barcelona, *Bishop* (*c.* 390)

St Pacian must have been born at the beginning of the fourth century, probably in Barcelona, since it was forbidden to ordain for the diocese those who had not been baptized within it. He had a wide classical culture, as his quotations from different Latin authors reveal, and must have belonged to a family of some means. He had married and had a son, Flavius Dexter, chamberlain to the emperor Theodosius, captain of the royal bodyguard under Honorius and author of a *Historia Omnimoda*. St Jerome (30 Sept.) was a friend of Dexter's and dedicated to him both his *Catalogue of Illustrious Men*, in which he included Pacian, and his *Apologia contra Rufinum*.

Pacian is chiefly remembered through his writings. Those that have survived are an exhortation to penance, a sermon on Baptism, two letters to a Novatian named Sympronian, and a treatise against the Novatian heresy, also addressed to Sympronian. The latter had initiated the correspondence, censuring the Church for allowing repentance and absolution for sins committed after Baptism and for assuming the title of "Catholic." Pacian's response emphasized the fidelity of the Church to the teaching and example of a merciful Lord, as revealed in the parables and in the welcome he gave to sinners. The bishop agreed with Sympronian that no one should sin after Baptism, but God has provided for the frailty of men in conferring on the Church the power of binding and loosing. The Church is not an élite gathering of the pure, but a humble people; it can be likened to a lost coin or a lost son, images too of its nature. It is a large house containing vessels of pure gold and silver but also vessels of baser material. A Christian should indeed be ashamed of sinning, but not of doing penance. Pacian used the context of Matthew 18 in an interesting aside to speak of Peter as the source of unity: "The Lord spoke to Peter, and Peter alone, so that unity should be founded on that one person. . . ."

As for the charge of assuming the title "Catholic," which the emperor Theodosius in 380 had forbidden to heretical sects, Pacian defends the Church's stand. Had there been no sects, it would have been unnecessary to designate the Church in this way, and he declares with resounding assurance, ". . . my name is *Christian*, but my surname is *Catholic*. *Christian* puts me in a certain class, *Catholic* gives me a certain character; the second is a testimonial, the first is a label." That the Church is Catholic means that it possesses unity of faith and everywhere observes the fullest obedience to God.

Pacian begs his correspondent to consider that even the restricted numbers of a heretical sect already point to its isolation, that the vitality of the Catholic Church is a clearer indication of the identity and fidelity of the church of Christ.

Pacian is an ideal adversary. He hates controversy, will condemn no one, never gives way to anger or bitterness. Now and again he is gently ironic, but he is serene in faith and confident in the truth, and his intentions are always irenic. He is a valuable source of information about the attitudes and practice of the early Church, providing a counterweight to the rigidity of Tertullian and his followers and an insight into the theology and spirituality of the Church before the advent of such giant figures as Ambrose, Jerome, and Augustine. St Jerome says that he died in the reign of Emperor Theodosius at a very advanced age.

AA.SS., Mar., 2, p. 4; C. Granado, *Pacien de Barcelone, Ecrits, S.C.*, 410, (1995); *Dict.Sp.*, 12, 17-20; *P.L*, 13, 1051-94.

St Catherine of Bologna, *Abbess* (1413-63)

Caterina de'Vigri was born in Bologna on 8 September 1413. Her father, Giovanni de'Vigri, a lawyer of outstanding ability, was a professor of jurisprudence at the university. He married Benvenuta, a devout young woman of the noble family of Mamellini. While she was expecting Catherine, her husband was summoned by the marquis Nicholas d'Este to attend him in Ferrara and be his representative to the Republic of Venice.

When Catherine was eleven years old, the marquis persuaded Giovanni de'Vigri to bring her to the palace as a companion to his own daughter, Margaret. The two became fast friends, pursuing their education and other activities together for two or three years. Here Catherine perfected her Latin and learned to paint exquisite miniatures—which can still be seen. When a marriage was arranged between Margaret and Robert Malatesta, prince of Rimini, the princess wished Catherine to accompany her, but by then Catherine had decided to consecrate her life to God.

Soon after returning home her father died, and almost immediately she joined a group of tertiaries of St Augustine at Ferrara; they lived a semi-monastic life under the guidance of Lucy Mascaroni. Catherine was about sixteen years of age, unlikely as yet to have encountered any enemies worthy of the name but already showing a grasp of the demands of a life of union with God. She wrote: "Since Jesus has deigned to call me to his service, I ought to do my very best to imitate him, following the royal way of the cross. I ought to try and love my enemies, to honour those who persecute me, willingly to serve those unwilling to serve me, knowing that blows and spittle rather than kind treatment are what I deserve." Generosity, the dominant note of her life, was evident very early on: "If you would have all, you must give all." So great was her fervour that she wondered whether she ought not to seek a life of greater solitude. In answer to her prayer for light she was told: "Each one, guided as she has been to it by the providence of God, should remain in the place where she has entered." She was most firmly bound to the group from then on, sharing in and contributing to its development.

There followed five years of struggle, which had far-reaching effects. The self-knowledge and the sense of realism she gained then made her an eminently practical guide in the ways of the spirit. Tried by fierce temptations but too sure of herself, she was foolhardy enough to think herself invincible. She imagined herself taunting the devil, "Know that you cannot tempt me without my recognizing your hand at work." She became immediately the subject of several demonic visions, which threw her into the greatest anguish. Both Our Lord and Our Lady seemed to be reprimanding her for her self-love and an imperfect obedience to the will of her novice-mistress—in reality the perfection of obedience implied in the criticism was no more than a caricature of religious obedience. Aridity compounded the anguish, as she felt herself rejected by God and discouraged to the point of despair. Her efforts to attain the required purity of spirit remained fruitless and sterile. Worse, the urge to blaspheme God, to doubt the truths of the Faith, especially the doctrine of the Real Presence, pursued her at every instant. During these five years also, compounding her personal problems, there were dissensions in the community concerning their future, some wanting to remain tertiaries of St Augustine, others wanting to adopt the stricter Rule of St Clare.

She was at one time baker for the community. The glare from the flames of the oven had begun to affect her sight: afraid that she might become a burden to the community later on if she went blind, she mentioned the difficulty to the superior, who, however, told her to remain at her post and leave her health to God. That too was taken as a lesson. When she was dying she exhorted her sisters, "We must bear [misfortune] with great courage for the love of Jesus Christ. Prefer suffering to pleasure, accept it with joy, always wanting more of it in order to become more completely conformed to him. This is only right in a truly Christian soul which is unworthy of the name of Christian if she refuses to carry the cross." The cross could come in unexpected ways. Catherine was so eager to be of service to others that she was sometimes accused of interference. She would on occasion intervene on behalf of others and earn a reprimand. As her motives were pure, she felt the injustice. Her equanimity could only be explained by a determined desire to endure all things, however contrary, for the love of Christ. "It means little," she wrote, "to wear a worn habit and walk with bowed head; to be truly humble one has to know how to bear humiliation. It is the touchstone of Christian discipleship." Her unlimited patience with others sprang from charity, but the logic of the human situation underpinned her pragmatic approach: "[So and so] has her defects, I too have mine. It is blindness on our part to expect others to have the same constitution of body and soul." Her policy was never to judge the intention or will of another but to accept the reality of a situation as an expression of God's will for her.

Catherine was fairly early on appointed novice-mistress and drew on her already profound experience of the spiritual life to form her charges. She wrote for them in 1438 her *Treatise on the Seven Spiritual Weapons,* as much an autobiography as a treatise, which shows her mastery of the principles of the spiritual combat. First published in 1475, it was reprinted often after her death and translated into other languages. She prefaces it with two conditions without which it would be useless to proceed: one must have the intention never to commit grave sin and a firm resolution to follow Our Lord in the way of the cross. The tools needed are diligence and perseverance. Distrust of oneself has to be balanced by total trust in God's love for his creature. Reflection on what Our Lord has suffered will give to those who love him the necessary courage, while the remembrance of death will keep them in a state of readiness. The thought of heaven is a stimulus, but the scriptures must be engraved on the mind for one's nourishment and guidance in this life. Many other directives have been preserved which are aimed at the acquisition of virtue but which can serve simultaneously to build up a rounded personality, free of self and directed toward the other—a personality of great charm such as she was herself.

About the beginning of her term as novice-mistress she had a remarkable vision, which is often represented in art and which may be described in her own words. Having obtained permission to spend Christmas night in church, "she went there as soon as she could, intending to recite a thousand *Ave Marias* in honour of Our Lady. This she did with all the attention and fervour of which she was capable. She was taken up with this until midnight, the hour when it is believed our Saviour was born. At this very hour she saw Our Lady appear, holding the infant Jesus in her arms, swathed in linen bands. This kind mother came to her and gave her Son to her. I leave you to picture the joy of this poor creature when she found herself holding the Son of the eternal Father in her arms. Trembling with respect but still more overcome with joy, she took the liberty of caressing him, of pressing him against her heart and of bringing his face to her lips. . . ."

The community had embraced the strict Rule of St Clare in 1432 and had moved to a more suitable building, but Catherine, together with a number of others, felt that regular observance would be better ensured if enclosure were established. This was resisted by the people of Ferrara, but eventually it was conceded by the authorities and finally sanctioned by Pope Nicholas V in 1452. In the meantime so many new candidates arrived that the nuns were unable to house them. The vicar general obtained leave from the pope to found other houses all over Italy, and the citizens of Bologna asked that a Poor Clare convent be set up in their city. To her consternation Catherine, a native of Bologna, was chosen as the superior of this new foundation. "I am not fit to look after the chickens," she protested, "how much less to care for those consecrated to God!" The party of sixteen arrived in Bologna on 22 July 1456.

Despite the strictness of the enclosure, the fame of Catherine's sanctity attracted so many candidates that room could not be found for all. Adjacent properties were bought and a building programme set in hand. In spite of the extra burdens this imposed on her, Catherine held herself and her community to the strict observance of the Rule. Her prayerfulness was in no way diminished by her many duties. For someone given to visions and other supernatural phenomena, it comes as a surprise to learn that she abhorred any exterior manifestation of such phenomena. She remained unattached to the joys and sweetness of prayer, not allowing herself to be overcome and lose consciousness. She herself confessed, "Had I allowed myself to give way, I would be always out of myself and more often than not unable to attend to my work."

Perhaps the trait that most evoked the love and loyalty of her community was her kindness. If she had to correct someone, she would accompany her after to the church and there pray with her until natural resentment had yielded to love and acceptance. When her term as abbess ended and a consultation of the community held, the only adverse comment against her re-election was that her very kindness undermined the rules. Whenever she could she visited the sick and performed innumerable services for them, even the most menial. Her spiritual charity went much further. Once when one of the novices confessed to her that she thought of abandoning her vocation, Catherine offered to remain in purgatory until the last day to pay her debts, to take upon herself all her sins, to give her a share of such spiritual wealth as she had, if only the novice would not abandon her vocation. Touched by the charity and sincerity of her superior, the novice changed her mind and stayed.

Catherine was equally ready to spend nights in prayer for anyone in need. Like Thérèse of Lisieux after her (1 Oct.), she prayed all night and obtained the repentance of an obstinate sinner due to be executed the next day. During the first years of the foundation many pushed their mortification too far and fell ill. The doctors despaired, but Catherine obtained their recovery by her prayers. Even before her return to Bologna, Catherine's own health had already been undermined. Seven years later she had arrived at the end of her course. On 25 February 1463, she spoke to the community for three hours, announcing her death and giving them her final instructions. Like the dying St John of the Cross (14 Dec.), her thoughts revolved around the virtue of charity: "It is impossible to please God without love. My beloved daughters, you must bear each other's burdens, then, and forgive each other any wrongs committed, enduring with an inexhaustible patience whatever results from differences of temperament. . . ." On the first Sunday of Lent she was attacked by violent pains and was obliged to take to her bed, from which she never rose again. She died on 9 March. Her passing was so peaceful that the watching nuns did not realize it until they perceived a sweet fragrance and noticed that her face had become as fresh and beautiful as that of a fifteen-year-old. Her body was buried without a coffin and remained in the ground for eighteen days, when it was disinterred, owing to the cures that were reported and the sweet scent that came from the grave. It was found to be incorrupt and has ever since been preserved in the chapel of the convent church in Bologna.

St Catherine was canonized in 1712 by Clement XI and is honoured as a patron of artists.

Léon, 1, pp. 394-437; J. Crasset, *Vie de Sainte Catherine de Bologne* (1863), an English translation of which is included in the Oratorian series. *Bibl. SS.*, 3, 980-2; *H.S.S.C.*, 7, 273-4. Contemporary Life by Sr Illuminata Bambi in MS, apparently still unpublished. See also E Henrion, "Una Educatrice franciscana del Quattrocento, Caterina di Vigri et il trattato delle armi spirituali," *Vita e Pensiero* 18 (1927), 486-95.

The miniatures executed by St Catherine are preserved in the convent. Two pictures of hers are still in existence; one is in the Pinoteca at Bologna the other in the Academy of Fine Arts at Venice. Bellini's painting of her with St Ursula and four companions is also in the Galleria dell'Accademia. There is a contemporary painted terracotta bust of a nun in the Galleria Estense in Modena, which is thought to represent her. A "curious Flemish painting of *c.* 1475 by the Master of the Baroncelli Portraits," in the Courtauld Institute in London, "shows her with three donors and also her body, dead but incorrupt, in the background": P. and L. Murray, *The Oxford Companion to Christian Art and Architecture* (1996).

St Dominic Savio (1842-57)

The Church has raised several child martyrs to the altars, but the case of Dominic Savio, who died of natural causes at the age of only fifteen, seems to be unique.

He was born at San Giovanni di Riva in Piedmont in 1842, the son of a blacksmith, and grew up wanting to be a priest. When St John Bosco (31 Jan.) began training youths as clergy to help him in his work for neglected boys in Turin, Dominic's parish priest recommended him. An interview took place at which Don Bosco was most deeply impressed by the boy: "I saw that the child was really filled with the Holy Spirit and I marvelled at the work of divine grace in one so young." In October 1854, when he was twelve, Dominic became a student at the Oratory of St Francis de Sales in Turin.

Dominic Savio was fortunate to have been committed to the care of so balanced a person as St John Bosco, for he might easily have developed into a young fanatic. Don Bosco insisted that prayer and penance be accompanied by cheerfulness and careful attention to daily duties, and he refused to allow Dominic to opt out of games. He guided him firmly toward an understanding of the human reality within which grace must operate, so that Dominic could later affirm, "I can't do big things, but I want all I do, even the smallest thing, to be for the greater glory of God."

Don Bosco used to say, "Religion must be about us like the air we breathe, but we must not weary boys with too many devotions and observances." True to that spirit, he forbade Dominic to inflict the least bodily mortification upon himself without express permission, explaining, "The penance God wants is obedience. There is plenty to put up with cheerfully—heat, cold, sickness, other people's tiresome ways. There is quite enough mortification for boys in school-life itself." Nevertheless he found Dominic shivering in bed one cold night, with all the bed-clothes save one thin sheet thrown off. "Don't be crazy," he said, "You'll get pneumonia." "Why should I?" replied Dominic, "Our Lord didn't get pneumonia in the stable at Bethlehem!"

Don Bosco had collected abandoned boys from the streets, boys who lived by their wits, who knew the seamier side of life and above all were without religious instruction or practice. The Oratory was by no means a haven of piety, even though Don Bosco willed it to become so by the force of example and the power of love. Dominic, who had a sure perception of the spiritual life and its moral demands and a clear grasp of the ways and means to foster the life of grace, was not spared a confrontation with evil. He was clear-sighted and forceful in his reactions not only in shielding himself but also in attempting to shield others from it.

He was scrupulous in observing the discipline of the house, and some of the wilder spirits did not like it when he expected them to be equally scrupulous. They called him a sneak and told him to "run and tell Don Bosco"—showing how little they knew Don Bosco, who would not tolerate tale-bearing. Likely enough Dominic laughed it off; he was always ready for a laugh, and sometimes this got him into trouble with the masters. But if he was no tale-bearer he was a good story-teller, and that endeared him to his companions, especially the younger ones.

To direct Dominic's attention away from himself or from a form of spirituality that might be turned in on itself, Don Bosco had been careful to nurture in him a truly apostolic spirit, and Dominic was indeed best remembered at the oratory for the group he organized there. This was called the "Company of the Immaculate Conception." Besides its devotional aims it helped Don Bosco in his work by undertaking various necessary jobs, from sweeping the floors to taking special care of boys who for one reason or another were misfits. When the time came, in 1859, for Don Bosco to form the kernel of his now world-wide Salesian Congregation, among the twenty-two present were all the original members of the Company of the Immaculate Conception—all, that is, except Dominic Savio.

Early on at the oratory Dominic prevented a brutal fight with stones between two boys who had exchanged insults and who were both determined to inflict maximum harm on the other. He had managed to extract from them a promise that they would not fight their duel without him, he for his part promising that he would not tell on them. His action at the crucial moment was characteristically direct. Holding up a crucifix between them, he said, "Before you fight, look at this, both of you, and say, 'Jesus Christ was sinless, and he died forgiving his executioners; I am a sinner, and I am going to outrage him by deliberately performing an act of revenge.' Then you can start by throwing your first stone at me!" They slunk away, protesting that they had no quarrel with him, and their hatred fizzled out.

The most important source for the details of Dominic Savio's short life is the account written by Don Bosco himself. In writing it he was careful not to set down anything that he could not vouch for, and he was particularly careful when dealing with the spiritual experiences that were accorded this boy, especially his extraordinary knowledge—of people in need, of their spiritual state, of the future. He recorded the occasion when Dominic went missing all morning till after dinner; he found him eventually in the choir of the church, standing in a cramped position by the lectern rapt in prayer. He had been there for about six hours, yet thought that early Mass was not yet over. Dominic called these times of intense prayer "my distractions." They would sometimes overtake him at play: "It seems as though Heaven is opening just above me. I am afraid of saying or doing something that will make the other boys laugh."

When his mother fell ill Dominic had a vision in which Our Lady told him she wished to cure her, so he went home to Mondonio. Both parents attempted to deflect him—a difficult confinement was not the moment for a visit by the fourteen-year-old youngster—but he merely embraced his mother, putting round her neck a scapular or medal of Our Lady. Though the worst was feared, she was subsequently safely delivered of a baby girl. On his death-bed Dominic was to suggest to his mother that the scapular be used in other cases like hers. Closeness to Our Lady was one of the most striking characteristics of Dominic's life. Don Bosco relates a dream or a vision of Dominic some time after his death, during which he asked his pupil what had given him the greatest consolation at the moment of death. Dominic replied, "The help of the loving and powerful Mother of God" and then went on to commend to the Congregation incessant prayer to Our Lady to obtain her help.

Don Bosco tells us that the needs of England had an important part in the boy's prayers. How this came about is not at all obvious. But then that other Dominic, Dominic Barberi (27 Aug.), even as a young peasant lad, also nourished a passionate desire to work for the conversion of England. By this time, it was nine or ten years since the latter had received Newman into the Church and four or five since Pius IX had restored the Catholic hierarchy in England. 1851 saw the last great outburst of anti-Catholic feeling in mainland Britain, but there were still formidable obstacles to be surmounted in rebuilding the Church. "Have we any right," Newman asked, "to take it strange if, in this England, the spring-time of the Church should turn out to be an English spring, an uncertain, anxious time of hope and fear, of joy and suffering, of bright promises and budding hopes, yet withal, of keen blasts, and cold showers and sudden storms?" (*Sermon on the Second Spring*). Don Bosco records one of Dominic's "strong distractions," in which the boy saw a wide plain shrouded in mist with a multitude of people groping about in it; there came toward them a figure in pontifical vestments carrying a torch that lighted up the whole scene, and a voice seemed to say, "This torch is the Catholic faith which will bring light to the English people." At Dominic's request Don Bosco related this to Pope Pius IX, who declared that it confirmed his resolution to give his attention to England.

Dominic's delicate health showed signs of deterioration in 1857, and in February he was sent home to Mondonio for a change of air. His complaint was diagnosed as inflammation of the lungs, and according to the practice of the day he was bled, and bled to excess. The treatment seems certainly to have hastened his end. He received the Last Sacraments, and on the evening of 9 March he asked his father to read the prayers for the dying. Toward the end of them he tried to sit up. "Good-bye, father," he murmured, "the priest told me something . . . but I can't remember what. . . ." Suddenly his face lit up with a smile of intense joy, and he exclaimed, "I am seeing the most wonderful things."

The cause of the beatification of Dominic Savio was begun in Rome in 1914. It met with some opposition, on the ground of his extreme youth. Pope Pius X, on the other hand, regarded his age as a point in favour of beatification. This view eventually prevailed; but Dominic Savio was not beatified till 1954, twenty years after the canonization of Don Bosco.

The definitive text of the biography written by Don Bosco is that published at Turin, ed. E. Ceris (1950). English translation by Mary Russel, 1934. Other Italian Lives are by Cardinal Salotti (1921) and Dom Cojazzi (1950), and among the French ones is A. Auffray, *Un Saint de quinze ans* (1950). There is an excellent short account by Fr. John Sexton (1950).

R.M.
St Vitalis, abbot of Rapolla in Basilicata (990)
St Bruno of Querfurt, bishop and martyr, see 19 June

10

ST JOHN OGILVIE, *Martyr* (1580-1615)

John Ogilvie was born in Drum, near Keith in Scotland, in 1580. His father, Walter Ogilvie, was the baron of Drum-na-Keith; he owned large territories in Banffshire and was the head of the younger branch of Ogilvies. His mother was Agnes Elphinstone, who came from a family generally loyal to the old religion. Her brother George entered the Society of Jesus shortly after John's birth, while her brother William died as a novice in the Society. Agnes died in 1582 when John was only two years old, and Walter then married Lady Mary Douglas of Lochleven, the daughter of Lady Douglas of Lochleven, Queen Mary's gaoler.

Like many Scottish families at that time, the Ogilvies were both Catholic and Presbyterian. Walter Ogilvie conformed to the Presbyterian faith and brought up his son a Calvinist. In 1592, when John was thirteen, he was sent by his father to the Continent to broaden his education. He travelled in Italy, France, and Germany and found as much religious tension as he had left behind, with the difference that, in France at any rate, disputed points were debated in public between protagonists of equal status. The open intellectual climate allowed the young Scot to weigh the arguments at leisure and to pursue them with scholars. According to a speech ascribed to him in a Scottish version of his trial, he went to consult Italian, French, and German scholars. On the Catholic side, the considerations that began increasingly to weigh with him after an initial period of confusion concerned the universality of the Catholic Church in time and space, its unity of faith, its holiness, the miracles attesting its claims, its theologians, and, above all, its martyrs.

In the course of the year 1596 John Ogilvie went to the Scots College at Louvain and asked to be received into the Catholic Church. He was instructed in Christian doctrine by the Jesuit Cornelius a Lapide, the famous scripture scholar, remaining in Louvain for two years until a financial crisis forced the college to send away its students. He then spent six months in the Scottish Benedictine monastery of St James in Regensburg, which he left that same year, 1598, for the Jesuit College in Olmütz. In November 1599 he became a novice of the Society at Brünn in Bohemia and was to remain in Austria until 1610, following the usual course of studies and training as a Jesuit. John Ogilvie was ordained priest in Paris in 1610. Across the Channel during that same year, James VI of Scotland had become James I of England and an Anglican; he established the Episcopal Church in Scotland and approved the consecration of Scottish bishops. In order to allay the fears of the Presbyterians, who thought they saw in the move a swing back to Catholicism, the Scottish government intensified the persecution of Catholics. The last two Jesuits working in Scotland were obliged to leave in 1611.

John Ogilvie wished to undertake the mission to Scotland, now more perilous than ever. He was less oblivious of the dangers than Aquaviva, the general of the Order, who was not inclined to expose him to certain risk. There was an embarrassing moment for them both when Ogilvie, under the mistaken impression that he had long been destined for the Scottish mission, began his preparations and was obliged to drop them when Aquaviva made his wishes known explicitly to the eager missionary. Ogilvie accepted the decision but continued to press his request. He did not have long to wait. In 1613 Aquaviva agreed to the mission, and Ogilvie set out, arriving in Scotland in November 1613 for a ministry that was to last only about nine months. He immediately went north to his own county of Banffshire, hoping to reanimate the loyalty of the nobles. Most of these had conformed, but he was received by the marquis of Huntly, a crypto-Catholic, at his castle of Strathbogie. He was able to minister to the Catholics in the district, but six weeks later he prepared to move on. He spent a short time in Edinburgh, at the home of the fervent convert William Sinclair, and then left for London on a mission that remains shrouded in secrecy. It seemed sufficiently important to him to justify a return to France to see his immediate superiors, who, however, were not prepared to go along with the project. He returned to Scotland in April 1614 in the company of the Jesuit Moffat and a secular priest named Campbell and went to Edinburgh. A trip to Renfrewshire resulted in the reconciliation of some of the gentry. In July he was in Glasgow, where he said Mass for the local Catholics, and he was back in Edinburgh in August. Mass was said at three safe houses in the town, and the beginnings of a congregation began to form. Ogilvie visited Catholics in prison and even penetrated the Castle prison, where Sir James Macdonald of the Isles was held under sentence of death.

Ogilvie's host, friend, and admirer in Edinburgh, William Sinclair, was subsequently to pay dearly for his hospitality to the priest with exile and the forfeiture of his goods. For all that, he remained Ogilvie's most loyal admirer and was to be a prime witness in the process for his beatification. For the moment he and his family, especially the children, Roger and Robert, succumbed to the spell of the Jesuit, who was completely dedicated to his work, fearless in exercising his ministry, yet witty and always ready with a jest or a good story to raise a laugh.

During the same month of August Ogilvie went to Glasgow and met the Catholics there, saying Mass in the centre established by Marion Walker, an intrepid Catholic. His ministry extended to the families outside Glasgow, to which he returned in September. After a short stay in Edinburgh he returned to Glasgow on 3 October, eager to receive five converts who awaited him.

Among these was Adam Boyd, an unsavoury character whose chronic need for money justified every expedient. Having laid his plans in concert with the archbishop of Glasgow, he arranged to meet the Jesuit on 4 October in the market square. Ogilvie arrived shortly before the time of the appointment and fell in with James Stewart, a Catholic. The two were conversing when the waiting Boyd made a signal to one of the archbishop's servants to apprehend the unsuspecting priest. Stewart attempted to protect Ogilvie, but this led to a dispute. A crowd gathered and bore the priest, in spite of his protests that the dispute did not concern him, to the provost's residence. There the archbishop of Glasgow, John Spottiswoode, came to meet him. As he entered the room where Ogilvie was held, the latter rose to his feet and was completely stunned by a blow in his face administered by the prelate, who immediately fastened on the crime for which his prisoner would have to die: "You are overbold to say your Masses in a reformed city!" Ogilvie was still an Ogilvie, one of the foremost families in the land, and his pride bristled as he replied with barely repressed indignation, "You act like a hangman, not a bishop, in striking me!" It would not be the last time that his dignity was affronted, but throughout his trial and torture he retained his self-respect and gave good measure for the insults and lies meted out to him. What was to win the sympathy of the populace was his courage, his keen mind, his quickness to parry the thrusts of his accusers and on occasion even to address the archbishop a telling *argumentum ad hominem,* but above all, his wit and humour. Moreover, Ogilvie had grasped the psychological value of making his gaolers laugh. Once they had laughed with him, they could not be totally against him. This did not avail to win him his freedom or even a mitigation of his torture, but it did create a faint sense of comradeship and common humanity, as the scene at his execution would show.

For presuming to answer back he was roughly manhandled by the servants and bystanders; he was rescued by Lord Fleming, who happened to be present. A search of his person yielded a Breviary, a silver reliquary, a ring-seal, some medicine, and a paper listing controverted points of religion. The next day his room was searched but yielded nothing, as a Catholic had hidden his portable altar and vestments, but when an exhaustive search was set in hand, this benefactor handed over the priest's belongings. They proved incriminating enough: a Mass kit, a list of names, probably of Catholics but most likely coded, a catalogue of vestments and other sacred objects left by his Jesuit predecessor in various safe houses, and a papal dispensation for those reconciled Catholics holding church property.

His trial lasted for five months. It was designed to serve other aims beyond that of proving the defendant's guilt. The prosecutors had to exculpate themselves from the possible counter-charge of persecuting someone purely for his religion, so the plaint of treason must be made to hold; it was vital also to round up recalcitrant Catholics; if nothing else, torture of the prisoner could be relied on to make him divulge the names of those who had given him shelter and had attended his Masses. The following day the proceedings began, conducted by judges and dignitaries, the majority of whom were holders of church property with a vested interest in keeping Catholicism at bay. Spottiswoode, who besides being archbishop of Glasgow was a privy councillor to the king, presided. The trial was to be a contest between the archbishop and the Jesuit mostly on a theological level, beyond the grasp of the rest of the court, but the first questions put to the prisoner were intended to implicate him from the start: "Have you said Mass in the king's dominions?"

To have done so made him immediately liable to the charge of treason. The prisoner replied, "If to do so is a crime it should be proved not by the word of the accused but by witnesses."

The court promised to produce the witnesses who were then under examination. Knowing that some of these might indeed incriminate him, the Jesuit replied, "Very well then, my denial would not invalidate such evidence nor shall I strengthen it by admissions until it seems good to me to do so." Questioned again about saying Mass, Ogilvie declined to answer:

"Thefts, treachery, murders, these belong to the king's forum, but the sacraments of religion do not."

"Why did you come to Scotland?"

"To unteach heresy."

"Who gave you jurisdiction since neither the King nor the Bishop did?"

"They are all laymen with their King and nothing more and can have no jurisdiction in the matter. Christ's sheep were committed to Peter's charge. . . . Hence comes my jurisdiction."

"It is treason to assert that the Pope has spiritual jurisdiction in the King's dominions."

"It is of faith to hold that."

"Do you dare to sign such a declaration?"

"Yes, and with my blood if need be."

Ogilvie had now said enough to be condemned for treason as defined by the laws of Scotland, and the trial should have ended there, but Spottiswoode was determined to press on and win more damaging statements. He asked the Jesuit, "Can the Pope depose a heretic king?"

He replied, "I am not bound to express an opinion save to one who has the authority to judge on controversies of religion—that is to the Pope or his delegate."

Pleased to have this statement concerning the supremacy of the Pope over that of the king in spiritual matters, Spottiswoode made now for the Jesuits' supposed weak point: what did Ogilvie think of the Gunpowder plot? He replied that he detested the assassination of kings and did not approve of the plot.

"But Jesuits and Papists teach these things."

Ogilvie quoted the Council of Constance in reply but brought the matter

95

nearer home by referring to the Presbyterian riots on 17 September. If Catholics were treasonable by reason of their status, what of those Presbyterian ministers who had pronounced the legitimacy of regicide?

"There are two thousand still in Edinburgh who bore arms on that day."

Ogilvie had had nothing to eat since the day before, had been beaten and incarcerated during the night, and had now been subjected to a gruelling examination. He began to shiver uncontrollably from the onset of fever. This first trial was brought to an end, and he was sent down to be near the fire. One of the bystanders hurled abuse at him for tarnishing the name of Ogilvie and wished he could throw him into the fire. The prisoner replied, "That would be welcome indeed; I am frozen." He continued the pleasantries until they were forced to laugh. Sent back to prison, he was left in peace for two days, then bound by the feet to a heavy iron bar, which forced him to remain lying on his back or sitting as he was too weak to drag it around. The dark and stench of the cell could only weigh the more heavily on him as he learned that those who had attended his Mass had been condemned to death and that it had been put about that he had betrayed them. For two months he endured these conditions and mental torture; on a cold day in December, he was led out to another trial, in Edinburgh. The relatives of those who had been condemned vented their grief and hatred as the party left Glasgow by pelting him with snow and mud.

The purpose of this second trial was to elicit from the prisoner the names of Catholics. He was questioned about his movements but declined to give the desired information: "I am not bound to answer; from one statement made to you, you would make the deductions which you need to the damnation of my soul, the offending of God and the ruin of my neighbour. . . . In betraying my neighbour I should offend God and kill my own soul. Furthermore, it would not help but harm me."

A method was devised to break the Jesuit's will, one moreover that would leave no trace of mutilation or mistreatment: he would be deprived of sleep until he chose to speak. Four of the archbishop's retinue were instructed to take it in turns to bring this about. The period lasted from 12 to 21 December—eight days and nine nights. At first pins and daggers were used to keep him awake and when these proved ineffectual after a while he would be propped upright and left to fall to the ground so that the shock and pain would jerk him back to consciousness. There was a constant stream of ministers and officials, menacing him with further torture, promising him rewards if he would comply, demanding the names they wanted. When they could no longer prop him up, they dragged him by his feet up and down. They did not give over until a doctor stated that he would die within a few hours. William Sinclair, who followed events closely and later spoke to his torturers, testified: "From the attendants who guarded him and the physicians who stood by him during his enforced vigil and others who witnessed his death I have heard that they marvelled how he had borne up to the very end such great sufferings with a spirit so brave and unflinching."

One night and one day's rest was given him before he was again summoned to another examination. Emaciated and deeply confused, but certain that his execution could not now be delayed, John Ogilvie had no time for niceties. To the remark that he had been treated with clemency in being deprived of sleep rather than in being subjected to the torture of "the boots," he retorted, "If you had examined me by the boots I might still have been carried to church or lecture-room and so earned my bread . . . but now the vigil has all but destroyed and killed my intelligence. What worse torture, indeed, save death could you have inflicted, since in my calling I need judgment and not limbs to serve Christ and the Church?"

"Unless you do the King's will, worse will follow."

" . . . I will not alter or add to anything I have said. What you are going to do to me by God's permission, do quickly. I beg no mercy. One thing only I ask, that what you do, you do quickly."

The Jesuit was returned to his cell, but not to peace. A deputy sheriff came to reproach him for his stubbornness, adding, "If I were king, you should be boiled in wax."

"No doubt if God had wanted to make you king he would have given you better brains."

But he drank the man's health and continued a pleasant banter, and even Spottiswoode had to laugh. The man not only bore Ogilvie no ill will, but as the party returned to Glasgow the following day, he invited the priest to look over his house and gardens. It was Christmas Eve 1614 when Ogilvie returned to the archbishop's prison cell and to a relatively easier régime. Spottiswoode treated him more humanely, hoping that kindness would now make him give in: "We could not have got anything out of you if we had not found your letters and belongings. It is maddening that you will not reveal anything while so many are working on the case and getting nowhere."

"To tell you the truth, I wish you had never got hold of even a suspicion of my existence," was the Jesuit's wry observation.

It was during this relatively quiet time that Ogilvie wrote his *Relatio Incarcerationis* for his brother Jesuits, smuggling it out page by page. At the same time King James was at work on his own compilation—questions intended so to snare the Jesuit that he could not avoid the gallows if he would stand by Catholic doctrine. In the circumstances they were merely hypothetical, with little relevance to Ogilvie's crime of saying Mass and converting the king's subjects to the Catholic faith: Did the pope possess power in spiritual and temporal affairs? Might he excommunicate and depose a monarch not of his church? Was it murder [after due process] to slay a monarch excommunicated and deposed by the pope? They were put to the prisoner on 18 January. In effect, it was not what Ogilvie had done but what he thought that was now under scrutiny. In keeping with his policy thus far, he refused to deny spiritual jurisdiction or supremacy to the pope but withheld answers to controversial questions that he regarded as beyond the competence of the tribunal. He added for good measure that he condemned the Oaths of Allegiance and Supremacy and demanded that this be registered by the clerk of the court and signed by himself.

Ogilvie's fate was sealed. His jailer, suspected of too great a fondness for him, was changed; even the archbishop's wife, found to be conquered by the Jesuit's charm, was sent away to Edinburgh. The public, informed by the gossip of the very gaolers who had tormented him, had come round to admiring him. His physical and moral courage was common knowledge throughout Scotland and beyond. The weight of the irons was therefore increased, and they were fastened the more securely. A last letter from Ogilvie to the general of the Society says simply: "My punishments are terrible and torments bitter. Of your fatherly love pray for me that I may die with a generous courage for Jesus who triumphed over all for us." The king fixed the day of his trial, which would be followed by the prisoner's death if he did not recant. The night before the trial an attempt was made by a Catholic gentleman to persuade Ogilvie to escape, but he would not agree to it.

The last trial covered no new ground save that the charge was now said to be based on the answers Ogilvie had given to the king's questions. The jury found him guilty of treason, and the sentence was pronounced: the prisoner was to be hanged and quartered. He was led to the gallows that afternoon, 28 February old style, 10 March, new style, 1615; to the last moment he was promised rich rewards if he would disown the pope's supremacy. The crowd, made up of both Catholics and Presbyterians, was enormous and unwilling to see so brave a man sent to an untimely death. So strong was the sympathy that the sentence was stayed and Ogilvie's body was not quartered. It was buried outside the town and said to have been exhumed later by the Catholic faithful.

John Ogilvie was beatified in December 1929 and canonized by Paul VI in 1976.

The quotations from the speeches and trials above are taken from W. E. Brown and P. McGlynn, *John Ogilvie* (1925), in which they are reproduced from research and trans. by P. McGlynn; J. Forbes, *Jean Ogilvie, Ecossais, Jésuite* (1885); G. Antonelli, *Il b. Giovanni Ogilvie* (1929); T. Collins, *Martyr in Scotland* (1955); *N.C.E.*, s.v.; *Bibl.SS.*, 9, 1132-5.

St Simplicius, *Pope* (483)

Simplicius, who succeeded St Hilarius (28 Feb.) in 468, was pope at a most difficult period, with mainly political challenges in the West and religious ones in the East. All the provinces of the West outside Italy had fallen into the hands of the barbarians, who were generally pagans or Arians. During his tenure of the papal office Rome itself was permanently occupied by Odoacer, the ruler of the Heruli. The Roman Empire had ceased to exist if only because the people had been too crushed by taxation and impoverished by devastating raids to offer any resistance to the conquerors, who, moreover, levied no taxes themselves. Simplicius was concerned to alleviate the miseries of the people and to sow the seeds of the Faith among the barbarian invaders. However, his position in a political vacuum rendered him impotent in face of the politically-inspired aspiration to greater power on the part of the see of Constantinople.

In spite of the occupation, the administration of the Church continued. Simplicius appointed Bishop Zeno of Seville as papal vicar for Spain, charged with seeing that the papal directives were duly observed. He built four new churches in Rome, two of which, San Stefano Rotondo and Santa Balbina, still stand; reorganized the services in the greater basilicas; and repaired many churches devastated in a third sack of Rome by the barbarian Richimer, who spared only St Peter's.

In the East he was engaged in a protracted struggle with the Monophysites, who successfully managed to place their own bishops in the key sees of Alexandria, Jerusalem, and Antioch. His protests fell on the deaf ears of the emperor Basiliscus, in sympathy with the heretics, and of Acacius, the patriarch of Constantinople, affronted by the Roman rejection of Canon 28 of the Council of Chalcedon, which, while paying lip-service to the primacy of Rome, in practical terms elevated the see of Constantinople over that of Rome. Simplicius had to endure much frustration as letters went unanswered and news of developments was withheld. With the advent of the emperor Zeno, better things might have been expected, but he and Acacius joined forces to bring about a compromise for the sake of peace. It fell to Simplicius' successor, St Felix (3 Mar.), to deal with this compromise. Simplicius died on 10 March 483 and was buried in St Peter's.

Duchesne, *Liber Pontificalis*, 1, pp. 249-51; Hefele-Leclerq, *Conciles*, 2, pp. 912-30; *N.C.E.* 13, p. 232; *Bibl.SS.*, 11, 1197; B. Mondin, *Dizzionario Enciclopedico dei Papi* (1995), p. 56; For the background see E. Duffy, *Saints and Sinners: A History of the Popes* (1997), pp. 37-8.

St Attalas, *Abbot* (627)

Attalas was a Burgundian of noble birth, confided by his parents to Aregius, bishop of Gap, for his education. Longing for a much stricter life than he found in the bishop's household, he left secretly for the monastery of Lérins, where he lived for some time. However, the life there was still not severe enough for him so he set out again, this time for Luxeuil, the monastery established by St Columban (23 Nov.). There he found all the austerity he craved and, in addition, the esteem and direction of the great Irish saint.

Having been ordered out of France by King Theodoric of Austrasia, whom he had rebuked for his vices, Columban moved on to Lombardy, taking his Irish companions as well as Attalas with him, and settled in Bobbio, a lonely spot in the Apennines, on land given them by King Agilulf of the Lombards. Columban was already seventy years of age at the time, and as he lived only one year after the foundation of Bobbio, much of the credit for the establishment and prestige of the great monastery is certainly due to Attalas, who succeeded him as abbot in 615.

However, once the authority of the saintly Columban was removed, murmuring against the austerity of the life began. Attalas would not be persuaded to relax the régime in any way but gave himself earnestly to prayer for his brother monks. He would not punish them either, so he let the malcontents depart. Eventually some returned, to be welcomed back by a loving father. According to Jonas, his biographer, Attalas was "a man beloved by all, of great fervour, great charity to the poor and the pilgrim. The proud he would resist, but he was humble with the lowly; he was not at a loss in conversation with the clever but with the simple he would speak of God's secrets. Wise when it came to knotty questions, firm when opposed by heretics, he was strong in adversity, disciplined in good times, always temperate and discreet. Love and respect he showed toward his subjects, wisdom to his disciples. In his presence no one could be either sad or unduly elated." Like Columban, Attalas fought against Arianism, which was prevalent in the districts about Milan.

As his final illness became more serious he asked to be laid outside his cell, beside which stood a cross he always touched on leaving or entering, and to be left alone. One monk remained at hand. The dying man prayed fervently for God's mercy, and, the other monk reported, he was then given a vision of heaven, which lasted for several hours. He was carried back to his cell and died the next day. He was buried at Bobbio beside St Columban. Later the body of St Bertulf (19 Aug.) was placed in the same tomb and the three holy men were venerated together.

AA.SS.OSB., 2, pp. 115-8; *AA.SS.*, Mar., 2, pp. 41-5; *P.L.*, 87, 1055-62; *M.G.H., Script. merov.*, 4, pp. 113-9.

Bd Marie-Eugénie Milleret, *Foundress* (1817-98)

Anne-Eugénie Milleret, foundress of the Religious of the Assumption, was born in the town of Metz in France on 26 August 1817, the fourth of five children. Her father, Jacques Milleret, a banker and one-time deputy of the Moselle, was an admirer of Voltaire, while her mother, Eleonore-Eugénie de Brou, of Luxembourg, no longer practised her Catholic faith but instilled in the young child a concern for honesty and uprightness. Although during Anne-Eugénie's childhood the family was well off, a certain austerity characterized their life. Courage, generosity, and self-control were expected of the children, and they were taught to care for the sick and respect the poor. With the death of her younger sister and a brother, Louis, her remaining brother, became Anne-Eugénie's childhood companion with whom she shared everything. She made her First Communion as a matter of social convention at the age of twelve. For her it was nevertheless a moment of grace and the beginning of a lifelong devotion to the Blessed Sacrament.

During the next three years tragedy struck the family. Anne-Eugénie contracted typhoid, which necessitated long months of rest at the château of Preisch, where the family lived for six months of the year. In 1830 her father faced bankruptcy; both the château and the family house in Metz were sold. Her parents, who had never got on very well together, separated. While M. Milleret and Louis remained together, Mme Milleret and her daughter went to Paris. For Anne-Eugénie, it was an enormous wrench, but during the months they were alone together she grew in intimacy with her mother. In 1832 Madame Milleret died from the cholera ravaging Paris. Anne-Eugénie was left alone at the age of fifteen. Her father arranged for her to stay with Mme Doulcet, a lady of high society in Châlons. The round of fashionable parties and soirées that now made up her life left her profoundly dissatisfied. Her fine mind found no intellectual stimulus in the society she was forced to keep, and she experienced a feeling of total emptiness. There was no one with whom she could share her preoccupations concerning the reality of God and the meaning of life and the longing she experienced to recover the relationship with God that her First Communion seemed to presage. Her father then decided to send her to Paris to his cousin Mme Foulon. This was a pious household but so narrow that the young girl felt even more confined.

The famous Dominican preacher Lacordaire had by then inaugurated a series of Lenten sermons at the cathedral of Notre Dame. Anne-Eugénie was expected to attend Lenten sermons, and she chose to go to Notre Dame for Lacordaire's second series. It was on the last day that the preacher's words struck home: "It is prayer that re-establishes our relationship with God. . . . Doubt is the beginning of faith." She was to say later that her vocation dated from these sermons at Notre Dame, which she dubbed her "appointment with grace." Her immediate desire was to consecrate herself wholly to God. Lacordaire understood the needs of this new penitent and advised her to embark on a course of reading, especially contemporary philosophical writers: de Maistre, Bonald, Bourdaloue, among others. He discussed the nature of the religious life with her but advised delaying any such step. Her immediate need was to pray, read, and wait. She waited for a year, during which the Eucharist was her mainstay.

Shortly before the following Lent, she had a dream. She was in a strange church, listening to an unknown preacher. A voice instructed her, "He will show you the way you must go." On going into the church of Saint-Eustache for the Lenten sermons, she recognized the church and the preacher of her dream, Abbé Théodore Combalot. A strange partnership was to ensue. She was only twenty years of age at this time, quiet, reserved, and intelligent; he was a fiery orator, ardent and impetuous. She was not attracted, yet it was to him that she had been directed. Combalot had for twelve years cherished the desire to found a Congregation of women that would be uncompromisingly contemplative in character and at the same time dedicated to the education of women, whom he regarded as the natural agents for the Christian renewal of society. It was a vision that she could share, though her modesty and intelligence suggested that she was hardly an apt instrument to carry out such a project. She was confirmed at Easter 1837 and seemed sufficiently strengthened to accept this unlikely vocation in spite of her own misgivings and the opposition of her father and brother.

She entered the novitiate of the Visitation nuns of Côte Saint-André in the south of France in 1838, finding in this community the attractive features of the spirituality of St Francis de Sales (24 Jan.): a warm, fraternal love, humility, gentleness, simplicity, and good humour. The tough programme of studies she now embarked on was to serve her well: scripture, Thomistic theology, Alphonsus Liguori's moral theology, the spirituality of St Augustine, and that of St Teresa. In addition she was given tuition in Latin, German, and English. She kept up a correspondence with Abbé Combalot and sometimes received visits from him. On one of these he was accompanied by Abbé d'Alzon, who later became her close friend and adviser. While enthusiastically in favour of the venture, d'Alzon was sharp enough to detect that the impulsive and authoritarian Combalot was more likely to hinder than help the foundation. But the latter was now engaged in recruiting the future members of the Congregation, and to good effect.

The Religious of the Assumption began community life on 30 April 1839 with Anne-Eugénie and Anastasia Bevier; fairly soon these two were joined by four others, among them the Irish mystic Catherine O'Neill, who was to hold the position of novice-mistress for forty years. They lived in conditions of great material poverty, not helped overmuch by a lack of training in domestic skills as well as frequent moves in search of the right premises. However, there was a willing spirit and an atmosphere of mutual respect and trust, simplicity and friendliness, which owed much to Anne-Eugénie's reverence for the work of grace in others. In principle all should have gone smoothly were it not for the idiosyncratic Combalot, whose contradictory directives turned obedience into a feat of spiritual gymnastics.

The first clothing ceremony took place in August 1840, and in 1841 Anne-Eugénie, now Sr Marie-Eugénie, was elected superior by the rest of the group. The new Institute was becoming known and gaining friends among the intellectual and socially sensitive Catholics of Paris sympathetic to its aim: Chateaubriand, Frédéric Ozanam (to be beatified in 1997; 8 Sept.), the Boré brothers, Jean Joseph Poujoulat, and many others. Indeed these contacts and the manifest interest of the group in social issues were to tease the conscience of the archbishop of Paris. However, an immediate problem that he had to settle was that of Combalot. Now that the need to establish the Constitutions of the Religious of the Assumption was making itself felt, Combalot had set to work and produced a thirty-page Introduction, without reference either to Sr Marie-Eugènie and the religious or to the archbishop. While incorporating much that inspired them all, it was a document that reflected his own special brand of rhetoric. The archbishop decided to act and appointed Abbé (later Bishop) Gros in Combalot's stead. Combalot refused to accept this and faced the group with a choice between Sr Marie-Eugénie and himself. He would take the group to Brittany and re-commence the foundation. By now the Sisters were too well bonded to come down on Combalot's side: although conscious of what they owed him, they were not prepared to do as he suggested. He left for Rome.

While the cohesion of the group was manifest, its viability was not so evident to the archbishop, who questioned their decision to pray the divine office rather than the more usual Little Office of Our Lady. He thought that combined religious and secular studies were too much of a burden, that consecrated women should not have so many contacts with the world nor be interested in social issues, that young women in a convent should have the protection of grilles. Moreover their poverty was so extreme that postulants were leaving, and the work of education had not even begun. Bishop Gros suggested disbanding. The group showed its mettle once more: what contemporary society needed was precisely a work of education, and if they were to engage in that, the Sisters would need to be well equipped; they, more than most, would need a solid basis of prayer. Bishop Gros acquiesced. A year later there were eight girls in the school, and Sr. Marie-Eugénie, at the age of twenty-five, wrote her *Counsels of Education* for the Institute.

The novitiate was formally opened in 1842, but concern about a too-contemplative orientation was raised again, this time by a new ecclesiastical superior dealing with the Constitutions. Sr Marie-Eugénie reacted with some asperity: "The more I go on, the less sympathy I feel for priests or pious lay-people. . . . Nothing that is big and broadminded resonates within them. Must I modify our own way of life so as to suppress everything in it that shocks their narrow minds?" 1844 saw the first five members of the Institute finally professed.

From 1850 the work of expansion began, continuing throughout the lifetime of the foundress. Schools and convents were established in England, all over France, in Spain, in Italy, in the Philippines, in Central and South America. Offshoots of the Religious of the Assumption also came into being. Those Sisters sent on the very first foundation in South Africa, a foundation that never succeeded, remained there and founded the Missionary Sisters of the Assumption. Abbé d'Alzon founded the Augustinians of the Assumption for men in 1845, and one of their members was to found the Little Sisters of the Assumption, while in 1855 the Third Order of the Assumption was begun in Nîmes. Later on, Abbé d'Alzon established the Orantes of the Assumption at a moment when Marie-Eugénie could not fall in with his request to send her religious to the Balkans.

In 1858 Sr Marie-Eugénie was elected superior general for life. By then the Congregation had established its identity and was flourishing. Her task from then on was to supervise its expansion and guide its members to holiness. But there remained one further step to be taken to anchor her work firmly within the juridical structure of the Church. In 1866 she petitioned Rome for approbation of the Institute, a move which did not win approval from the Gallican elements of the Church in France. The ecclesiastical superior of the Institute,

Fr Véron, would not co-operate; indeed he withheld material required for the dossier and proceeded to undermine Marie-Eugénie's position. He went so far as to plan the expulsion of the Congregation from Paris. The superior general offered to resign, but the situation was suddenly reversed when Fr Véron died. Approbation was accorded the following year. This step was important to the foundress, whose understanding of the Church inspired the aims of the Institute: "It is an ardent love for the Church and for our society, so far from God, that has given birth to this work. The irreligion of three-quarters of the people makes the work of education necessary." For her there was no Christ without the Church. The Church is his body and the source of life, transcending its historical accidents or any contemporary understanding of its reality.

The Congregation of the Religious of the Assumption enshrines a high ideal of Christian education. It envisages nothing less than the advent of the Kingdom of Christ in every individual, whether teacher or student. Marie-Eugénie saw people as a whole. Piety would never be enough to bring about the reign of Christ; all the powers of mind and heart had to be cultivated and engaged in the effort to bring all things into subjection to him. Only a fully alive, fully committed human being is capable of the act of total dedication to Christ. A spirit of freedom, intellectual inquiry, social awareness, mutual respect, and warm-hearted appreciation of the other are the singularly attractive fruits of the guidance of the Congregation of the Assumption by its foundress.

Marie-Eugénie Milleret died on 10 March 1898 and was beatified by Pope Paul VI on 9 February 1975. The Congregation numbers 1,500, distributed in 207 communities and thirty-one countries.

Les Origines de l'Assomption (1898); Hélène-Marie Bories, *Marie-Eugénie Milleret* (1992, private publication); L. Lovat, *The Life of Eugénie Milleret de Brou* (1925); C. C. Martindale, *The Foundress of the Sisters of the Assumption* (1936); M. Poinsenet, *Feu vert au bout d'un siècle, Mère Marie-Eugénie Milleret de Brou* (1971); *Dict.Sp.*, 15, 671.

R.M.
SS Caius and Alexander, martyrs of Syria (first century)
St Kessog, bishop of Luss in Scotland (*c.* 566)
St Amenavag, martyr at Karenberdak in Armenia (1335)
St Drotté, abbot in Paris (*c.* 580)
SS Peter Ch'oe Hyong Hyeng and John Baptist Chon Chang-un, martyrs in Korea (1866)—see 20 Sept.

11

St Sophronius, *Patriarch of Jerusalem* (*c.* 550-639)

Recent scholarship now accepts that Sophronius, patriarch of Jerusalem, is the same person as Sophronius the Sophist. This makes him one of the most engaging personalities of his time, cultured, open-minded, and passionately concerned for orthodoxy.

Sophronius was born in Damascus around 550. Although he left his native city at an early age, lived mostly elsewhere, and travelled widely, he was always proud of his birthplace, "where Paul arrived unseeing and left with sight restored, where a fleeing persecutor became a preacher; the city which hid the apostle as he was being hounded and let him out in a basket through a window, so sharing the graces of the saints and winning greater fame. . . ." The major part of his education must have been acquired in Damascus, where he would have been steeped in both Greek and Syriac culture.

Sophronius toyed with the idea of becoming a monk and visited the monastery of St Theodosius in Judea, where he met John Moschus, a professed monk there with whom he struck up a friendship that endured for forty years. It is difficult to gauge the reciprocal influences. Sophronius was undoubtedly the more cultured of the two, but he looked up to Moschus as to his spiritual guide and mentor. Perhaps their greatest tie was the concern they shared for the integrity of the Faith as definitively enunciated by the Council of Chalcedon. They also began a remarkable partnership in monastic journalism, as Moschus was fired by the desire to continue the stories of the lives of the Desert Fathers for the benefit of coming generations. The upheavals of the Middle East during their time propelled the two friends from one region to another, one monastery to another. Between 578 and 584 they were in Egypt, where Sophronius studied under the Aristotelian Stephen of Alexandria and they enjoyed the friendship of Theodore the philosopher and Zoilus, reader and calligrapher. Some of Moschus' anecdotes date from this stay in Egypt, and it is clear that Sophronius accompanied him on his visits to various hermits and monasteries. It may have been at this time that Sophronius began to lose his sight. Despairing of obtaining help from doctors, he visited the shrine of SS Cyrus and John (31 Jan.) at Menuthi and was cured. In gratitude he wrote the accounts of seventy miracles wrought by these saints, the last being an account of his own cure.

It is difficult to reconstruct the movements of the two men after 584. Sophronius became a monk at the monastery of St Theodosius, as he says in his work on the miracles of SS Cyrus and John. John Moschus is known to have stayed in a monastery in Sinai for ten years and to have visited the monasteries of Cilicia and Syria. When the Persians began their incursions into the Roman Empire in 604, Moschus took refuge at Antioch on the Orontes in Syria, and subsequently Moschus and Sophronius were together in Egypt, where they stayed for about ten years and were active in the service of the patriarch of Alexandria, John the Almoner, appointed to the patriarchate in 610. Both were staunch supporters of the patriarch, a Chalcedonian in a largely Monophysite Egypt.

The Persians seized the Holy Places in 614, and Egypt was their next destination. John the Almoner left for Cyprus together with Sophronius and John Moschus. These two visited the other islands as well and finally made their way to Rome. There John Moschus fell ill and confided the manuscript containing his collection of monastic anecdotes, *The Spiritual Meadow,* to Sophronius. He also asked his friend to see that he was buried on Mount Sinai or, failing that, in his monastery of St Theodosius in Palestine. The year was 619.

The Emperor Heraclius had already been on the throne for nine years. Much of his energy was directed against the Persians, but like other rulers before him he understood that without doctrinal peace the empire could not hold together. With the agreement of Sergius, patriarch of Constantinople, he favoured a Monothelite faith, which he was indeed to impose on the whole empire in 638. For the Chalcedonians the signs must have portended the extinction of all their hopes, but Sophronius acted with vigour. He had confronted Cyrus of Alexandria in 633 when he was planning to bring about a union with the Monophysites on the basis of Monoenergism (the belief that there is only one source of activity in Christ), though with little result. He went to Constantinople to see Sergius, but he merely incurred his wrath.

In 634 Sophronius was elected patriarch of Jerusalem, which meant that he could now fight from a position of relative strength. Sergius was canny enough to suspect that Sophronius would be in touch with Rome, so he decided to get his word in first. Unfortunately, Pope Honorius gave more attention to Sergius than to Sophronius, whose synodical (the letter sent round by a new patriarch to fellow-bishops setting out his theological position and seeking to establish communion with them on the basis of that position) arrived later. However, Sergius became more and more openly heretical, and Sophronius felt he must return to the fray. He would have wished to submit the facts to Rome himself, but the Saracens were advancing on Jerusalem, and he could not leave. Instead he commissioned Stephen of Dora to go to Rome and speak in his stead. An old man now, Sophronius led him up the hill of Calvary and there adjured him to act. Stephen relates to the fathers of the Lateran Council, meeting in 649:

> There he bound me with unbreakable bonds: "If you neglect or despise the faith now under threat, you will have to render an account to the One who,

though God, was crucified in this holy place, when at his awesome coming he will judge the living and the dead. As you know, I myself am prevented from making this journey by the invasion of the Saracens. . . . Go without delay to the other end of the earth until you come to the apostolic see, the foundation of orthodox teaching. Tell the holy men there, not once, not twice, but many times, what is going on here; tell them the whole truth and nothing but the truth. Do not waver, ask them, earnestly beg them to use their God-given apostolic wisdom to come to a definitive judgment and, following the canons, destroy the novel teaching inflicted on us." Awed by the solemn appeal Sophronius made in that fearful and venerable place and considering the episcopal dignity which by the grace of God had been conferred on me, I travelled to Rome without a second thought. I am here before you for the third time now, prostrate before the apostolic see begging, as did Sophronius and so many others, "Come to the help of the embattled Christian faith."

After a wait of ten years in Rome, Stephen at last saw the heresy condemned by Pope St Martin I at this same Lateran Council.

Sophronius negotiated the surrender of Jerusalem with the Saracens to avoid a massacre of the population and died a few months later. Besides his Lives of the Alexandrian martyrs Cyrus and John he left several sermons, a fine prayer for the blessing of the water on the feast of the Baptism of the Lord, and hymns and odes of considerable merit. His tropes for Holy Week are said to have been the source of the *Improperia* in the liturgy for Good Friday.

Quotation above trans. from *AA.SS*, Mar., 2, pp. 64-71; the same material is also in *P.G.*, 87/3, 3141-2; *Triodion* (1879); *Dict.Sp.*, 14, 1066-73; D. J. Chitty, *The Desert a City* (1966); C. von Schönborn, *Sophrone de Jérusalem: Vie monastique et confession dogmatique* (1972); H. Chadwick, "John Moschus and his friend Sophronius the Sophist," *J.T.S.* 35 (1974), pp. 41-74; John Moschus (trans. J. Wortley), *The Spiritual Meadow* (1992); *O.D.C.C.* (1997), p. 1519.

St Eulogius and the Martyrs of Córdoba (between 822 and 859)

At the end of the seventh century the Church in Spain possessed an extraordinary vitality. By then the Romano-Hispanic population had assimilated the Suevi and the Visigoths, and after a long struggle Spain had largely rid itself of Arianism and kindred heresies. The bishops of Seville, Zaragoza, and Toledo, together with the impressive series of councils held in Toledo, were the great lights of the Spanish Church and had fostered a spirituality at once Catholic and local. The presence of heresy had served to bring christology and trinitarian theology into focus, while the Church's splendid liturgy nurtured a warm piety. The monastic life was well developed, channelling that tendency to austerity and mysticism still characteristic of the Spanish Church.

Waves of Islamic invasions were already beating against the walls of the Byzantine Empire and submerging Christian communities in North Africa. By 711 the Muslims had overrun almost the whole of Spain. This did not bring about the end of of Christianity there, but the changes wrought by the Moorish presence were immense. Córdoba became the capital, from which was disseminated a Moorish civilization beneficial in many respects even as its thrusts tore at the Christian heart of the country.

The peninsula had never known such opportunities for trade nor dreamed of the exotic materials that adorned the mosques, palaces, and castles built by the occupiers. The fountains of marble and jasper were only part of huge systems designed to bring pure water to the town, where roads were now paved, gardens delighted the eye, and bridges arched the Guadalquivir. Schools for poor children and public baths were established and the police organized. As the Moorish hold on the country was consolidated, the court became the centre of artistic and intellectual life, although only the occupiers and those prepared to identify themselves with them were the beneficiaries. It was not Moorish practice to annihilate subject populations, nor indeed to suppress their customs and religion, but controlling them was an imperative. In the long term the inevitable collaboration with the occupying power was perceived as emasculating what was most essential to the indigenous population, provoking not merely resentment but desperation as its proper values were threatened with extinction. Conversions to Islam, for whatever reasons, disheartened the beleaguered Christians. Daily life was irksome even if the occupiers were moderate men. In addition to general taxes needed to support building projects, there was the hated poll tax levied on all non-Muslims. In order to survive, some knowledge of Arabic was necessary; in order to get on, fluency was essential, and this could not be acquired without steeping oneself in Arab literature, impressive then even if the best was to come only in the following century. Some took up Moorish studies with enthusiasm in a genuinely eirenic spirit, and not a few Christians and Jews held high posts in the administration, official reluctance notwithstanding. Intermarriage between Muslims and Christians was a complicating factor, particularly when the religious allegiance of the children was in question. The offspring of a Muslim father were deemed to be Muslim; if they opted for Christianity, they were judged apostates and subject to the death penalty.

Christians found themselves living under the régime of a monotheistic religion, and there were those who wondered what difference there was between themselves and the Moors. Furthermore, if Christians were revolted by the life of luxury and pleasure endemic to the court, there were fervent Muslims who were just as revolted by it. On the other hand, the person of Mohammed could not but appear to most Christians as usurping the position of Christ. If loyalty to Christ were ever to breach the restraints it would be expressed in a repudiation of the Prophet, and this too carried the death penalty. The Christian clergy, educated in their own establishments and in touch with Christian tradition, saw the issues fairly clearly. The Moors too knew that the clergy would be the natural centres of resistance. One way to neutralize the possibility of resistance was to control appointments to the sees. No bishop could take office without the emir's approval or without paying a fee. Bishoprics could be bought outright. Reccafred, the archbishop of Seville, was regarded as a creature of the Moors by the radical party of Christians, though it is impossible to judge how far, if at all, he was truly compromised. At one point Eulogius, a priest at the basilica of St Zoilo in Córdoba, gave up saying Mass to avoid the impression that he was in communion with him, and he had this to say to those who made a point of emphasizing the tolerance of the Moors: "Can it really be said that we co-exist peacefully when they destroy our basilicas, insult priests, and oblige us to pay an intolerable tax every month? None of us can go among them safely or live with them in peace. None of us can cross the rampart without being plastered with insults. When we are obliged to leave our little corner on some household errand to the market or forum and they see we are clerics, they hurl insolent abuse at us as if they had taken leave of their senses, not to speak of the children who pursue us through the streets pelting stones."

Eulogius belonged to an old "senatorial" family, which may indicate Roman stock but could also mean that the family had given members of senatorial rank to the service of the town. In the new situation the family was considerably reduced in status but clung to its Christianity. Destined to the priesthood by his mother, Eulogius was enrolled at the age of seven in the school attached to the basilica of St Zoilo, where he pursued his studies in preparation for an ecclesiastical career. Intelligent and studious, he was soon dubbed "master of the teachers." He sought elsewhere in Córdoba for teachers who might further his studies, and it was thus that he met Abbot Esperaindeo, a semi-hermit and patristic scholar, a lover of the Faith, a man who prized the Latin language and Iberian culture. Esperaindeo was too gentle to hate, but he could feel nothing but revulsion toward the Arab conquerors and all they had brought to Spain. He wrote a biography, no longer extant, of the first martyrs to suffer in the ninth century under the Moors (822), the brothers Adulphus and John. His influence on Eulogius must have been considerable. The *Memorialis Sanctorum,* which Eulogius began in 851 and which covers the period 851-9, may well have been intended as a continuation of the work begun by Esperaindeo. In the abbot's circle Eulogius met a young man of about the same age, Pablo Alvaro, with whom he felt an immediate sympathy, whose predilections and aspirations he shared, especially his love of theological debate, and who from the first moment became his friend and confidant. Eulogius went on to be ordained, while Alvaro married.

Eulogius was also a man of prayer and penance: Alvaro speaks of his passing whole nights in prayer. He was a frequent visitor to the several monasteries on the outskirts of Córdoba, where he found like-minded spirits who kindled his fervour and whose fervour he in turn sustained. One of these monasteries asked Eulogius to draw up a monastic Rule for them. His friendship with the communities was of paramount importance in the history of the Córdoban

martyrs, since many of these came from such monastic groups. Equally important for one who was to become, in Alvaro's words, the *incitator martyrum et
laudator,* the instigator of martyrs and their eulogist, was his appointment as
head of the school attached to St Zoilo. Young Christians were to be fired by
his passionate loyalty to the Faith and to the culture it had fostered over the
centuries. He assumed quite naturally the leadership of the radical Christians,
advised them, protected them, accompanied them to their execution, and later
wrote their *acta*, casting them in the heroic mould of the Roman martyrs.
Eulogius was at once hagiographer, apologist, and propagator of the ideal of
martyrdom.

It was not an ideal that won the approval of the entire Christian community,
whose inclination was rather to lie low. Why substitute for a reasonable if
uncomfortable *modus vivendi* with the Muslim occupiers a régime of reprisal?
The Muslims themselves were nonplussed by Christians courting death and
laughing in the face of torture; they not only sought the help of Bishop Reccafred
but called for a council of bishops in order to halt the movement. Martyrdom
could not but inflame everyone's mind, Muslim and Christian alike. However,
some of the martyrs quoted Our Lord's words, promising to repudiate before
his Father those who refused to testify to him before men as one of the driving
motives of their actions, and Eulogius was quick to point out that antiquity had
known those who actively sought martyrdom in their zeal to witness to Christ.

The first person to be executed in the 850s became a martyr almost by
chance. The priest Perfectus belonged to the basilica of St Acisclus, also a
centre of Christian education, and was fluent in Arabic. Accused of calling
Mohammed a false prophet, he denied the charge for fear of death but regained his courage in prison and was subsequently beheaded on 18 April 850.
A few weeks later it was the turn of Isaac (3 June), a Christian of noble and
wealthy parents, so proficient in Arabic that he held one of the highest posts in
the administration of the affairs of the local population. He had suddenly
abandoned everything, entered the monastery of Tábanos, and just as suddenly
left after three years to confront his erstwhile colleagues; he was sentenced for
insulting the Prophet and was beheaded. His body, suspended by the feet, was
exposed for several days and finally burnt to ashes and thrown into the
Guadalquivir so that no one could salvage the smallest relic. Eulogius does not
give any names but implies that other Christians suffered with Isaac. There is
explicit mention, though, of a young man named Sancho, a one-time captive
and then a volunteer in the royal regiment, who was impaled two days later.

This savage sentence failed to destroy the precedent set by Isaac. Indeed, the
urge actively to court martyrdom gathered momentum. The Monday following
Isaac's execution six others came forward. Peter was a priest, Walabonso a
deacon; both had come to Córdoba to pursue their studies and were then
ministering to the needs of the nuns of Cuteclara. Sabiniano and Vistremundo
were from the monastery of St Zoilo, the one a monk of long standing, the

other a recent entrant, who "ran toward martyrdom," as Eulogius says. Habentius was an anchorite of the monastery of San Cristóbal who lived an exceedingly penitential life; Jeremiah, an old man now, was the founder of the monastery of Tábanos. They declared their solidarity with Isaac and Sancho and reiterated the denunciation of the Prophet. Jeremiah was cruelly beaten, almost to death, and all were beheaded (8 June), their bodies exposed for a few days then burnt and thrown into the river without a trace.

The deacon Sisenando followed them on 16 July. His body was recovered and buried in the church of Saint Acisclus. Paul the deacon, at once a charitable and charming young man, had been a pupil at the school of St Zoilo. He taxed the Muslims with empty knowledge and their Prophet with madness, confessing Christ to be truly God. He was seized and put in a cellar where he found a priest named Tiberino, imprisoned there for twenty years. Paul was martyred on 20 July, and a few days later Tiberino was restored to his home town. Paul's body was left unburied outside the palace walls but was later recovered together with that of Theodimir the monk, who was martyred on 25 July; both were laid to rest in the sanctuary of St Zoilo.

Flora and her brother were children of a mixed marriage. Their Muslim father had died, so the boy, Muslim by force of law, was head of the family. Their Christian mother brought up Flora and her sister to be fervent believers. Spied on by her brother, Flora and her sister ran away to stay with safe Christian families. Her brother unleashed a persecution of Christians suspected of harbouring them; many of the clergy were jailed and the convents targeted. Flora returned to her home and dared her brother to do his worst. He took her to the *cadí*, before whom she confessed her faith, declaring that there was no question of apostasy as she had been a Christian from infancy and had furthermore vowed to remain a virgin for love of Christ. The *cadí* had her violently struck and severely whipped. She was imprisoned in the family house but, having recovered somewhat, managed to escape and with her sister remained in hiding for six years until she came before the *cadí* once more.

María, the daughter of a converted Moorish mother and a Christian father, whose brother Walabonso had been martyred, had become a nun in the monastery of Cuteclara. Informed by another nun that Walabonso had appeared to her and asked her to tell his sister that she must put aside her grief as they would be seeing each other shortly in the joy of heaven, María prepared to give herself up to the *cadí*. She went into a church to pray for strength and there she met Flora, who was preparing to do the same thing. The *cadí* was at once saddened and astonished by the spirit of these two women and sent them to prison with prostitutes for their companions.

If Isaac was the forerunner and the guiding light of the martyrs, Flora and María were their glory. Eulogius himself was taken prisoner in October or November of 851 together with Saul, bishop of Córdoba, and several abbots and priests rounded up after Flora's earlier escape. From prison Eulogius wrote a long letter, known as the *Documentum Martyrii*, to the two women also in prison, exhorting them to stay the course. It is a noble work, at once passionate and restrained, in which Eulogius highlights the gospel texts and those of St Paul that speak of loyalty to Christ; it bears comparison with St Cyprian's *Exhortatio ad martyres*. There was the danger that the women might be raped. Eulogius repeats for them St Augustine's statement that virginity is a quality of the soul which can never be destroyed if there is no interior consent to its violation. The letter gives us an insight into the passionate zeal of this apostle of martyrdom, tempered by the tender admiration he feels for Flora. The women were taken before the *cadí* again, but as they would not be deflected from their purpose they were finally condemned to death. María's body was found and taken to Cuteclara; Flora's was never recovered, though their heads were preserved in the basilica of St Acisclus.

In January 852 Gumesindus, a priest, and Servus Dei, a monk-hermit, confessed their faith and were martyred on 13 January. Aurelius, son of a Moorish father and Christian mother, had remained a loyal Christian. He married Sabigotho, a daughter of Muslim parents who had become a Christian when her widowed mother married a Christian. The two practised clandestinely to avoid the charge of apostasy. A kinsman of Aurelius named Felix, who had once lapsed but had repented, married Liliosa, the daughter of Christians. The marriage was a very happy one, but they too practised their faith in secret and for the same reason. It happened one day that Aurelius was in the forum when John the merchant was put on show. This John had been arrested for having sworn by Mohammed—a familiarity he had considered good for business. Not quite qualifying for the death penalty, he was beaten almost to death and publicly humiliated. Aurelius was moved by the spectacle of John's courage and underwent a conversion. From then on, he and Sabigotho were more openly Christian and prepared themselves for their own martyrdom. George, a monk of St Sabas in Palestine on a begging tour for the support of his monastery, found his way to Spain and to the monastery of Tábanos, where he met Sabigotho, who immediately exclaimed, "This monk is destined to join the contest with us!" The women deliberately attracted attention by going unveiled to church, and an informer told the *cadí*. Soldiers sent to Aurelius' house, where the group was assembled, ordered the Christians out. George was not taken, so he challenged the soldiers who struck him violently. Although wounded, he followed the others to the tribunal. The four refused to deny Christ. Offered bribes to recant, they maintained their refusal and were condemned to death. George was in danger of being left out again—he had not been heard actually insulting the Prophet—so he made good the omission then and there and was included with the others. All five died on 27 August 852.

The monk Cristóbal was a pupil of Eulogius who had entered the monastery of Saint Martin. Fired by the courage of the martyrs who had preceded him, he sought out a *cadí* and attempted to annouce the good news of Christ, threatening the Moors with hell-fire if they would not believe. The *cadí* ordered him imprisoned and chained. Another monk, Leovigildis, from the monastery of SS Justus and Pastor, also came to the city seeking martyrdom. First he went to beg Eulogius' prayers, then presented himself before the *cadí*, who had him beaten, chained, and thrown into prison, where he found Cristóbal. They were beheaded on 11 September 852, such remains as there were after the bodies had been burnt being placed in the basilica of St Zoilo.

Emilia and Jeremiah were brothers who had been educated at the school attached to the basilica of St Cyprian. One was a deacon, the other a simple layman, and both knew Arabic. When they came before the *cadí*, Emilia spoke against the Prophet at length, which only provoked a greater anger against them. The two were imprisoned and beheaded on 15 September 852, and their bodies were exposed on the other side of the river. While these were still in jail, they were joined by two others, Rogelio, an old monk, and Servio-Deo, a native of the East who had settled in Córdoba. They had made a pact never to abandon each other until they shed their blood as martyrs. Mixing with the crowds, they went into a mosque and preached the gospel, denouncing Islam. The crowd turned on them and would have torn them to pieces had not a *cadí* who was present intervened. He ordered them to be chained and put in prison. As a punishment for having entered the mosque they were sentenced first to dismemberment and then to decapitation, the sentence being carried out on 16 September 852.

By now both Christians and Moors were revolted by the loss of life, wantonly pursued—in the eyes of some on both sides—by a fanatical, hysterical, and suicidal minority. The Moors' solution was to increase penalties and put pressure on the bishops, whom the king had convoked to council, to condemn the martyrs and to forbid anyone to seek martyrdom by denouncing the Prophet. Eulogius found himself at the centre of the controversy, as he was considered the one responsible for the movement. The bishops produced a formula to satisfy the government while not explicitly condemning the movement. Then King Abd al-Rahman II died and was succeeded by the far more severe Muhammad I in September or October 852. He immediately dismissed all the Christians holding administrative posts at the court and enacted a series of laws designed to break their spirit. Churches built or repaired within the preceding three hundred years were to be destroyed (this at a time when the mosque of Córdoba was being considerably enlarged), taxes on the Christian population were to be increased, and military pensions were to be suppressed. Inevitably some Christians abjured their faith.

Fandila, a student at Córdoba who had entered the monastery of Tábanos, presented himself to the *cadí*, spoke of the gospel, and denounced the Prophet. He was beheaded on 13 June 853. Next day the priest Anastasius and the monk Felix were killed. Hardly had they died when Digna, a nun of Tábanos, appeared before the *cadí* and asked why her brothers had been killed in that way. Is it, she asked, because we adore God and faithfully worship the Trinity, Father, Son and Holy Spirit, and reject everything else contrary to this confession? The *cadí* was so angry that he did not even allow her the usual time of reflection in jail. She was beheaded immediately. Benildis, a middle-aged woman, was executed the day after.

Columba, a nun of Tábanos, who had been given permission to lead an eremitical life and had continued to do so even when transferred to Saint Cyprian after the destruction of Tábanos by the Moors, slipped out one day and asked her way to the *cadí*'s house. He received her calmly and just as calmly she explained her faith. He was quite taken aback by her gentleness and could not bring himself to condemn her. Instead he sent her to the palace where she was heard by a council of satraps. They condemned her to death, which took place on 17 September 853. Her body was recovered and placed in the church of St Eulalia. The news of her martyrdom reached the nun Pomposa, who also longed for martyrdom. Her parents, knowing this, had kept her always in their sight, but that night her brother left the main gate open and she slipped out. At daybreak she entered the city and went to the *cadí*, confessed her faith and repudiated the Prophet. She was beheaded on 19 September. Her body was recovered only some twenty days later and buried at Columba's feet.

Ten months later Abundius, a priest, was apprehended. Interpreting this as a call to martyrdom, he suffered bravely. His martyrdom in July 854 was followed by that of Amador, Peter, and Louis and, perhaps in 855, of the old man Vitesindus (15 May), a repentant apostate. Another aged priest, Helias from Portugal, suffered together with two young monks, Paul and Isidore, on 17 April 856. Argimirus, an official in the Muslim administration who had retired to a monastery, was summoned to answer a charge of disrespect to the Prophet while in office, brought against him probably by someone with a grudge. He perished on 28 June 856.

Aurea, of Muslim extraction and too highly connected to be touched by the persecution, had been a nun of Cuteclara for over thirty years when members of her family from Seville denounced her to the *cadí*, to whom she was related. He promised her full honours if she would apostatize and if she would not, torture and death. At this point Aurea gave in and was given her freedom, but she returned to her convent and, far from repudiating her faith, became more attached to it than ever, bemoaning her moment of weakness. She was denounced again to the *cadí*, who exploded with anger at the thought of her treachery. She was sent to prison in chains and beheaded by decree of the emir on 19 July 856. Her body was exposed and then thrown into the river, from which it was never recovered.

There were three brothers living in the province of Cabra, one of whom was a Christian and one a Muslim. The third was Rodrigo, a Christian and a priest. One night the first two came to blows over religion. Rodrigo intervened, only to be knocked unconscious in the fray. The Muslim had him placed on a stretcher and carried through the streets, while he announced that his priest brother wished it to be known before he died that he had renounced his Christian faith and returned to Islam. Rodrigo recovered and was very angry indeed when he heard what had taken place. He fled to the hills outside Córdoba and lived there for five years. At the beginning of 857 he came into Córdoba in his priest's garb and was recognized in the street by his Muslim brother, who had him taken to the *cadí*. He was thrown into prison, where he befriended Salomon, a repentant apostate. Learning of their friendship, the *cadí* ordered that they be separated. Later he tried to tempt them into abjuring the Faith by promises of favours but failed to persuade them and pronounced the sentence of death on 13 March 857. As usual, precautions were taken to deny the Christians the satisfaction of honouring the martyrs' relics, but these were eventually found and buried with great rejoicing.

Though besieged on many sides by threats to his empire, the emir Muhammad never ceased the fight against the Christians. However, in 858 all was quiet. Both Eulogius and Alvaro had accepted that voluntary martyrdom should not be encouraged. Eulogius had been elected to the see of Toledo, which he was never to occupy. The *acta* of Rodrigo were the last to be written by him and were incorporated in his latest apologetic work, *Liber apologeticus martyrum*. Alvaro brought the history of the Cordoban martyrs of this period to a close with accounts of the martyrdom of Eulogius himself and Lucretia.

Lucretia was born of rich and noble Muslim parents. She had one Christian relative, a nun who had instructed her in the Faith and had her baptized. Her family tried every conceivable stratagem to bring her back to her Islamic origins. Unable to escape from a carefully guarded house, she sent a message to Eulogius describing her plight. He advised her to seek an occasion to escape, which presented itself when a relative was getting married. She proposed to attend the marriage and was allowed to do so. When she failed to return, a search was set in hand. Eulogius had her moved frequently and by night from one safe house to another. One night she came to his house wishing to speak to his sister, Anulona, with whom he lived. They spent the night in prayer and waited for the person who was due to take her back at first light. Her escort came too late after sunrise for them to attempt to move through the town, so it was decided that she should stay in hiding there that day. Shortly after, the house was surrounded by police, and both Lucretia and Eulogius were taken.

The *cadí* demanded of Eulogius his reasons for harbouring the young girl. He answered that it belonged to his office to help anyone who requested instruction in the Faith, that he was even prepared to instruct the *cadí* himself if he so wished. He was ordered to be whipped, but he would not accept the ignominious penalty: "Do you think you are going to destroy my body with a whip? If you want to return my soul to God, you had better whet your sword. I am a Christian, just as I have always been. I confess that Christ, son of Mary, is the true Son of God." Eulogius was then sent to the palace, where a tribunal of palace officials was hastily improvised. One of these, distressed to see such a good and eminent man in danger of execution, tried to persuade him to abjure, promising that he would see to his safety. Eulogius thanked him, "If you only knew what awaits us!" He made one further confession of faith before the assembly and was condemned to death. As he was led out, one of the eunuchs struck him on the cheek. Eulogius offered his other cheek but was hurried out of the chamber by the soldiers. Arriving at the place of execution, he knelt down, extended his arms, made a large sign of the cross, prayed silently, and offered his neck to the sword. It was 11 March 859.

Four days later, scorning the bribes offered her, Lucretia, still strong in faith, was beheaded and thrown into the Guadalquivir. Her body would not sink but remained plainly in view. The Christians buried St Eulogius in the basilica of St Zoilo and Lucretia in that of St Genesius. In 1305 their remains were translated to the cathedral of Oviedo.

P.L., 115, 703-966; 121, 527-8; *AA.SS.*, June, 1, pp. 317-19. Note the privileged place held by Isaac in the Spanish martyrologies; there is a separate entry for him in the present work, 3 June. J. P. de Urbel, *A Saint under Moslem Rule* (1937), pp. 99ff; E. Colbert, *The Martyrs of Córdoba* (1962); K. B. Wolf, *Christian Martyrs in Muslim Spain* (1988); *Dict.Sp.*, 4, 1110-12; *Anal. Boll.* 108 (1990), p. 210; for Isaac, *Bibl. SS.*, 7, 919-20; for Eulogius, *Bibl.SS.*, 5, pp. 218-9; for the other martyrs, *ibid.*, 4, pp. 173-5; J. A. Coope, *The Martyrs of Córdoba* (1995).

St Oengus, *Abbot and Bishop* (Ninth Century)

Oengus, compiler of the earliest Irish martyrology, is thought to be the first person to have been called a "culdee," or "God's vassal," a Celtic term used subsequently to designate someone living an exceedingly penitential life.

He came of Ulster royal stock and was born about the middle of the eighth century. In early youth he entered the famous monastery of Clonenagh in Leix, which under abbot Melaithgen then enjoyed a reputation for sanctity, learning, and the great number of its monks. Oengus made such good progress both in his monastic life and in his studies that he was considered unrivalled on both counts. However, he had but one ambition: to fly from the world and be free to practise his austerities. He left Clonenagh and retired to a cell at Dysartenos some seven miles away but was pursued by visitors, so he abandoned his hermitage and made his way south.

The story is told that on his way he came to the church of Coolbanagher, where he had a vision of angels around a particular tomb singing most sweetly. He asked the parish priest to tell him what was special about the man buried there. "Nothing," the priest replied, "save perhaps that on getting up in the morning and before going to bed at night he would pray to all the saints he had ever heard of and could remember." It immediately flashed through Oengus' mind that he might some day compile a list of saints in metrical form as an easy way to recall them to mind—and incidentally win himself as good a reward as that of the poor man in the churchyard.

He carried on with his journey and came to the monastery of Tallaght near Dublin. Concealing his identity, he asked to be received as a servant. He was accepted by the abbot, St Maelruain, and for seven years he toiled at the meanest and most laborious tasks, but he was happy. However, he was unmasked by a schoolboy. It happened that the lad was playing truant because he had not learnt his lesson. He came to the barn where Oengus was and asked if he might stay there. Oengus even lulled him to sleep. When he awoke he knew his lesson perfectly. That, at least, was what he told the abbot, who questioned the boy after hearing him repeat the lesson with unusual fluency and intelligence. The abbot then ran out to the barn and embraced Oengus affectionately, divining or eliciting from him that he was the missing Oengus of Dysartenos. Upbraided for the misplaced humility that had deprived the community of the benefit of his learning and experience, Oengus fell on his knees and begged the abbot's pardon. From that moment the two saints became the closest of friends. They collaborated on the *Martyrology of Tallaght*, considered to be the oldest of the Irish martyrologies and probably providing the basis for Oengus' further work. He then set about composing the metrical hymn known in the Irish language as *Félire* and in Latin as the *Festilogium*. It does not seem to have been circulated before the death of St Maelruain in 787. Other valuable works by Oengus are the collection of *Pedigrees of the Irish Saints*, with topographical notes and references to ancient churches, and *Saltairna-Rann*, a collection of 150 poems on the history of the Old Testament.

Oengus remained in Tallaght for some years, but after the death of St Maelruain he returned to Clonenagh, where it is said he succeeded Maelaithgen as abbot and received ordination as bishop in accordance with the practice prevalent in Ireland at the time. As he felt his end approaching he withdrew to Dysartenos. The exact date of his death is contested, but it is not thought that he lived to a great age.

Colgan's *Life of St Oengus* is reprinted in *AA.SS.*, Mar., 2, pp. 84-87. The *Félire* was published for the Henry Bradshaw society, 1880. See also Healy, H. Lawlor, and R. Best, *Martyrology of Tallaght* (Henry Bradshaw Society, 1931), with review by P. Grosjean in *Anal.Boll.* 51 (1933), pp. 117-30. D. Pochin-Mould, *The Irish Saints* (1964), pp. 228-41, treats together SS Maelruain and Oengus. See also P. O'Aigin, "The Tallacht Martyrologies Redated," *Cambridge Medieval Celtic Studies* 20 (1990), pp. 21-38.

Bd Thomas Atkinson, *Martyr* (*c.* 1546-1616)

Thomas Atkinson was born in the East Riding of Yorkshire (or possibly in Leeds) about 1546 and educated at Douai College. He was ordained at Laon in 1588 and sent on the English mission that same year. His ministry, which was confined to Yorkshire, covered a period of twenty-eight years. They were years of hardship and fatigue, as he travelled on foot over the countryside seeking shelter from Catholic households but not always finding it. Sometimes he travelled at night in all weathers, sometimes he slept in a bed, at other times he had to be content with sleeping in an outhouse. On one frosty night he broke a leg and was unfortunate enough to have an incompetent doctor to set it. After this he had to use a horse.

He was about seventy when he was arrested leaving the house of Mr Vavasour, with whom he had been staying at Willitoft in the East Riding of Yorkshire. The family was taken into custody with him. He was brought before the president and judges of the assizes being held at the time, but he would not acknowledge his priesthood for fear of compromising his hosts. He did not deny it either, so the onus of proof rested with the court. After his arrest he had been searched and found to have on his person a rosary and a copy of indulgences granted by the pope. These were considered enough proof, and the jury brought in a guilty verdict. He was hanged, drawn, and quartered at York on 11 March 1616; he was beatified in 1987.

M.M.P., p. 339; Anstruther, 1, p. 13. See also the entries under 4 May and 25 October in the present work.

SS Mark Chong Lu-bai and Alexius Ou Syei-Yeng,

Martyrs (1866)

Mark Chong was born in Korea in 1794 of a noble family. He became a teacher, married but had no children, and was subsequently widowed. He chanced to witness the martyrdom of two Catholic priests and marvelled at their joy. He then began to read Catholic books and asked for Baptism. Appointed a catechist, he carried out his duties conscientiously and looked after the sick and orphans as well. He remarried but chose to live in poverty with his new wife and adopted son. He helped Catholics escape when persecution was unleashed, but he himself remained at his post. He was arrested on 25 February 1866 and was severely tortured. He was beheaded on 11 March 1866.

Alexius Ou Syei-Yeng was born in 1847 of a wealthy noble family. Hearing about the Catholic faith from a catechist, he ran away to meet Bishop Berneux (8 Mar.) in a remote village. The bishop sent him to the catechist Mark Chong for instruction and then baptized the young man himself. Harshly treated on his return, Alexius decided to leave his family altogether. He stayed with Mark Chong, translating the catechism and other texts. On New Year's Day 1866, Alexius was with Mark Chong when all the Catholics in the village were arrested. Alexius denied his faith and was released but repented immediately. He went to Bishop Berneux, who was in prison, and confessed his apostasy as well as his part in beating a catechist to death. He was re-arrested, endured the torture with courage, and was finally beheaded at the age of twenty-two on 11 March 1866.

M.S.K. p. 143; see 20 Sept. for a general treatment of the martyrs of Korea.

R.M.

St Agapa, martyr at Antioch in Syria (fourth century)

St Constantine, king and martyr of Scotland (sixth century)

St Vincent, martyr at León (630)

St Vindicianus, bishop of Cambrai (*c.* 712)

St Benedict, bishop of Milan (725)

St Firmanus, abbot of Macerata near Piceno in Italy (992)

St Peter, hermit of Gubbio in Italy (before eleventh century)

St George the Younger, pilgrim of Constantinople (tenth century)

Bd John Baptist Righi, O.F.M. of Massaccio (1539)

Bd Dominic Cam, martyr (1859); see "The Martyrs of Vietnam," 2 Feb.

12

St Pionius, *Martyr* (? 250)

Pionius was a priest of Smyrna and a true heir of the spirit of St Polycarp (23 Feb.), whose memory he revered. He was an eloquent man, well read both in profane literature and in the scriptures, a teacher, and clearly a leader of men who had brought many to the Faith.

Pionius provided a refuge in his own house for Sabina, who had run away from a pagan household where she had been ill-treated for her faith. Asclepiades was also with them on the day of their arrest. Pionius had a dream warning him of his impending fate, and in a gesture part defiance and part acceptance of martyrdom he draped himself and his companions with chains about the neck. They had prayed and had consumed blessed bread when Polemon, the temple chief, burst in with his men. They were interrogated by him in the forum before a crowd of people and invited to offer sacrifice to the gods, but they refused. When Asclepiades was asked what God he worshipped, he replied, "Jesus Christ." "Is that another god?" Polemon asked. Asclepiades said, "No, he is the same God that the others have confessed"—a clear declaration of the divinity of Christ. When Sabina heard talk of the stake, she merely smiled and was threatened with exposure in the brothel. "God will be my protector there," she said.

Polemon had the three sent to jail, where they found three other Christians, but he returned with an officer of the cavalry and some soldiers to take them by force to the temple. Pionius protested at the illegality of the proceedings: they could not be forced out of the prison save by order of the proconsul. Someone lied, "The proconsul has sent a message that you are to be transferred to Ephesus." Pionius asked for proof and, at that, was overpowered by the officer. They were dragged to the marketplace and threw themselves on the ground to avoid being pushed into the temple. It took six men to take Pionius in, head downward. There were more interrogations and lively exchanges between Christians and the crowd. Garlands were put on them, but the Christians tore them off, refusing also to eat sacrificial meat. As nothing more could be done, they were then sent back to prison.

When the proconsul, Quintilian, arrived in Smyrna Pionius was summoned to appear before him. After the usual interrogation and his refusal to sacrifice Pionius was tortured. Again asked to sacrifice, he refused once more and was then condemned to be burned immediately at the stake.

Pionius hurried to the stadium and removed his clothes; his body showed no signs of the recent torture. He stretched himself out on the gibbet and allowed the executioner to drive in the nails. A final effort was made: if he would change his mind, the nails would be taken out. "I think they are there to stay," was the reply, "and the sooner I die, the sooner I shall rise again." While the firewood was being piled about him, Pionius closed his eyes so that it was thought that he had fainted, but he was praying silently. He opened his eyes finally and said, "Amen," his face quite radiant as the flames leapt about him. Finally, with the words "Lord, receive my spirit" and a single spasm, he quietly gave up his soul to God.

A.C.M., pp.137-67, for Greek text and translation. A Latin version was published by Ruinart. The author of the account of the trial and martyrdom declares that he is an eyewitness of the events and offers definite dates which place them in the reign of the emperor Decius, but Eusebius speaks of Aurelius as the emperor at the time. Despite the contradictory evidence, the narrative is considered by scholars to be authentic. For the question of date see further, H. Grégoire in *Anal. Boll.* 69 (1951), pp. 1f. See also L. Robert, *Le Martyre de Pionius* (1994).

SS Peter and Companions, *Martyrs* (303)

The emperor Diocletian was in Nicomedia when he heard that there were Christians in his own household. He arranged a simple test to flush them out: images of the gods were set out, and all were ordered to offer sacrifice. The Christians refused, and the first to incur the emperor's vengeance was Peter, his majordomo. Stripped naked, Peter was suspended in the air and scourged until his bones showed; vinegar mixed with salt was then poured into the wounds. Dorotheus, who was in charge of the imperial bedchamber and Gorgonius, another high official, remonstrated with the emperor for singling out Peter: "His faith is ours also." Then they took their stand: "Up to now we have fought for you but from now on we shall serve the God who made us." They and another official named Migdon were tortured and put to death. In the meantime Peter, who remained undaunted, was cut down, trampled underfoot, and finally roasted on a spit. He uttered no cry of pain in his terrible agony.

Several other names are noted in the various martyrologies together with those above and it is possible that they all suffered on the same occasion.

Euseb., *H.E.*, 8, 6; *AA.SS.*, Mar., 2, p. 105.

St Innocent I, *Pope* (417)

Innocent was a native of Albano, but beyond that nothing is known of his personal life. He succeeded Pope St Anastasius I in the year 401, and for the sixteen years of his pontificate played an active part in the affairs of the Church. His quick response to current problems shows him to have been capable, energetic, and vigorous.

He was conscious of the unique position of the See of Rome in relation to the other sees of the Church and quick to assert the papacy as universal arbiter, especially of doctrinal matters. We find him writing to St Victricius (7 Aug.), bishop of Rouen, that "greater causes" were to be referred to Rome and to the Spanish bishops in the same vein. He also instructed several bishops to see that their clergy observed celibacy after the Roman example. He supported John Chrysostom (13 Sept.), who had been unjustly removed from his see of Constantinople by the Oak Tree Synod in 403, refusing to recognize his intruded successors. He tried to get the emperor Arcadius to have him reinstated, and after John's death he urged the see of Constantinople to place him in the diptychs as a sign of communion.

After the bishops of Africa had condemned Pelagianism at the councils of Carthage and Milevis in 416, they wrote asking the pope to confirm their decisions. The pope did so, adding that "in all matters of faith bishops throughout the world should refer to St Peter, as indeed you have done." The papal confirmation was announced by St Augustine (28 Aug.) to his flock at Hippo: "Two councils have written to the Apostolic See about this matter, and the reply has come back: the question is settled." This is the source of the well-known saying, *Roma locuta, causa finita est*. Subsequently Pelagius drew up and sent to Innocent a confession of faith, which arrived after the pope's death.

During Innocent's pontificate, on the night between the years 406 and 407, the barbarians crossed the Rhine. Four years later Rome was taken and sacked by the Goths under Alaric. The pope was in Ravenna at the time, having gone there with a deputation to persuade Emperor Honorius to make peace by buying off the invaders. He died on 12 March 417.

AA.SS., July, 6, pp. 548-61; Fl-Martin, 4, pp. 243-7 (1945); E. Duffy, *Saints and Sinners: A History of the Popes* (1997), pp. 31-2.

St Paul Aurelian, *Bishop* (573)

The Life of St Paul Aurelian was written by Wrmonoc, a monk of Landévennec, in the ninth or tenth century. The author says that he based his work on an earlier Life, but the extant document seems to be in parts a conflation of other Lives, and much remains uncertain. However, the broad lines of Paul's career are supported by the traces of his existence and cult found in some place names.

Paul Aurelian was born in Wales and educated together with St David (1 Mar.), St Samson (28 July), and St Gildas (29 Jan.) at Ynys Byr by St Iltyd (6 Nov.). As a young man he chose a solitary life and spent many years in prayer and study. Ordained priest, he gathered round him twelve companions, who lived in cells near his own. With them he left for Brittany, stopping to see his nun sister, Sitofolla, in Cornwall. Although there are no traces of the existence of Sitofolla or her monastery, there is a settlement named Paul close to the western shore of Mount's Bay.

The group came to the island of Ushant, where they landed at a place now named Porz-Pol. There they lived for a while, moving on later to the mainland to Ploudalmézeau and finally to the island of Batz, where a monastery was built. Paul's ministrations to the local population were so much appreciated that he was looked upon as a possible bishop. Withur, the local lord, had recourse to a trick to obtain his consent. He sent him with an urgent letter to King Childebert in Paris, containing a request that Paul be consecrated a bishop. In spite of the candidate's protestations, King Childebert had him consecrated and sent him back to Léon. Paul continued to live the same austere life, his only food being bread and water except on great festivals when he added a little fish.

He resigned his office some years before his death but outlived two of his followers whom he had ordained to succeed him in the episcopacy. He lived to extreme old age and died in his monastery at Batz. He was said to be endowed with the gift of prescience and, according to Wrmonoc, foretold the incursions of the Northmen. The name of his episcopal seat, Léon, was changed to St-Pol-de-Léon in his memory.

A tenth-century MS of Wrmonoc's Life was printed by C. Cuissard in *Revue Celtique* 5 (1883), pp. 417-58, and a later eleventh-twelfth century MS in *Anal. Boll.* 1 (1882), pp. 209-58; see also 2 (1883), pp. 191-4; G. H. Doble, *St Paul of Léon* (1941), and his *Lives of the Welsh Saints*, ed. D. S. Evans (1971).

St Theophanes the Chronicler, *Abbot* (817)

Theophanes was the son of Theodota, of whom nothing is known, and Isaac, imperial governor of the islands of the White Sea. Isaac died early, and the boy was brought up by his mother, with the emperor having some say in the future of the child who would one day possess an enormous fortune. It was this fortune that seems to have tempted a close associate of the emperor Leo Chazares to make preliminary arrangements for a marriage between the boy and his own twelve-year-old daughter, who was sent to live with her future mother-in-law. When Theodota died, pressure was put on the couple to marry. They went through with the ceremony but determined to remain celibate, and when Theophanes' father-in-law died, they separated definitively. After they had distributed their wealth, she went to a convent of her choice, and he embarked on his own monastic career.

Theophanes received the monastic habit in Sigriano and later built a monastery on his own property on an island named Calonymus (Calomio). After six years he returned to Sigriano, set up another monastery there, and became its *igumen*. In 787 he was invited by the patriarch Tarasius to attend the Second Council of Nicea and support the use and veneration of sacred images. His biographers draw attention to the contrast between his sackcloth and the rich vestments of the bishops assembled there, many of whom had known him when he was a very rich young man indeed. For all that he cut a fine figure, according to St Theodore the Studite (11 Nov.), who depicts him at the time of his monastic conversion: "He abandoned, home, town, and country, and this in the prime of life; tall, handsome, in the best of health, admired for his qualities of soul no less than for what struck the eye."

Theophanes practised a thorough asceticism, giving many hours to prayer. He was also a man of study. The chronicle of world history he composed, perhaps between 810 and 815, has, more than anything else, thrown the spotlight on his very holy life and quasi-martyrdom. Working on material already prepared by George Syncellus and drawing on Socrates, Sozomen, Theodoret, and the chonicles of Constantinople, he compiled a history covering the years 281-813. The first part is straightfoward history; the second is composed of chronological tables, the dates of which have been filled in, sometimes incorrectly, by another hand. In spite of its deficiencies, the work is considered superior to the majority of Byzantine chronicles that have come down to us.

His quiet was shattered when Leo the Armenian, recalling Theophanes' friendship with the court and his now high reputation in the religious world, tried to get his support for his Iconoclastic policies. Although suffering agonies with the stone and other complications he went to Constantinople when summoned. With a mixture of threats and inducements, Leo tried to win him over. Theophanes merely laughed: "I am an old man now, riddled with pain, and not likely to be seduced by any of the material advantages I rejected when young. My monastery and my friends? I place them in God's hands. You are wasting your time if you think you can frighten me into compliance as if I were a child under threat of the birch." Others were sent in an attempt to wear him down, but he remained unbowed. He was condemned to be scourged and imprisoned. After receiving three hundred stripes, he was thrown into a prison cell and for a period of two years deprived of everything. His illnesses became acute, and he was finally banished to the island of Samothrace, where he did not survive beyond another seventeen days. He died on 12 March 817.

The biography of the saint by Methodius was edited by D. Spyridon in 1913. The Lives previously known seem to be dependent on this, although the two Lives reproduced in the *AA.SS.*, Mar., 2, pp. 210-25, are divergent. A panegyric delivered by St Theodore the Studite can be found in *Anal.Boll.* 31 (1912), pp. 11-25, and his letters referring to Theophanes in *P.G.*, 99, 1197ff. See *Anal.Boll.* as above also for the *Chronographia*, pp. 148-56.

St Symeon the New Theologian, *Abbot* (949-1022)

He who sees God is entitled to speak of God. It is in this sense that St Symeon is a theologian. He was dubbed "new" by his contemporaries, perhaps contemptuously, but the designation held, for in the eyes of many he contributed to a spiritual renewal of the Byzantine Church. That Church always has been and still is predominantly monastic in character. At the time of the abbot Symeon, most of the theological controversies of earlier centuries had had their hard edges softened and their divisive power diminished, but there remained a high degree of esteem for the monks as guardians of orthodoxy and models of spirituality.

George, as he was probably named, was born in 949 in Paphlagonia in Asia Minor of a noble provincial family of means with connections to the imperial court of Constantinople. At eleven he was sent to the capital to live with his uncle Basil, who held a position at the court to which George might also have aspired. However, after the completion of his secondary schooling he declined to go on to a higher education. He also declined an introduction to the court. His motives are not clear but were not overtly religious. He writes in the third person of himself emerging from his teens: "He was called George and was not very old—about twenty—and he lived in Constantinople in our own time. He cut a fine figure of a man, was so polished in dress, appearance, and comportment that no one would have imagined him descending to anything unbecoming." In retrospect, he considered he had led a dissipated life. Addressing God, he says, "Of my own accord I threw myself into the abyss, escaping far from your grasp. . . . In your mercy you set me on my quest, you brought me out of the deep, you raised me to a greater excellence. . . ."

A reading of the Lives of the saints made him realize his state of soul and resolve to find someone who could lead him to God. He was directed to the monastery of Studium in the city and to the monk known as Symeon the Devout. With great tact, Symeon allowed him to advance at his own pace. A turning point was reached when he requested some spiritual reading and was given the work of Mark the Hermit entitled *The Spiritual Law*. He was struck by Mark's advice faithfully to follow the inspirations of grace: "Heed your conscience if you would be healed. Do whatever it bids you, and you will profit by it." From then on he never went to bed leaving undone anything urged on him by his conscience. During the day he administered the household of a patrician, visiting the palace daily, but at nights his conscience bade him pray: "Thus, wounded by love and desire for the Lord, he sought the supreme Beauty." An overwhelming perception of the presence of God, experienced as an irruption of light, impressed him profoundly on one occasion during this period, and he returns to it again and again in his writings. However, his resolve remained weak, and he fell back again into a worldly and dissipated life in which he struggled vainly for a period of six or seven years. He attributes his release from this servitude to the prayers of his spiritual father, to whom he was once again restored. In the meantime his uncle had died, and George was his own master. He decided to become a monk and about the age of twenty-seven entered the monastery of Studium.

Studium was a cenobitic community in the tradition of St Basil, re-founded in the ninth century by Theodore the Studite (11 Nov.). There Symeon the Devout took charge of the new candidate, who as a mark of esteem for his spiritual father took the name of Symeon. All his writings witness to a fervour that seemed to know no decline from the heady heights of his first weeks. Love of the Blessed Virgin, reverence for the Eucharist, and the study of the scriptures were bolstered by the constant, even intransigent demands, down to the smallest details, he made on himself to conquer his self-will. Later he would advise beginners to observe a disciplined deportment and to exercise strong control over the instincts of greed and selfishness: "Take your portion of food without scrutinizing it; do not begin to eat before the seniors or before grace is said; do not stuff; eat less than you are tempted to. Eat what is put before you without choosing. Do not seek first place, remembering that to be the last is to be the first." He makes Christ say to the novice, "If you, a man, wish to become God, to attain eternal life and be with me, humble yourself as I humbled myself for you. . . . If you are ashamed to imitate God, how will you reign with him?" Attentiveness to the office was of primary importance, so that "nourished and strengthened, you may arrive at compunction of heart, humility, and the illumination of the Holy Spirit."

Symeon the younger was soon receiving graces of a mystical nature. A second irruption of light, linked with a profound experience of God, occurred during his novitiate at Studium. It is not possible to establish an exact chronology of these spiritual experiences, as his later accounts of them are imprecise as to order and vary in detail. In a general way these visitations seem to have been frequent if intermittent, leaving behind an immense pain of loss. It was not until he had an experience of Christ speaking from within the very depths of his own being that he arrived at a state of union with him and a permanent awareness of the divine presence.

Two features of the situation in which the novice found himself were producing ripples in the community. The obviously intense relationship between the two Symeons, stronger on the younger man's side because of his dependence on the other, had a jarring and disturbing effect in a cenobitic setting of some formality; also, the novice might have been thought more suited to an eremitical than to a cenobitical life, as he required many hours of solitary prayer. The *igumen* attempted to normalize the situation by forbidding the younger Symeon access to the older monk, but in young Symeon's eyes this was tantamount to a denial of grace. Only the expulsion of the novice resolved the situation. Symeon then sought entry to the monastery of Saint Mamas, of the same tradition as Studium and in fact not very far away. It was a small community, living in a half-ruined monastery, under an elderly and saintly *igumen*. Symeon the Devout continued to direct the novice, who three years after his entry was elected *igumen* to succeed the old man on his death and was at the same time ordained priest.

It was an astonishing choice and may be accounted for by Symeon's own fervour as a monk and perhaps by the state of the community. Symeon set himself to rebuild the monastery without delay, and it was not long before his spiritual fire, warmth of personality, and approachability had won many new recruits. It was the custom in Eastern monasteries for the *igumen* to address the community after the office of Prime on the subject of monastic spirituality and observance. The addresses made by Symeon, the *Catecheses*, were copied down and even circulated to interested persons in the capital. These addresses provide much of our knowledge of the intimate aspirations and mystical experiences of the New Theologian. His inaugural address is, fittingly, a hymn to charity, for it is this supreme virtue, love of God and love of the brethren, that underpinned his life and motivated his actions. He was not to find the task easy: "Our burdens are beyond counting. I am overwhelmed by them, body and soul. The worst of all is the loneliness and the measureless concern I feel for the brethren."

Nicetas, Symeon's biographer, said that he was uneducated. This was certainly not so. He may not have gone on to receive a higher education and—a point which would later be seen as capital—did not follow any course of ecclesiastical studies, but he had fairly quickly assimilated a monastic culture, studied the scriptures assiduously, and imbibed the whole ethos of worship and liturgy. Called on to bring others to spiritual maturity, he drew on his own experiences, urging his brothers with relentless logic toward the fullness of the Christian life. His limitless enthusiasm invested monastic observance with a life-and-death quality. Half-measures were no measure at all. Symeon cannot bear it when he encounters resistance to the demands of the monastic life. It is contrary to all common sense when monks pledged to asceticism fight over a morsel of bread or indulge in murmuring when they have promised to bear all things for Christ. There is not much point in distributing our goods, he argues, if we do not pass through the crucible of tribulation, and if we refuse we shall never be free with the freedom born of the consolation of the Holy Spirit. Imitation of Christ by patience and perseverance will win us further grace from the Holy Spirit. Compunction and repentance are the gate through which we leave the darkness and enter into light. We may not say that the gift of tears is merely a question of temperament, that compunction is unattainable, or that divinization by grace is beyond our reach. If we do, we condemn the scriptures. It is heretical to say that no one among us, in our own time, can obey the gospel precepts and do as our Fathers did and become contemplatives, seeing God. The difference between the saints and those who regard such a programme as impossible is that the saints had their will turned toward the good, were full of zeal, patience, humility, and love of God. A Christian who does not know Christ, who does not consciously see him and live with him in fullest intimacy, is no Christian at all.

Symeon might be accused of saying that contemplation is not a gift freely given by God but something attainable by our own effort. Given the enthusiasm with which he presents his programme of sanctity, it is more likely that he is urging his monks to the realization that the more they love God and the more willing they are to bear hard and harsh things for Christ, the closer God will draw to them. God will not withhold his gifts from one who loves him, certainly not the supreme gift of the Spirit by whom and in whom one is led into the mystery of the Godhead.

A defensive note is discernible in the discourses made to the community. It is clear that Symeon was meeting opposition to what may have been regarded as a simplistic view of the demands of the spiritual life. He finds himself obliged to defend the authenticity of his mystical experience against those who consider him exaggerated, if not presumptuous, and far too exigent for the ordinary run of people. Symeon saw himself, though, as "a poor man, full of love for his brothers, who having asked an alms of a merciful friend of Christ [Symeon the Devout] and having received some coins, ran joyfully to his companions in the same state of unhappiness to tell them quietly, 'Run, hurry up, so that you too may receive something.'" Yes, he does claim that the Spirit speaks through him, but has not Our Lord himself said that in defending our belief in him, it is not we but the Spirit speaking through us? Is Symeon proud, is he deceived? But Symeon too has the mind of Christ. This is how we know that God is in us, by the Spirit he has given us. The mutual love of Father and Son is a conscious union. They are in us, so it follows that the union with us is likewise a *conscious* union. This conscious union of the believer and God is for this life, not just for the next: "Come and learn that it is not only for the future but somewhere under your eyes, before your eyes, at your feet, that the indescribable treasure lies."

Symeon felt the opposition keenly and wished to resign: "My exhortations go unheeded, my reprimands are rejected, my criticisms hated, my corrections are corrected and I am pursued as if I were an enemy. I think of resigning, but each time my heart bursts into flames and then I see myself caught in a circle. I feel the hurts you inflict on me as much as you feel your own. It is I who burn for you . . . life is unlivable." A clique of some thirty monks thought so too, and one morning, as he was speaking to the brothers, a group made as if to fall on him and drag him off. He remained perfectly immobile, smiling quietly as he looked his would-be aggressors in the eye. Cowed, they went off to the patriarch Sisinnios to obtain the removal of their *igumen*, who had now governed them for fifteen years. The rebels were in fact expelled, but Symeon would not agree to closing the door to their return as the patriarch had wished. He stayed at his post for another ten years, resigning in 1005 after an igumenate of twenty-five years. He was consistent to the end: "I am innocent with regard to you. I have not refused to tell you what our Lord Jesus Christ by his holy and adorable Spirit said to me, showed me and laid down concerning the gifts and sublime charisms of God his Father—I have not hidden my talent!"

Had Symeon's influence remained restricted to this monastic setting, he would no doubt have ended his days quietly at Saint Mamas. However, he was a public figure, with his writings well known and with many in the capital regarding him as their spiritual father. One personage in Constantinople,

Stephen, one-time bishop of Nicomedia, who held high office within the patri-arch's administration and had an entrée to the synod, perhaps because he held a professorship in the city, did not look favourably on the activities of the *igumen* of Saint Mamas. The two men were diametrically opposed. A few fragments of Stephen's writings that survive speak of the existence of free will and the faculties of the soul, which shows his philosophical concerns, while Symeon was unable to distinguish between the domains of reason and faith. There is no record of all the objections Stephen harboured, which can be divined only from Symeon's replies in his work of controversy, the *Theological and Ethical Treatises*. However, according to Nicetas, some of Stephen's hostil-ity was directed against Symeon's introduction of the liturgical commemora-tion of his deceased father in God, Symeon the Devout. This action was spon-taneous but tantamount to a private canonization and could not go unchal-lenged. In the Ethical Treatise No 9, Symeon in response indulges in what might be regarded merely as an *argumentum ad hominem,* were it not that it enshrines his attitude vis-à-vis the institutional Church, which picks up and pushes to its logical limits his conception of the non-mystic Christian as no Christian. To appreciate the sarcasm of the passage it has to be remembered that a retired cleric, such as the ex-bishop of Nicomedia, was regarded as having the status of a monk. The *igumen* speaks to him as he might to one of his own monks:

> Have you renounced the world, brother, and the things of the world? Are you now poor, docile, estranged from your own self-will? Have you attained sweet-ness of disposition and acquired humility? Have you reached the summit of fasting, prayer and watching? Have you attained total love of God and do you look on your neighbour as another yourself? . . . Do tell me! If you are ashamed to say No, or in your modesty would rather not answer, then I shall answer for you. . . . And if you yourself have not as yet attained the divinizing virtues to such a degree, how then do you dare open your mouth and speak? How can you, a catechumen, want to teach and try to treat at length things you know nothing about and have never learnt? . . . May God take form in you—what is this but a prayer that God may transform, recreate and change us into the likeness of his godhead? To my knowledge that is what happened to Symeon the Devout, who lived the ascetic life in the monastery of Studium. I am certain of it from my own experience.

This was too much for a prelate and a professor. Symeon was exiled—it was said with reluctance—by Sergius II, patriarch of Constantinople. He took up residence in the oratory of Saint Marina, near Paloutikon on the Asiatic side of the Bosphorus. Although he was reinstated in 1010 or 1011 he chose to remain where he was, refusing a bishopric, the offer of which he may have interpreted as a means to silence him and which may well have been so intended. He built a monastery in the place of his exile and spent his last years completing his works of controversy. During this time he also composed the majority of his hymns. While the note of controversy is never completely absent, these breathe a spirit of love and desire that remind us that we are listening to the outpourings of a great mystic.

There were other objections to Symeon's ideas, judging from his attempts to deal with them in his theological and ethical treatises. Due weight must be given to these objections, which touched on principles of jurisdiction and the consequent power to administer the sacraments independently of the subjective state of soul of the minister. Such principles did not enter the purview of someone not trained as a theologian. It must be noted also that Symeon is not without contradictions. His statements are never nuanced, though opposite positions can be found in the selfsame writings, providing a necessary corrective. Such claims as that unworthy clerics cannot administer the sacrament of Confession, or that grace does not exist where there is no consciousness of it, stem from his single-minded conviction that mature Christians, if they have accepted the logic of commitment to Christ, must necessarily have attained not only to union, but a conscious union with him. It is the attitude of the monk whose only criterion is sanctity, whose own vocation calls for complete self-giving and a total correspondence of what is with what is professed.

Symeon lived in his exile without bitterness, in perfect peace of soul and with no recriminations, revered for his gifts of prophecy and healing. In one of his hymns he thanks God for his suffering: "I thank you, Lord, for my suffering; it is unjust, but if what I suffer really is just, then let it compensate for my sins and effect the cleansing of my innumerable faults. I pray you, Lord, never let me be assailed by temptations and afflictions beyond my strength. Grant that I may never succumb and give me the strength I need to bear them." He died on 12 March 1022. His relics were brought back to the monastery of Saint Mamas in 1052.

The biography of Symeon the New Theologian was written by his disciple Nicetas Stethatos. Although not completely reliable, it is our main source of information, but it can be supplemented and corrected by the autobiographical details that are contained in Symeon's own writings. See I. Hausherr, *Orientalia Cristiana* 12 (1928), 45; *S.C.*: *Catechèses*, 96, 104, 113; *Traités Théologiques et Ethiques*, 122, 129; *Hymnes*, 156; *Les Chapitres Théologiques, Gnostiques et Pratiques*, 56. Symeon's works are also to be found in different places in *P.G.*: 120, 321-710; 95, 284-304; 96, 853-6; 152, 270-81. Mark the Hermit, *De Lege Spirituali, P.G.*, 65, 906-30. For Symeon's writings available in English see P. McGuckin, *The Practical and Theological Chapters and the Three Theological Discourses*, Cistercian Studies, 41 (1982), and G. A. Maloney (1975) for the hymns. *Dict.Sp.* 4, 1387-1401; 2, 1762-1911.

Bd Joseph Tchang Ta-Pong, *Martyr* (*c.* 1754-1815)

Tchang Ta-Pong Tchen-ouan was born into a pagan family in Tou-yun-fou in the province of Kouy-tcheou in China around 1754. There were two younger brothers, Tchang Takouy and Tchang Hiao-ta.

Tchang Ta-pong was a deeply religious man. A Buddhist initially, he went on to embrace Taoism. For some unknown reason he left Tou-yun-fou when he was about forty years of age and went to live in Kouy-yang, the capital of the province. There he entered into partnership with Ouang, a silk-merchant whose eldest son had been sent to Peking to compete in the written exams. The younger Ouang gained a degree but, more importantly, was baptized in 1796, receiving the name of Xavier. On his return to Kouy-yang he converted relations and friends and tried to persuade Tchang Ta-pong to follow suit. However, it was a catechist, Laurent Hou, who convinced Tchang Ta-pong of the truth of the Catholic faith.

Once intellectually convinced, there were practical hurdles to be surmounted. The first of these was a second marriage, entered into when his first wife failed to give him an heir. He had already had a son by this second wife when he became a Christian, but he provided her with a dowry and saw her married to another Christian. His family, fearing for their positions and their fortunes, proved less accommodating, but Tchang Ta-pong would not abjure his faith. In the meantime, Xavier Ouang's uncle, angered by his nephew's conversion, denounced him as a spoiler of the public peace and thus initiated a period of persecution. Tchang was able to elude the police, but Ouang, who had been forced to buy them off to shield his son, forbade any prayer or act of religion on his premises. To be free of such restraints, Tchang left Ouang and set up on his own as a money-changer. He was received as a catechumen in 1798. With the help of other Christians he bought an isolated house where they could assemble or a missionary priest could be concealed. He himself was baptized in 1800, taking the name of Joseph. Two years later he received his First Communion.

In 1800 Joseph's brothers, reacting strongly to the dishonour they claimed he had brought on the family, denounced the Catholics at a meeting of highly-placed mandarins and caused many of them to be arrested, including the catechist who had converted Joseph, Laurent Hou. Warned of the dangers, Joseph escaped but later returned and began a period of intense apostolate, making many converts. He visited the poor and the sick, assisted the dying, and buried the dead. At the request of the faithful he was appointed school-master and catechist in 1808. When persecution broke out again in 1811 he escaped to Hin-y-fou, but his son Antony was arrested. Pressed to reveal his father's whereabouts, the eighteen-year-old boy refused, declaring, "If my father has committed a crime, I take the responsibility for it: let me bear the punishment you intend to inflict on him." The boy was exiled within the province but died the following year. To throw the police off the scent, Joseph then set out for the north of the province. Though he was warmly welcomed by the Catholics there, the bishop urged him to return to support his own flock. He did so, continuing his work of evangelization under extreme pressure.

In 1814 his brother-in-law revealed his whereabouts to the police, and he was taken and thrown into prison. He was brought before four tribunals and ordered to abandon his faith. This he resolutely refused to do, even when his brothers and nephews besought him to do so. They collected a considerable sum of money to buy his release, but as he told them, "You cannot buy my soul and I cannot agree to your buying my body." In conformity with the imperial decrees of 1811, 1812, and 1813 against Catholicism, Joseph Tchang Ta-pong was condemned to death. The condemnation was sanctioned by the governor and viceroy of the province in November 1814 and by the emperor in January 1815. News of this final approval was brought to Kouy-yang in March. It was conveyed by the prefect to the prisoner, who listened silently, then thanked the mandarin and retired to prepare himself for death. He refused his relatives' offer of the customary farewell banquet, desiring only to be left alone to pray. He was led to his execution by a troop of soldiers on 12 March 1815. A tall, dignified man with white hair and beard, he stood head and shoulders above the group. His face was bathed with tears. One of the Christians pushed his way through in order to encourage him, but he replied, "Yes, I am crying, but they are tears of joy! Pray for me all the same." He was stretched out on a cross and the noose put round his neck when his relatives begged him again to abjure. "I cannot," he replied. "Do not cry," he added, "I am on my way to heaven."

Joseph Tchang Ta-pong was beatified in May 1909.

AAS 1, (1909), p. 455; P. A. Launay, *Les 35 vénérables serviteurs de Dieu—Annamites, Chinois;* G. Wang, *Martirologio della Chiesa cattolica in Cina* (1968), pp. 31-6.

Bd Aloysius Orione, *Founder* (1872-1940)

Luigi Giovanni Orione was born on 23 June 1872 in the village of Pontecurone in Piedmont, Italy. His father, Vittorio, was a road-mender and often away for long periods, but his mother, Carolina, amply made up for this by her efficient management of the household. Vittorio had served in the Piedmontese army under Charles Albert, but Garibaldi was his hero. As the recipient of largesse from the liberal Ratazzi, who owned a property in Pontecurone, Vittorio followed the prevailing anticlericalism, but he was an honest man. Carolina was illiterate, a woman of profound faith, exceptional intelligence, and energy. The description of her left by Don Orione evokes in surprising detail that of the perfect wife in the book of Proverbs. There were four children. The second son, christened Luigi, died in infancy, and his name was given again to the fourth child.

Carolina was afraid for her youngest son. Possessed of a formidable energy, he stubbornly pursued his own way, no matter what the consequences. She prayed fervently that such energy might be channelled in God's cause and believed her prayers answered when he announced that he would become a Franciscan friar. Having received some grounding in Latin and other elementary subjects from the parish priest, he seemed likely to be a good subject, but an unpromising postulancy culminated in an attack of pneumonia that left him weak and listless. His health was pronounced unequal to the Franciscan life, and he was sent home. The suggestion was then made that he should go to Don Bosco.

Aloysius went to the Salesian College at Valdocco in 1886. Don Bosco, who had only two more years to live, accepted the young boy as one of the group whose Confessions he heard regularly. Aloysius wrote later, "I have always thought it was not for nothing that the Lord allowed me go to Don Bosco and get to know him and the first generation of Salesians. If there is anything good in this Congregation of ours, we owe it to Don Bosco." However, a vain priest among the Salesians put the young boy off joining them, which led finally to his decision to enter the diocesan seminary of Tortona.

His youthful intolerance was further put to the test at the seminary, where there was a fair share of indiscipline and laxity and, inevitably, a certain ganging-up against him because of his supposed prudishness. He held resolutely to his course despite petty persecution and in time found that he was winning over the better-disposed seminarians. Among these was Carlo Sterpi, who was to become his collaborator for fifty years and later his successor. He did well in his studies and even became an avid reader of Italian classical literature. Having obtained leave to remain in the seminary during the holidays, he began at this early stage to search out the underprivileged, the sick, and the suffering. He visited the hospitals, as he had once done with his parish priest at Pontecurone. He was not allowed to visit the prisoners in the local gaol so decided to lighten their lot instead by playing the mandolin for them outside the walls. His unconventional charity was soon delated to the bishop—and not for the last time.

His father was now worn out by hard labour and could no longer support him at the seminary. A job as sacristan in the local cathedral provided for his needs and also gave him the chance to get to know the young urchins in the neighbourhood. Soon he had organized catechism classes, outings to shrines around the city, and various sports for his boys. These had a tendency to regard the cathedral as their legitimate playground, and soon the bishop had to be invoked to put an end to their romps. The bishop gave Aloysius a disused building, and all should have been well. As luck would have it Aloysius gave an outspoken address supporting the temporal power of the papacy, which, given the politics of the time, was asking for trouble. The bishop was blamed by the prefect, who demanded that the seminarian discontinue his work with the boys. The "Festive Oratory," as it was called, had to be dissolved. It was not yet a year old. Aloysius was devastated.

His next venture was a school for poor boys in San Bernardino. The bishop, who on principle was a firm supporter of Catholic Action, allowed him to go ahead but then, fearful of the consequences from a secular government determined to keep education under its own control, felt inclined to withdraw. Aloysius had already found the rent and had a pupil. With thirty more pupils, he even thought he might go on to make a bid for an empty convent formerly used as a barracks. The matter was referred to the mayor, the prefect, then to the government in Rome, which unexpectedly agreed to the venture. The Collegio Santa Chiara was opened in 1891 with 150 boarders and day-boys.

Don Luigi Orione was ordained in April 1895. The pattern of his life was already becoming clear. His "Little Work of Divine Providence," though not a canonical entity nor even a blueprint in his own mind, was nevertheless coming into being. The blueprint was to be determined by the demands made on his seemingly inexhaustible charity and equally inexhaustible resourcefulness.

Don Orione's visit to Sicily at the invitation of the bishop of Noto was to provide the priest with yet another inspiration. The bishop wished to offer him some buildings intended for a theological seminary as a school. He also offered him farm land for an agricultural centre, a line of development Don Orione had already embarked on with those students of Santa Chiara who showed less aptitude for book learning. But in Sicily he met two hermits who gave him the idea that his very active Congregation might profit from a contemplative branch of hermits. Unexpectedly his own bishop thought it was a good idea too, but he suggested that the hermits should be used to train good farmers. He also had reservations about Don Orione's schemes. Should he embark on so many? Why not just concentrate on the hermits, say, and their usefulness as farmers? Agricultural schools were all very well and good, but he had no resources to run them. He had begun a paper to publicize the work of Catholic Action, and now he was working on a centre for higher studies in San Remo! In addition, Don Orione, having become a popular preacher, was always absent. Since that was so, the "work" did not need to tie up any priests. The bishop sent out Orione's helpers to parishes and wanted the ordinands in his care to be absorbed into the diocesan seminary.

The work was paralyzed. The bishop asked Don Orione to come for an interview and wished him to acknowledge that he, the bishop, was in the right. The priest renewed his willingness to obey his superior. That was not what the bishop had asked, and again he pressed Orione to concede that he was acting rightly. Orione replied that the bishop, acting as he did, should not in conscience say Mass on the morrow. The "work" was the work of God, and the proof of it was Don Orione himself, a worthless instrument. Six weeks later, in 1903, the bishop signed the decree approving the Congregation of the Little Work of Divine Providence. Orione's aims, though always marked by an infinitely receding horizon, were to gain in clarity. He wrote later:

> To respond to its basic aim, this work should centre its activity in working-class areas, preferably in the most run-down quarters of the great industrial cities. Since it exists in order to help the unfortunate, it should flourish among them. Those who belong to it should consecrate their work to the poor and

offer their lives in sacrifice to Christ out of love, and for the salvation of their brothers. Nor should they forget truth and justice, which flow naturally from love. The Little Work exists for acts of service rendered out of love. It trusts that God will help it to carry on its work for the moral and material well-being of the most abandoned. Its motto is that of St Paul, "The charity of Christ urges us on," and its programme is that of Dante, "Our love excludes no one." It receives with open arms, then, those who can find no one to give them something to eat, a bed, or words of comfort. It wishes by every means to benefit all in order to lead them to Christ.

This was undoubtedly the agenda he had set himself to follow. It was his charity, not intellectual discussions, that won the Modernist Alfieri back to the Church. Orione was not interested to know why a priest, or anyone else, was in difficulties; his only concern was to hold out a helping hand. In this he was well within the tradition of the Piedmontese Church as it had been shaped by such giants as Francis de Sales (24 Jan.), Don Bosco (31 Jan.), Leonard Murialdo (30 Mar.), and Joseph Cottolengo (29 Apr.), and to which he would make his own special contribution.

In 1906, Don Orione had his first audience with Pope Pius X. The two men had much in common and instinctively admired each other. Aloysius spoke of his intention of sending missionaries abroad, but the pope asked him to undertake missionary work instead among the neglected slum-dwellers outside the Porta San Giovanni. It was not until 1913 that he sent missionaries to South America. Two years after this first visit the pope summoned him again. Had he become suspect, having received into his houses those homeless priests accused of Modernism or otherwise unfrocked? He was certainly not in favour, either with the clergy or with the anticlericals. In the event, the pope dismissed him with his blessing.

The most difficult years of Don Orione's life were the three from 1909 to 1912 spent in Messina, following the earthquake of December 1908. He had made enormous efforts to work with all, Catholics, non-Catholics, Freemasons, to rebuild the city, but his presence as a northerner was never really understood or accepted. In the end he felt he had to resign his post. He found himself in another devastated region, this time in the Abruzzi in 1915, where very few survived another devastating earthquake. The conditions were subhuman. It fell to him to find a place for some five thousand orphans. He collapsed with fatigue but returned after a ten-day break. Again there were tensions among relief workers. He saw himself as a beast of burden, there to provide help of the meanest sort, as he explained to an orphan whom he was befriending: "My vocation in life is to learn how to live like one of God's little donkeys, a real little donkey of Divine Providence."

Hitherto he had always borrowed nuns from other Congregations for special projects, but now he felt the need to have nuns of his own to carry out his charitable works. He recruited two women so unlike each other that the plan seemed sure to fail: a young aristocrat, Contessa Giuseppina Valdettaro, and Catarina Volpini, a washerwoman, who brought along her crippled brother. They began in San Bernardino and were to become known as Little Missionaries of Charity. After ten years the Contessa left to found her own Congregation, but the Little Missionaries of Charity by then numbered two hundred. A Cistercian nun whom Don Orione had consulted about the possibility of having his own nuns had said to him, "Yes, but they ought to be like rags in God's hands . . . rags with which to dry the tears of suffering humanity." The Congregation undertook the humblest work: scrubbing, cooking, sewing, mending, teaching small children, and looking after orphans, the infirm, the aged, the blind, the mentally handicapped. Like Don Orione himself, they existed only to respond to every form of human misery. Don Orione followed this venture much later in 1926 with a community of nuns, all blind, known as the Sacramentine Sisters, who were to be devoted to prayer and perpetual adoration.

Not until 1921, after the First World War, did Don Orione visit South America. The needs among the 200,000 Italian immigrants in Brazil were immense; as usual, he was most concerned about the children. Going on to Argentina, he received offers of land and premises in Buenos Aires for parishes, orphanages, and agricultural schools. He returned to Buenos Aires in 1934 to view the expansion that had since taken place and to encourage the foundation of further hospitals, orphanages, and a new church.

The First World War and the inter-war years in Italy were not easy. However, Don Orione would not tolerate any dependence on the Fascists: "I do not wish the government to have any say in our works of charity, for that would only adulterate and pervert them. Our spirit and theirs have nothing in common." Once a highly-placed official offered to mediate with Mussolini in order to save one of the Congregation's houses in Genoa. Don Orione would not agree to it: "That is not Our Lord's way." It was this hard-headed choice of "the Lord's way" that made Don Orione so remarkable. He was by nature fiery, rebellious, self-willed, impatient, even explosive, hugely intelligent, and dynamic. Once when he heard a report of an injustice committed by Mussolini, he burst out, "If I were not wearing a soutane, I would lead an army and unseat that man!" He realized full well that Mussolini was endowed with all the gifts of a demagogue, but his own commitment to Christ and to his neighbour, for the sake of Christ and in accord with the methods of Christ, remained irrevocable.

He foresaw a terrible future looming: "A frightful cataclysm may be about to change the face of the world. What will emerge from the ruin? Let us be truly sons of Divine Providence and trust wholly in God. We are not amongst those doom-sayers who think that the world will end tomorrow. Corruption and evil are indeed rampant, but I still maintain that God will triumph in the end." He did not live to see the end of the Second World War nor to savour the satisfaction of pontifical approbation of his Institute, given in 1955. In 1940 he was slowly relinquishing his hold on the Congregation he had founded, without, however, losing his priestly concern for the salvation of others. A prayer in one of his notebooks discovered after his death may fittingly echo the spirit that animated his varied apostolate: "Lord, set me down at the gates of hell so that by your mercy I may keep them shut against all comers."

He died on 12 March 1940 and was beatified by Pope John Paul II on 26 October 1980. His remains are preserved in Tortona. His Congregation, now numbering about four thousand, is found everywhere in Italy and on all five continents.

S. Clissold, *Some Call It Providence* (1980); D. Hyde, *God's Bandit* (1957); Giorgio Papasogli, *Vita di Don Orione* (1974); Domenico Sparpaglione, *Don Orione* (1978); *Dict.Sp.*, 11, 962-64; *Bibl.SS.*, 9, 1234-7.

R.M.
St Alphege, bishop of Winchester (951)
St Bernard, bishop of Foro-Claudio in Capua (1109)
St Serafina of San Gimignano in Tuscany (1253)
Bd Jerome Gherarducci, Augustinian friar of Recanati, near Piceno in Italy (1369)
Bd Justina, recluse of Arezzo (1319)

13

BD AGNELLUS OF PISA (1236)

Bd Agnellus, founder of the English Franciscan province, was admitted to the company of friars by St Francis (4 Oct.) himself when the latter visited Pisa, probably in 1211. A friary was founded in the town, and there Agnellus found himself carried along on the full tide of early Franciscan fervour.

At the chapter of 1217 it was decided that the friars should go to France. Francis wished to go with the group and did indeed accompany them some of the way, but in a chance meeting with Cardinal Ugolino, the future Pope Gregory IX (1227-41), he was persuaded that his place was rather in Italy. Francis himself nominated Agnellus, then a deacon, as the leader of the group, which was to proceed as planned. The abbot of Saint-Denis gave the friars the use of a house, and in a very short time this friary opened other houses in the region around Paris, of which Agnellus was the *custos* (custodian) for some years. However, the most significant step taken by Agnellus in Paris was to begin another friary there for Franciscan students at the university, thus initiating the association between the Franciscans and the most influential educational centre of the Middle Ages.

Seven years after his arrival in France, in 1224, Francis designated Agnellus leader of another founding group of eight friars, this time destined for England. There were three Englishmen in the group, one of whom, Richard of Ingworth, was a priest. The company of friars was hospitably received by the monks of Fécamp on the French side of the Channel, who in addition paid their fares to Dover, where they disembarked on 10 September 1224. They went on to Canterbury, where they were lodged in the Poor Priests' House, sleeping in a building used as a school by day. While the boys were there the friars were penned up in a small room at the back, and only after the students had gone home could they come out and light a fire. It was winter, and they must have suffered considerable discomfort, especially as their fare consisted of no more than bread and diluted beer. Their cheerfulness and fervour won them the admiration of Stephen Langton, the archbishhop of Canterbury, who saw in them an embodiment of the spirit of the apostles and referred to them as Brothers of the Order of the Apostles. Eventually they received a gift of land from the warden of the Poor Priests' House. It was swampy and undrained, but there they built themselves huts in which they lived for some fifty years.

The two English friars, Richard of Ingworth and Richard of Devon, together with two Italians, had set out immediately for London. They were warmly received by the Dominican friars, who lodged them for about a fortnight until they could hire a house for themselves in Cornhill. The two Richards then pressed on to Oxford, while Agnellus went up to London. A year later the friars at Cornhill moved to a house on Stinking Lane—a name that reveals something of the locality—which was to be enlarged in 1229 to accommodate the influx of vocations. Agnellus was himself strongly imbued with St Francis' ideal of poverty and would not allow the friars to accept more land than was strictly necessary or to have spacious buildings. Later, when an infirmary was built on to the friary in Oxford, he made the ceiling so low that there was barely enough room for an average man to stand upright.

While recruitment may have been the primary purpose of the push to Oxford, the school of theology Agnellus set up there was to be of immense significance for the English province as well as for the university of Oxford. Agnellus himself was not a scholar, nor indeed could it be said that St Francis was an enthusiastic advocate of study, being rather concerned that his friars might lose their simplicity by falling prey to empty ambition. Learning was a good thing, provided it did not extinguish the spirit of prayer or impede the work of the Holy Spirit. The English province so far absorbed the spirit of Agnellus that, even though its academic standing was of the highest in the Order, its zeal for poverty was equally outstanding. Haymo of Faversham, an English Franciscan who had entered the Order in Paris, was the leader of the group that challenged and overthrew Elias, the controversial master general, whose want of a sense of poverty had outraged the majority of the friars; the English province kept a steady balance during the subsequent conflicts within the Order concerning this question of poverty, and they could be counted on to be outspoken on the matter at the general chapters. John Buralli wished that "such a province might be placed at the centre of the world that all might follow its example."

The coming of the Franciscans to Cambridge contributed to the establishment of a faculty of theology there, although Cambridge never achieved quite the same importance in the Franciscan world. The names of Oxford scholars connected with the Franciscans still evoke a splendid era: Robert Grosseteste, whose services as lecturer Agnellus secured almost at the inception of the school and who could be said to have established its reputation, was followed by four other secular masters until the Franciscans themselves took over the post of lecturer. Among these were Adam Marsh, Thomas of York, Richard Rufus of Cornwall, John of Wales, and the intellectual giants Roger Bacon, Duns Scotus (8 Nov.), and William of Ockham.

Agnellus could not foresee the intellectual brilliance that would characterize the English province nor indeed the spiritual influence of so many men dedicated to the ideals of St Francis. What was important was that he lived those ideals and communicated a vibrant example of what it was to be a Franciscan to the young English friars whom he received into the Order. His reputation for sanctity was no less high among the laity. He was a friend of King Henry III and was chosen for his gentleness and tact to negotiate with the rebellious Earl Marshall. His health is said to have been undermined by his efforts in this cause and by a last painful journey to Italy. On his return to Oxford he succumbed to a bout of dysentery and died there at the age of forty-one, after crying out for three days, "Come, sweetest Jesus." His cult was confirmed in 1892.

The narrative of Thomas of Eccleston, *De adventu Fratrum Minorum,* together with the Chronicle of Lanercost and the *De conformitate* of Bartholomew of Pisa, provide the basic sources of information. See also A. G. Little, *The Grey Friars in Oxford,* (1892); E. Hutton, *The Franciscans in England* (1933); Father Gilbert, *Bd Agnellus and the English Grey Friars* (1937); John R. H. Moorman, *The Franciscans in England* (1974).

St Leander of Seville, *Bishop* (*c.* 600)

Spain lay at the periphery of the Roman Empire yet seemed to attract to and intensify within itself all the turmoil once experienced at the centre. The fourth and fifth centuries saw the antagonisms between Catholic and Arian, barbarian and Roman, Byzantine and Goth played out on the western edge of the Mediterranean world.

Leander, bishop of Seville, by the force of his faith and discreet intervention, was able to resolve some of this antagonism and so give Spain a period of peace in which Catholicism could take root and flourish. He was born into a noble Arian family. His father was one of the great magnates of the Visigothic kingdom, a duke or governor of the eastern province whose capital was Cartagena. In the mid-sixth century a noble named Athanagild called in the Byzantines to come to the help of the Catholics persecuted by the Arians. The Greeks took possession of the coast and made Cartagena their base, so Leander's family fled to Seville. There his mother subsequently embraced the Catholic faith. Her children were brought up fervent Catholics, judging from their subsequent careers. Fulgentius became bishop of Ecija, Isidore (4 Apr.) succeeded Leander himself as bishop of Seville, while their sister Florentina became a nun, and all are reckoned as saints. There is a legend that there was another sister who married the Arian king Leovigild, but this seems doubtful.

Even as a boy Leander had undoubted charm and a way with words, but he decided to enter a monastery, where he spent three tranquil years in prayer and study. On the death of the bishop of Seville in around 578, the populace stormed the monastery, took Leander to the cathedral of St Vincent, and seated him on the episcopal throne. His main concern as bishop was to fight the Arian heresy. Providence played into his hands. King Leovigild had two sons, Hermenegild and Reccared. In 576 Hermenegild married Ingonde, the Catholic daughter of Sigebert of Austrasia and Brunehaut. Goswinthe, the queen, a rabid Arian, despised and maltreated her daughter-in-law, so Leovigild sent Hermenegild away to oversee the region of the Bética. At Seville the prince met Bishop Leander, who received him into the Catholic Church. An angry King Leovigild summoned his son back to Toledo. Instead, Hermenegild came to an understanding with the Byzantines. A reign of terror ensued as Leovigild launched a persecution against the bishops in particular. He pursued Hermenegild, besieging Seville for two years. When the city was taken, Hermenegild's life was spared, but he and his family were exiled. He escaped and collected an army, which was routed by his father's forces. This time Hermenegild was beheaded (and subsequently honoured as a martyr; 13 Apr.).

Leander left Spain in 583 for Constantinople, on an embassy to the emperor possibly connected with these events. The outcome of his visit is unknown, but we do know that there Leander met St Gregory the Great (3 Sept.) and struck up a friendship with him. It was at Leander's request that Gregory set down in writing the conferences he had given on the Book of Job to the group of monks who accompanied him. He sent them to Leander later, after many revisions, with a letter of dedication, as well as a copy of his *Pastoral Care.*

King Leovigild died in 586. The legend that he had had a death-bed change of heart and that he had confided his son Reccared to Leander seems to be unfounded. It may be that Reccared was already secretly harbouring feelings of sympathy for the Catholics while his father was still alive. In any case, Leander's return to Seville and the new king's open adherence to Catholicism meant the inauguration of a new era. The two worked together for a Catholic Spain. There followed a series of councils, which envisaged a restoration to orthodoxy as well as a renewal of morality. Reccared was present at the first council called after his accession, the third of Toledo. Leander presided and preached a sermon of thanksgiving, *De triumpho ecclesiae,* which is extant. By the strength of his arguments Leander persuaded many Arian bishops to abjure their heresy, although Reccared is known to have deposed the less amenable ones. At this same council the Nicene Creed was appointed to be said at Mass in order to reinforce the faith of the people. The practice, which Leander probably witnessed in the Church of Constantinople, eventually spread to the whole Western Church.

Leander also worked to convert the Suevi, the tribes that dwelt in Galicia and had initially been converted to Catholicism by St Martin of Braga (20 Mar.) but had subsequently been perverted by Leovigild. Gregory, by then pope, wrote an affectionate letter to Leander, congratulating him on the blessings bestowed by God on the Church in Spain, and sent him the *pallium.*

The only other composition by St Leander that has come down to us is his *De institutione virginum,* which he had written for his sister Florentina. It is also called the *Rule of a Monastic Life.* Though dependent on Cassian and other monastic writers, its practical approach gives it an immediacy that makes it still worth reading.

Leander died in around 600, and his relics rest in a chapel of Seville Cathedral. In Spain he is honoured as a Doctor of the Church. He is represented with a flaming heart or a triangle in one hand to denote his preaching against Arianism. Gregory had made him a gift of an image of the Virgin, and he is sometimes depicted with this image.

AA.SS., Mar., 2, pp. 271-5; *D.C.B.*, 3, pp 637-640; 4, pp 536-8; *D.T.C.*, 9, p 95; H. Leclerq, *L'Espagne Chrétienne* (1906); *Año Cristiano* (1933-5), pp. 286-92. His Rule for Nuns and homily are trans. C. W. Barlow, *Iberian Fathers*, 1 (1969), pp. 175-235. There is a recent study in Italian by L. Navarra, *Leandro di Siviglia* (1987).

St Heldrad, *Abbot* (*c.* 842)

Heldrad was born in Provence of a noble and well-to-do family. While still quite young he inherited a large fortune, much of which he spent on charitable projects. He built a church and hospice, where all guests were received without charge, and also laid out a beautiful garden whose produce was available to all comers. However, finding himself burdened with too many administrative problems, he decided to get rid of all his wealth. Part of it he gave to the Church and the rest to the poor. He then set out in search of a monastery of strict observance where he might enter.

He went through Provence, then Aquitaine, then on to Spain, and finally came to Italy. There he heard of Novalese, an observant monastery of five hundred monks, strictly governed by the holy abbot Ambulf. Heldrad was received into the abbey, and soon, we are told, he had thoroughly grasped the Rule of St Benedict, the sayings of St Columba, and the writings of St Basil. He was given charge of the vineyards, and it was not long before he was given the habit. Later he was charged with the training of the young monks.

After Ambulf died Charlemagne's son Hugh was appointed abbot, but he was so often absent that the abbey would have suffered greatly had it not been for Heldrad, who acted as administrator with so much success that he was elected abbot on Hugh's death. As abbot he did much for the monastery. Within the fortified enclosure he erected a tower, the upper part of which served as a signalling-station while the lower part contained the treasures of the house and the famous library, which was his special care. The monastery already looked after the Mont Cenis pass, but Abbot Heldrad established another hospice on the Lautaret pass, now called the Monestier de Briançon.

St Heldrad died about 842. He was held in such veneration that his relics were long carried in procession in the valley of Novalese at Rogationtide. His cult was approved in 1903.

Nearly all that can be learned about St Heldrad can be found in C. Cipolla: *Monumenta Novaliciensia Vetustiora* (1898), including a ninth-tenth century rhythmical Life and the eleventh-century prose Life that appears in *AA.SS.*, Mar., 2. pp. 326-33.

St Ansovinus, *Bishop* (840)

Ansovinus was born at Camerino in Umbria, Italy. After ordination to the priesthood he retired to a solitary spot at Castel Raimondo near Torcello and soon acquired a reputation for sanctity and miracles.

When he was in Italy, the emperor Louis the Pious chose him as his confessor, and he approved his election to the see at Camerino. Ansovinus accepted the election on condition that he be exempted from the obligation to conscript soldiers for the imperial army, which he considered unbecoming for a bishop and contrary to the law of the Church. He proved a wise and prudent pastor. He was always generous to the poor, but in times of famine he managed his resources so well that there was always something for the needy. He is also credited with the gift of healing.

He was in Rome when he was seized with a fever, which seemed likely to prove fatal. In spite of the protests of his friends, he insisted on returning home to die among his people, reached Camerino, and was able to give a last blessing and receive the *viaticum* before he expired.

The Life by Eginus, *AA.SS.*, Mar., 2, pp. 316–22, is an unconvincing document consisting mainly of miracles, but the *cultus* of St Ansovinus is recognized. See also M. Santoni: *Culto di Sant' Ansovino* (1883).

BB Françoise Tréhet and Jeanne Véron, *Martyrs* (1794)

These two religious were martyred in the town of Ernée (Maine-et-Anjou) during the French Revolution.

Françoise Tréhet was born in Saint-Mars-sur-la-Futaie on 8 April 1756 of a family of well-to-do farmers, while Jeanne Véron was born in Quelaines on 6 August 1766. They both entered the Congregation of the Sisters of Chapelle-au-Riboul, dedicated to the education of young girls and to works of charity. Because of their grey habit, the Sisters were known familiarly as "the little grey nuns."

Around 1783 Françoise was sent to Saint-Pierre-des-Landes to open a school, where she was later joined by Jeanne. The two taught and looked after the sick. Françoise was a strong character. With her lively intelligence she was quick to see the evil that would come upon both Church and country through the Revolution. Jeanne was noted rather for her gentleness and charity. No denunciation or complaint had been lodged against the two religious, but they were put on a list of persons destined for the guillotine. They were arrested at the end of February or the beginning of March 1794 and held in Ernée, Frances in prison and Jane, gravely ill, in a hospital, until their respective trials. Frances appeared before the *Commission Clément* on 13 March. Accused of having nursed the Chouans (Royalists), she replied that both Chouans and Blues (Revolutionary army) were her brothers in Jesus Christ and she would refuse her help to neither. Required to pronounce the words "Long live the Republic!" she refused and was condemned to the guillotine. The judgment handed down by the commission noted that she had "concealed non-conforming clergy and had fed and protected the Chouans." The sentence was carried out the same day. She was thirty-seven years old.

Jeanne was brought to the tribunal on 20 March in a chair as she was paralyzed and seemed even to be dying. She refused to take the oath. The judgment was the same as for Françoise. She had to be carried to the guillotine. She was twenty-eight years of age.

Cesbron, *Les Martyrs de Laval* (1955). For a general treatment of the martyrs of the French Revolution, see the entry for 2 Jan., "Martyrs of the French Revolution."

R.M.

SS Macedonius, Patricia and Modesta, martyrs in Nicomedia (third century)

St Sabinus, martyr in the Thebaid (fourth century)

St Christina or Iazdo, martyr in Persia (sixth century)

St Pientius, bishop of Poitiers (sixth century)

SS Roderigo and Solomon, martyrs—see "The Martyrs of Córdoba," 11 Mar.

Bd Peter II, abbot of Cava, Campania (1208)

14

St Matilda, (*c.* 895-968)

A descendant of the celebrated Widukind who led the Saxons in their long struggle against Charlemagne, Matilda was the daughter of Dietrich, a Westphalian count, and of Reinhild, a scion of the royal Danish house. She was born about the year 895 and confided to the care of her paternal grandmother, abbess of the convent of Erfurt. There she grew into a beautiful, learned, and devout woman.

In due course she married the son of Duke Otto of Saxony, Henry, called "The Fowler" because of his fondness for hawking. The marriage proved to be a singularly happy one, with Matilda exercising a restraining influence over her husband. Just after the birth of their eldest son, Otto, Henry succeeded to his father's dukedom, and when, about the beginning of the year 919, King Conrad died childless, he was raised to the German throne.

Henry was constantly at war, and both he and his subjects attributed his successes as much to the prayers of his devout queen as to his own prowess. She lived like a religious in the royal palace, generous and loving to all. Her husband, who trusted her completely, rarely checked her liberal almsgiving or resented her pious practices. He died in 936, and on hearing the news Matilda immediately took off the jewels she was wearing as a sign that from that moment she had renounced the splendour of her state.

Five children had been born to Henry and Matilda: Otto, later emperor; Henry the Quarrelsome; Bruno (6 Oct.), who became archbishop of Cologne; Gerberga, who married Louis IV, king of France; and Hedwig, the mother of Hugh Capet. Henry had wished his son Otto to succeed him, but Matilda, who had always favoured her younger son, Henry, persuaded a few nobles to vote for him. However, Otto was chosen and crowned. Unwilling to accept the decision, Henry raised a rebellion against Otto but eventually had to sue for peace. He was pardoned by Otto and, at Matilda's request, was made duke of Bavaria. Henry's grandson Henry (the Good; 13 July) was eventually to become emperor when Otto III died without issue.

The queen was now living a life of almost complete self-abnegation, but her bounties continued on a lavish scale, and this drew criticism. Otto accused her of wasting the crown revenues, required an account of her expenditure, and set spies to keep a check on her movements and donations. To her chagrin, Henry, her favourite son, allied himself with his brother against her, both proposing that she should take the veil. She bore it all patiently, even remarking with a touch of wry humour that it was a consolation to know that her sons were united, even though it was only in order to persecute her. To remove any further cause for complaint, Matilda handed over her inheritance to her two sons and retired to the country residence where she had been born. No sooner had she gone than Duke Henry fell ill and state affairs began to deteriorate. It was generally interpreted as a punishment for the ill treatment meted out by the two leaders to their mother. At the urging of the nobles and clergy, Otto's wife, Edith, persuaded him to ask his mother's forgiveness and restore all he had taken from her. Matilda forgave both her sons and returned to court, resuming her works of mercy. Henry continued to be a source of sorrow. He revolted a second time against Otto and later cruelly put down an insurrection of his own Bavarian subjects. When Matilda saw him for the last time in 955, she prophesied his death and begged him to repent before it was too late. When the news of his death came it almost prostrated her.

Otto showed his restored trust in his mother by leaving the kingdom in her charge when he went to Rome to be crowned emperor. The last family gathering took place in Cologne at Easter 965. The emperor Otto was there, together with Matilda's other surviving children and grandchildren. After this, she spent most of her time in her monastic foundations, especially Nordhausen. At the end of 967 a fever that had troubled her for some time suddenly became worse. Realizing that she was dying she sent for Richburga, her one-time lady-in-waiting, now abbess of Nordhausen, and told her that she must leave in all haste for Quedlinburg, explaining that it had long been decided by her husband, Otto, that that was to be their burial place. The last move took place in January 968. Her grandson, William of Mainz, visited her, heard her Confession, and anointed her. Wishing to give him something as a present, Matilda asked abbess Richburga if there was anything available. Since all her property had now been distributed to the poor, nothing was left but her own winding sheet. "Give that to Bishop William," she said, "He will need it first. . . . When I die, the popular proverb will be proved true: relatives always find the wherewithal for a wedding-dress or a funeral." Bishop William died twelve days before his grandmother, on 14 March 968. Her body had been laid out and taken to church when messengers came from her daughter Gerburga with a cover embroidered with gold, just right for draping the casket. Matilda's body was buried beside that of her husband at Quedlinburg. She was venerated locally as a saint from the moment of her death. She is often represented with a church in her hands or a bag of money because of her generous gifts to the poor and to the religious communities she founded.

M.G.H. contains the best text of the two ancient Lives of St Matilda, the older in *Scriptores*, 10, pp. 575–82, the more recent in *Scriptores*, 4, pp. 283–302. See also *AA.SS.*, Mar., 2, pp. 351–64; L. Clarus, *Die hl. Mathilde* (n.d.); L. Zöpf, *Die Heiligenleben im 10 Jahrhundert* (1867); L. E. Hallberg, *Ste Mathilde* (n.d.). Further information may be gleaned from the contemporary chroniclers and charters.

Bd James Cusmano, *Founder* (1834-88)

Giacomo Cusmano was born on 15 March 1834 in Palermo, Sicily. He studied medicine, became a doctor, and was also ordained priest.

Profoundly affected by the poverty of the island and its recurrent famines and epidemics, disturbed too by the prevailing social conditions, he determined to give his all in a spirit of love of God and neighbour to ameliorate the situation. He began by opening a House of the Poor, then launched a larger venture aimed at improving the social order, the Society for the Poor Man's Portion, which, like the grain of mustard seed, was to become an immense tree. He did not hesitate to beg in the streets of Palermo to obtain funds and supplies for the poor who thronged to him. Like all the works of God, his ran into difficulties, which worried him greatly, but his immense trust in God and strength of character brought him through.

He founded the Institute of Servant Sisters of the Poor and the Congregation of the Missionary Servants of the Poor, training his spiritual sons and daughters in the practice of charity within the framework of the evangelical counsels. His rules and letters of direction, a combination of firmness and gentleness, are of great ascetical value. The recurrent advice he gives his correspondents is to live in the presence of God and in union with him, receive everything from his hands, and do everything for love of him and for his glory.

An epidemic of cholera swept Palermo, and Fr James exhausted himself helping the poor victims. He prayed unceasingly, "Lord, strike the shepherd, but spare the flock." His health was irremediably impaired as a result of his ministry, and he was barely fifty-four when he died on 14 March 1888. He was beatified by Pope John Paul II on 30 October 1983.

N.S.B. 1, pp. 214-5; *Osservatore Romano*, 31 Oct. 1983.

R.M.
SS James and Marian, martyrs at Tell-dara, Persia (347)
St Alexander, martyr at Pidna, Macedonia (*c.* 390)
St Lazarus, bishop of Milan (fifth century)
St Lubin, bishop of Chartres (*c.* 557)
St Paulina, nun at Fulda (1107)
Bd Eve of Liège, recluse (*c.* 1265)—see under Bd Juliana, 5 Apr.
Bd James Capocci, archbishop of Naples (1308)

15

St Zachary, *Pope* (752)

Among the signatures to the acts of the Roman council of 732 is that of the deacon Zachary, who would succeed Gregory III (10 Dec.) as pope nine years later. His father, Polychromius, a Greek, lived in Calabria. Like most of his predecessors in the papacy for the previous one hundred years, Zachary was of Greek origin, but he would be the last—and the last to retain a sense of loyalty to the Byzantine Empire. During his short tenure there would be a shift of power from the East to the West to which his own actions were to contribute.

In the East the Inconoclastic policies of the Byzantine emperors not only unleashed persecution on their own peoples but provoked opposition in the Greek-held territories in Italy, where Greek refugees were numerous and where the heavy imposition of taxes by the Byzantine government—without benefit of Byzantine protection—were straining ties to the empire to breaking point. Lombard dukes, moreover, were intent on destroying Byzantine rule in Italy and on carving out new duchies there for themselves. Further afield, Boniface (5 June), who saw himself as an emissary of the pope to the Germanic races, was creating a new Christian people in Germany imbued with his own attitude toward the papacy; and the Franks, impressed by the indefatigable English missionary, were prepared to follow his lead.

Four days after the interment of Gregory III, on 3 December 741, Zachary was elected pope and consecrated—without reference either to the Byzantine emperor or to the exarch of Ravenna, the most powerful Byzantine in Italy. Nevertheless he felt obliged to inform the emperor of his election. Constantine V had suceeded Leo III, but Zachary's envoys arrived in Constantinople while a coup was in progress. Constantine was in fact reinstated and received the envoys courteously. The pope asked for the rescinding of the decrees against sacred images and the restitution to the Roman patriarchate of the provinces wrested from it by Leo III. Constantine ceded the fairly wealthy territories of Nymphaea and Normia to the papacy, but no more.

However, the pope immediately set himself the task of making peace with Liutprand, king of Lombardy. Disowning the policy of Gregory III, he abandoned the dukes of Spoleto and Beneventum and offered the king the services of the Roman army in his struggle with the duke of Spoleto in return for the domains Liutprand had formerly siezed. The old king, a faithful Catholic, was impressed by the pope, who had come to see him personally, and restored the territories forthwith, entering into a twenty-year treaty of peace with the duchy of Rome.

In 743 Liutprand made an attempt to subjugate the exarchate of Ravenna. He first took the cities of Cesena and Imola and prepared to march on Ravenna. At the urgent request of the exarch and of the neighbouring bishops, Zachary sent an embassy to the king to ask him to desist, and when that failed, he himself went to see him and obtained the cancellation of the march on Ravenna together with the restitution of the two cities to Byzantium. Zachary intervened again in 749, this time with Ratchis, Liutprand's successor, and succeeded in calling off attacks on Perugia and the Pentapolis. Ratchis subsequently became a monk and was succeeded by his brother Aistulf, who, however, did not allow himself to be deflected from his aim of subjugating the exarchate. When Zachary died it no longer existed.

That Aistulf would look beyond Ravenna to the duchy of Rome itself might have occurred to Zachary, but during his reign the means to defend the papal territories were already being prepared. Zachary had always maintained close links with Boniface, fully supporting him in his missionary work and even appointing him legate to the Frankish Church. The Merovingian dynasty had by then become powerless, with Charles Martel and his son Pepin mayors of the palace in name but the real rulers of the realm. It was a co-worker of Boniface, Burchard of Wurzburg, who put to the pope the loaded question concerning Pepin's sovereignity over the Franks: Should those who actually hold power not also lay claim to the royal titles? Zachary agreed that they should and opened the way for Pepin to declare himself king. Boniface anointed him such in 751, and in 754 the then pope, Stephen II, renewed the anointing. In 756 the pope received back from Pepin the lands recovered by the Franks.

Zachary's activity was wide-ranging; his letters to Boniface and to Pepin, with their precise instructions and clear decisions, are useful for the history of canon law. He also held two councils in Rome, in 743 and 745. In the course of the latter he upheld Boniface's condemnation of the heretical bishops Adalbert and Clement. Still sensitive to the unity of the Roman empire and keen to keep contacts between East and West, he translated the *Dialogues* of St Gregory the Great into Greek, but he also found time to organize the agricultural exploitation of ecclesiastical lands. He erected no new buildings but refurbished many, especially the Lateran and Santa Maria Antiqua, where there is a portait of him with a square nimbus. He is also linked with Monte Cassino, which he helped finish and himself consecrated. He died on 15 March 752, a gentle and peace-loving pope who sought to change the course of events more by persuasion than by force.

Fl-Martin, 5, pp. 419-23; Dan-Marrou, 2, p. 58; B. Mondin, *Dizionario Enciclopedico dei Papi* (1995), pp. 90-1; E Duffy, *Saints & Sinners: A History of the Popes* (1997) pp. 68-9.

St Louise de Marillac, *Foundress* (1590-1660)

Louise de Marillac, under the direction and inspiration of St Vincent de Paul (19 July), launched one of the most impressive movements to alleviate and remedy the sufferings of the poor in the history of the Church. The foundress of the Sisters of Charity gave permanence to their ideals and made possible the continuance of their work in the centuries that followed.

Louise de Marillac was born in 1590 in France, probably at Ferrières-en-Brie, where she was baptized. Her father was Louis de Marillac, a member of the lesser nobility; her mother's identity is unknown. Louise's contract of marriage as well as the documents attesting the financial settlements made by her father in her favour reveal that she was his natural daughter, but they make no mention of her mother's name. Louis' first wife, Marie de la Rozière, died in 1588 or 1589, and he married Antoinette Le Camus in 1595. Louise was born then in the interim between her father's first and second marriages. She mentions neither her stepmother nor her natural mother, which suggests that she lacked the comfort of a mother and recognition from her father's family. Nothing is known of her very earliest years. While still young she was sent to the royal Dominican convent of Poissy where her great-aunt, Louise de Marillac, was a nun. There she received the rudiments of an education in the humanities and the arts and mixed with the noblest families of France. This suddenly came to an end around 1604, perhaps on the death of her father. She was then entrusted to a "poor spinster" who ran an orphanage of sorts where she was to be taught "those things which a woman ought to know." It is clear that the family did not envisage her future as being with them. Michel de Marillac, her uncle, was occasionally in touch with her by letter but kept his distance.

Louise not only learned what she was supposed to learn but helped organize the work in order to supplement her guardian's paltry income. We know that she painted and found time not only to read but also to cultivate a life of prayer. At some point she resolved to become a nun, but her director at the time was wholly opposed to her entering a convent on account of her poor health. She was then and ever afterwards subject to stomach upsets, resulting perhaps from inner emotional turmoil. It would have been strange had she remained unaffected by a situation that denied her any real personal identity and any status despite her father's acknowledgement of her as his daughter. If she could not enter a convent, the only course open to her was that of marriage. The de Marillacs were willing enough to find her a suitable husband, which would bring to an end any further responsibility for her.

Antoine Le Gras, secretary of the household to the queen, seemed a good match, neither too exalted nor too lowly. The marriage took place in February 1613 in the presence of the groom's family and some members of her own and brought Louise some years of relative stability and happiness. She was required to attend at court and to entertain, and as Mademoiselle Le Gras (the title *Madame* being accorded only to the higher nobility) she was accepted socially by the de Marillacs. Her son, Michel, was born in that same year of 1613. Louise proved an excellent mother and wife and managed her household prudently and efficiently. Even then, she considered it a duty to look after the needs of the poor. Her worldly success, such as it was, was short-lived. Louise's first great trial and one that dogged her for the greater part of her life was her son, who was ungainly, slow-witted, and unstable. Further disaster struck when the queen was banished and Antoine lost his job. He found employment managing the estate of the d'Attichy children on the death of their parents, one of whom was Valence, Louise's aunt. In an excess of zeal he pledged his own assets to restore the estate and eventually forfeited them. The d'Attichy orphans were not grateful, resenting Le Gras' position and even reminding Louise that she was in debt to the family for favours received. Antoine then fell ill with a terminal disease, and Louise had to nurse him for four or five years. These accumulated misfortunes plunged Louise into a crisis of self-doubt. She saw them as a punishment for having married when she had made a promise not to do so. The situation could hardly have been improved by her taking another vow to remain a widow should her husband die. Temptations followed thick and fast: she was tempted to leave him there and then and to abandon her director; she found it impossible to believe in the immortality of her soul and finally even in the existence of God. An interview with St Francis de Sales (24 Jan.) in Paris, between 1618 and 1619, calmed her only temporarily.

Louise's regular director at the time was the bishop of Belley, himself a disciple of St Francis de Sales. He tried to bring her round to a more rational frame of mind, but he himself was no longer close at hand in Paris. He asked "Monsieur Vincent" to take on the responsibility for her direction. Vincent de Paul, who never made a decision on the spur of the moment, was non-committal. In the meantime Louise, imprisoned in her depression, prayed earnestly to St Francis de Sales, who had died the year before. On Pentecost Sunday 1623 she was suddenly set free, grasping by an interior illumination that her present duty was to her husband. She understood that one day she would take vows in company with others of a like mind, that her work would be the service of the poor, and that God would send her a director. She wrote later, "[God] showed me who he was to be. I was reluctant, but I accepted."

Antoine Le Gras died in 1625. Now in straitened circumstances, Louise moved to the rue St Victor in the parish of St Nicholas Chardonnet, where she was fairly near the Collège des Bons Enfants, a seminary where she would shortly place her son and where Vincent's Mission Priests were then working. She was to spend two years marking time while Vincent waited for God to show them both how and when they should proceed. She renewed her vow of widowhood, adding to it vows of poverty, chastity, and obedience. Still very much wrapped up in her little concerns, Louise spent the time in various pieties: she belonged to several confraternities, each with its special programme; she bound herself to thirty-three acts of adoration a day in honour of the thirty-three years of Our Lord's earthly life; she went to Mass and communicated when permitted to do so. Her rule of life was rigidly observed. She sewed and knitted articles for the poor whom she visited in their homes. Vincent was concerned about the narrow and circumscribed outlook of his penitent but allowed himself only the occasional objection to her tying herself up in knots: "Go patiently, go prudently and be as happy as you can." Mademoiselle Le Gras could not really be happy. An unwanted child, reluctant wife, unfulfilled mother, she had never had the chance to transcend and lose herself in anything bigger than her immediate worries. Now that she was free, even her religion, dominated as it was by scruples, was a species of prison. Vincent must have divined nevertheless that there was a fire smouldering within her. She was capable of love and fidelity and, above all, she was ready to obey.

Louise saw the work of the Mission Priests at close hand, and she could hardly have failed to be touched by the ardour of their founder as he reached out to the poor so that they too might have the gospel preached to them. The day came when she asked to be able to serve the Mission in whatever way her director would decide. Vincent decided to use her to oversee the Ladies of Charity he had established in the parishes where he had served. In those of Paris they were the instruments he would use for the launching and sustenance of the first thoroughly-organized works of charity the capital had ever seen. Outside the capital these Ladies were the better-off in the parish, concerned about or awakened by Vincent to the plight of the uneducated, unevangelized, and uncared-for poor in their midst. He gave these Ladies a skeleton programme and left them to pursue the work locally. Inevitably, without his presence, their zeal faltered, and the work was done haphazardly if at all. In 1629, then, he sent Louise on her first mission: to judge the state of the Charities in the outlying parishes where they had been set up, to rectify what was wrong, and to increase their effectiveness where possible. She spent four years on this mission and in the process became a different woman. Much of her time was spent in the open air. She knew fatigue but learned how to manage it. She came into close contact with human wretchedness but judged carefully by what strategies it could be allayed. She learned to be diplomatic in dealing with local or clerical officials and even discovered that she had no mean talent for public speaking. No longer living in an imaginary world but in direct contact with real life, she learned to be simple and direct. Scruples and fear became a thing of the past. Later she could write to one of her charges, "Try to neutralize your scruples by taking up other interests; instead of confronting them, pray to the Holy Spirit to give you joy." Perhaps one of the more significant signs of her new *persona* was the decision to reclaim her maiden name. Although she was always referred to as Mademoiselle Le Gras, she now signed herself Louise De Marillac. Vincent too watched with joy as this formerly melancholy, constricted woman blossomed into a co-worker in whom he could have absolute trust. He said to her once, "God alone knows, Mademoiselle, what he has done for me in giving you to me; in heaven you will know!"

Louise came to see that the Ladies of Charity would never persevere in carrying out their programme of good works unless they had help from women wholly dedicated by their vocation to the immediate performance of acts of service to the poor. The Ladies might contribute or find the funds to help the poor and organize the distribution of aid, but they were less ready to wash the sick, dress their sores, and feed them. Vincent deplored the habit of some Ladies of sending their maids to do what they were not always prepared to do themselves. An outstanding example of what might be done by a dedicated if uneducated person was that of Marguerite Naseau. She learned to read in order to teach other girls of her village and performed the humblest tasks for the afflicted. (She was to die of the plague, caught while nursing its victims in Marseilles.) Louise carefully watched the young and generous girls who came forward to help and was eager to form them to the special service of the sick poor. Nothing less than a new type of religious seemed called for, and Louise saw Marguerite as a model. With his habitual caution Vincent called for reflection. He himself was confessor to the nuns of the Visitation in Paris and knew that St Francis de Sales had burnt his fingers over the question of active religious, which he had been the first to propose. To the Church of the day, to be a religious meant being enclosed within walls and grilles and long hours of worship in choir. What Louise and Vincent envisaged was something totally different. The only way these workers might win acceptance was to forego altogether the status of religious. Vincent was to repeat time and time again to the assembled Sisters that they were not religious and were never to aspire to be such. In words that have become famous he described them as "a community with no other monastery than the houses of the sick, with no cells but lodgings or the poorest room, with no chapel other than the parish church, with no cloister other than the streets. . . . [The Sisters of Charity] are enclosed only by obedience, make the fear of God their grille and have no veil apart from their modesty. . . . The one aim of the religious is the attainment of personal perfection; the objective of the Sister of Charity is the comfort and salvation of her neighbour."

By the end of 1633 Louise had gathered together in her own small house a group of young girls who had volunteered to work under the Ladies of Charity for the direct service of the poor. Vincent was convinced that only village girls, providing they had the necessary spirit, would do:

True country girls are very simple. They are not artful in the way they speak, nor do they use words with a double meaning. They are not stubbornly attached to their own opinions or intent on getting their own way, and they believe with great simplicity whatever they are told. We may observe in real country girls a great degree of humility. They never vaunt their possessions or tell you how well connected they are; they do not regard themselves as having cultivated minds and they behave modestly. Some may be better off than others but they do not live better than the rest and all live on equal terms together.

These were inestimable advantages, but the girls had to be trained not only for a specific task but to a spiritual awareness that the service of the poor was a loving service of Christ, who was to be found not only in the persons of the poor but in those of their sisters. Louise found herself teaching the girls to read and write, to live with each other, imparting not only Christian doctrine but the desire to love God above all things communicating her understanding of this new vocation, at once religious and as exacting as any monastic rule in the matter of obedience and personal poverty while at the same time oriented toward a total subjection to "the poor, who are our masters." That there have been so many heroic examples of charity among the Sisters then and through the centuries is a testament to the teaching and example of Louise de Marillac. Vincent loved to speak of the young Sister who, when deputed to help in the household of a highly-placed Lady of Charity, asked humbly to be excused the honour: "I have left my parents and come here not to serve the rich but the poor."

Through forming others in this way Louise herself grew into the vocation of a Sister of Charity. A year after the training had begun, Vincent allowed her to make a private vow to dedicate herself wholly to the needs of these girls whom she had come to love utterly and devotedly. Her attitude may be divined by her rejection of the title of "superior" in favour of that of "Sister Servant." Nothing distressed her so much as the failure on the part of some to persevere, although Vincent comforted her with the thought that some degree of loss was inevitable. He himself helped in the process of formation through the *Conferences* he addressed to the assembled Sisters, which Louise attended. Her own letters to those sent out on a mission show her constant concern for every aspect of their lives.

As the numbers of "Daughters of Charity," as they were first called, increased and they were sent out on various missions, Louise's administrative responsibilities likewise increased. From 1634 until her death in 1660 she studied and supervised every new venture: the opening or taking over of existing hospitals in Paris and in the provinces, orphanages and the rescue of abandoned babies, free schools, refuges for the insane, homes for the old, hostels for vagrants and beggars, soup kitchens, the care of soldiers on the battlefield, criminals condemned to the galleys. Her mastery of detail, good judgment, and discernment were qualities exercised not in isolation but in close collaboration with Vincent and the Ladies of Charity.

Throughout those years the situation was immensely aggravated by bouts of civil war, which hit the poor more than most but also dried up the contributions of the rich. The Company of Sisters continued to develop despite these conditions. Vincent allowed a few Sisters to take vows in 1642, to be renewed every year. The Company was approved by the archbishop of Paris in 1646 and by Parliament in 1658. In addition to the formation of the Sisters, Louise conducted retreats for those Ladies who had come to value her spiritual gifts. More and more her own self-dedication led her into the mystery of Christ and to a close union with him. Carried on the wave of a grand movement in which she recognized herself as no more than an instrument, Louise no longer sought to control her own spiritual progress but yielded herself to the designs of Providence. She could not have uttered these words had she not herself vividly experienced their reality: "When we are set free from all attachment to this world and to the senses, from all attachment to our own self-love and our own free will and even from attachment to our delight in Christ and in his presence, when we have created a complete void within ourselves, the Holy Spirit will come into it and make us live with a divine life." Louise had begun life not knowing who she was. She had lived for many years with an interior void, suffering the pain of rejection and the helplessness of belonging nowhere and to no one. It fell to Vincent to draw her out of this black hole into the light and love of God's presence. As she grew in love of the crucified Christ she could freely re-enter the void in token of her willingness to be crucified with Christ: "I desire to be completely extinguished through the annihilation of my whole inner life. . . ."

Vincent consented reluctantly to direct a penitent and gained a collaborator who entered fully into his life's work. They worked as one to fulfil God's will as this became evident at every stage. Louise herself would not take a single step without Vincent's approval; it is clear that she gave him in return as much as she received from him. The great work of charity that is their legacy would not have been what it is had they worked alone.

By 1659 both saints were becoming infirm. Louise wrote in January 1660: "No desires, no resolutions. The grace of my God will accomplish in me whatever he wills." For six weeks she lay prostrate. She made one request to Vincent, that she might see him before she died. He himself was very weak and unable to walk. He sent her the simple message: "Go in peace." She died on 15 March 1660 at the age of sixty-eight, and she was canonized by Pius XI on 11 March 1934. In 1960 she was declared the patroness of Christian social workers. Her remains are now in the convent of the Sisters of Charity in the rue du Bac in Paris. Physically small—just under five feet—her greatness is seen today in her numerous Sisters in all continents and in other Congregations largely inspired by hers.

M. Gobillon, *Vie de Mlle le Gras* (1676); M.C. Richemont, *Histoire de Mademoiselle Le Gras* (1883); Mgr Baunard, *La vénérable Louise de Marillac* (1898); *Dict.Sp.*, 9, 1081-4. Quotations are taken from the three following works: J. Calvet, trans. G. F. Pullen, *Louise de Marillac* (1959); L. Sullivan, *Spiritual Writings of Louise de Marillac* (1991); *Vincent de Paul and Louise de Marillac, Rules, Conferences and Writings*, C.W.S. (1995). All the lives of St Vincent de Paul, especially that by P. Coste, *Saint Vincent de Paul et les Dames de la Charité* (1917), include information about St Louise. See also *H.S.S.C.*, 8, 166-71.

Bd William Hart, Martyr (1558-83)

William Hart was born at Wells in Somerset in 1558, the eldest son of a mother who had lapsed from the faith. He went to Lincoln College, Oxford, and later to Douai. When the College moved to Reims in 1578, he made the journey on foot together with his companions in spite of great suffering due to the stone. Unable to obtain relief in any other way and keen to ensure a place eventually on the English mission, he submitted to surgery and astonished even the doctors by his courage. Later he was sent to Rome, where he was ordained. He returned to Reims in May 1581, and from there he set out for England at the end of that same month.

His ministry was centred on York and the country round about. He was a man of great charm and eloquence, outstanding for his love of the faith, his cheerful spirit, and the unstinting service of his fellow-Catholics, especially those imprisoned in York Castle for their Catholicism. He brought them the sacraments and the encouragement of his own strong faith while attempting to alleviate their physical sufferings in every way he could. Once while at Mass in the castle, during which some Catholics were arrested, he managed to escape by letting himself down the wall into the moat where he was up to the chin in mud and water. Six months after this incident, on St Stephen's day 1582, he was arrested and imprisoned in the same castle, where he remained until his execution.

At his trial he was found guilty of high treason and condemned to be hanged, drawn, and quartered. He spent the six days that remained to him fasting and praying. Importuned by two Protestant ministers even at the gallows, he asked politely but firmly, "Be so kind as to let me be quiet this short time I have to live." He died on 15 March 1583 and was beatified in 1886.

M.M.P., pp. 72-8; Anstruther, 1, p. 155.

St Clement Mary Hofbauer (1751-1820)

St Clement Mary Hofbauer was the first to establish the Congregation of St Alphonsus Liguori north of the Alps and is regarded as the second founder of the Redemptorists. He, more than anyone else, is credited also with the collapse of "Josephinism," the Austrian equivalent of Erastianism, which treated ecclesiastics as functionaries of the State.

Johannes Hofbauer was born in Tasswitz in Moravia in 1751, the ninth of the twelve children of a grazier and butcher who had changed his Slavonic surname of Dvorak to Hofbauer and who died when Johannes was six years old. As a child, Johannes wished to become a priest but, lacking the means, was apprenticed to a baker at the age of fifteen. Later he went to work in the bakery of the Premonstratensian monastery at Bruck. The self-sacrifice he showed during a time of famine won him the favour of the abbot, and he was allowed to attend the abbey school. After the abbot's death he became a solitary until

Emperor Joseph's edict against hermitages obliged him to take up his old trade, this time in Vienna.

Twice he went on pilgrimage to Rome together with his friend Peter Kunzmann. On the second occasion they obtained permission from Bishop Chiaramonti of Tivoli (later Pope Pius VII) to settle as hermits in his diocese. After a few months Johannes realized that his real vocation was to be a missioner, and he returned to Vienna. One day, after he had served Mass at the cathedral of St Stephen, he offered to call a carriage for two ladies detained in the porch by a downpour of rain. This chance meeting led the ladies to finance not only his studies for the priesthood but those also of his friend Thaddeus Hübl. The two went on pilgrimage to Rome (Johannes' third), where they joined the Redemptorists. They made their profession and were ordained in 1785, with Johannes taking the names Clement Mary in religion.

Clement Mary was sent by his superiors to begin a mission in Courland in Lithuania. He set out northward with Thaddeus. On the way he met his old friend Peter Kunzmann, still a hermit in Tivoli but then on pilgrimage. Kunzmann decided to join them as a lay brother, becoming the first Redemptorist novice to be received north of the Alps. At Warsaw the papal nuncio gave them the church of St Benno for their use, but in order to secure their services for a ministry to the several thousand German-speaking Catholics in the city who had been without pastors since the suppression of the Jesuits, he wrote to Rome and obtained the postponement of the mission to Courland. The Redemptorists began their work in Warsaw in the utmost poverty. As they did not even have beds, the two slept on the table while Brother Emmanuel used a chair. They had to borrow pots and pans for their cooking. At first they preached in the streets, but when this was forbidden by the government they remained in St Benno's, which became the centre of a continuous mission. Although their work was primarily with the Germans, Clement Mary wished to help everyone. The arrival of the first Polish novice, John Podgorski, helped greatly in their outreach to the Poles. Five sermons were preached every day, three in Polish and two in German. Both Protestants and Jews were converted, and another church, Holy-Cross-in-the-Fields, was given them for their use.

Clement Mary was also concerned for the children of the poorer classes who were suffering great privations as a result of war. He opened an orphanage near St Benno's and begged alms for their support. On one of his begging expeditions, a man who was playing cards in a tavern replied to his appeal by spitting in his face. Clement Mary was unmoved and said to him, "That was for me. Now please let me have something for my poor children." The man later became one of his regular penitents. A school for boys was also founded, while confraternities and other associations helped to ensure their continuance. As the community itself increased, Clement Mary sent out missionaries to Courland, their original destination, to other parts of Poland, Germany, and Switzerland, though none of these initiatives was destined to survive Napoleon's suppression of the religious Orders. He intended to leave for America in 1806 and encouraged others to go in his place.

After twenty years Clement Mary had to give up his work in Warsaw also. A police agent risked his life to warn the Redemptorists of their impending expulsion, so they were prepared for the official visitation when it came on 20 June 1808. They were taken to the fortress of Cüstrin on the banks of the Oder. Such was their influence on their fellow-prisoners and on the people outside who used to crowd round the prison to listen to the Redemptorists' hymns that the authorities decided to send them away. Each member was to return to his native country. Clement Mary, however, determined to settle in Vienna in the hope of establishing a Redemptorist house there in the event of a repeal of the laws of Joseph II. After great difficulties, including another imprisonment on the Austrian frontier, he reached Vienna, where he was to live and work for the last twelve years of his life.

After ministering unobtrusively in the Italian quarter, he was appointed chaplain to the Ursuline nuns and rector of the public church attached to their convent. There he was free to preach, hear Confessions, and perform all priestly duties. Soon from this centre fresh vigour began to flow into the religious life of Vienna. His confessional was besieged not only by the poor and simple but by ministers of state and university professors. Clement Mary and his friends and penitents, one of whom was Prince Ludwig of Bavaria, were mainly responsible for defeating the attempt to create a national German Church, independent of the pope, at the Congress of Vienna. Perhaps his crowning work was the establishment of a Catholic college whose students went on to occupy important positions in every field or to become priests and monks.

All through his life Clement Mary had a great devotion to the sick. He is said to have attended two thousand death-beds. He was summoned to rich and poor alike and never refused a call. His attitude to Protestants was perceptive and appreciative. He wrote in 1816 to a friend, "If the Reform in Germany grew and held its ground, it was not due to heretics and philosophers but to men who truly aspired to interior religion."

In spite of his good works and public spirit, Clement Mary remained the object of hostility to the supporters of "Josephinism." Once he was forbidden to preach, and he was accused of being a spy for the Vatican. The Chancellor asked that he should be expelled, but Francis I heard such a good report of him from the archbishop and from Pope Pius VII that he not only forbade any further annoyance of the Redemptorists but even spoke of a legal recognition of the Congregation. Clement Mary's two great objectives were thus practically attained, the Catholic faith was once more in the ascendant, and his beloved Congregation would be established on German soil. He predicted: "The affairs of the Congregation will not be settled until after my death. Only have patience and trust in God. Scarcely shall I have breathed my last when we shall have houses in abundance."

By 1819 he was still working, even though he suffered from several illnesses. On 9 March he braved a snowstorm in order to sing a requiem Mass for Princess Jablonowska, who had helped him when he was in Warsaw. Six days later he died. All Vienna crowded the streets to do him honour as his body was borne to the cathedral. He was canonized in 1909 by St Pius X, who declared him patron saint of Vienna.

There are biographies in German by A. Innerklofer, M. Meschler, and M. Harringer (this last appeared in Eng. trans. in 1883), but the best is that of J. Hofer, *Der Heilige Klemens Maria Hofbauer, Ein Lebensbild* (1921); See H. Castle, *Life of St Alphonsus Liguori* and Berthe, *Saint Alphonse de Liguori* (trans. 1905); *H.S.S.C.*, 9, 218-24; *Bibl.SS.*, 4, 49-51; the Life by Honnermann (1936) described as "*romanzata*" was trans. into English by J. Galvin (1952).

Bd Placid Riccardi (1844-1915)

Tomasso Riccardi was born on 24 June 1844 to Francisco Riccardi and Maria Stella Paoletti at Trevi in the diocese of Spoleto in Umbria, a region of Italy which gave to the Church two illustrious pairs of saints, Benedict and Scholastica, Francis and Clare. He was the third of their ten children. The family was well-to-do, and the boy was given a good education at the exclusive Collegio Lucarini until the age of fourteen. When the college showed signs of losing its character, he was withdrawn and continued his studies at home under private tuition.

There was little in his adolescence to single him out particularly. As a young man of a good and devout family, he was well behaved and fairly pious. He had been attracted to a young woman named Nina, whose eccentric uncle, however, put an end to any budding romance by forbidding him the house. If consolation were needed, the young man found it in his love of music, concerts, the theatre, and his preference for fine clothes. Yet it was at this period that he joined the Confraternity of the Holy Family and became a Franciscan tertiary.

Having completed his studies in 1863, he enrolled at the Angelicum in Rome to study philosophy. When he paid a farewell visit to Don Ludovico Pieri, his spiritual director, he had a shock when the priest said gravely, "In Rome you will develop a vocation and become a religious." This prediction seemed to touch a raw nerve. The young man retorted that should such a vocation present itself, he would not hesitate to choke it off. His violence may have been no more than an expression of the unresolved turmoil already raised by the question in his own mind.

The ordered life of study and the influence of the Dominicans now played a part in quietly effecting an interlude of interior peace. He was in the midst of his exams when this was shattered by the summons to military service. He wrote asking for a few days' grace to complete his exams, and thinking that he might be exempt as a resident of Rome, he went to visit Loreto. There he experienced the conviction that God was indeed calling him to the religious life. Afterwards, he went to the Jesuit house of Sant'Eusebio and followed the Spiritual Exercises. This seems to have been decisive.

He asked to be admitted to the Benedictine community of St Paul-outside-the-Walls on 12 November 1865. Two months later he entered the novitiate, receiving the name of Placid. It was not easy to yield his independence of mind and unreservedly put himself in the hands of his novice-master, and he strongly resisted doing so initially. After a period of reflection, he submitted himself with a good grace to his direction. This was perhaps the decisive victory over himself that set him on the path of self-abnegation he was never subsequently to abandon. He himself saw it as an immense grace that had set him free. Ildefonsus, Cardinal Schuster (30 Aug), his biographer, asked the then novice-master how it was a young man could have risen so quickly to such a degree of abnegation. The novice-master replied that Placid drew his strength from continuous prayer: "He prayed much, and he prayed well; that is all." Throughout his life, this was indeed his passport to the other virtues. Later in life, when relatively freer, he spent seven hours a day in prayer and often prayed for whole nights before the Blessed Sacrament.

He made his first profession in 1867 and embarked on his studies for the priesthood. Minor orders in 1868 was followed by the subdiaconate and diaconate in 1870. The day he was made deacon the troops of the *Risorgimento* entered Rome and claimed it as the capital of a united Italy. A new, strongly anticlerical government required the clergy to be conscripted along with the rest. In fact, following his failure to answer the summons to report to Spoleto for his military service, Placid was now classed as a deserter. In spite of an amnesty to cover such cases, Placid found himself in prison in Florence in November 1870. A royal pardon was finally obtained, but he remained liable to military service. However, his health was judged deficient by the military doctors, and he was released from jail in January 1871. Solemn profession and the priesthood followed in March 1871.

The subsequent life of Dom Placid is outwardly unremarkable and can be quickly told. For the first ten years after his profession he was occupied in teaching and supervising the young *alumni*. He formed part of the team of confessors appointed to minister to the people visiting the basilica and was also a confessor to the nuns of Santa Cecilia in Trastevere. In 1881 his health again broke down. By 1884 he was better, but he was plagued with the Roman "tertian fever" ever after. He was then appointed vicar of the Benedictine nuns of San Magno in Amelia, an appointment he held until 1894 apart from a break of two years. His duties were those of chaplain, ordinary confessor, and guardian of internal discipline. As the monastery had become lax in its observance, his task was no sinecure, and indeed the numerous ascetical writings among his papers reveal how conscientiously he worked toward the interior reformation of those in his care. He was also confessor to the bishop and to many of the clergy and taught regularly at the seminary as well as the convent of the *Maestre Pie* in the town.

In 1885 he was recalled by the Holy See to be the novice-master at St Paul's under conditions that were unusual. A novice who claimed to be the recipient of visions and ecstasies and other supernatural phenomena had been received at St Paul's. The novice-master believed these phenomena genuine, as did the abbot and some in the community. Others, indeed the majority, were uneasy. Dom Placid Riccardi was instrumental in proving that the young man was an impostor. That question resolved, the novice-master had to be replaced, and Dom Placid was appointed in his stead for two years.

1894 saw him transferred to Farfa, a once-splendid monastery in the Sabine hills, now derelict. Dom Placid, together with two lay brothers, lived in the grange of Sanfiano, about four miles from the monastery. He was expected to serve the abbey church and its pilgrims as well as the rural population, pre-serve what remained of the abbey, and restore what could be restored. To this task he gave all his attention and energy for twenty years.

Dom Placid came to Farfa at fifty years of age, mature in years and well advanced in the ways of the spirit. While the abbot had not seemed to be choosing an eremitical way of life for him, the new charge gave Dom Placid a solitude he could not have had in the larger community of St Paul's. By then he would have qualified, in the words of St Benedict, as one of "those who not in the first fervour of their religious life, but after long probation in a monas-tery . . . go out well-armed from the ranks of the community to the solitary combat of the desert." His intense life of unremitting prayer had first led him into that other desert in which self-will was gradually displaced by the effort to obey in humility and purity of heart. In this second desert his love of God and neighbour grew into a living flame that seemed to render any virtue effortless. Once, at Sanfiano, one of the Brothers who lived with him was asked what Dom Placid was doing. He replied, "Obeying everybody, even the dog on guard at the front door!" Personal poverty, abstemiousness in food and drink, physical mortification, were the continued expressions of the purity of heart he sought in prayer. While at Farfa he walked two hours daily to visit a priest in order to make his Confession. However, he was anything but a sad saint. He radiated joy and peace, was affable and approachable, and was known to enjoy a good joke. To observe him was to absorb from his life and countenance the spiritual programme of the Rule of St Benedict.

Placid was much loved by the people for whose needs he was now responsi-ble. They came to the abbey as much to see him as to venerate the Madonna for which it was famous. He was also appointed confessor to the Poor Clares at Fara Sabina and later to the Barberini Franciscans also. As at Amelia, he was endlessly consulted by the clergy on all sorts of problems. At the beginning of 1912 the abbot decided that the small community should move from the grange to the abbey. As Placid was becoming infirm, he sent a younger monk to help him. This monk construed his charge otherwise and virtually assumed the role of superior of the little community, even taking over Dom Placid's apostolate among the rural population, who deeply resented the change. It was a final trial before he returned to St Paul's.

On the feast of St Gertrude, 17 November 1912, Dom Placid suffered a stroke after Mass, which left him helpless for two years and four months. He returned to the monastery of his profession on 12 December 1912, unable to feed or help himself in any way. His patience seemed inexhaustible, his gratitude for the services rendered most touching. He died quietly on 15 March 1915 and was buried two days later. Instead of the usual toll at his funeral, a peal of bells rang out. It happened to be the day on which the Lenten *statio* was held at St Paul's, and the bell-ringers, forgetting the funeral, rang to announce the *statio*. Asked whether the peal should be cut short, the abbot replied, "Let it be. If we do not ring for Dom Placid, for whom should we ring?"

His body was exhumed and identified in 1938 and found to be incorrupt. He was beatified by Pope Pius XII on 5 December 1954.

Ildefonsus Schuster, *Profilo Biografico del Monaco D. Placido Riccardi* (1922); Pietro Gorla, *Il Servo di Dio Don Placido Riccardi* (1936); Romanus Rios, *Benedictines of Today* (1945).

R.M.
St Menignus, martyr at Parius in the Hellespont (*c.* 250)
St Matrona, martyr at Thessalonica in Macedonia (third/fourth century)
St Hesychius, bishop of Vienne (*c.* 490)
St Cessator of Limoges (eighth century)
St Lucretia, martyr—see "St Eulogius and the Martyrs of Córdoba," 11 Mar.
BB Monaldus, Francis and Anthony, Franciscan martyrs at Arzenga, Armenia (1314)

16

ST JOHN DE BREBEUF, *Martyr* (1593-1649)

Jean de Brébeuf was born on 25 March 1593 in Condé-sur-Vire, a small village in the *département* of La Manche in France. He was already sufficiently educated in the humanities and in philosophy to have moved on fairly swiftly to ordination after his entry into the Jesuit novitiate of Rouen in late 1617. He was considered to have such frail health that he was restricted to teaching and that only for two years. He was ordained probably in March 1622 and was then made bursar of the Jesuit college at Rouen.

De Brébeuf was in his fifteenth year when Quebec was founded by Samuel Champlain in 1608. Frs Biard and Massé, the first two Jesuits to be sent to New France, as Canada was then called, left France in 1613 but returned about two years later after attacks by the English. Biard never went back, but Massé was to be one of the four Jesuits who, at the request of the remaining Franciscan missionaries for further help, were to go out in 1625. The other three were John de Brébeuf, Charles Lalemant, and Buret, a lay brother. From then on Fr de Brébeuf had continually to bear the most appalling physical hardships any man can be called on to endure—as indeed had all his co-missionaries—and finally to be martyred after sustaining tortures of astounding cruelty. His health must have improved a great deal since his novitiate days to have made this possible, but he also harboured a desire for martyrdom that made light of lesser pains.

The Jesuits were inclined to give most of their attention initially to the Hurons, the most peaceable and sedentary of the Indian tribes and therefore the most amenable to evangelization. De Brébeuf was keen to begin work among them, but not long after their arrival the Jesuits learned of the death of one of the Franciscans at the hands of the Hurons. It seemed more prudent not to deal with them at that moment. In October of that year de Brébeuf left Quebec to live instead with the Algonquin Indians during the winter, braving the filth and vermin of their smoke-filled tepees. Like them, he slept on fir branches strewn on the snow in a confined space packed with human bodies and dogs. During the day he hunted with them in the ice and snow, eating their unfamiliar food and starving when there was none available. He hoped to get to know the Indians intimately and learn their language so as to discover a point of insertion for the Christian doctrine he had come to pass on to them. He discovered only too quickly that "the noble savage" did not exist *per se*; only the grace of Christ would bring such a one to birth. Unable initially to utter a word to make himself understood, he was made the butt of their ridicule. The Indians even deliberately taught him to use foul words without telling him their meaning. These minor manipulations of their guest could not hide from him the extent to which the Indians themselves were the slaves of superstition and the playthings of their sorcerers. However, he persevered with his task and was actually able to compose an Algonquin grammar and dictionary during his five-month stay with them.

In the summer of 1626 he persuaded the Hurons to take him together with de Noue, a fellow-Jesuit, and a Franciscan, to their lands. The only method of transport was the canoe, but even that was useless to negotiate the thirty-five to forty rapids. At each of these the canoe and all baggage and provisions had to be carried overland until the next point at which the travellers might take to the water again. De Brébeuf's sojourn was not easy: the Franciscan went off to work with another tribe, while de Noue, unable to make any headway with the language, went back to Quebec. Unaided and alone, de Brébeuf translated an existing catechism into Huron. He earned the title of Sorcerer—which was later to serve him ill—when in a time of drought he suggested prayers to the Christian God and rain fell. He made some excursions to the Petuns at this time. His stay was brought to an end when he was summoned back to Quebec. The colony found itself at the mercy of a French Huguenot in the service of the English. Champlain and de Brébeuf returned to France, the latter to Rouen, where he took his final vows in 1630. New France passed into the hands of the English until it was ceded back to France in 1632.

Champlain returned to the colony in 1633, John de Brébeuf accompanying him. The Hurons agreed to have missionaries among them only after they had been severely trounced by the Iroquois, the fiercest and most aggressive of the Indian tribes. Four Jesuits together with their lay helpers set out for Huronia in 1635 on a nightmare journey. The canoes were separated, and de Brébeuf was abandoned by his guides in an uninhabited region. He found his way to Ihonitiria and to those who had known him before and were prepared to welcome him in their midst. He stayed for three years. That same year an epidemic broke out for which the missionaries were blamed. Often ill themselves and under the external threat of death, they ministered for over a year to the sick and baptized the dying. On four occasions councils were held to decide on the death of the missionaries. At the funeral banquet he himself provided prior to his expected death, de Brébeuf spoke eloquently about God, heaven, and hell. His execution was stayed. In 1637, in their darkest hour, the first healthy adult was baptized. He proved to be an exemplary Christian. As the Indians accepted the recommendation to segregate the sick, the epidemic eased, but de Brébeuf moved the mission centre in 1638 to Tenaustayoe. In time the missionaries could move more freely among the Hurons and the work of evangelization proceeded for the few years before the tribe was annihilated by the Iroquois.

The Neutrals were a tribe not unlike the Hurons; they were so called because they refused to support either the Hurons or the Iroquois in their wars. In 1640 de Brébeuf set out with three others to make contact with this tribe, unaware that hostile Hurons had gone ahead to prejudice the Neutrals against them. Every village shut its doors against them. One night, as the temperatures were dropping dangerously low, they pushed their way uninvited into a cabin, only to be faced with a group ready to flaunt the rules of hospitality and kill them. Other villagers joined the group. De Brébeuf addressed them and calmly went on talking as arrows were aimed at him. His courage won the day, and they were unharmed. A squaw received them with great kindness while a snow-storm raged for over three weeks, though she showed no signs of wanting to be a Christian. However she did give them precious help with their work on the dialects. On his return journey de Brébeuf fell on the ice and broke his collar-bone, which may account for three years sedentary work in Quebec.

The Iroquois were becoming increasingly daring, and it seemed necessary to contact the missionaries working in Huronia. In 1644 de Brébeuf set out. The following year he was to be found among the Huron refugees fleeing the Iroquois, but it was clearly evident that unless all the tribes united against the Iroquois, there was little hope of saving them or the scattered missions. In 1648 two massacres took place requiring a re-siting of the mission. This new site was breached on 16 March 1649. De Brébeuf and Gabriel Lalemant (17 March) were in another village four kilometres away, but that too was taken. The Iroquois massacred the inhabitants without pity, but their prize was the Sorcerer himself.

Nine years before this, John de Brébeuf had made a vow to Christ: "I vow in the presence of the Eternal Father and the Holy Spirit . . . never to shirk the grace of martyrdom if, in your mercy, you offer it some day to your unworthy servant . . . and when I am about to receive the stroke of death, I bind myself to accept it from your hand in the joy of my heart." He had had many intimations that his self-offering had been accepted and would not have been surprised when the moment came.

The priests were stripped naked, bound, and had their nails torn out. As they were led to the mission-site the Iroquois lined up on either side, raining blows on the men with knives, clubs, and stones. Led to the stake at which they were to be burned, the men showed no fear. De Brébeuf fell on his knees and kissed it as he would an altar at the beginning of Mass. As the flames whipped about him, the warriors plunged heated prongs into his flesh or applied fire-brands to his body. Strips of flesh were cut away, roasted in the same fire, and then eaten by his tormentors. Not a word or groan escaped him; he tried only to encourage the other Christians. Infuriated that he showed himself uncowed, they cut off his nose and lips, broke his teeth with clubs and forced a fire-brand into his mouth. An apostate Huron brought cauldrons of boiling water to "baptize" the baptist. A belt of bark, saturated with pitch was tied around his waist and set afire, and red-hot tomahawks were hung around his neck. Still there was no sound. The victim was then scalped and hot ashes shovelled on the wound. Finally he was struck on the head with a tomahawk, which ended his agony. They tore out his heart and drank his blood, thinking they might thus assimilate his indomitable courage.

John de Brébeuf was canonized in 1930. His feast is kept together with the other martyrs of North America on 11 October.

See the entry for 11 Oct. for a fuller treatment of all the martyrs of North America and for the bibliography.

BB John Amias and Robert Dalby, *Martyrs* (1589)

John Amias (or Anne) and Robert Dalby were two Yorkshire men who studied for the priesthood at Douai College in Reims and were sent on the English mission.

Amias, a widower, was ordained on 25 March 1581 and returned to England with Bd Edmund Sykes (23 Mar.) on 5 June of the same year. He ministered for seven or eight years before being arrested. Robert Dalby, who had been a Protestant minister, was arrested as he landed at Scarborough in 1588. The two were tried at the same time, condemned to die because of their priesthood, and led to their execution together. All were astonished at the alacrity and joyousness with which they lay on the hurdle, refusing to be bound as was customary.

An eyewitness account of their martyrdom runs thus:

This year on the 16th of March, John Amias and Robert Dalby, priests of the College of Douay, suffered at York as in cases of high treason, for no other cause but that they were priests ordained by the authority of the See of Rome, and had returned to England, and exercised there their priestly functions for the benefit of the souls of their neighbours. I was myself an eye-witness of the glorious combat of these holy men, being at that time a young man in the twentieth year of my age; and I returned home confirmed by the sight of their constancy and meekness in the Catholic faith, which by God's grace I then followed. For there visibly appeared in those holy servants of God so much meekness, joined with a singular constancy, that you would easily say they were lambs led to the slaughter.

They were drawn about a mile out of the city to the place of execution, where being arrived and taken off their hurdle, they prostrated themselves upon their faces to the ground, and there employed some time in prayer, till [Mr Amias] being called upon by the Sheriff, rose up and with a serene countenance walked to the gallows and kissed it, then kissing the ladder went up. . . . He then turned to the people, declared that the cause of his death was not treason but religion. But here he was interrupted and not suffered to go on. Therefore composing himself for death, with his eyes and hands lifted up to heaven, forgiving all who had any ways procured his death, and praying for his persecutors, he recommended his soul to God; and being flung off the ladder quietly expired. . . . All this while his companion, Mr Dalby, was most intent on prayer; who being called upon, immediately followed the footsteps of him that had gone before him, and obtained the like victory.

They were hanged, drawn, and quartered on 16 March 1589 and beatified in 1929.

Anstruther, 1, pp. 7-8, 96, with further refs. See also the general entries on the martyrs of England and Wales, 4 May and 25 Oct.

R.M.
SS Hilary and Tatian, martyrs at Aquileia (third century)
St Papas, martyr at Seleucia in Isauria (fourth century)
St Julian, martyr at Anzarba in Cilicia (fourth century)
St Eusebia, abbess of Hamage, Artois (680)
St Gregory, bishop and hermit of Pithviers (*c.* 1000)
St Heribert, bishop of Cologne (1021)
St Chrystodoulos, archimandrite at Eubea in Greece (1100)
Bd John Sordi/Cacciafronte, bishop and martyr of Vicenza (1181)
Bd Torello, hermit (1282)

ST PATRICK
Red saltire on silver field

17

ST PATRICK, *Bishop* (Fifth Century)

Christianity came to south-east Ireland very early on, brought there either by British or Gaulish traders and missionaries. In 431, before the arrival of St Patrick, St Palladius (7 July) had been sent by Pope Celestine to the Christians there, although nothing further of his ministry is known. St Patrick, who was then not the first in the field nor Ireland's unique evangelizer, later concentrated his efforts on the north and set in place a native clergy who ensured the continuation and spread of his work. For lack of hard evidence one cannot assert that he was a monk, despite the legends concerning his stay in Lérins. His was an episcopal Church, which from the beginning clearly encouraged the monastic life, so prominent in succeeding ages—but perhaps the most enduring feature of Irish Christianity through the centuries is its missionary spirit, which assuredly owes much to Ireland's patron saint.

The career of St Patrick is obscured by later legend, and it is impossible to assert more than a few historical facts with any confidence; these are more prudently drawn from his own writings than from his seventh-century biographers, Tírechán and Muirchú, or other even later sources. Contemporary scholars have themselves not arrived at any consensus concerning his dates, his movements, or his missionary activity except in a general way but are agreed on the authenticity and unique value as source-material of his two writings, the *Letter to the Soldiers of Coroticus* and his *Confession*.

Sub-Roman fifth-century Britain retained its Latin character even as the empire itself was in decline, though its frontiers became increasingly porous without Roman defences. South of Hadrian's wall, toward the north-west, lay the town of Carlisle, where it is presumed Calpornius, Patrick's father, was an alderman, and in whose vicinity was the village of Bannaventa Berniae, containing the family villa and the homestead where Patrick was reared. His grandfather, Potitus, was a priest, while Calpornius was a deacon. The three generations thus bore Latin names and were Christian ministers, which indicates both civil and ecclesiastical structures firmly in place and the family's good standing within them. Moreover, there were slaves on the estate, a sign that the family was fairly wealthy. Patrick's comments might suggest a not very observant household and, as far as he was concerned, a not particularly religious upbringing. However, he must have been baptized and have attended religious services, since he tries to interpret his capture as a punishment for not having listened to the exhortations of the priests.

Patrick was not yet sixteen when a band of Irish raided the property. He was taken with some of his father's slaves and eventually found himself in the north-west of Ireland—although there is a strong tradition that it was in the north-east in the present Co. Antrim. He lived in exile for six years, herding his master's livestock—the Antrim tradition placing this on the slopes of Mount Slemis. The experience was definitive in shaping the spiritual features of one of the most remarkable of missionaries. To the son of a decurion conscious of his *Romanitas* and position in society, the status of a slave was deeply humiliating. He may not have been aware of it during his captivity, but for the rest of his life Patrick grieved for the education he had not had. Barely articulate in his own tongue, he was forced to adopt another. Nostalgia for his own country, people, and kin, plus loneliness and poverty and exposure to the harshness of the climate brought him to that degree of denudation where God alone is found to be the sole, inalienable treasure of the spirit.

Prayer became Patrick's sustenance. He declares that the call to prayer was so insistent and such a source of joy that he would willingly face frost, snow, or rain to pasture the animals while he gave himself up to it. The love and fear of God, he says, took over more and more as his faith deepened and the Spirit worked within him. His subsequent history bears out the impression that during these years he learned to be a passive instrument in God's hands. He came to regard his captivity as a blessing, his life of prayer as pure, unmerited grace. There is no mention of friendships formed, of conversations held with those of his own age, of any attempt to kindle in others the fire that burned within him; yet the summons, when it came, to return to Ireland presupposes that he had made some impression on those around him.

"Soon you will go back to your own country . . . see, your ship is ready," was the message he received one night in his sleep. He escaped at that point, at the age of twenty-two, and trekked some 188 miles "in the power of God who guided [his] way" until he found a ship preparing to set sail. After three days at sea, the vessel came to port in some unidentified spot. Captain and crew disembarked, and for twenty-eight days the group, with Patrick among them, walked without finding any human being or human habitation. As their food was running out the captain challenged Patrick, as a Christian who believed in an almighty God, to obtain food for them. Patrick's answer sums up the programme he had set himself over the last six years: "Turn with faith to the Lord my God, to whom nothing is impossible. . . ." They came upon a herd of swine which, with the discovery of wild honey, tided them over.

It is not clear whether this desolate region was in Britain or Gaul. Patrick had been promised in his dream a speedy return to his own country, but there remains the possibility of a landing and sojourn in Gaul. In old age, when he was writing his *Confession,* he admits to having felt the desire not only to return to his native land but also to see the men of God in Gaul. In any case he found his way back to his family. It was their joy at seeing him and their earnest plea

169

that he should never again leave them that precipitated the very thing they most feared. Patrick saw "in a vision of the night someone apparently coming from Ireland . . . bearing many letters, one of which he gave [him]." Patrick read the letter containing the voice of the Irish and seemed to hear "the voices of those around the wood of Foclut, near the Western Sea." They begged him to return: "Come, and from now on walk with us." Patrick was deeply moved. Later he received confirmation that the plea was divinely inspired: "He who gave himself up for you, he it is that speaks in you."

It was not merely a call for companionship. Patrick had nothing else to give but the faith that was in him. He refers in his *Confession* to his time as a deacon, which indicates that he had decided to follow the accepted stages of preparation for ordination. His mission to Ireland must have been approved also by his "seniors," who were later to regard it as incumbent on them to reprove him, and whose decision must have promoted him to the episcopate. There were some who questioned the prudence of his venture, and Patrick, never sure of himself, was lured into doubt: "I did not immediately yield to what was pointed out to me and [to] what the Spirit suggested. And the Lord had pity on me among thousands of thousands, because he saw in me that I was ready, but that in my case for these [reasons] I knew not what to do . . . because many were hindering my mission—not for the sake of malice, but because it was not a wise thing in their opinion, with which I too agreed because of my lack of education. I did not readily recognize the grace that was then in me, but now I know what I ought to have done at the time."

Nevertheless, with some foresight, Patrick sold his patrimony to obtain funds for his mission, declining to accept any support from his home church, and set out for Ireland—either in the 430s or in the 450s—this time as the slave of Christ and with the firm determination never to leave his adopted country. It is impossible to deduce from his own writings the progress of his evangelization or even to indicate the places where he worked. The tradition is that he went to the north and worked in Ulster, Leinster, and Munster and that Armagh was the privileged place of his ministry. Patrick himself throws out only a few general remarks. He reveals that there were times when his life was imperilled, and that on one occasion he was taken prisoner, chained, and apparently condemned to death. He had to make presents to local chieftains and to their men to act as guides. He travelled to the furthest regions of the inhabited world and was amazed at the harvest of souls: "Among you and everywhere I travelled for your sake, amid many perils, even to remote places beyond which there was no one and where no one had ever penetrated, to baptize or ordain clergy, or to confirm the people. . . ." That he, Patrick, should be the instrument of God was equally a matter of astonishment: "I am greatly a debtor to the God who has bestowed on me such grace that many people through me should be born again to God, and that everywhere clergy should be ordained from a people newly coming to the faith." He was astonished that grace worked so powerfully on the young who spontaneously chose to be monks and virgins despite parental opposition. Nowhere does Patrick's tenderness show to such advantage as when he relates the Baptism of a "blessed Scottish maiden, nobly-born, very beautiful, of adult age, whom I baptized" and who subsequently determined to embrace virginity.

Patrick's love for his converts was to lead him to over-react when the soldiers of Coroticus snatched some of the new Christians of his flock to sell them into slavery. He knew the horrors of slavery only too well, knew that the young who had pledged virginity might find the pressures on them beyond their strength, and mourned those Christians who had died in the fray. What angered him was that the raid was carried out by Christians and Romano-Britons like himself. In his *Letter to the Soldiers of Coroticus* he went so far as to excommunicate the perpetrators. It may have been that in thus acting *ultra vires* Patrick brought down on himself the ire of the British bishops, who thought it as well to take a good look at the activity of this lone missionary. Messengers brought to Patrick the suspicions that had surfaced: He had refused to accept financial help from his own Church; was this normal? Had he accepted the mission for his own personal enrichment? Was it true that he accepted gifts from his converts for the administration of the sacraments of Baptism and Ordination? These suspicions were buttressed by the betrayal to the synod of a secret sin confessed by Patrick to a dear friend some thirty years before this when he was a young lad, hardly knowing the difference between right and wrong. Patrick never clearly reveals the sin to the reader, but judging from the context it may have concerned some small dishonesty. Patrick sent back a rebuttal of these accusations. What we hear in the *Confession* is his recollection in old age of his self-defence, but it still rings with anger and dismay. Indeed it precipitated a crisis of faith: "When I was attacked by some of my seniors who came and urged my sins against my laborious episcopate I was strongly driven to fall away, here and for ever."

Yet at the end of his life, so rich in grace for himself and for the people he had brought to God, Patrick longs for even more difficulties to surmount: martyrdom would satisfy him best: "I desire enough and too much, and am prepared that he should give me 'to drink of his cup,' as he has granted to others that love him . . . and if I have ever imitated anything good on account of my God whom I love, I pray him to grant me, that with those proselytes and captives, I may pour out my blood for his name's sake, even though I myself may even be deprived of burial, and my corpse most miserably be torn limb from limb by dogs, or by wild beasts, or that the fowls of heaven should devour it. I believe most certainly that if this should happen to me, I shall have gained both soul and body."

Patrick ends his *Confession:* "I beg of those who believe and fear God, whoever shall deign to look into or receive this writing, which Patrick, the sinner, unlearned indeed, has written in Ireland, that no one may ever say, if I have

171

done or demonstrated anything according to the will of God, however little, that it was my ignorance [that did it]. But judge ye, and let it be most truly believed, that it has been the gift of God." Patrick died on 17 March, probably at some time in the latter half of the fifth century.

The penitential pilgrimage to Connaught's Croagh Patrick, which commemorates the saint's probably legendary forty days' fast, may reflect his very real ascetic bent. The pilgrimage to Station Island on Lough Derg in Co. Donegal, which has its origins in the twelfth century, is characterized also by the same spirit of penance. However, the cult of St Patrick is by no means restricted to Ireland. Wherever Irish missionaries have gone—and their remarkable zeal has taken them to every corner of the globe—they have taken with them devotion to the apostle of Ireland.

C. H. Wright, *The Writings of St Patrick*, from which the above quotations are taken (1889); L. Bieler, *Libri Epistolarum Sti Patricii* (1952); C. Thomas, *Christianity in Roman Britain* (1981); R. P. C. Hanson, *The Life and Writings of the Historical St Patrick* (1983); *idem*, "The Mission of St Patrick," in J. P. Mackey (ed.), *An Introduction to Celtic Christianity* (1989, n.e. 1995), pp. 22-44; N. D. O'Donoghue, *Aristocracy of Soul, Patrick of Ireland* (1987); D. M. Dumville, *St Patrick A.D. 493-1993* (1993); D. R. Howlett, *The Book of Letters of Saint Patrick the Bishop* (1994). The famous hymn known as "St Patrick's Breastplate" dates, in the form in which it has come down to us, from the eighth century and cannot be associated with him.

St Gertrude of Nivelles, *Abbess (c. 626-59)*

Gertrude was born around 626, the younger daughter of Pepin of Landen and Bd Itta. Pepin, an Austrasian noble with vast possessions, was the majordomo of the palace of Austrasia and governed the realm in the name of Dagobert, son of Lothair II, who had been established by his father in Metz. Itta was likewise wealthy but also deeply religious. Their first daughter, Begga (17 Dec.), married the son of St Arnulf of Metz, and their son, Grimoald, was to succeed his father as majordomo.

When Gertrude was about ten years old, her father gave a feast attended by Dagobert and other nobles of the realm. One of these asked that Gertrude be given to his son in marriage. Gertrude was summoned and asked, in the young man's presence, to give her consent. She answered that she would marry neither him nor any other man as she was already committed to Christ. On the death of Pepin in 640, Itta retired to her own property at Nivelles, taking Gertrude with her, and on the advice of St Amand (6 Feb.) founded a double monastery there. She asked Amand to give her daughter the veil.

Itta governed the monastery for about seven years and then handed over the reins to Gertrude, who proved an able abbess, esteemed not only by the nuns of the community but also by the many visitors, the poor, strangers, and pilgrims. Among those whom Gertrude welcomed to the abbey were two Irish monks, St Foillan (31 Oct.) and his brother St Ultan (2 May), who were to work closely with her. Chased out of their monastery of Burgh Castle in Norfolk by Penda, king of Mercia, they travelled to Péronne, where another brother, Fursey, had been buried. They were received in the course of their travels by Gertrude and Itta, who probably obtained from Grimoald a grant of land in Fosse-la-Ville for them to build a monastery. They acted as chaplains and advisers to Gertrude. It was after having said Mass for the community that St Foillan was assassinated in 655 while returning to his own monastery. Itta had preceded him in 652.

The abbey prospered under Gertrude's direction. She so organized her administrative responsibilites that freedom for prayer and reading was always safeguarded, but her penances were extreme and finally led to a breakdown in health. She handed over the government of the monastery to her niece, Wulfetrude, daughter of Grimoald. Her own reputation was so great that even while she was alive some of her monks, endangered at sea, invoked her name and were saved.

As her death approached, apparently in a state of fear at the approaching judgment she sent a message to St Ultan at Fosse. He told her that she would die the next day during Mass but must have no fear as she would be welcomed by St Patrick on his feast, by the angels, and by many other saints. She died on 17 March 659 at the age of thirty-three and was buried in the church of St Peter, one of the three at Nivelles. At the end of the seventh century her tomb was moved when the church was enlarged for the convenience of the many pilgrims. In 1046 the Emperor Henry III placed it in a new church which was itself restored after the second World War.

St Gertrude has always been venerated in Belgium and the Low Countries. From the eleventh century she has been regarded as the patron saint of travellers, probably owing to her care for pilgrims and to the miraculous deliverance of her monks at sea. Before starting on a journey it was the custom to drink a stirrup-cup in her honour. She was also invoked on behalf of the dying. Her feast on 17 March marks the beginning of spring and the beginning of work in the garden, and so she became the patron saint of gardeners, called upon to protect the fields and gardens especially against rats and mice—no one really knows why. A sixteenth-century stained-glass window in the diocesan museum of Strasbourg shows her seated reading, with three mice chewing her habit.

See *M.G.H.*, 2, pp. 447-74; *AA.SS.*, Mar., 2, pp. 590-602; *H.S.S.C.*, 4, pp. 136-40.

St John Sarkander, *Martyr* (1576-1620)

John Sarkander was born on 20 December 1576 in Skoczow, near Ciaszyn, in the Habsburg Empire. His father, Grzegorz Maciej Sarkander, was of Czech origin, while his mother, Helena Gorecka, was Polish. His Baptism took place not in the parish church, which was occupied by Protestants at the time, but in a small church adjacent to the hospital, which was in Catholic hands, so the religious controversies of the age, which were to play so large a part in his martyrdom, thus immediately made themselves felt in his life.

His father died when John was only thirteen. Left with the problem of how to secure a Catholic education for her four sons, Helena Sarkander decided to settle in the more Catholic Moravia. John attended the Catholic parish school in Przybor, where they had made their home, and in 1593 at the age of seventeen went on to further his education at the Jesuit college in Olomouc. After obtaining a degree in philosophy he went to Graz for his studies in theology. He was ordained in 1609.

For the space of seven years he was assistant priest in various parishes until in 1616 he was appointed parish priest in the mostly Protestant town of Holeszov. Since the fifteenth century the district had been a hotbed of the Hussites, followers of the reformer and declared heretic Jan Hus and home also to the Bohemian Brothers, a group initially concerned to obtain the chalice for the laity but subsequently linked with the Hussites and later with the Lutherans. The local landowner, Baron von Lobkovitz, had wrested from these sects the church to which Sarkander had been assigned on the advice of the Jesuits. The baron's action was manifestly in breach of the charter, the *Majestát,* issued by King Rudolf of Bohemia in 1609, which guaranteed freedom of worship to Catholics and Hussites as well as the signatories from the other sects to the so-called *Bohemian Confession.* However, in a non-centralized administration in which local nobles had a free hand such an action would not have seemed unnatural, although in 1618, two years after Sarkander's appointment, a supposed violation of the charter roused the Protestant estates to bring to trial two governors who were subsequently thrown out of a window (the "Defenestration of Prague"); this was followed by a widespread rebellion in Bohemia and the replacement of the royal governors by directors. These refused to support King Ferdinand II, who succeeded his uncle, Rudolph, in 1619. At that point Moravia held aloof from the rebellion.

The new parish priest threw himself into his pastoral activity and received hundreds of converts into the Church. In so doing he incurred the enmity of a powerful neighbouring landowner, Bitowsky von Bystritz, a violent anti-Catholic and rival of Lobkovitz. There was a violent reaction on the part of Hussites and Protestants, too, and several attempts were made on the parish priest's life. In 1618, at the beginning of the Thirty Years War, a revolt broke out in Moravia as well. The Protestants seized the reins of government and set about destroying Catholic institutions. Lobkovitz was arrested and the Jesuits expelled. In the meantime Ferdinand II was deposed, and the throne was given in 1619 to the Calvinist Frederick V, elector of the Rhine Palatinate.

On the advice of parishioners and friends, Sarkander left for Poland, staying on in Cracow for some months when he heard that the Lutherans had occupied his parish. As soon as he thought it prudent, he returned to his flock, but the country was effectively at war. In February 1620 Polish troops known as the Lissovtchiks passed through Moravia, pillaging as they went. They were an élite army of light cavalry, as cruel as they were efficient, sent by the Polish king at the request of the kaiser to help put down the rebellion in Bohemia. In an attempt to identify his people as Catholic to this approaching force, John Sarkander went out to meet them at the head of his parishioners, carrying the Blessed Sacrament. The Poles immediately turned aside, and Holeszov was saved. Not so their parish priest. He was at once accused of collaboration with the enemy by Bitowsky and indeed, as a presumed agent of von Lobkovitz, of having, during his recent visit to Poland, negotiated the expedition of Polish troops to the country. He was arrested by order of Frederick V on 13 February 1620. The commission that tried him was composed entirely of Hussites and led by Lobkovitz' Protestant successor, Hetman Zerocin. They called on him to disclose who had brought the Polish troops into the country and what Baron von Lobkovitz, who was known to be his penitent, had told him in the confessional. Sarkander denied having anything to do with the coming of the Poles and refused absolutely to divulge anything said in the confessional. "I know nothing," he said, "and nothing has been entrusted to me in the holy sacrament of penance. Anything that may have been confided to me in that way is not retained in my memory. I have buried it in oblivion, out of veneration for the inviolable seal of confession, and I would choose, with God's help, to be torn in pieces rather than sacrilegiously to violate the seal of confession." He was then subjected to the rack in its severest form, and four days later he was racked again. After this second racking he was burned with torches. The following day he was racked for a third time and afterwards covered with feathers which had been dipped in a mixture of pitch, sulphur, and oil and then set on fire. He survived this atrocious treatment and lingered on for a month, reduced to helplessness but praying continually. He died on 17 March 1620 and was beatified in 1859. In May 1995 he was canonized in Olomouc by Pope John Paul II, who used the occasion to ask forgiveness of non-Catholics for the wrongs Catholics had inflicted on them in past centuries and pledged forgiveness on the Catholic side for the wrongs done to Catholics. This went some way to mollify the Czech Brethren, who had previously declined to meet the pope during this visit.

John Scintilla, a Catholic magistrate of Olomouc, who was obliged by his position to be present at the first session of the commission which tried the martyr, afterwards drafted for Cardinal von Dietrichstein the report which is the main source of our information. See the *Nota biograficzna* in Zofia Kossak, *Bl Jan Sarkander* (1995); *The Tablet*, 27 May 1995, p. 684.

St Gabriel Lalemant, *Martyr* (1610-49)

Gabriel Lalemant was born in Paris in 1610. He followed his uncles Charles and Jerome into the Society of Jesus and, like them, also went to New France as a missionary. His profession took place in 1632. He added to it a fourth vow to devote his life to the Indians and waited for fourteen years before it could be fulfilled. Once ordained, he was appointed chaplain to the Jesuit college of La Flèche, taught philosophy for a year, and supervised studies at Bourges from 1644 to 1646, when at last he went to New France after having begged his superiors for years to allow him to join the mission there. It is little wonder that they hesitated to grant his request, as he was frail and delicate in appearance. His uncle, who was the superior in Quebec, likewise hesitated for some time to allow him to go to Huronia as he had requested. However, Lalemant's spirit was anything but fragile. A written prayer of his to Christ gives a glimpse of his understanding of the deepest demands of his missionary vocation: "Let your blood, which was poured out for the savages no less than for ourselves, be effectually applied to them for their salvation, and let me cooperate with your grace and be immolated for them."

He spent two years in Quebec during which he followed every scrap of news of events in Huronia. In 1649 he was at Brébeuf's (16 Mar.) side at one of the mission centres in Huronia when the Iroquois were bearing down hard on the Hurons. Thereafter his story is that of de Brébeuf, his own tortures exceeding in barbarity those of the older man. Unlike Brébeuf, whose agony at the hand of the Hurons lasted for three hours, Gabriel Lalemant's was to endure for fifteen. Finally a blow of the tomahawk brought him release. It is said that when his sister, a Carmelite nun, heard of his martyrdom she sang the *Magnificat* in thanksgiving. His mother, a widow, there and then decided to consecrate her life to God. Gabriel Lalemant was canonized in 1930. His feast is kept on 11 October, together with the other martyrs of North America.

See the entry for 11 Oct. for a fuller treatment of all the martyrs of North America and for the bibliography.

R.M.
St Agricola, bishop of Chalons-sur Saône (580)
St Paul, martyr in Cyprus (*c.* 770)
Bd Conrad, hermit of Molfetta in Apulia (1154)

ST CYRIL OF JERUSALEM
Gold moneybag (he sold church property to feed the poor) on green field

18

ST CYRIL OF JERUSALEM, *Bishop and Doctor* (*c.* 315-86)

St Cyril of Jerusalem was a man of gentle and conciliatory disposition whose lot it was to live at a time of bitter religious controversy. Nothing is known for certain of his early life, but he was born about 315, perhaps in Jerusalem. He had an excellent education and was thoroughly versed in the scriptures, of which he made great use, some of his catechetical instructions consisting almost entirely of carefully interwoven biblical passages. Some of the references to the "angelic life" suggest that he may have been a monk or at least point to an understanding of the monastic life. He was ordained priest in 345.

It was as a priest that he delivered the *Catechetical Instructions* for which he is so well known and esteemed. Twenty-four of these sermons have survived. The first nineteen are explanations of Christian doctrine, delivered during Lent in Constantine's basilica of the Holy Cross to the catechumens preparing for Baptism at the Easter Vigil; the rest are explanations of the Christian mysteries given to the newly-baptized after Easter in the *Anastasis,* or Church of the Resurrection. These homilies are invaluable as a witness to the teaching and ritual of the Church in the mid-fourth century.

Cyril became bishop of Jerusalem in 350 or 351. The circumstances of his appointment are obscure and, if Jerome is to be believed, not altogether in order, but it is noteworthy that at the Second Ecumenical Council of Constantinople Cyril is referred to as "long since canonically appointed by the Bishops of the province," among whom Acacius, bishop of Caesarea, must have been foremost, as he was considered to hold the first place among the bishops of Palestine. Initially, Acacius may have held mildly Arian views, but his position was veering toward an outright Arianism, although the party he had founded, the Homoians (*omoios,* similar), aimed at a middle position between Arian and semi-Arian. Cyril's position differed from his in that he held the orthodox view of Christ's divinity without, however, ever using the word *homoousios* (of a like nature), defined by the Council of Nicaea.

Disagreements between Cyril and Acacius began over the question of precedence. The Council of Nicaea had designated Jerusalem as a "succession of honour," but without prejudice to the rights of the metropolitan of Caesarea. This was ill-defined at best, and Acacius did not look kindly on a suffragan bishop preceding him in honour. He summoned a synod to Caesarea, to which Cyril declined to go, either because it was packed with Arians or because he judged it beneath him to be judged by other than a patriarchal synod. In his absence he was arraigned on three counts: of insubordination, of the sale of church property to feed the poor in a time of famine, and finally of being a *homoousian*. Cyril was condemned and driven out of Jerusalem. He made his way to Tarsus, where he was warmly received by Silvanus, a semi-Arian, and where he remained pending an appeal to a higher court. Two years later his appeal came before the Council of Seleucia, which was made up of semi-Arians, Arians, and a small number of orthodox. Cyril was there, much to the displeasure of Acacius, who departed in high dudgeon. Thinking better of it, he returned to present his case, but he himself was deposed and Cyril reinstated.

Acacius then persuaded Emperor Constantius to summon another council. Fresh accusations were made, including one most likely to incense the emperor. Cyril was accused of having sold a gold-brocaded vestment given by Constantine to Makarios of Jerusalem, which was subsequently seen worn by a comedian on stage. Cyril was exiled again, but on the death of Emperor Constantius in 361 his successor, Julian, recalled all the bishops his predecessor had expelled, and Cyril returned to his see.

There he watched with some amusement Emperor Julian's attempt to rebuild the Jewish temple, declaring that it would come to nothing. Preternatural occurrences, earthquakes, visible balls of fire, collapsing walls, and the like were attested not only by church historians but also by the pagan Ammianus Marcellinus. However, the bishop did not remain long in his church. In 367 the Arian emperor Valens decreed the expulsion of all the prelates recalled by Julian. For a third time Cyril was exiled to some unknown place. When the Catholic Theodosius I became caesar of the East, Cyril returned for good, to find Jerusalem torn with schisms and party strife, overrun with heresy, and the scene of crime. The Council of Antioch, to which he appealed for help, sent him St Gregory of Nyssa (10 June), who did not stay but wrote in his *Warning against Pilgrimages* a vivid description of the morals of the Holy City at this period.

In 381 both Cyril and Gregory were present at the Council of Constantinople, the second ecumenical council of the Church. The Nicene Creed was promulgated in an amended form, and Cyril, who subscribed to it with the rest, accepted the term *homoousios*, which had come to be regarded as the test of orthodoxy.

He is thought to have died in 386, at the age of nearly seventy, after an episcopate of thirty-five years, sixteen of which were spent in exile. Of his writings, the only ones that have survived are the *Catechetical Lectures*, a sermon on the healing at the pool of Bethsaida, a letter to Emperor Constantius, and three small fragments. He was made a Doctor of the Church in 1882.

See *AA.SS.*, Mar., 2, pp. 623-32, and the manuals of patrology. J. H. Newman's preface to the *Catechetical Discourses* (Library of the Fathers, 1845), is still of value; A. Fortescue, *Greek Fathers* (1908); F. L. Cross, *St Cyril of Jerusalem's Lectures on the Christian Sacraments* (1951); *O.D.C.C.* (1997), pp. 442-3.

St Braulio of Zaragoza, *Bishop* (651)

Braulio was born into a noble and wealthy Romano-Hispanic family and brought up in the household of his brother John, bishop of Zaragoza. He completed his studies in Seville at the college founded by St Isidore (4 Apr.), whose intimate friend and collaborator he became. When Bishop John died in 631, the neighbouring prelates elected Braulio as his successor.

The new bishop sought to extirpate the Arian heresy, which continued to flourish even after the conversion of King Reccared (see St Leander, 13 Mar.). As a pastor he taught and encouraged his people conscientiously. So great was his eloquence that people said they saw the Holy Spirit, in the form of a dove, resting on his shoulder while he preached. Besides being an eloquent preacher he was also a keen controversialist and carried conviction no less by his absolute sincerity than by his reasoning. He took part in the Fourth Council of Toledo, which was presided over by his friend St Isidore (4 Apr.), as well as in the fifth and sixth councils. This last commissioned him to write on its behalf to Pope Honorius I in defence of the Spanish bishops who had been reprimanded for negligence. Rome was impressed by his dignified stance no less than by the elegance of his style. These councils of Toledo were just as much concerned with affairs of State as with those of the Church, and it is not surprising to find Braulio also corresponding with the king. It was he who suggested to King Chindaswinthe that he nominate his son, Recceswinthe, as his successor so as to avoid the turmoil that generally accompanied the customary vote for the succession.

Braulio hated luxury of any kind. His clothes were rough and plain, his food simple, and his life austere, but his generosity to the poor knew no bounds. He hated flattery: "It often happens that human opinion is unfair; we regard an evil man as good and a good man as evil. . . . I know that I am not what you make me out to be." His many extant letters of condolence reveal a man of warm heart and profound faith. While he sympathized wholly with all the pain of bereavement, he would swiftly point beyond it to the joys of heaven that must be the lot of those who have died in Christ. Excessive grief for dead relatives or friends is unchristian: "You must put aside your grief now because it is an offence against a good Lord." The close of his own life was troubled by infirmities, especially by failing eyesight, which must have been a heavy trial for one so dedicated to study.

Braulio was the most impressive writer of the Visigothic Church in Spain after St Isidore. He helped the latter compile his *Etymologies* and later revised them. His extant works include a life of St Emilian (12 Nov.), with a poem in his honour, the Acts of the martyrs of Zaragoza (16 Apr.), and a collection of forty-four letters. His affection for St Isidore and his concern to build up his already impressive library are evident from these letters. He shows sympathy with and an understanding of the monastic life. He disapproves of the imposition of a superior on a community for fear of the quality of the obedience likely to result, and he can be severe toward an abbot who takes his responsibilities too lightly. Aspects of his spiritual doctrine come through: justice and severity should always be tempered with patience and goodness. Braulio's approach is, above all, christocentric: what is important is the love and imitation of Christ. He encourages his sister, Pomponia: "Let all our love be directed to Christ, all our energies channelled into serving him so that interiorly we may be consoled by him who suffered for us and will never leave us to ourselves." His reconstruction of the prayer life of St Emilian during his forty years as a hermit is a reflection of his own. Aspirations, ejaculatory and affective prayer, according to him, dispose one to contemplation.

Braulio died in 651. His relics were transferred to the church of Our Lady of the Pillar in 1275. He is the patron of Aragon and one of the most famous of Spanish saints.

AA.SS., Mar., 2, pp. 634-7; *P.L.*, 80, 639-720; *Dict.Sp.*, 1, 1925; C. H. Lynch, *St Braulio* (1938). A critical edition of his letters was published by J. Madoz (1941).

St Edward, *Martyr* (979)

Edward was the son of King Edgar the Peaceful and his first wife, Ethelfleda, who died a few years after the child was born. He was baptized by St Dunstan (19 May), who was then archbishop of Canterbury and in effect the king's prime minister. When Edgar died, an attempt was made by some disaffected thanes (probably an antimonastic faction, to judge from subsequent events) to install the ten-year-old Ethelred, the king's younger son by his second wife, Elfrida. Dunstan resisted the move, favouring Edward, the king's first-born, whom he crowned.

Edward himself was only a youth, but he had a vile temper and a propensity to violence that did not endear him to others. One chronicler refers also to his mother's status. King Edgar had delayed his coronation out of a sense of his own unworthiness, but about two years before his death, he and Elfrida were consecrated king and queen by St Dunstan. Etheldred was therefore the offspring of a true queen, while Edward was not.

Although Dunstan backed Edward with all the prestige of his position and guided him in his government of the kingdom, feeling against the king persisted. Aelfhere of Mercia and others attacked the monasteries, scattering the monks and thereby damaging Dunstan's work, previously aided and abetted by Edgar. These attacks may be read as a reaction to the continued alliance between the crown and the archbishop of Canterbury and fear of an emergent monasticism too well endowed and consequently too powerful for the thanes. According to St Oswald of Worcester's (28 Feb.) biographer, a plot was hatched to kill the king. Three years into his reign, Edward was assassinated. The chroniclers of the time are all agreed that murder had been done. William of Malmesbury and Oswald's biographer are more explicit. The latter attributes the deed to Ethelred's retainers, the former to the mother, Elfrida. Given the disaffection of Aelfhere of Mercia and his support for Ethelred against Edward, the conspiracy may have had a wider base. In any case, it was at the castle of Corfe-Gap in Dorset, where Elfrida was staying with her son, that the chance for the kill presented itself. Edward called at the castle after the hunt to see his half-brother, and as he rode up, unescorted, he was presented with the stirrup-cup. He was stabbed by a retainer at a sign from Elfrida. He spurred his horse, but one foot slipped the stirrup, and he was dragged by the other and so died. No one was ever charged with the crime, but Elfrida is said to have become a nun at Wherewell in order to expiate her crime.

Edward was a martyr only in the broad sense of one who in the pursuit of duty has suffered unjustly. A cult based on the reports of miracles at his tomb in Shaftesbury, to which his relics had been translated, soon sprang up. He is portrayed with a dagger in his left hand. His feast is now kept in the diocese of Plymouth, while some of his relics are kept in an Eastern Orthodox church at Brookwood in Surrey.

See the *Anglo-Saxon Chronicle*, Florence of Worcester, Osbern the Hagiographer, Eadmer, and the author of the "Life of St Oswald" in the *Historians of the Church of York* (Rolls Series), 1, pp. 448-52; F. M. Stenton, *Anglo-Saxon England* (1943); R. M. Wilson, *Lost Literature of Medieval England* (1952); R. Humble, *The Saxon Kings* (1980); C. E. Fell, *Edward King and Martyr* (1971); D. Hill (ed.), *Ethelred the Unready* (1978); S. Ridyerd, *The Royal Saints of Anglo-Saxon England* (1988).

St Salvator of Orta (1520-67)

Salvator was born in the town of Santa Coloma near Gerona in Spain. He came of poor parents who both worked on the night shift in the local hospital, receiving the sick poor. Their son was known to his school friends simply as "Hospital Salvator." He lost both parents while still a child and migrated to Barcelona, where he worked as a shoemaker.

At the age of twenty he became a Franciscan of the Observance in the friary of Santa María in Barcelona. During the day he was employed in the kitchen, where his humility and prayerfulness witnessed to a deep desire for a life of intimacy with God; during the night he actively sought that intimacy in prayer. After his profession he was sent to the friary of Santa María de Jesús at Tortosa, where he was successively cook, porter, and mendicant. The cures he worked while out begging soon made him known to the entire population of the town. So many crowds besieged the friary daily begging his intercession for their ills that his superiors sent him under a false name to a remote community in the mountains, not far from the town of Orta. There Salvator spent most of the twenty-seven years of his religious life, but not in the obscurity that had been planned for him. Crowds, informed of his presence no one knew how, converged on the convent and demanded the humble Brother. In his usual way he enjoined them to go to Confession and Communion and then made the sign of the cross over them, and they were cured. Over two thousand pilgrims arrived every week. Again the friars complained of the disturbance caused by the crowds, and once again Br Salvator was sent to another house, this time Reus, where exactly the same thing happened. The crowds arrived apparently with certain knowledge of the Brother's presence at Reus. Eventually he returned to his first convent in Barcelona, where the prodigies continued. A friend there once warned him of the danger of vainglory. Salvator replied, "I am but a sack of straw, whose value remains the same whether it be in the attic, or in the basement, or in the stable!"

However famous he might be, however many people, royalty or commoners, came to see him, from Spain, Portugal, France, Br Salvator remained the same. He always walked barefoot, scourged himself daily, and kept long and rigorous fasts. He was especially devoted to Our Lady and to St Paul, who it is said appeared to him on several occasions, notably on his death-bed.

Salvator was sent by his superiors to Sardinia, where he fell seriously ill. He died at Cagliari in 1567, at the age of forty-seven. Venerated as a saint during his lifetime, he was eventually canonized in 1938.

See *AA.SS*, Mar., 2, pp. 665-894, for the biography by D. Serpi, promoter of the saint's cause; Léon, l, pp. 470-83.

BB John Thules and Roger Warren, *Martyrs* (1616)

John Thules was born at Whalley in Lancashire in 1568. His parents were William and Anne Thules, and his elder brother, Christopher, also became a priest. John was educated for the priesthood at Douai College, which was then in Reims, and ordained in Rome in March 1592.

Returning to England, he was taken prisoner in Northumberland around July 1593 but escaped from detention and took up work first in Essex and then in Lancashire. There he was once again arrested and committed to the county gaol at Lancaster. Among the Catholics imprisoned there at the time was one Roger Warren (usually known as Wrenno), a weaver. These two made their escape one evening from the prison during a mass break-out and walked all night, thinking that they had put a fair distance between themselves and the town. They had actually gone in a circle and were quite near it; they were re-arrested and made to appear at the Lent assizes soon after. John Thules was condemned for being a priest and exercising a priestly ministry in the country, Roger Warren for having harboured and assisted priests.

On their way to execution attempts were made to force them into a church, which the younger and stronger Warren managed to resist. They were offered their lives if they would take the Oath of Allegiance, but both refused to do so. Another attempt was made as Fr Thules was mounting the ladder, but again he refused. Roger Warren's rope broke as he was swung off the ladder, and he fell heavily to the ground. Quickly recovering, he knelt in prayer. Someone suggested to him that he had been providentially saved so that he might yet take the oath. He insisted that he had not changed his mind and this time ran to the ladder and went up as fast as he could. The sheriff asked why he was in such a hurry. "If you had seen what I have just now seen, you would be as much in haste to die as I now am," replied the martyr.

They were hanged, drawn, and quartered on 18 March 1616 and beatified in 1987. Three criminals were dealt with in the same way before Warren, and all the bodies were thrown together into the square so that Catholics should not be able to identify the remains of their martyrs.

Anstruther, 1, pp. 354-5, with further refs.

Bd Martha Le Bouteiller (1816-83)

Martha was born in the village of Percy in France on 2 December 1816 and entered the small community of St Marie Madeleine Postel (16 July) in 1841, at the age of twenty-five. She was not particularly gifted in any way, but she had a good constitution, a will to work, and a desire to serve God with all her heart.

The postulant was given the habit on 14 September 1842, aptly receiving the name of Martha, for her life was to be one of service to the community and its dependants in the everyday running of the house. During her year of novitiate she was sent to help the small group of Sisters at the sanctuary of Our Lady at La Chapelle-sur-Vire. There, while washing the linen in the icy river, she fell in. Her legs were so affected as a result that she could hardly walk and suffered silently for a whole year.

Professed in 1844, she worked first in the kitchen, then in the garden and on the farm and in the ill-lit cellars where she looked after the cider and other provisions, earning the nickname of "Sister Cider." During the Franco-Prussian war the children were sent away and the convent opened to the French soldiers, especially the wounded, who would otherwise have had little shelter or attention. Somehow Sr Martha managed to feed all the many extra mouths for almost six months.

A special relationship beween Mother Placide and Sr Martha was an enormous source of strength to the superior, but to Sr Martha, bearing the burden of two, it could spell much suffering. The years of Sr Marie's ascendancy over the community (see St Placide Viel, 4 Mar.), the lack of understanding on the part of some, and the constant absences of the superior, were a source of pain to her. Instinctively she understood Mother Placide's actions; intuitively she grasped what others did not. When Mother Placide was at the point of death, Sr Martha could not join her Sisters in giving her a final embrace. It was perhaps her only moment of weakness, if one can call it that. Her own death followed six years later in 1883. She was at her work when she collapsed; she was anointed and died in one of the parlours close at hand.

Like Mother Placide, Sr Martha had fully imbibed the evangelical spirit of the Congregation from its foundress. She had accomplished nothing in an external sense; she had merely lived the life as laid down by St Marie Madeleine Postel and had grown to full stature loving God and her neighbour. Hers was a radiant example of fidelity lived out in utter simplicity, a model of sanctity within the reach of all. She was beatified by Pope John Paul II on 4 November 1990.

L. Canuet, *Une fille de Sainte Marie-Madeleine Postel et de la Vénérée Mère Placide, Soeur Marthe, 1816-1883* (1931).

R.M.
St Tetricus, bishop of Langres, Burgundy (572)
St Fridian, bishop of Lucca, Tuscany (588)
St Leobardus, hermit of Tours (*c.* 593)
St Tetricus, bishop of Auxerre, Burgundy (706)
St Vahan Goltnaci, martyr at Rusafah in Syria (737)
St Anselm, bishop of Lucca, Mantua (1086)

ST JOSEPH
Gold-handled carpenter's square, silver blade and Madonna lily,
on blue field

19

ST JOSEPH (First Century)

Not until the fifteenth century was there a liturgical feast of St Joseph observed in Rome, and not until the sixteenth century was there a feast authorized for the Universal Church. For all that, it is fair to say that devotion to St Joseph has never been wanting.

The Church was fully preoccupied with the great christological controversies during the first five centuries, yet there appeared as early as 150 the *Protevangelium of James*, the first apocryphal writing to attempt to flesh out Matthew's and Luke's accounts of the infancy of Jesus. Between the second and eighth centuries four more apocryphal gospels followed. Although historically worthless, they were to influence both the East and the West up to the Middle Ages, and even today one can still see contemporary statues of St Joseph holding the lily associated with him in these apocryphal tales. These writings witnessed to an interest in the human setting of the Holy Family and of the characters that appear in the canonical Gospels.

St Joseph was commemorated in the Eastern Church during the Christmas season, and he had his place also in the Advent liturgies of the West. The Copts observed a feast of St Joseph in the seventh century. He began to appear in some martyrologies of the ninth century, notably those of Reichenau and of Oengus the Culdee (11 Mar.), but not in the liturgical calendars until the tenth century and then only in local celebrations. In England a feast was observed at Ely, Winchester, and Worcester before 1100. The thirteenth and fourteenth centuries showed an increase in liturgical devotion as Servites and Franciscans observed a feast on 19 March here and there in Europe. With the accession to the papacy of the Franciscan Pope Sixtus IV in 1479, the feast on 19 March was introduced into the Roman Church. In the following century it was extended to the Universal Church by means of the revised Breviary and Missal enjoined by the Council of Trent, which ensured Roman liturgical usage everywhere.

These liturgical developments owed much to spiritual writers and popular preachers, some still dependent on the apocryphal writings, such as Ludolph of Saxony and the anonymous *Meditations on the Life of Christ*, but others more concerned with the scriptural and doctrinal implications of the position of Joseph within the Holy Family. Jean Gerson, the most articulate of those who sought more recognition of St Joseph, was followed by Cardinal d'Ailly, Isidor of Isolani, and Suarez, to name the more prominent propagators of his cult. St

Teresa's (15 Oct.) devotion to St Joseph was carried by the discalced Carmelites to France, where in the seventeenth and eighteenth centuries Bérulle, Olier, St Francis de Sales (24 Jan.), the Jesuits, and the Franciscans all contributed to its spread. From Spain also the devotion spread to the New World; already in 1555 St Joseph was made the patron of Mexico, while in 1678 he was named Protector of the Missions in China. During the seventeenth and eighteenth centuries many new congregations took St Joseph as their patron, and innumerable churches and convents were dedicated to him. At the close of the First Vatican Council in 1870, Pius IX made him Patron of the Universal Church, while John XXIII inserted his name in the Roman Canon (1962) in the course of the Second Vatican Council. The feast of the Patronage of St Joseph, initially celebrated by the Carmelite Order, was extended to the Universal Church in 1847 but was abolished in 1956 and replaced by that of St Joseph the Worker (1 May). St Joseph now holds an eminent place both in the hearts of the faithful and in the official liturgy of the Church.

As will be remarked again on the feast of the Annunciation, the gospel material does not provide a *verbatim* report of what happened, above all during Jesus' early years. The evangelists are concerned to present their views of salvation history, and these are but loosely hinged to a biographical framework. Writing some time during the latter half of the first century or early in the second, they were living in the time after the resurrection and had experienced the working of the Holy Spirit within the community. Their convictions concerning the person of Jesus were reflected back into their accounts: he is the risen Christ "who in the order of the spirit, the spirit of holiness that was in him, was proclaimed Son of God in all his power" (Rom. 1:4). Lacking concrete detail, they construct events to bear a theological rather than a biographical significance. They use Old Testament incidents, or merely Old Testament echoes whose primary resonances illuminate and subserve a Christian understanding of salvation achieved, and they see in the past prefigurements of their own contemporary situation.

Luke gives his account from Mary's standpoint, while Matthew's concentrates on Joseph, but the two evangelists are agreed on some basic points: Jesus is conceived without human intercourse by Mary through the action of the Holy Spirit and is accepted by Joseph as his son, thus receiving from him an extrinsic but legal paternity, through which he is recognized as of the race of David and a lawful claimant to messianic status. Matthew's genealogy of the Christ situates him within the history of the chosen people. He begins with Abraham and through the Davidic line reaches Joseph, but there he abandons the formula: "Eliud was the father of Eleazar, Eleazar the father of Matthan, Matthan the father of Jacob; and Jacob was the father of Joseph . . . " adding in apposition to Joseph, "the husband of Mary, of whom was born Jesus who is called Christ." He follows this with an explanation of the strange appearance of Mary in a list of male progenitors.

186

Mary is betrothed to Joseph, but he had not yet taken her to his house for the marriage when it became clear that she was pregnant. Given the quasi-marital rights conferred by betrothal, the situation was serious. The Book of Deuteronomy (22:13-21) deals expressly with the infidelity of a betrothed woman should her husband tax her with misconduct and publicly defame her, and it prescribes stoning if she is found guilty. However, given the ease with which divorce was obtainable and in later times the several grounds on which a husband might divorce his wife, there were other ways than that laid down in Deuteronomy or in Numbers (5:11-31) to deal with the situation. Being an upright man, Joseph felt he had to terminate the engagement and so "banish the evil from among you," as Deuteronomy has it. Uprightness required him equally to do no injustice to a fellow-Israelite. When Tamar was condemned as a prostitute, it was Judah who proved to be unjust. When God decreed that the son of their adulterous union should die, it was not because Bathsheba had acted sinfully and was to be punished—it was David. Joseph then was unwilling publicly to defame Mary, whose fidelity he could not do other than question but whose innocence remained a possibility. With the aid of two witnesses, he could quietly serve her with a writ of divorce. This course he decided to follow.

Using the Genesis story of the patriarch Joseph, Matthew now exploits the tradition of the "man of dreams" and by means of it shows that Joseph is not only deflected from his decision by a supernatural revelation of the nature of Mary's pregnancy but is given specific instructions about his role in the unfolding of a divine plan. He is expressly bidden to take Mary to his own home, thus completing the marriage arrangements; he is told to name the child, thus becoming its father. From then on the responsibility for the welfare of mother and child rests with him. He will be no ordinary child: "She has conceived what is in her by the Holy Spirit . . . and he will save his people from their sins." Moreover, this conception and birth had been predicted by Isaiah and will realize the presence of God among his people.

The character and history of Herod the Great make it not implausible that there had been a massacre of infants on his orders, but the evangelist is concerned to present the events of his second chapter as a replay of Israel's Exodus experience. First the child is proclaimed Messiah king by the Magi, who take up the proclamation of the one-time *Magos* Balaam (Num. 24:17): "A star from Jacob takes the leadership, a sceptre arises from Israel." The Magi, described in terms drawn from the sixtieth chapter of Isaiah, prefigure all those Gentiles who have accepted and will accept the King of the Jews, a title Herod considered his own. Its usurpation by another rouses not only his murderous instincts but also the antipathy of the whole of Jerusalem, a pointer to the opposition that will one day be openly manifested toward the Messiah. In another dream, Joseph is instructed to escape into Egypt with the child, for Herod is determined to have him killed.

Like the patriarch of old, Joseph takes refuge in Egypt until such time as he is recalled by the providence that had sent him there. Pharaoh also had sought to destroy the Hebrew male population, and Moses, who escaped the first massacre, later had to hide again from him in the land of Midian. Now the life of Christ, the new Moses, is likewise threatened. On the death of Pharaoh, the Lord instructed Moses to leave his refuge, "for all those who wanted to kill you are dead." Joseph is told in yet another dream: "Go back to the land of Israel for those who sought the life of the child are dead." So Joseph arose and together with the child and his mother left for the promised land, thus re-living the Exodus: "Out of Egypt I have called my son."

Although children were not obliged to go up to Jerusalem at the Passover before the age of thirteen, the family seems to have done so regularly together. It was on one of these occasions that Jesus, when he was twelve years old and presumably already into the thirteenth year, marking his majority, remained behind in the Temple while his parents returned home to Nazareth in separate groups. On coming back to the Temple they found him among the teachers, and Mary upbraids him for his lack of consideration: "Your father and I have been anxiously looking for you." By giving Joseph the title of father, she makes it clear that he had indeed fulfilled the duties of fatherhood as the angel of the Lord had commanded; for this reason alone he merited the consideration of his son. The boy's reply shows that the consciousness of his divine sonship and of his special vocation is already stirring his adolescent enthusiasm. He is constrained by his own destiny: "Did you not realize that I must be about my Father's concerns?" They do not understand, and he accepts that the time is not ripe. Since Joseph stands in for his heavenly Father, Jesus may not begin his mission without a parental blessing. He returns with Joseph and Mary to Nazareth and is subject to them. When he did emerge from these hidden years, Joseph was apparently dead, his work accomplished. The Christ whom we meet in the Gospels was thus formed by Joseph, together with Mary, in the family home, through the discipline of work and worship in the village of Nazareth.

St Joseph is many things to many persons. St Bernard (20 Aug.) says disarmingly: "When we do not know how to pray we turn to St Joseph." For her part, St Teresa of Avila thought that there was no better teacher of prayer: "Whoever wants a master to teach him how to pray, let him take this glorious saint as guide and he will not go astray," but his care extends into every area of existence: "To other saints our Lord has given power to help in one sort of need, but this glorious saint, as I know by experience, helps us in every need. I cannot remember ever having asked him for anything which he did not obtain for me." Considered to have had a most holy death in the presence of Jesus and Mary, he has long been invoked as the patron of a happy death, but his most glorious title to veneration remains that of Guardian of the Universal Church.

Dict.Sp., 8, 1289-316; H. Strack and P. Billerbeck, *Kommentar zum Neuen Testament aus Talmud und Midrasch* (1926-61), 1, pp. 304-5; F. L. Filas, *The Man Nearest to Christ* (1944); D. J. Harrington, *The Gospel of Matthew* (1991); R. E. Brown, *The Birth of the Messiah* (1993); *O.D.S.*, (1997), pp. 274-5.

The prevalence of the figure of St Joseph in art is directly related to devotion to him, as it gained ground from the fourteenth century onward. The majority of Italian masters from then on included St Joseph in their representations of the Holy Family, as did the Spanish and Flemish artists, although the Virgin always retains a position of prominence. Sympathetic portrayals are those by Murillo in two versions of *The Two Trinities*, an earlier one (*c.* 1640) in Stockholm and a later (*c.* 1670-2) in the National Gallery, London. In this unusual subject, the Father and the dove of the Holy Spirit are above, and the Virgin and St Joseph below, with the Christ Child common to both groups. The most impressive contemporary monument to St Joseph is the basilica in Montreal, Canada, which owes its inspiration to the saintly Brother Andrew Bessette (6 Jan.).

The Martyrs of Mar Saba (797)

Stephen the Wonder-worker (not the Stephen commemorated on 31 Mar.), known also as *The Poet,* was a hymn writer in the tradition of the monks of Mar Saba. At the request of the *igumen* Basil he wrote a description of the martyrdom of twenty of his fellow-monks at the hands of the Arabs, which he himself had witnessed. It was not the first time that the community of Mar Saba had suffered martyrdom. Forty-four of their number had been massacred by the Persian armies in 614 (16 May), but the community was once again flourishing (and indeed exists to this day).

Syria and Palestine had been lost to the empire ever since the defeat of the emperor Heraclius in 636 at the hands of the Persians, but by the end of the century Persian rule had given way to Arab domination. At the end of the eighth century the Arab capital had moved from Damascus to Baghdad. Its caliphs, already remote, were more concerned with their far-flung empire than with law and order in Palestine. The Arabs who were devastating the country, burning monasteries and despoiling churches, were probably no more than marauding groups that could operate with impunity. Mar Saba seems to have been initially spared, as these groups succumbed to internal dissensions, but the community lived in great fear. Yet they considered that it would be an act of cowardice to run away, given the Lord's saying that his disciples should not fear those who could only kill the body. They were conscious too that the monastery would soon be rendered uninhabitable for future generations should they abandon it to inevitable pillage.

Combining forces, a group of some sixty armed Arabs approached the monastery early one morning. Some Fathers attempted to divert them, explaining their peaceful vocation as hermits who had abandoned the world. They had in the past extended their hospitality to Arabs and were prepared to do so now. However, these men only wanted money. The monks protested that they had none, which so provoked the Arabs that they let loose a hail of arrows, wounding some thirty monks. The attackers then made for the cells, which they set on fire. Seeing a party coming to the rescue, they made off with what spoil they could.

A few days later, as the Fathers were keeping the vigil of Palm Sunday in church, there arrived two sturdy monks covered with sweat from their efforts to get there, sent by the Fathers of the Old *Laura* to warn them that the Arabs were coming in even greater numbers that night. Two other monks arrived later, one an old Father with a companion, bringing a letter from the Fathers of the monastery of St Euthymius to say that a group of Arabs was on the way. Two groups of Arabs were then planning to converge on Mar Saba.

As some pages are missing from the MS we do not know what happened between Sunday and Holy Thursday. The story takes up with the Arabs attacking the community of monks on the Thursday. They fell on them with every imaginable weapon, including stones, and not one was spared some more or less severe injury. The victims were herded into the church, but some, unable to endure such violence, escaped into the caves or mountain clefts. A few succeeded in remaining completely hidden. John, the guestmaster, escaped; he had already sustained several wounds and was almost half-dead, but they recognized him and seized and dragged him by his feet from the top of the cliff over the rocky and stony paths down to the church, where they dumped him with barely a breath of life left. That was to be finally snuffed out by the fumes of the fire, which also destroyed his companions.

Sergius was a Damascene, perhaps the sacristan, certainly under the personal direction of the *igumen*, who knew where the sacred vessels had been buried. As he saw the wounded monks being driven into the church, he suspected they would be tortured and so escaped, fearing he might not be strong enough to keep the secret. He was quite a long way off when the guards posted for the purpose of tracking down the fugitives spotted him. Sticking their sword-points into his sides they tried to force him back to the monastery. In a spurt of courage he replied steadily, "I shall not return just because you order me to. You ordered us into church today but it was neither to pray nor to worship God." They were astonished at his spirit but keeping up the threats went on ordering him to return. As he would not yield, they tore off his clothes and threatened to cut off his head, but he retorted, "I shall not go back at your bidding, but if you want to cut off my head and Christ allows you to do so, there is nothing to stop you." At which he bared his neck to the sword, as another Brother captured with him later related. Sergius was struck three times with the sword. Heavy stones were piled on his body so that it was completely broken by their weight. He was thus the first to die.

Some of the Fathers hid in a cave which the Arab scouts suspected was a hiding-place. One of their number, Patrick, went out and gave himself up and tried to persuade the Arabs that he was the only one to have taken refuge there. He ran toward the church to draw them off; there he was to perish with the others. Most of the monks had been forced into the church or into the adjoining guesthouse, where the Arab leader now demanded money in exchange for their lives and the safety of their church. The monks protested that they did not have the sum demanded nor ever would have anything like it; they offered all they had—their clothes and whatever might be found in their cells. Angered by this answer, the Arabs laid hold of the bursar and put him against the wall with his arms extended in the form of a cross, the men holding their bows taut and arrows at the ready. However many the threats, the monks stood by their statement that they had no money or valuables.

Stephen speaks often of the mutual charity that bound these men together, instancing, in addition to Patrick's noble act, their protection of Thomas the doctor. He was the *igumen* of the Old *Laura* at the time and was known by name to the Arabs, who ordered the monks to identify him. No one would do so. Having had enough of their resistance, the Arabs then herded the Fathers into a passage off the church, which had had an exit into the guesthouse in the time of St Saba but which had subsequently been sealed. At its entrance they piled thorns and brushwood and set them on fire so that the monks within were suffocated by smoke. At intervals their tormentors would summon them to come out through the flames, question them again about hidden treasures and drive them back. They would then pile on more fuel. At last, seeing that they could in no way elicit information about valuables from any of them, they pillaged the cells, guesthouse, and church and then made off.

Sergius died by the sword; eighteen others died of suffocation; to their number must be added another monk who died soon after, having refused to be treated by a surgeon.

AA.SS., Mar., 3, pp. 2-12,* gives Stephen's Greek narrative, and a Latin translation is on pp. 167-78.

Bd John Buralli (1208-89)

Giovanni Buralli, the seventh minister general of the Franciscans, was born of a humble family at Parma in Italy in 1208 and was educated by his priest uncle. He was already teaching logic in the city when at the age of twenty-five he became a follower of St Francis (4 Oct.), whose ideals of poverty and simplicity he clung to all his life. He was sent to Paris for further studies and, after he had been ordained, to teach and preach in Bologna, Naples, and Rome.

Francis' followers, even during his lifetime, could never agree on the practical implementation of the founder's vision of a life of poverty as a way of imitating the poor man of Nazareth. For some, especially among his first disciples, there was no doubt that poverty was to be a literal fact in the life of a friar; allied to this poverty was a life of prayer often taking an eremitical form, which nevertheless allowed for an apostolate of the word. For others, poverty was likewise important but ultimately unsustainable in the radical form lived by Francis. If preaching was to form part of the life, studies were necessary; if studies had to be pursued, a cave or a hut was an unpropitious setting for the purpose. Franciscan life evolved toward the friary, in which a community of friars could pursue their studies and for which some revenue, if only in the form of gifts, was necessary. However, from time to time a nostalgia for what seemed the authentic Franciscan ideal would take hold of individuals or groups of friars. In the time of John Buralli, such a group existed and was known as the "Spirituals." They had been harshly treated by Crescentius of Iesi, who as minister general did not call a general chapter in 1247 as he should have done, perhaps to avoid a confrontation. Pope Innocent IV intervened and summoned the chapter at Lyon. Crescentius did not appear, and John Buralli, who was accepted by all the parties, though claimed by the Spirituals as one of themselves, was elected in his place.

John's views were in fact moderate, though he tended to come down on the side of the Spirituals. One of his first gestures was to approach this group and invite them back into the fold. To them he appeared indeed as a deliverer from the tyranny of Crescentius, from whom they might expect a return to primitive Franciscanism, but as one of the Spirituals expressed it with some realism, he had really come too late. Friaries had already been built, relaxations and privileges had become too entrenched to be dislodged. For one vexed question, though, John sought an immediate solution: since the friaries could not hold funds, these might be invested in the Holy See and administered by procurators—a statute authorized by Pope Innocent IV.

John Buralli determined to visit all the friaries in Europe to see for himself how the Rule was being observed, how he could restore discipline where needed, and how he could heal the divisions. He set out in 1248 on foot, dressed in his coarse habit, with a few companions. Outside the friaries he would never allow his position to become known. He was so unassuming that on coming to a house he often helped the Brothers with the meanest chores. Brother Salimbene, who was very close to him, describes him as physically robust, with a sweet expression, polished manners, and full of charity. The minister began his general visitation in England, then crossed over to France, visiting Burgundy and Provence, and then went south to Spain. In 1249 he presided at his first general chapter in Metz, at which he insisted on the observance of the Constitutions and acceptance of the Roman Breviary and Missal. He would not add to the Constitutions, thinking that the existing regulations were quite adequate. He sought rather to protect the Franciscans from outside authorities such as papal legates or cathedral chapters electing friars to episcopal posts without reference to the Order's own powers of jurisdiction.

His work was interrupted in 1249 by an order from Pope Innocent IV to go to the East to help the cause of reunion. After two years in Constantinople he returned to deal with the business of the Order, in particular a storm of hostility that had broken out in Paris. William of Saint-Amour, a secular doctor of the university, had whipped up feeling against both Mendicant Orders and their strange conception of poverty, attacking them in his pamphlet *De novissimorum temporum periculis*. He suggested that the friars were the false prophets announcing the arrival of Antichrist. The Franciscan minister general addressed the university professors, disarming them with his gentleness and persuasiveness; his adversary, who was expected to deliver a riposte, merely blurted out "God bless you."

Two rulings obtained by John Buralli from Pope Innocent IV contributed greatly to the spiritual influence of the friars in the Middle Ages. Franciscan oratories were henceforth to become collegiate churches, which meant that the friars could there exercise a full priestly ministry, thus attracting the devout laity, whom they would encourage and direct in the pursuit of holiness; benefactors affiliated to the friars could share in the suffrages of the Order, which would act as an incentive for its support.

John governed the Order for ten years. His personal integrity, transparency, and simplicity endeared him to most. In the long run his sympathies with the Spirituals told against him. The "large observance" judged that with him the Order would not develop in the direction they wished. Whether intentionally labelled or not, he was delated to the pope as being a Joachimite. He may well have been strongly attracted to Joachim of Fiore, given his own love of simplicity and humility, his abhorrence of legalism and power-seeking, but the Franciscan Gerard of Borgo San Donnino, who had written the *Introduction to the Everlasting Gospel*, which went far beyond the positions held by Joachim himself, had just been condemned in 1256, and there were lively memories of this in 1257. John Buralli sensed that he no longer had the support of the whole Order to continue as minister general, and it may be that the papal Curia was also urging him to step down. He did so in the chapter of that year. Asked to say whom he would recommend as his successor, he suggested Bonaventure (14 July), who was in fact elected and became known as the second founder of the Franciscans. Buralli was subjected to an interrogation concerning his supposed Joachimite beliefs and was acquitted. John had thirty more years before him. This period may have been the happiest in his career. He retired to the hermitage of Grecchio (where St Francis had prepared the first Christmas crib), leaving it only occasionally at the request of the pope.

Hearing that the Greeks were abandoning the union agreed to in 1274, John, now eighty years of age but armed with the approval of Pope Nicholas IV, offered to go and discuss the situation with them. When he reached Camerino, he realized that he could not go on. He died there on 19 March 1289. Many miracles were reported at his tomb, and his cult was approved in 1777.

Salimbene's text is published in *M. G. H.*, 32. There are two biographies in Italian: B. Affó (1777) and L. da Parma (1909). See also Léon, 1, pp. 493-513; J. Moorman: *A History of the Franciscan Order* (1968).

Bd Mark of Montegallo (1425-96)

Marco, son of Chiari de Marchio d'Ascoli, was born at Fonditore, a commune of Montegallo in Italy. He studied under the humanist Enoch d'Ascoli and later at the universities of Perugia and Bologna, graduating as a doctor of law and medicine. From 1448 he practised medicine in Ascoli. Urged by his father, he married Chiara de Tibaldeschi in 1451, but a year later, when his father had died, the two separated by mutual consent to follow their respective religious vocations. She entered the convent of Poor Clares in Ascoli, while he joined the Friars Minor.

Mark did his novitiate at the friary of L'Eremita at Valdisasso near Fabriano and almost immediately after was appointed superior of Santa Maria de San Severino. It was here that he heard a voice saying to him, "Go out, Brother Mark, and preach about love." This became his dominant theme as he tramped up and down the country for forty years, from Sicily to the valley of the Po. His zeal was indefatigable, and he often combined healing of bodies with that of consciences. Everywhere he went he tried to make peace between the many factions that were at this time tearing the country apart.

He was above all concerned for the poor. In common with Bd Bernardino of Feltre (28 Sept.), he promoted the *montes pietatis*, originally pawn-shops which made small loans to the poor upon pledged objects but which later developed into banks for money loans at minimal or zero rates of interest. In order to set up this kind of bank in Vicenza, Mark preached there with such eloquence that all the money required was collected in a day, and the office was built and launched within the year. Besides the house at Vicenza, other loan-banks and hostels were started at the friar's instigation, notably one at Fabriano which a friend of his built and another at Perugia, founded by St James of the Marches (28 Nov.).

Kind as Brother Mark was to others, he was merciless to himself. Even on his journeys he omitted none of his customary penances, often spending most of the night in prayer. At Camerino, where the plague was rife, he assured the people it would cease if they repented. They flocked to Confession, and the plague did indeed come to an end.

During his term as provincial of the Marches, he incorporated into the province the new monastery of Poor Clares, founded at Camerino by Julius Caesar Varani. There he installed the prince's daughter, Bd Baptista Varani (7 June), and other nuns from the convent at Urbino. It is likely that he undertook the spiritual direction of Bd Baptista on the death of Bd Peter of Mogliano (25 July), who had succeeded him as provincial, as one of her letters to him is extant. She also dedicated to him her spiritual autobiography and her *Treatise on the Mental Sufferings of our Lord*.

Brother Mark preached the Lenten sermons for the second time in Vicenza in 1497 with particular fervour. About the middle of Lent he was seen to gather all his little belongings together into a bundle, as if he were going on a voyage. That very night he was taken ill. As he lay dying he asked to have the Passion read to him, and at the words, "bowing his head he gave up the spirit," he yielded his own soul to God. It was the feast of St Joseph.

He was buried in the friary church of St Blaise. When the community moved to the city, his remains were moved to a chapel in the new church dedicated to him.

AA.SS., Mar., 3, pp. 71-74; Léon, 1, pp. 530-4 (1885); *Dict.Sp.*, 10, 283-4. *Bibl.SS.* 8, 739-40.

Bd Marcel Callo, *Martyr* (1921-45)

Marcel Callo was born in Rennes in Brittany on 6 December 1921, the second of nine children born to Felicité Marie-Josèphe and Marcel Callo, into a family of modest means. Madame Callo hoped that her first-born son, Jean, would be a priest, and he was in fact to be ordained in Rennes shortly after Marcel had been taken to Germany in 1943.

Marcel was not a brilliant pupil. He was capable but tended to work in spurts. Despite his lack of application, he obtained the necessary certificates to enable him later to take up an apprenticeship in the town. He could be a bit of a tease and had his normal share of cuffs in the classroom. An altar-server for seven years, he became a member of the Eucharistic Crusade, which left its stamp on his spirituality. The Eucharist always remained central to his life. At the age of ten-and-a-half he made his solemn Communion and was confirmed a year later. At home he was affectionate and trusting, particularly toward his mother, whose faith and understanding helped him toward spiritual maturity. The Scout movement, which he joined in 1933, touched off his enthusiasm, and he remained a Scout at heart all his life.

Apprenticed to a local printer in 1934, Marcel was thrown into a milieu that caused him some anguish. An upright and pious family life and the healthy atmosphere of the Scouts had not prepared him for the salacious or blasphemous conversation of a hardened adult world. He kept up regular Confession and attendance at daily Mass and gradually came to terms with his surroundings. Despite his hours of work at the printshop, he continued to perform the heavy work of the house to ease his mother's burden, handing over his salary to her for the upkeep of the family.

A year later, at the age of fourteen, he faced a momentous decision. Abbé Martinais, who was recruiting to the *Jeunesse Ouvrière Chrétienne* (Young Christian Workers) young men of a more spiritual outlook to counter what he saw as an unfortunate militancy for workers' rights divorced from its apostolic aims, invited Marcel to join his section. Marcel, who was genuinely happy with the Scouts, was reluctant to do so. However, both the priest and his mother, who was unhappy with Marcel's frequent outings with the Scouts, prevailed. Unable to cut himself off totally, Marcel decided to be both Scout and *Jociste*. In time, as he grew into the ideals of the J.O.C. and became more and more committed, he let his affiliation with the Scouts lapse. From then on, his whole desire was to bring his worker-comrades to Christ and Christ to them. The subsequent drama of his life and its dénouement in the concentration camp at Mauthausen were but the consequences of his apostolic zeal and devotion to duty.

On becoming president of the group, Marcel was able to give full scope to his zeal and to his undoubted gifts of leadership. He became the friend and confidant of all his group members, the soul of all their activities. Abbé Martinais testified to the complete reorientation of the group effected by Marcel Callo: "Under [his] presidency the section became a centre of intense Jociste life, a group of numerous and active young men," though it was not easy to uphold evangelical standards in a milieu that regarded the Christian worker as a traitor. Marcel's formula of consecration shows the motivating love behind all his activity: "O Christ, I want to become more and more a J.O.C. guide, a pure and joyous and first-rate combatant. In my great love for my brothers, I want to win young workers. I want to live in you, Jesus. I want to pray with you. For your sake I want to give all my strength and all my time, in all the circumstances of my life."

During eight years of *Jociste* activity, 1935-1943, Marcel Callo gave his utmost, but he also received much from the movement. The help and guidance of Abbé Martinais was never lacking; there were regular retreats and days of recollection, but above all there was the doctrine of the Mystical Body of Christ that sustained the *Jociste* movement and inspired its best workers. That Marcel was among these, there could be no doubt, as his comrades were the first to say, "I have never heard anyone say anything nasty of him"; "No one ever had anything with which to reproach him"; "He was a model for us"; "I did not see any failing in him. True, he was lively and he did get carried away, but it did not last. He was the first to acknowledge that he had gone too far." At twenty-one years of age, Marcel became engaged to Marguerite, a fellow-*Jociste*. They planned to announce their engagement on the occasion of his brother Jean's ordination.

Meanwhile, by 1943 the war had closed in on Rennes, with Allied bombing of munitions factories, depots, and railway lines. The first casualty to affect the Callo family was the death of Madeleine, the third child, in one of the raids. Simultaneously, Marcel was requisitioned for work in Germany. It would have been possible to go into hiding and evade the summons, but that would have exposed his father and his brother, just about to be ordained, to reprisals. In the end he decided that God was calling him to a missionary task in Germany. He left Rennes on 19 March for Thuringia. Some eighty Bretons were among a group of Frenchmen who were distributed in the barracks of the largest camp at Zella-Mehlis. The French were assigned to the Walther armaments factory, where 3,000 to 3,500 workers were employed for ten to eleven hours a day. The rest of the time they spent in the barracks, cold and hungry. The deportees or prisoners, whatever their nationality, were treated as a subhuman species by the guards. In the year preceding Marcel's arrival there had been one Mass and one collective absolution. Adding to his chagrin were the volunteer French prostitutes who had followed the deportees. Marcel arrived physically and morally depressed, suffering from food-poisoning. A finger had been damaged in a machine; he was plagued with toothache, migraines, and the colic. His wallet was stolen, and he had news that his family had been bombed out of the house where they lived. The first three months thus proved a difficult initiation, but he recovered and became the Marcel Callo of old, renewing his fervour and determination to win others for Christ. He referred to this time of trial in one of his letters later: "The two months after my arrival were extremely hard. I had no taste for anything. I was without feeling. I was conscious of opting out little by little. Suddenly Christ made me snap out of it. He made me understand that what I was doing was not good. He told me to get on and see to my comrades. Then my *joie de vivre* returned."

There were other *Jocistes* among the deportees and in other camps in the region. Soon they were in touch with each other planning their various apostolates. Marcel began organizing Masses with a German priest who knew French and could hear Confessions. He brought others to make their Easter duties and had soon arranged a monthly Mass to which the deportees and prisoners could go. His *Jociste* group met in the woods. There were other groups and other activities: the *Amicale française de Zella-Melhis*, to whose theatrical section Marcel belonged; the football team in which he played. He taught his comrades other games, always to provide healthy distractions and to build up a network of contacts to enable news of Masses to circulate. Meanwhile the Gestapo were following events and probably reading his many letters. Clandestine associations had been forbidden, and inevitably the day came when the Gestapo pounced. The occasion was provided by the list of *Jociste* leaders found on the Vallée brothers, *Jocistes* themselves, who had been arrested. Marcel's name was on the list.

When asked why he had been arrested the Gestapo replied, "He is too much of a Catholic." Marcel asked a companion to write to his family and say that he had been arrested because of his Catholic Action, and he himself wrote, "You know how this accident came about. Moreover, I expected it." With eleven other *Jocistes* he was sent in April 1944 to the prison of Gotha, where he remained until October. Hard labour was imposed, but there were moments of joy. Letters were sent, parcels received. They heard of the invasion of Normandy. Once they were able to receive the Blessed Sacrament. Marcel exclaimed, "Communion. Immense joy!" After July 1944 there were no further letters. In his last one to his family, his faith is undimmed: "Happily, I have a Friend who does not leave me for a moment and can support me when things

197

are difficult or too much. With him, all can be borne. How grateful I am to Christ for having marked out for me the way in which I now am. What fine days I have to offer him. I offer all my suffering and difficulties for you all, my dear parents, my little fiancée, for Jean, that his ministry may be fruitful, for all my friends and comrades. Yes, it is good and a source of strength to be suffering for those one loves."

The thought that he should have to pay the ultimate penalty seems not to have surfaced in Marcel's letters. On the contrary, he often spoke of his return and of the prospect of having his own family. The transfer to the concentration camps of Flossenburg and then Mauthausen in October 1944, however, can have left him in no doubt of the final outcome. In the former a hundred bodies were burned every day, and the scent of burnt flesh pervaded the camp; the living were no more than walking skeletons. On 26 October he was sent to Güsen I, a camp of twenty-one hectares housing twenty thousand prisoners, where he spent ten hours a day sorting rivets for airplanes in an airless underground factory. In November he was transferred to Güsen II, where the conditions were even worse. A short spell of four to five hours sleep was terminated with whips. There followed a two-hour wait for some black liquid and an endless roll-call in the freezing cold. This was followed by twelve-hour shifts in the underground factory. Marcel had lost his glasses and could not even see where he was going. Any awkwardness was regarded as attempted sabotage and punished by twenty-five lashes. Most victims doubled up after four or five lashes and were then kicked mercilessly. Marcel underwent this punishment four times, but never swore at his guards, as most of the others did. From December onward the food was no more than beetroot leaves and unwashed potato peelings. One mess-tin of soup was passed round six men. By now Marcel was suffering from oedema and attacked by boils in addition to his chronic stomach trouble. He prayed continually and was prepared to share his paltry ration with others. He attempted to rally his companions: "Christ is with us. We must not give in. God is looking after us."

Suffering from chest pains, Marcel was admitted to the infirmary for a first stay from 5 to 20 January 1945. There might be unnoticed corpses among the five assigned to a single bed; forty to fifty died every day. He had to return to the infirmary later, this time to die. There the sick were left naked in temperatures well below freezing, suffering as they were from typhus and dysentery. According to the testimony of Colonel Tibodo, who watched over his last hours: "I only knew Marcel Callo for a few hours before his death. . . . Enough for me to state that this young man was much above the ordinary run of youths. He was still conscious when I knew him. There were latrines in the blocks. He fell in, but I was there and was able to take him back to his pallet without anybody seeing. It was then that I realized that he was not like other young men. I knew his name because he told me what it was, but unfortunately I do not remember the other things he said. If I remembered him—and I have been through several camps and have known many prisoners—it was because Marcel Callo had a really supernatural expression. What I am saying does not come anywhere near the reality. His look was rather a look of hope, hope in a new life.... It expressed a profound conviction that he was going toward a blissful end. It was an act of faith and hope in a better life. Never have I seen in a dying man an expression such as his.... He had the face of a saint."

Marcel Callo died on 19 March 1945, two years to the day since his departure for Germany. According to the statement of the camp doctor he died of tuberculosis, following on dysentery caused by weakness and starvation. As there was no longer any coal to fire the incinerators by the month of March, it may be concluded that his body was buried in a common grave by the side of the camp, where a cross now stands. He was beatified by Pope John Paul II on 4 October 1987.

Paul Gouyon, *Marcel Callo, Témoin d'une génération, 1921-1945* (1981); François Marion, *Marcel Callo, jociste et confesseur de la foi* (1961); Jean-Baptiste Jégo, *Un exemple, Marcel Callo* (1947) and *Marcel Callo, témoin du Christ* (1967). *Bibl.SS.*, Suppl. 1, p. 240.

R.M.
St John of Panaca, abbot of Spoleto in Umbria (sixth century)
St Alchmund, martyr of Lilleshall in Scotland (800)
Bd Isnard of Chiampo, O.P., of Pavia in Lombardy (1244)
Bd Andrew Gallerani, layman of Siena in Tuscany (1251)
Bd Sybillina Biscossi, recluse of Pavia (1367)

ST CUTHBERT
Gold cross, silver lions, on blue field

20

ST CUTHBERT, *Bishop* (*c.* 634-87)

At Pentecost in the year 563 St Columba (9 June) arrived in Scotland with twelve other Irish monks. There, already established in the region of Dalriada, was a community of Irish settlers, among them kinsmen of his own clan, who gave him land on the island of Iona to build a monastery and evangelize the surrounding country.

Ethelburga, the Christian daughter of Ethelbert of Kent, arrived in Northumbria in 625 as the bride of its king, Edwin, accompanied by the Roman Paulinus, to whom the region apparently owed its first formal evangelization. When Edwin was killed in 633 by the nominally Christian Cadwalla and the pagan Penda, Paulinus fled to Kent, taking the queen and her daughter. Cadwalla pressed home his victory by slaying the two royal princes, Osric and Eanfrid, who had assumed power after Edwin. Eanfrid's brother, Oswald (9 Aug.), then fought and vanquished Cadwalla and ruled Northumbria until 642. Conscious of the damage inflicted on the country's nascent Christianity, Oswald appealed to Iona for monks to carry on the work of evangelization initiated by Paulinus— but it would take the entire seventh century to achieve a fusion in the Northumbrian church of the two Christian traditions, Irish and Roman.

Iona sent a missionary who failed, and then St Aidan (31 August), a gentle monk who won the affection of all. Bede cannot find high enough praise for this poverty-loving, itinerant bishop, whose discretion, humility, self-denial, and zeal were surpassed only by his affability and approachability. Many other Irish monks worked with him to evangelize the country, but it is his spirituality that informs that of seventh-century Northumbria. Even Wilfrid (12 Oct.) is not entirely a stranger to it, though it is most genially expressed in Boisil, Eata, Herebert, and above all in Cuthbert. Bede has only one fault to find with Aidan: he did not observe Easter at the proper (*i.e.*, Roman) time, but allows that it cannot be held against him. On the island of Lindisfarne, the gift of Oswald, Aidan established a monastery on the Irish model within sight of the castle of Bamburgh, residence of the Northumbrian kings. While he lived, he was the sole bishop of all Northumbria, but his successors had to fit in with the political fortunes of its two halves, Bernicia and Deira, and the ecclesiastical divisions into three, and later, five dioceses.

Cuthbert, an Anglo-Saxon, was born about 634, the year Oswald began to rule. Nothing is known of his parents or the place of his birth, though casual remarks of his biographers suggest that he may have come from a well-to-do family. He became a monk not at Lindisfarne as might have been expected but at its daughter-house of Melrose, whose prior, Boisil, he must have known and esteemed, since it was his presence there that determined his choice of monastery. Abbot Eata was away at the time, and it was Boisil who in 651 welcomed the new candidate as he arrived on horseback and armed with a spear—perhaps a last flourish of worldly status. Boisil exclaimed spontaneously, "Here comes a servant of the Lord!" Boisil himself looked after the young man and, assured of his vocation, petitioned the abbot to allow him to receive the tonsure and join the community. Cuthbert not only set out to follow the regular monastic round but even to surpass the others; however, a cautionary aside shows that even he suspected his limitations: he would give up strong drink but not his meals on account of the manual work he was expected to do.

In 660 King Ahlfrith donated some land to Melrose for a new foundation at Ripon. Eata selected the still young Cuthbert for the founding team, appointing him to the sensitive post of guestmaster. Apart from the hagiographical conventions observed by the anonymous biographer and by Bede himself on the subject of angelical visitations, Cuthbert is shown entering with ease into relationships with his guests. Bede writes that he was affable and pleasant in his manner, and although his conversation revolved round the lives of the monks of old, he occasionally introduced autobiographical incidents, sometimes openly declared as such, sometimes disguised. This gift of easy exchange constituted one of his most endearing traits and most valuable pastoral assets. However, an openness to the enthusiasts for Roman practices did not at this point enter into Cuthbert's perspective or, more importantly, into Abbot Eata's. After long exposure to Roman customs in Kent, Gaul, and Rome, Wilfrid had returned to Northumbria in 658, zealous to convert his countrymen to Roman ways, especially to the Roman date of Easter. Alhfrith himself was convinced and wished his foundation at Ripon to conform to the Roman practice. Eata preferred to cede his place rather than capitulate. The monks of Melrose returned home, and Ripon was handed over to Wilfrid.

As in much of the century, the population was at the mercy of periodic visitations of the plague. Cuthbert fell victim to it on his return, and Boisil watched with concern while the whole community prayed for the young monk's cure. Hearing that there had been an all-night vigil for his recovery, Cuthbert got up from his sick-bed, convinced that such prayers could not but have been efficacious. In fact, he got up too soon and ever after suffered the consequences, but his youth probably pulled him through the worst. Boisil, himself dying of the plague, assured Cuthbert that he would never again fall victim to it but suggested that in the time remaining before his own death they should together study St John's Gospel. The picture of these two monks—Boisil, straining to communicate to the younger man his own zeal for holiness, Cuthbert, eager to assimilate the words of his master in Christ—is one of great poignancy. Bede says that they avoided controversial questions, concentrating rather on the things of "faith, working through love." In those last days Boisil spoke to Cuthbert too of his future career, even predicting his appointment as bishop— a prophecy the younger man carefully kept to himself.

On Boisil's death Cuthbert was appointed prior of Melrose. Perhaps in conscious imitation of Boisil, he combined a fervent monastic life with visits to the neighbouring hamlets, preaching and teaching. His openness and manifest goodness won many to Christ. A story related of him while he was prior of Melrose illustrates his single-minded pursuit of self-conquest through secret prayer and penance. He had been asked by the abbess of Coldingham to visit the community and speak to them about the things of God—Cuthbert always willingly met requests for help from women. While there, he spent the night in prayer as usual, but in the icy sea with the water right up to his neck. Another monk, curious to see what he was up to, had followed him and watched the proceedings. To his amazement, when Cuthbert came out of the water, two otters came to wipe him dry and warm his limbs, so that he was ready to attend the offices in church.

Cuthbert's biographers relate many miracles that compassion for the sufferings of others impelled him to perform, but the attraction to hidden prayer now began to dominate his life. The Life by a monk of Lindisfarne says that he had made an attempt to become a solitary while still at Melrose, but that Eata, on becoming abbot of Lindisfarne after the departure of Colman (18 Feb.) with those other Irish monks not prepared to accept the Roman date of Easter, prevailed on him to take up the position of prior there. It proved to be no easy task, for the monks of Lindisfarne were in a rebellious mood, although it is not certain what their grievances were. The Irish in Northumbria may have felt threatened by Wilfrid and his party. The Synod of Whitby, in that very year of 664, had decided to adopt the Roman date for Easter. Eata and Cuthbert accepted this, as had indeed the majority of Irish elsewhere. Wilfrid was also keen to introduce the Rule of St Benedict. Bede writes, "Now there were certain brethren in the monastery who preferred to conform to their older usage rather than to the monastic rule. Nevertheless [Cuthbert] overcame these by his modest virtue and his patience, and by daily effort he gradually converted them to a better state of mind. In fact very often during debates in the chapter of the brethren concerning the rule, when he was assailed by the bitter insults of his opponents, he would rise up suddenly and with calm mind and countenance would go out, thus dissolving the chapter, but none the less on the following day, as if he had suffered no repulse the day before, he would give the same instruction as before to the same audience until, as we have said, he gradually converted them to the things that he desired." And Bede adds, "for he was a man remarkable for the strength of his patience and unsurpassed in bravely bearing every burden whether of mind or body." Was Cuthbert entrusted with the task of introducing the Benedictine Rule? Or of merely revamping the Rule of St Columba, adding elements from that of St Benedict?

Or of reforming a community which had become lax? Cuthbert's anonymous biographer writes, "He arranged our rule of life which we composed then for the first time and which we observe even to this day along with the rule of St Benedict." As in many other monasteries at the time, the observance would have been a hybrid affair, the Benedictine Rule being grafted on to the unwritten Rule of St Columba and only gradually displacing it.

Cuthbert had spent twelve years on Lindisfarne in obedience to Abbot Eata, "following the contemplative amid the active life," when he felt he must yield to the call of the desert and take up the solitary life. He did so, says Bede, "with the good will of that same abbot [Eata] and also of the brethren," retiring in 676 first to nearby "Cuthbert's Isle" and later to the more remote isle of Farne, where Aidan used to spend the weeks of Lent. He remained there for nine years. The solitude was so absolute that it was deemed to be a haunt of demons where no human being could safely dwell. On the landward side there was nothing but steep rock-face, on the seaward side there was a gentler shore with one possible landing-place, but nothing to break the view of the distant horizon. Cuthbert decided that even this must be blotted out. He built a round house, digging deep into the rock so that its floor was below ground level. Its walls then rose so high that the hermit could see nothing but the sky. He also built a small cabin near the landing-place where visiting monks might stay. At first his brethren helped him to construct these dwellings and kept him supplied with provisions, but he preferred to grow his own food rather than be served at the expense of others. The soil was poor, supporting only barley, and on this he lived. His first biographer, sensing the heavy burden of such solitude, says: "In all conditions he bore himself with unshaken balance." There were many who sought him out in his retreat for advice, spiritual counsel, healing, even knowledge of the future.

In 684 the Synod of Twyford, which assembled in the presence of King Ecgfrith and under the presidency of Archbishop Theodore of Canterbury, elected Cuthbert unanimously to the bishopric of Hexham, whose current bishop it had just deposed. Messages were sent to him, but the hermit made no move. Ecgfrith, with other members of the synod, went to Farne and begged him in the name of the Lord to accept, while the archbishop waited. Cuthbert yielded to their importunity. He had spent nine years strengthening his faith through prayer; two years of active duty now gave him the opportunity to express that deepened faith through the works of love. Eata, himself bishop of Lindisfarne, knew more than most what was being asked of his one-time prior. He offered to take the bishopric of Hexham and give the bishopric of Lindisfarne to Cuthbert, perhaps on the grounds that that diocese was better known to the hermit. With great simplicity Cuthbert took up his duties. He dedicated churches, ordained priests, consecrated virgins, preached and taught, looked after the poor, all the while preserving his own frugal way of life. His compassion overflowed especially on the sick and sorrowful, the bereaved, and the plague-stricken. He himself prepared Queen Eormenberg for the shock of King Ecgfrith's death in battle, and afterwards gave her the veil. The vocabulary used here by his biographers owes much to the life of St Martin, the ideal monk-bishop, but there can be no doubt that Cuthbert had earned the affection and esteem of his people and of his community.

On a visit to Carlisle for the veiling of Queen Eormenburg Cuthbert saw his old friend and fellow-hermit, Hereberht, for the last time. They used to meet once a year, but now Cuthbert made it plain that this would be their last meeting. Overcome with grief, Herberht begged his friend to pray that they might be united in death, as in life they had been united in the bonds of friendship, and Cuthbert obtained this favour for his friend. He spent Christmas of 686 with the community at Lindisfarne as an act of farewell, then immediately after retired to his bleak dwelling on Farne to spend the next two months and three weeks preparing for his death. The monks saw him off. One of them ventured to ask when they would see him again, to which he replied, "When you bring my body back." Bede shows him happy to chat with the now-frequent visitors from Lindisfarne as if he were eager to show them these last marks of his affection. He fell ill on 27 February. The following morning Abbot Herefrith called to say that he was returning to Lindisfarne. He found Cuthbert obviously ill but thought that he was suffering from an old complaint. To his surprise, Cuthbert began to instruct him about the disposal of his body. Hearing this, Herefrith asked whether he ought not to leave some monks behind to look after him, but Cuthbert, with a tinge of sadness, would not have it. They left, and, still troubled, Herefrith asked the community to pray for their bishop in his last hours. For five days a storm prevented the abbot from returning. When he did, he found Cuthbert in the cabin at the landing-stage, to which he had dragged himself notwithstanding the vile weather and his own weakness. Cuthbert explained, "It happened through the providence and will of God that, destitute of human society and help, I should suffer some afflictions. . . . My adversaries have never persecuted me so frequently, during all the time I have been living on this island, as during these five days." Had he come to the cabin to spare the monks the further steps to his cell, or had he attempted to advance by however short a while the human comfort he needed at that moment? The abbot did not dare question the dying man as to the nature of his dark night but did what he could to minister to his physical needs. Cuthbert was taken back to his dwelling where he died later that afternoon, 20 March 687. He had been a bishop for only two years, a monk for thirty-six.

Abbot Herefrith had wrung from Cuthbert the permission to bring his body back to Lindisfarne. So many miracles were reported at his tomb that in 698 the community decided to exhume his remains and put them in a shrine where they might be more easily venerated—an act tantamount to canonization. To the stupefaction of all, Cuthbert's body was found incorrupt and fully flexible; even the clothes in which he had been buried were in perfect condition. The outer vestment and sandals were replaced, and a new wax-cloth used to wrap the body, which was placed now in a wooden coffin above ground.

In 875, the extraordinary peregrinations of Cuthbert's relics began when attacks by the Vikings forced the community of Lindisfarne to abandon their monastery. A party carrying the relics wandered over the north of England for seven years until it arrived in Chester-le-Street. There a church was built and there the relics rested for 113 years, when they were removed to Ripon in 995, again to escape the Vikings. Four years later they were enshrined in the church at Durham built by Bishop Aldhune. The advent of William the Conqueror into Yorkshire precipitated another move, this time to Lindisfarne, but the relics were brought back to Durham in 1070. Thirteen years later a Benedictine community was introduced into the church of Durham and began building a new church. A temporary shrine was erected and, finally, in 1104, before the actual completion of the church, the body was translated to the new shrine prepared for it. Before the translation, the coffins were opened for an examination of the relics. There were three coffins: an outer tomb, a chest with leather covering and, within this chest, the wooden coffin of 698. Within this wooden coffin, on an inner lid, lay St Cuthbert's Gospel book, very probably the copy known as the Stonyhurst Gospels, which had been written and illustrated at Wearmouth and Jarrow. The body of Cuthbert, still incorrupt and flexible, lay on its side to allow room for other relics, judged from written sources to be the head of St Oswald, the bones of St Aidan, and those of Cuthbert's successors in the bishopric of Lindisfarne, saved from violation by the Vikings. The other relics were removed and the body of St Cuthbert, together with the head of St Oswald, replaced. Other objects that had been found were also replaced: a portable silver altar, a finely-worked chalice, corporal and paten, an ivory comb, and a pair of scissors.

When the shrine was despoiled between 1537 and 1539 by the commissioners of Henry VIII and the coffins opened, the body of St Cuthbert was found to be still incorrupt. A leg was broken during the proceedings. The body was reburied in 1542 in the place where the shrine had stood. This grave was opened in 1827 by the Anglican authorities of the cathedral. Under the first slab, some soil was found, then another slab with the name of a fifteenth-century monk incised on its underside. The coffins had disintegrated, bones were found in one of the coffins, but a single skeleton lay at the bottom, wrapped in silks, which fell apart when handled but of which some fragments remain; this skeleton was assumed to be that of St Cuthbert. The chalice, paten, and scissors were missing; a pectoral cross, not hitherto mentioned, broken but with the pieces aligned, was found. This fine reliquary, made of gold and garnets, is kept in the Treasury at Durham Cathedral with most of the other Cuthbert relics. The bones were reinterred in a new coffin the same day. The grave was reopened in 1899 and a medical examination of the bones made, from which it was concluded that the skeleton was that of a man of about fifty years of age, whose skull would have predated an eleventh-century type. Traces of a tubercular disease were found. The whitish substance still adhering to the bones was taken to be evidence of a mummified condition of the corpse as a result of embalmment, a process thought to have been aided by burial in the sandy soil of Lindisfarne. The pieces of fabric were proved to date from the seventh century.

The accumulated evidence gained through these examinations is strong, but it did not win total acceptance. Catholic tradition has known of many saints, ancient and recent, whose bodies have remained incorrupt in testimony of their sanctity without benefit of embalmment. Moreover, St Cuthbert's body rested in the ground for only eleven years and remained enshrined above ground for more than 800. The surprise of the monks on finding the corpse intact in 698 is inexplicable had they embalmed the body only a few years previously. If the body, with its wrappings and its vestments, was still incorrupt when the shrine was despoiled at the Reformation and the body left in the revestry for some time, it is possible that a substitution could have been made either then or during the interregnum, with the saint's vestments being transferred to the substituted skeleton. Some English Catholics have long believed that such a substitution did take place and that the real body of St Cuthbert is hidden elsewhere in the cathedral. "Secrets" are alleged to exist noting its location. However, one secret has been tested by excavation and proved worthless. The other two appear late in written sources and may be equally unreliable. The suggestion that the vestments were changed at the time of the substitution, while not impossible, seems far-fetched.

The cult of Cuthbert, the most popular saint in the north of England, remains strong today. 135 churches in England and seventeen in Scotland are dedicated to him, while the window in York Minster featuring the saint remains an outstanding example of late medieval Cuthbert iconography. The Lindisfarne Gospels, associated from very earliest times with the shrine, is now in the British Museum, while the National Trust has care of the Farne Islands, now a wild-life sanctuary.

Bede, *H.E.*, 4, 27-32; B. Colgrave (ed.), *Two Lives of St Cuthbert* (1940); W. Levison, *England and the Continent in the Eighth Century* (1946); C. F. Battiscombe, *The Relics of Saint Cuthbert* (1956); P. Hunter-Blair, *The World of Bede* (1970); D. Kirby, *St Wilfrid at Hexham* (1973); *Northumbria in the Days of Bede* (1976); E. Power, "St Cuthbert and St Wilfrid" in D. H. Farmer, (ed.), *Benedict's Disciples* (1980; n.e. 1995), pp. 52-69; *The Age of Bede* (1983); B. Ward, *Miracles and the Medieval Mind* (1987); "The Spirituality of St Cuthbert," in *St Cuthbert, his Cult and his Community*, pp. 65-76, eds. Bonner, Rollason & Stancliffe (1989); H. Mayr-Harting, *The Coming of Christianity to Anglo-Saxon England*, 3d ed. (1991); *O.D.S.* (1997), pp. 120-2. There is a manuscript of the Life by a monk of Lindisfarne (*c.* 700), dating from the eleventh/twelfth century, in the library of University College, Oxford.

The earliest representation of him is a sculpture in Carlisle Cathedral, dating from the tenth/eleventh century. The window in York Minster is fifteenth-century.

St Martin of Braga, *Bishop* (*c.* 520-79)

St Martin of Braga is said by St Gregory of Tours (17 Nov.) to have been the foremost scholar of his age, while the Christian poet Venantius Fortunatus (14 Dec.) described him as having inherited the merits as well as the name of St Martin of Tours (11 Nov.). He was born around 520 in Pannonia, the birth-place of his namesake. Some scholars, thinking this too much of a coincidence, have attributed the statement to a scribal error, but it appears in his epitaph, which he is said to have composed himself.

As a young man he went on pilgrimage to Palestine. There is no precise information as to what he did while he was there, but it is probable that he came to know the monastic way of life and became a monk there, as this alone explains his later zeal in establishing monastic foundations. There, too, he may have met pilgrims from Spain, whose stories of the half-pagan, half-Arian Germanic tribe of the Suevi, also originally from Pannonia but settled in Galicia for the last fifty years, may have induced him to go there with the purpose of converting them. These Suevi had once been Catholic under King Rechiarius but during the reign of King Remismund were lured into Arianism by Ajax, an apostate bishop from Gaul. In addition, although the Romano-Hispanic population was not well represented in Galicia, such elements as were there were affected by Priscillianism, a Gnostic-Manichaean heresy that had earlier affected much of Spain.

Martin's arrival in 550 coincided with the translation of the relics of St Martin of Tours to Orense. The son of king Chararich was cured through the intercession of St Martin of Tours, whereupon the king renounced his Arianism and embraced the Catholic faith. His successor Theodimir was much more active in resisting Arianism, so with the support of the monarchy, it became possible for Martin to undertake the work of converting the tribe.

Martin founded several monasteries but seems to have fixed his base at the monastery of Dumium, of which he was abbot and which eventually, in 556, became the seat of the bishop. He was later appointed to the bishopric of Braga, in present-day Portugal, which made him the metropolitan of all Galicia. He was present at the First Council of Braga in 561, then in his capacity as bishop of that see he presided over the second, held in 572. At this council the bishops were able to say, "There is no doubt now that, through the grace of Christ, there is but one faith in the province," but they remained concerned about the presence of paganism.

Besides his work as a missionary, Martin wrote some treatises intended to serve the pastoral needs of his young church. He made a collection of eighty-four canons, mostly Greek but also Spanish and African, which proved to be of great importance in the history of medieval canon law. Whether or not he purposely intended his teaching to have a progressive character, his treatise *Formula vitae honestae*, addressed to King Miro and, like the *De ira*, based on the moral treatises of Seneca, represented the pursuit of the naturally good and virtuous life. His *Pro repellenda iactantia, De superbia,* and *Exhortatio ad humilitatem,* on the other hand, introduce his readers to Christian spirituality. Martin says to his people, "When you have done some good deed, whatever it may be, keep a careful guard over your heart lest in consenting to the praise of others, you grow in self-esteem and self-satisfaction. Nor should you actively seek glory for some good deed, for the nature of glory is like the shadow cast by your body: chase it, and it will fly from you, flee from it, and it will follow you. Whatever good you do, ascribe it to God, the giver of all you have." For his monks he collected the *Sententiae Patrum Aegyptiorum* and, with the collaboration of Paschasius, one of the community at Dumium, the *Verba Seniorum.*

The task of converting the entire tribe of the Suevi was probably beyond the capacity of any one person or of one single generation. Martin's *De correctione rusticorum* reveals how aware he was of what remained to be done. The lack of adequate instruction, combined with his own relative isolation, meant that pagan superstition still existed. His attitude to this lingering paganism is quite different, though, from the violent methods of the Visigoths. Persuasion, not coercion, was his preferred policy and the burden of his counsel to Bishop Polemius, for whom the sermon was written.

It is to Martin's everlasting credit that he tried and succeeded in the task of re-evangelization beyond what could have been expected. He died in 579 at his monastery in Dumium. His relics were translated to Braga in 1606.

Gregory of Tours and Venantius Fortunatus are the principal authorities for the life of St Martin. See *AA.SS.,* Mar., 3, pp. 86-91; *P.L.,* 72; 83; 84; *Dict.Sp.,* 10, 678-80; *N.C.E.,* 9, 303; C. W. Barlow, "Writings of Martin of Braga," in J. M. F. Maricq, *Leaders of Iberian Christianity* (1962), pp. 105-13; A Ferreiro, "The Missionary Labours of St Martin in 6th c. Galicia," in *Studia Monastica* 23 (1981); "St Martin of Braga's Policy towards Heretics and Pagan Practices," in *American Benedictine Review* 34, 4 (1983).

Bd Hippolytus Galantini, *Founder* (1565-1619)

Ippolito Galantini, the son of a Florentine weaver, was born on 14 October 1565 and eventually took up his father's trade. As a child he developed a remarkable talent for memorizing and repeating sermons. When he was twelve, Archbishop Alexander de'Medici—later Pope Leo XI—reorganized the teaching of Christian doctrine in the diocese, appointing Don Jacopo Ansaldi to oversee its implementation. Don Jacopo recognized the boy's potential and took the unprecedented step—in view of his age—of appointing him master of Christian doctrine at the church of Santa Lucia sul Prato. With the help of other like-minded youths Hippolytus would organize catechism classes for the poor and uneducated children of the neighbourhood. He was to hold different posts in other lay institutes, but this first confraternity endured beyond the stage of youthful enthusiasm to play a vital role in the city of Florence.

He later tried to join the Capuchins but was not accepted as a candidate because of his poor health. However, he became a member of the Third Order of St Francis, which gave him the religious dedication he desired and left him free to follow his calling as a catechist. At the age of seventeen he was nominated director of the *Compagnia di Santa Lucia,* a lay association existing in several parishes, which he reorganized and to which he attracted many new recruits. After some years he felt obliged to resign on account of the jealousy he seemed to have provoked. He accepted the position of guardian in a similar organization attached to the Franciscan church of Ognissanti and was concerned not only with religious instruction but also with all the needy members of society, especially during the famine of 1590. He later worked for the church of San Domenico in Palazzuolo and the Oratorio dei Bini, while still concerned with his own confraternity.

Without influence, money, or learning, Hipolytus succeeded in founding a Secular Institute devoted to teaching the faith to children and uninstructed adults. He composed a Rule for his associates about the year 1602, and his example inspired others all over Italy to imitate his work. Although it was generally referred to as the *Compagnia d'Ippolito,* or more popularly as the *Vanchetoni,* his society was in fact renamed, at the request of Pope Clement VII, the *Congregation of St Francis for Christian Doctrine.* The citizens of Florence, recognizing the excellent work he had done, made it possible for him to build a chapel in 1603 for the use of his Institute on a site accessible to the poorer classes, who could receive from the Confraternity a complete course of Christian education. His writings include "Exercises of the School of the Spirit," published in 1831.

Hippolytus had a great devotion to the Blessed Sacrament and received Communion almost daily, contrary to the usual practice of the period. His spiritual life was indeed hidden with Christ in God, but after his death many spoke of the miracles he had worked. He was only fifty-five when he succumbed to a painful illness. His sufferings were alleviated by heavenly visions, and he died while kissing a picture of his crucified Lord on Good Friday, 20 March 1619. His tomb in Florence soon became a place of pilgrimage. He was beatified by Pope Leo XII in 1825.

D. Marsella, *De B. Hippolyto Galantini* (1826); Léon, 1, pp. 513-6; N. de Robeck, *Among the Franciscan Tertiaries* (1930); C. Hallack and P. Anson, *These Made Peace* (1957); *Bibl.SS.*, 5, 1355-6.

Bd Francis Palau y Quer, *Founder* (1811-72)

Francisco Palau y Quer, the seventh of nine children, was born in 1811 at Aytona in the region of Lérida, Spain. He entered the seminary of Lérida in 1828 and the Carmel of discalced friars in Barcelona in 1832. He took solemn vows in 1833, the year of Ferdinand VII's death. The king had left no male heir, and a dynastic war broke out between Ferdinand's brother Charles and his widow, Maria Cristina, acting as regent for her daughter Isabel. The disputants were backed by the two political parties vying for power: the anti-religious, anticlerical liberals, who rejected the Salic law and supported the regent, while the more traditional elements sided with Charles. Although the liberals prevailed in the long run, they split up into two factions, liberals and moderates, alternately holding the reins of government. However, there was little difference between the two factions in their attitude to the Church, which was forced to surrender its estates to finance the dynastic and colonial wars. The religious houses were despoiled, and in one instance a community of friars was massacred at Madrid in 1834.

Francis pursued his studies in the normal way, but in 1835 he was forced to leave the friary, which was never re-established in his lifetime. Ordained priest in 1836, he began his apostolic ministry in Catalonia. He was imprisoned by liberal sympathizers in the castle of Monjuich; freed the following year, he went into a long exile in France (1840-51), where he divided his time between apostolic activity and periods of intense solitude. He wrote some of his books while in exile and was spiritual director of a group of young people in Notre Dame de Livron, in the diocese of Montauban.

On his return to Spain in 1851, when a new Concordat with Rome was signed by the Spanish government, he took up his apostolic ministry once more, founding the "School of Virtue," a model of catechetical teaching, in Barcelona. The school was accused of complicity in the strikes organized by the trade unions and was brutally suppressed by the civil authorities. As director, Fr Palau was internally exiled to the Belearic Islands for six years (1854-60). Released from exile, he went on to found two Congregations, the Missionary Carmelites and the Missionary Carmelites of St Teresa, in the Balearic Islands. Both in the dependent islands and on the mainland he preached popular missions, promoting devotion to Our Lady, the perfect model of Holy Church. He died in Tarragona on 20 March 1872; in 1947 his relics were translated from the cemetery to the church of his Congregation.

The outstanding characteristic of his spirituality was his love for the Church. He wrote: "The day I became a priest was the day I was ordained for your service, became one with you, the Church, and since that day I no longer belong to myself. I am yours, together with everything I do." He valued solitude for the chance to commune with the Church's mysterious reality; he embraced action in order to serve it by every means at his disposal: preaching, catechetics, exorcisms, the pen of the writer or the journalist. All his apostolic works were motivated by this one resolve, "To love and serve the Church in the poor, the sick, children, youth, the family. . . ." He left several works, some of which are pastoral and pedagogic in nature, some autobiographical and spiritual.

His ideals live on in the Congregations he founded, now working in four continents. He was beatified by Pope John Paul II on 24 April 1988.

N.S.B. 2, p. 168; *Dict.Sp.*, 12, 107-12; 4, 1186, 1188. Life by A. della Madonna del Carmine (1993 and 1979); *Bibl.SS.*, Suppl. 1, 1006-7; F. Holbörk, *Die neuen Heiligen der Katholischen Kirche*, 3 (1994), pp. 21-3.

R.M.

SS Paul and Cyril, martyrs at Antioch in Syria (n.d.)

St John, bishop of Jerusalem (417)

St Urbicius, bishop of Metz (*c.* 450)

St Thomas, bishop of Constantinople (610)

St Wulfram, bishop of Sens (*c.* 700)

St Nicetas, bishop of Appolonia, Bithynia (733)

St Arc'il, king and martyr of Notkore, Georgia (786)

Bd Ambrose Sansedoni, O.P., of Siena (1287)

St John Nepomucene, priest and martyr of Prague (1393)

Bd Baptist Spagnuolo, O.F.M., of Mantua (1516)

Bd Jeanne Véron, martyr in the French Revolution (1794)—see 13 Mar.

21

St Nicholas of Flüe, *Hermit* (1417-87)

Nicholas von Flüe (Bruder Klaus) holds a unique place in the esteem and affection of the Swiss. He was born near Saschseln in Unterwalden in 1417 to a much-respected family of well-to-do farmers, owners of the Klüster Alp in the Melchthal and of the estate of Flüeli on the Sachsterberg, from which they derived their surname. His father, Henry, also held a civil post in the cantonal service. His mother, Emma Roberto, was a native of Wolfenschiessen, perhaps of Italian ancestry.

Emma was a deeply religious woman who initiated her two sons, Nicholas and Peter, into the spirituality and practices of the "Friends of God" (*Gottesfreunde*). A movement begun in the previous century by mystics and preachers such as Johann Tauler, Henry Suso (25 Jan.), and Henry of Nordingliden, it sought the personal sanctification of its practitioners through a deep interior life. Its aim was union with God through prayer, meditation on the passion of Christ, renunciation, and the service of one's neighbour. Although there would in time issue from the Friends a society with heretical, separatist tendencies, this was not characteristic of the generality of Friends, who set out to avail themselves of all the helps of the Church, however much its image might be defiled by unholy clergy. The brotherhood of Friends, loosely held together through personal contacts or existing in groups around a spiritual director, was to be found all along the Rhine, in Germany, Switzerland, and the Netherlands, among clergy and religious but predominantly among the laity. Nicholas never sought to evade the military duty that his position in a family of landed farmers imposed on him. Fifteenth-century Switzerland was not yet a single country but a collection of cantons at war with each other, forest cantons especially at loggerheads with the cantons of the towns. When occasion arose, all farmers had to take to arms against the towns in an expression of solidarity. In his twenties Nicholas was alternately farming and fighting, taking part in the battles of this period whether against the towns, the Austrians, or the French. He is recorded as intervening dramatically in the battle against the Austrians in 1460. An attempt by these to lay claim to Swiss territory had provoked a retaliatory invasion of the Thurgau. The Austrians were routed, but the town of Diesenhofer held out stubbornly. In the end the Austrians rushed to take refuge in a Dominican convent, where, according to the convention of Sempach drawn up by the Swiss themselves for the conduct of war, they should have been safe from enemy fire. The convent was fired on anyway. Seeing this, Nicholas is said to have cast himself before a crucifix, praying for the safety of the inmates. He then argued the illegality of the action with the officers and obtained a cessation of fire. The convent was indeed burned, but those within were spared.

By this time Nicholas had married. He was to leave his wife and children twenty-five years later, but he could hardly forsee this at the time, and there would have been compelling reasons for him to take such a step. The spirituality of the Friends was a lay spirituality above all. Nicholas himself was illiterate, and there could have been no question of joining the ranks of the clergy or even religious. As the elder son he would have been expected to marry and to carry on the family line and the work of the farm. The marriage was probably arranged by his parents as a matter of course, and he would have felt obliged to obey. Be that as it may, his marriage to Dorothy Wissling, from the village of Sachseln, proved to be a happy one. She bore him ten children, five boys and five girls. Marriage did not in any way affect Nicolas' ascetic habits. He fasted as he always did and every night after a short sleep rose to pray, going out-of-doors to do so or remaining indoors in bad weather. While he was still with his family he underwent a trial, the nature of which remains obscure but which may have been one of doubts against the faith. Fr Imgrund, parish priest of Stans and his director, helped him through it, teaching him also to meditate on the passion of Our Lord, an exercise that was to become a staple of his spiritual life as a hermit.

Nicholas' standing was high in the canton of Unterwalden. He sat on a board of fourteen magistrates to dispense justice, although he was to resign when a majority opted for what he considered an injustice. Asked to be mayor more than once, he steadfastly refused, saying, "One is safer below than on the heights." However, he was always in demand as a counsellor and an intermediary. He was chosen as one of five arbiters appointed to settle a dispute between the parish of Stans and the monastery of Engelberg and even to make representations to the clergy over a question of excessive tithing.

In obedience to what seemed to him a supernatural call to contemplation—he was the recipient of many visions and revelations—he used at times to withdraw into solitude in the valley of the Melch. When he was about fifty he felt irresistibly drawn to abandon the world altogether and to spend the rest of his days in solitude, far from home. His wife made no objection, seeing in it a call of God. In 1467, then, with the consent of his director and family, he left everything and set off barefoot and bareheaded, dressed in a grey-brown tunic and armed only with a staff and a rosary. His destination seems to have been Alsace, where there was a settlement of the Brothers. Before crossing the frontier he received hospitality from a peasant, who turned out to be one of the Friends of God and who dissuaded him from going on. He explained to him that the Swiss, with a reputation of being savage soldiers, were regarded with hostility. Nicholas turned back to seek a corner in his own part of the world.

On his return journey he was suddenly seized with severe gastric pains, after which he became quite unable to eat. He subsisted for another twenty years on only the Blessed Sacrament. To the parish priest of Kerns he once said, "The body and blood of Christ are my only food. He dwells in me and I in him. He is my food, my drink, my health and medicine." Though he had always fasted, this new condition was not one he had willed on himself; he saw it as a gift from God for his own good purposes. Such a prodigy was to bring on him the suspicions of many. Both ecclesiastical and civil authorities spied on him to catch him out secretly eating but had to acknowledge that his fast was genuine. Thomas, bishop of Ascalon, once set a trap for him. In what seemed an amicable conversation, he asked Nicholas which was the most important of the virtues. Unhesitatingly, the hermit replied that he considered obedience the most important. The bishop then required him in the name of obedience to eat the meal he had brought. Nicholas obeyed, and in a few moments was convulsed in agony.

Later that autumn, hunters who had been looking for game in the Melchthal brought home news that they had come upon Nicholas on his pasture land of the Klüster, where he had made himself a shelter of boughs under a larch. His brother Peter and his friends went to plead with him not to remain there to die of exposure, and he was persuaded to move to Ranft, another part of the valley, where the people of Obwalden built him a little cell with a chapel attached. This was consecrated in 1469. At first he went to Mass on Sundays and holydays to Sachseln, but later, with the alms provided by the people, it became possible for daily Mass to be said in the chapel by a permanent chaplain. The pattern of his life was simple. He rose at midnight and prayed into the morning, when he would walk in the forest; later, when Ulrich of Swabia, a disciple hermit, set up another cell in the region, he would visit him. The afternoons were given to visitors, and then he prayed again until time for his repose, which lasted for a few hours only and was taken on a wooden plank with a stone pillow. Some of the hermit's visitors have left accounts of their interview with him, and that written by Albert von Bonstetten, dean of the monastery of Einsiedeln, is particularly interesting. He describes the recluse as tall, brown, and wrinkled, with thin grizzled locks and a short beard. His eyes were bright, his teeth white and well preserved and his nose shapely. He adds, "He praises and recommends obedience and peace."

As a counsellor both in practical and spiritual matters, Nicholas gained a reputation far beyond the borders of Switzerland, but his impact on his countrymen was immediate and sometimes decisive. At this epoch the Swiss Confederation had just passed through the most glorious phase in its history. In the space of six years the sturdy mountain-folk had vindicated their independence and, at the invitation of Louis of France, had routed the hitherto unconquered Charles the Bold, master of the two Burgundies and nearly the whole of Belgium. However, quarrels arose over the distribution of the payment money by

Louis of France to the cantons in return for their victory over his enemy, and again between the forest cantons and the towns over the proposal to include Fribourg and Soleure in the township alliances. At length agreement was reached on most points and was embodied in a document known as the Edict of Stans. On the subject of the inclusion of Fribourg and Soleure, no agreement could be reached, and feeling ran so high that it seemed that the question would have to be settled by arms. Deeply distressed, Fr Imgrund suggested seeking a final opinion from Nicholas of Flüe, to which the delegates agreed.

His suggestion was no casual or sudden inspiration. As we know from the protocols of the Council of Lucerne, a city which occupied an ambiguous position between the forest cantons and the townships, it had at an early stage in the strife sent delegates to Brother Nicholas to obtain his advice, and it is quite possible that other districts had done the same. It has even been suggested that the Edict of Stans, a most statesmanlike charter, may have been drafted in the hermit's cell. The delegates were preparing to leave Stans when the parish priest begged them to re-assemble to consider the proposals of the hermit of Ranft. No one could explain how the hitherto unyielding delegates put aside their differences and arrived at an agreement within the hour. Each side yielded something: the forest cantons withdrew their objections to the towns joining the township alliances, subject to certain conditions, and the towns gave up their plans to push further centralization. Nicholas of Flüe is credited not only with saving the country from a self-destructive civil war but also with creating an attitude of mutual tolerance that enabled the Swiss Confederation not only to endure but to remain united in the face of the divisive religious controversies of the century to come. Letters of thanks from Berne and Soleure to the hermit are still extant, as well as a letter from Nicholas' son John thanking Berne for a gift, which he said would be used for the chapel.

Six years after the Council of Stans, Nicholas was seized with his last illness, which lasted only a week but caused him intense suffering. He died peacefully in his cell in the presence of his parish priest, Ulrich his disciple, his wife, sons, and grandsons. Nicholas' son John became the parish priest of Stans, while one of his grandsons was to become a hermit in the self-same cell of Ranft. Nicholas was canonized in 1947; his tomb is at Salchsen.

Robert Durrer, a scholar with an unrivalled knowledge of the Swiss archives, published two quarto volumes, entitled *Bruder Klaus,* in the early part of this century. They contain all the available material on the life of Nicholas von Flüe. See also *AS.SS.,* Mar., 3, pp. 395-437; G. R. Lamb, *Brother Nicholas* (1955); M. L. von Franz, *Die Visionem des Niklaus von Flüe* (1959).

Bd Thomas Pilchard, *Martyr* (*c.* 1557-87)

Thomas Pilchard was born about 1557 at Battle in Sussex and educated at Balliol College, Oxford, going on to the degree of Master of Arts in 1579. He studied for the priesthood at Douai College, which was then at Reims, and was ordained at Laon in 1583. He was sent on the English mission two months later. He is described as being "of a most gentle disposition, more than moderately learned, a remarkable pattern of priestly life." He was easily recognized because he had "a decided squint." After a ministry of only two years he was arrested in London and banished from the country in 1585. He returned to the mission in January 1586 and worked for another two years, when he was again arrested and brought to trial. He was condemned for being a priest and for exercising his priesthood in England. He was hanged, drawn, and quartered at Dorchester, where he had been captured, on 21 March 1587. He was beatified in 1987.

Anstruther, 1, p. 276, with further refs.

Bd Matthew Flathers, *Martyr* (*c.* 1560-1608)

Matthew (or Major) Flathers was born at Weston in Yorkshire, the son of John and Agnes Flathers of Leeds. He was educated at University College, Oxford, obtaining his B.A. in 1590, and then studied for the priesthood at the College of Douai. He was ordained at Arras in 1606 and three months later was sent on the English mission. He was arrested in that same year and banished from the country. He soon returned to his ministry in Yorkshire and was again caught at Upsall Castle, in 1607, and charged with being a priest. Another priest from Douai, William Mush, and the widow who had sheltered them both were arrested and charged with him. All three were condemned for refusing to take the Oath of Supremacy, but the sentence was carried out only on Matthew, who was hanged, drawn, and quartered with great barbarity on 21 March 1608. He was beatified in 1987.

Anstruther, 2, p. 111.

Bd Benedicta Frassinello, *Foundress* (1791-1858)

Benedetta Cambiagio Frassinello was born on 2 October 1791 in Cilli, a small canton of Langascio in Liguria, Italy. She was the fourth of the five children of Guiseppe Cambiagio and Francesca Ghiglione. They were a family of small farmers, of a simple and genuine faith. The children were brought up strictly but in a loving environment. Nothing is known of her schooling, but she had a lively mind and loved reading, which she used to increase the rudimentary knowledge she may or may not have acquired in school.

Napoleon annexed Liguria in 1805. His troops were but the latest to have pillaged or destroyed the country, and many Ligurians were forced to leave their plots of land and look for a safer existence elsewhere. In 1809 the Cambiagio family went to live in Pavia, where they opened a greengrocer shop on the high street. Benedicta was involved in the venture, which was to earn the family their living, and was soon engulfed in a non-stop round of activity, leading to a gradual spiritual atrophy she found unendurable. She felt herself being drawn by God, with the gospel passages she had learnt by heart taking on the character of an urgent appeal addressed to her personally: "Come. Get away. Leave. . . ." The Lives of the saints she was reading fascinated her, whetting her desire to respond immediately to the call. Convinced that she was being summoned to a life of solitude and prayer, she left the house one day without saying a word to anyone and retired to a shanty in a rock cavity near a stream. Like the Desert Fathers, she lived on roots and wild berries. Her parents set out in search of her, and eight days later she was back at home, abandoning what she was later to call a "veritable fantasy." Nevertheless, she retained the desire for the religious life and while awaiting an opportunity for its realization gave herself up to prayer and penance under the guidance of her spiritual father, Giacomo De Filippi, a canon regular of Somascha.

Benedicta's excessive penances, which were gradually affecting her health, alarmed her parents, who decided to marry her off to a Ligurian who seemed to be fond of her. Giovanni Battista Frassinello was illiterate but intelligent and clever with his hands. Above all, he was a good Christian. Benedicta tried to oppose her parents' plans, but to no avail. Yet deep within her she was certain that God's providence was directing her life; this certainty led her to abandon herself totally to his mysterious will—an abandon which would become the dominant feature of her spirituality. The marriage took place on 7 February 1816.

The new couple took Benedicta's sister, Maria, who suffered from an incurable illness and had been abandoned by her husband, into their home and lovingly looked after until her death. Giovanni and Benedicta themselves, after two years of marriage, decided to lead celibate lives on the model of the family at Nazareth. A common ideal now bore fruit in their lives, which were more and more turned toward others. Benedicta was tormented by the desire to rescue and rehabilitate the young prostitutes who every evening congregated outside the university of Pavia to lure the students. She spoke to the bishop, Mgr Tosi, of the moral problem the university students raised and of the urgent need to deal with it. She also talked to her confessor about the seriousness of the situation; to appease her he merely replied, "One can only bow to the inevitable."

Maria died on 9 July 1825 and the Frasinellos were now free to execute the plan they had long prayed and thought about: to enter the religious life. With the approval of Mgr Tosi Benedicta entered the Capuchin convent of Capriolo nel Bresciano toward the end of July 1825, while Giovanni took the habit of a lay brother with the Somaschi Canons in December of the same year. Benedicta plunged happily into the life of silence and prayer she had so longed for since her adolescence, while the community was edified and sustained by her presence and energy. One night, it is said, the convent was attacked by a band of ruffians trying to get into the enclosure. They battered the entrance door, which was about to give when Benedicta opened it. Barring their way, she demanded in a peremptory voice, "What do you want here?" Clearly they were not expecting such a determined show of resistance and melted away.

As time went on, Benedicta became aware of a call to an apostolate among the young after the manner of St Jerome Emiliani (8 Feb.). The community tried to dissuade her, but she became so ill that the bishop intervened, telling her to return to her family—a strange decision apparently dictated by a dream. Returning to her home in a dying condition, Benedicta too had a vision. Her parents were at her bedside waiting for her to breathe her last when suddenly her face lit up and her lips moved as if she were speaking with someone. When she came to herself she related a conversation with St Jerome Emiliani, who asked her to dedicate her life to imperilled young girls. She consented to do so, and her health was quickly restored.

More than ever convinced that God was mysteriously guiding her steps, Benedicta settled into a run-down house on 29 September 1826, together with a small group of seven traumatized young girls and some adults who were interested in the work she proposed to do. They had practically to beg their way. In order to protect Benedicta from her distraught parents, who considered their daughter's decision a smirch on the honour of the family and determined to make her abandon her vocation, Mgr Tosi asked Giovanni Battista Frassinello to return to his wife. He returned to Pavia, and the couple renewed their vow of chastity before the bishop. The number of inmates soon reached a hundred. A rich proprietor, Angelo Pozzi, impressed by Benedicta's work, helped her to acquire and run another house. The lay character of the venture was thus underlined, the bishop and parish priest having only an advisory role. The new institution came to be called "Benedicta's Hospice," and the young girls the "Benedictas." This first attempt at a preventative social measure in Pavia was soon legally approved and registered as an institution in the public interest.

The team under Benedicta's direction constituted a real community, sharing the same ideals and dedicated to the service of the young girls in distress whom they welcomed. Benedicta gave the community a Rule closely related to a monastic Rule, which inculcated obedience, repentance, humility, prayer, cultivation of the interior life, unconditional abandonment to Providence, and, above all, a great love of the girls. The material means available to the foundress were scant, and there would be many an opportunity to testify to the sudden interventions of Providence. It was not unusual at meal-times to suggest that the inmates form a procession in the garden or make a visit to the chapel before going to the refectory, where the plates had nothing on them. A benefactor always seemed to arrive at that moment, and sometimes in the strangest fashion.

In 1838 the bishop, whose health was deteriorating daily, set up a commission to help him in the administration of the diocese. Several of its members were linked with either the Jansenist or the Josephist movements in Pavia.

These saw Benedicta as a rabid opponent of their different views and did not hesitate to disseminate the most far-fetched calumnies concerning the foundress of the hospice. The frequently heard "They say . . ." finally succeeded in creating widespread hostility toward her. When it was learned that she had helped a young man financially to complete his studies, she was accused of being an immoral person herself. The worst calumny came from one of the young inmates. According to her, the directress had taken the girls by force from their families, exploited, and maltreated them. Some of them had died of fatigue and hunger and were buried in the cellars. This calumny was to bring Benedicta to court; on her way to the court sessions not only insults but stones were hurled at her by a crowd of hooligans. Mgr Tosi, now thoroughly prejudiced against his erstwhile collaborator, obliged her not only to leave the *casa* but the town of Pavia as well. On 16 July 1838 she signed a legal act of transfer of rights of ownership and direction of the house on the Via S. Giovanni to the bishop. In a spirit of obedience she declared in the same act her intention to resign from the institution in order to take a rest. The Institute would henceforth be called the *Pia Casa delle Figlie della Carità*.

The following day she left the town together with Giovanni Battista and five co-workers. Their journey should have led them to Rivarolo (Liguria), where two years before two priests had requested the foundress to begin work there on the same lines as those of Pavia. As another religious community had preceded her to Rivarolo, she agreed to set up house in Rocco Scriva, her husband's birthplace, and work there in accordance with the dictates of her unusual charism: to come to the help of the young, especially girls, whose poverty exposed them to the danger of prostitution. She opened a school, an orphanage, and a day-school. It is at Rocco above all that the "Religious Family of Benedictine Sisters of Providence" was born, as if spontaneously, and grew to maturity. A Rule was drawn up, the definitive text of which was submitted to ecclesiastical approbation in 1845. Its outline is similar to the Rule drawn up in Pavia, but this was destined not just for one community but for a Congregation called to spread beyond the narrow confines of Liguria. The definitive title of the Congregation became Benedictine Sisters of Providence of Rocco Scriva, the adjective Benedictine referring to the fact that the Congregation chose St Benedict as its patron. Its special work was to welcome the most vulnerable young girls into its houses and to receive as many as they could feed. The Rule was approved in 1856 by the archbishop of Genoa, the Institute being canonically approved on 29 March 1926.

In 1847 Benedicta sent two Sisters who had come with her from Pavia, Giustina and Maria Schiapparelli, to Voghera, a town in Piedmont, to look after their father and blind sister. They were soon to learn that the moral and social conditions there were no different from those in Pavia. With the encouragement of their superior and in the spirit of the Institute, they began work and had soon set up an establishment for the education of girls. The foundress often visited and advised them, leaving them as much freedom and initiative as they needed. Benedicta's charism expressed in her own Congregation was quite special to her, but the fact that the new religious family had gone its own way was unimportant. What counted above all was that saying of Jesus which determines the goal of any apostolic work, "that they may have life and have it more abundantly." In 1905 the house in Voghera became an independent Congregation, the Benedictine Sisters of Providence of Voghera.

Benedicta was recalled to Pavia in 1851, Mgr Tosi having been replaced. She acquired the one-time Benedictine monastery of Santo Gregorio, where she organized a house for young girls, a school, an orphanage, and a boarding-house. Again, she was subjected to persecution and again she was asked to leave the city and her work there. She left two companions to carry on and set out for Quirico, where there was a school for girls, but she never arrived. Obliged to stop at Ronco because of a heart attack, she died there on 21 March 1858, then the feast of St Benedict.

If there is one striking feature in Mother Benedicta's life, it is her ever-constant availability to God and his providence. Each sign from God has its own "why," its own importance. Benedicta lives on in her Institute, which has houses in several Italian cities, in Spain, and in Peru. Her relics were destroyed in the Second World War by Allied bombing, which wrecked the cemetery where her body lay. Benedicta Frassinello was beatified by Pope John Paul II on 10 May 1987.

Giulio Venturini, *Benedetta Cambiagio Frassinello* (1986). Four other biographies have been published in Italian between 1861 and 1981, and there are MS biographies also in the archives of the Institute.

R.M.
St Serapion, martyr at Alexandria (first century)
SS Trophimus and Thalus, martyrs at Laodicea in Syria (fourth century)
Martyrs of Alexandria, Egypt (339)
St Lupicinus, abbot of St Claude in the Jura (580)
St James, martyr at Constantinople (824)
St John, bishop of Valence (1146)

22

St Nicholas Owen, *Martyr* (1606)

Nicholas Owen, also known under the names of Andrewes and Draper, was probably one of the four sons of Walter Owen, an Oxford carpenter, from whom he would have learned his extraordinary craftsmanship. Of the sons, Henry became a printer and distributor of Catholic books, while Walter and John became priests. Nicholas worked with the Fathers of the Society of Jesus for many years before becoming a Jesuit lay brother in 1597. He was a small man, affectionately known as "Little John" or "Little Michael." A packhorse once fell on him, breaking his leg, which was badly set, leaving him with a limp for the rest of his life. For all his lack of stature he must have been very robust in order to have accomplished the work that he took on over the years.

He is first heard of in connection with St Edmund Campion (1 Dec.), whose servant he may have been and whom he had defended against the charge of treason. As a consequence of this he himself was imprisoned in 1581, at first alone, then later in another prison with three others. The conditions were so harsh that one of these died, but the body was never removed. On his release Nicholas disappears from view, but from 1586 to 1606 he was in the service of Fr Henry Garnet, the Jesuit provincial, and he travelled extensively with him, staying in the houses of recusants, where he constructed hiding-holes for the hunted missionary priests.

Dates are not available for the construction of the various hiding-holes, which saved innumerable priests from the scaffold and Catholic families who harboured them from dispossession of their property. Owen must have spent a considerable amount of his time on this work, to judge from their great number and still greater complexity. He set out to construct uniquely-designed hiding-places whose points of entry would be so disguised as to defy discovery by the most assiduous pursuivant, which would hold one or two men with the minimum of discomfort for several days, would ensure both light and air to the fugitives, and would contain an adequate supply of food. Owen would communicate before he began a job and would pray continually as he worked. As a measure of precaution he never discussed his work so that no one could ever divulge anything concerning it, whether lightly or under torture; he would pretend to be engaged on repairs in some other part of the house during the day and would work on the hiding-holes during the night. This often involved breaking down walls and moving huge stones unaided. When a hiding-place was completed, only he and the owner of the house would know where it was and where its entrance was to be found. Fr John Gerard wrote of him, "I verily think no man can be said to have done more good of all those who laboured in the English vineyard."

Nicholas went to be with Fr Gerard in London in 1594 to help him with the purchase of a house. The business had been completed, but before moving in they stayed in lodgings and while there were betrayed by a trusted servant of the Wiseman family of Braddocks in Essex. John Frank had already tried to betray Fr Gerard at Braddocks but had failed, thanks to Nicholas' hiding-hole. He tracked the priest to his London address and acted as the bearer of an urgent letter. Having confirmed the whereabouts of his prey he called in the pursuivants. Both Fr Gerard and Nicholas Owen were arrested and detained separately. Nicholas and a companion, Richard Fulwood, were racked "for three hours together, having their arms fixed into iron rings and their bodies hanging in the air." No information was extracted from them, and eventually Owen was freed on payment of a bribe. He continued to see Fr Gerard, who as a result was consigned to the Tower in 1597. Nicholas Owen was one of the party abetting Fr Gerard's spectacular escape from the Tower and may even have helped to devise it.

Feelings ran high against Catholics in the aftermath of the Gunpowder Plot at the end of the year 1605. Four Jesuits took refuge in Hindlip Hall in Worcester-shire: Fr Garnet, Fr Oldcorne, Ralph Ashley, and Nicholas Owen. Robert Cecil, the secretary of state, knew of their whereabouts but did not act until all the conspirators had been executed. He then instructed the local justice of the peace, Sir Henry Bromley, to make a thorough search of the house. Bromley arrived with a hundred men. The priests had entered one hiding-hole, Owen and Ashley another. For a week the searchers combed the house, sounding and pounding the walls in vain. After a week, Owen decided to give himself up, hoping that the search for the priests might be called off. He slipped out of the closet unperceived, but the men were not satisfied with the catch. They spent another week searching for the priests, who by now had spent two weeks in hiding and had no more food. Eventually they found their hiding-place. Fr Oldcorne and Br Ralph Ashley were hanged, drawn, and quartered in 1606 in Worcester; Fr Garnet and Nicholas Owen were taken up to London. The former was tried and executed in May 1606. Nicholas Owen was not tried; instead, he was to be tortured without mercy for the invaluable information he more than anyone else could give about the houses harbouring priests and providing facilities for Masses. He was taken to the Tower and tortured every day for six days. He already had a hernia as a result of his heavy manual work, so an iron band was fixed round his body to ensure that he did not die before his torturers could elicit the information they wanted. Iron gauntlets were fixed to his wrists, and he was hung up by these for six hours at a time. Weights were added to his ankles. Confessions concerning his relationship to Fr Henry Garnet were wrung out of him, but he said nothing that was not already known to the authorities. Not a word of his work escaped him; he would merely repeat under torture the words "Jesus" and "Mary." Under the strain of the hanging his body finally burst open and he died in terrible agony on 22 March 1606. It was put about that he had committed suicide—a statement no one believed. His jailer was more truthful: "The man is dead; he died in our hands."

Nicholas Owen was beatified in 1929 and is one of the Forty Martyrs of England and Wales canonized by Pope Paul VI in 1970.

P. Caraman, S.J. (trans.), *John Gerard: The Autobiography of an Elizabethan* (1951); M. Waugh, *Blessed Nicholas Owen* (1961); A. Fraser, *The Gunpowder Plot* (1997). For a general treatment of the Forty Martyrs of England & Wales, see 25 Oct., with bibliography.

St Paul of Narbonne, *Bishop* (*c.* 290)

Gregory of Tours (17 Nov.) in his history of the Franks relates that in the time of the emperor Decius Paul of Narbonne was sent from Rome with several other missionaries to evangelize Gaul. Two of the band, St Saturninus of Toulouse (29 Nov.) and St Dionysius of Paris (9 Oct.), were martyred, but St Paul of Narbonne, St Trophimus of Arles (29 Dec.), St Martial of Limoges (30 June), and St Gatian of Tours (18 Dec.) died in peace after lives of great holiness during which they converted the people and witnessed the spread of the faith.

AA.SS., Mar. 3, pp. 369-74.

Bd Francis Chartier, *Martyr* (1762-94)

François-Louis Chartier was born in Marigné in the *département* of Maine-et-Loire, France, on 6 June 1762. He became a secular priest and was appointed to the post of curate in the parish of Soeurdres, about five kilometres from his birth-place.

When under the Civil Constitution on the Clergy, promulgated in 1790, all clergy were required to take an oath of loyalty to the State, he refused and would not reveal where he had hidden his chalice. He acknowledged celebrating Mass and administering the sacraments and protested that the extinction of non-conforming clergy in particular amounted to persecution. It was an act directed against the Catholic, Apostolic, and Roman Church. This earned him immediate condemnation and he was guillotined in Angers on 22 March 1794.

For a general treatment of the martyrs of this period, see "Martyrs of the French Revolution," 2 Jan.

R.M.
SS Callinicus and Basilissa, martyrs in Galatia (third century)
St Basil, priest and martyr at Ancyra, Galatia (362)
St Lea, widow of Rome (c. 383)
St Benvenuto Scotivoli, bishop of Osimo, Piceno (1282)

23

ST TURIBIUS OF MOGROVEJO, *Bishop* (1538-1606)

Turibio Alfonso de Mogrovejo was born in 1538 at Mayorga in the province of León in Spain, the son of the governor of Mayorga, Luis Alfonso de Mogrovejo, and Doña Ana Morán y Robledo. He studied at Valladolid and then at Salamanca, winning a scholarship in 1571 to the *Colegio Mayor de San Salvador* in Oviedo. He chose to specialize in law, either because he was genuinely attracted to it or in emulation of his uncle, Juan Pérez de Mogrovejo, a famous jurist in his time. Obtaining a licentiate both in civil and canon law in 1573, he then went on to teach, holding meanwhile the post of counsellor of the Inquisition in Granada and later in 1575 that of acting president of the tribunal.

In that same year of 1575 the death of Jerónimo de Loaiza, archbishop of Lima, made it necessary for Philip II to find someone to replace him. His choice fell on Diego Gómez de la Madrid, inquisitor in Cuenca. However, the queen wished Diego Gomez to remain in Spain, and he was appointed bishop of Badajoz. The king's next choice fell on Turibius, although he was not a cleric, having received the tonsure only. Turibius' high intellectual and moral qualities were not unknown; what was to emerge from his years in Peru was a type of sanctity seen most clearly in his contemporary, Charles Borromeo, the reforming bishop of Milan (4 Nov.): zealous for the reformation of the Church, pastorally concerned for clergy and people, conscientious yet always diplomatic, humble and long-suffering, a good organizer, and totally dedicated to the task in hand. Pope St Pius V (30 Apr.) dispensed Turibius from the usual preparatory steps to ordination so that he was able to receive minor and major orders within a short space of time, followed by episcopal consecration. He set sail in 1580, arriving in Panama in the New Year. There he embarked again, reaching Paita on the northernmost section of the Peruvian coastline, where he disembarked and travelled from then on overland to his see in Lima. It was the first of his many voyages through the country for which he was to expend every ounce of his energy. He arrived at his destination in May 1581.

The Spanish colonists had already been there for over fifty years. The last Inca chief was beheaded in 1571, but the system of government by viceroys had been in place since 1555 and would remain until 1824. These were subject to the Council of the Indies, which sat in Spain, so that communication was slow and the process of adjudication between appellants to the king or council protracted and cumbersome. The Church was to a great extent in the power of the viceroys but ultimately in that of the king, whose hold on ecclesiastical matters was tighter in the New World than in the mother country. However, the kings of Spain acted with zeal for the spread of Christianity and the protection of the Indians against oppressive colonists. If there were abuses in such a remote part of the world, there was much on which the second archbishop could build.

For the most part the Peruvian Indians belonged to an agricultural society and had led a settled existence under the Inca rulers long before the Spaniards arrived. For them it was a question of exchanging one set of rulers for another. The Indians on the periphery, however, were violent and aggressive; evangelization, relatively straightforward among the sedentary population, proved more difficult and protracted with these. A system of Indian parishes, known as *doctrinas*, was in place and staffed mostly by religious. On his arrival Turibius found Franciscans—the first religious to arrive in Peru—Mercedarians, Dominicans, Augustinians, and Jesuits, who had already made an immense contribution to the task of evangelization. In 1565 the Dominicans were petitioning the king for funds to establish a university. An Augustinian friar held the chair of native languages, established by the Viceroy in 1569, and books were already being published in Aymara and Quechua, the two most widely used Indian languages.

Lima, the centre of Spanish colonial power in South America, had been made a metropolitan see in 1546, initially with jurisdiction over the whole of Spanish South America. A third council of Lima, to embrace the entire ecclesiastical administration, had been mooted under Turibius' predecessor some time before. Turibius' first act, after having consulted his chapter and the provincial superiors, was to convoke the council for 1582. In the meantime he set about a visitation of the archdiocese, beginning with a journey to the region south and south-east of Lima. He returned in Lent, when he held a local synod to launch the preparations for the council. After Easter he set out again over the Andes to the province of Huánuco, never previously visited by any prelate, returning fifteen days before the council.

Forty-four constitutions were issued by this Third Council of Lima, the first under Turibius, many of which were concerned with ecclesiastical administration. As might have been expected, the reforms promulgated by Trent were not welcomed by the entire body of clergy, and Turibius found himself delated both to the king and to Rome. The latter decreed some modifications but upheld the council in its condemnation of absentee parish priests and those who trafficked in Indian slaves. A more difficult case was that of the bishop of Cuzco, an openly simoniacal cleric. The assembly was divided on what should be done. The archbishop decided to refer the case to Rome, but this was opposed by the bishop's supporters. Faced with their intransigence, he left the assembly, which continued to meet without him. He had no choice but to condemn the subsequent meetings as invalid, and he invoked the secular authority to intervene and rescue the files concerning the bishop. The viceroy failed to support him, and he in turn excommunicated four dissident bishops. The authorities then required the archbishop to lift the excommunication. In the interests of peace and in order to avoid any intransigence on his own part, he later did so and officially reopened the council but exposed himself to the insults of the dissidents, who denied his presidency and treated him as if he had been the one excommunicated. The situation was resolved by the death of the bishop of Cuzco and a reprimand from the king addressed to the four bishops in question. However, the council was more important for its instructions concerning the pastoral care of the Indians. It insisted that all who held a parish—not just a few scholars—should learn the Indian language in order to teach the catechism adequately and hear Confessions. It directed that a new catechism be drawn up and translated into Aymara and Quechua. This catechism, published in Spanish as well as in the two Indian languages, was approved by the archbishop in 1584 and proved the most important directive issued by the council. Other documents concerning Confession, the impediments to marriage, the care of the dying, and the place of Indian rites, were to be drawn up to ensure uniform instruction and practice. Indians were permitted to become cantors, sacristans, and catechists, although the priesthood was still withheld from them.

Turibius himself learned to speak Quechua to facilitate his apostolate, which, in accord with the Laws of the Indies of 1542, was to be directed mainly to the Indian population. The next requisite was to make contact with his widely-dispersed flock. During the twenty-four years of his pastoral activity, he travelled three times over the eighteen thousand square miles of his territory, traversing the Andes, seeking out the Indian villages in the high valleys as well as on the humid coast, crossing swollen rivers or desert plains, urged on always by his apostolic zeal. After his third voyage in 1598 he himself wrote to Pope Clement VIII that he had personally visited the country on many different trips, "getting to know and minister to my flock, correcting and remedying abuses where necessary, preaching on Sundays and feast-days to both natives and Spaniards in their own tongues and confirming a vast number of people, travelling more than five thousand two hundred leagues, often on foot, on unsafe roads and over rivers, overcoming every difficulty, sometimes going without food or sleep; going to the remote parts where there are Christian Indians (often at war with other Indians) to whom no prelate or Visitor had ever come." José de Acosta, writing of the obstacles to evangelization in Peru at this time, confirms that the routes were more suited to goats and deer than to men; that the Indian dwellings were more like sheep-pens and stables than human lodgings. Turibius normally stayed in the presbytery, but not every village had one, and he would then accept the hospitality of the Indians, contenting himself with the local fare. He received all who wished to see him with great affability. His work done, he would leave without delay for fear of burdening the local Christians. He accepted no gifts—rather was he assiduous in dispensing alms to the needy everywhere. He was especially noted for the delicacy with which he came to the aid of impoverished Spaniards. His voyages took place in 1584-90, 1593, 1598, 1601, and—the last, during which he died—1605. In 1593 he began a diary in which he noted the condition of the various parishes. He never omitted to say Mass even in the most trying conditions. It is said that he himself baptized and confirmed half a million persons, including St Rose of Lima (30 Aug.) and St Martin de Porres (5 Nov.).

In between journeys Turibius summoned not less than ten, perhaps as many as thirteen diocesan synods, and three provincial councils. Trent had recommended yearly synods, which in the missionary context proved difficult to realize. As it was, complaints were made to the king about their excessive number. Nor were the provincial councils particularly liked by the civil power, as they were thought to undermine the royal patronage. However, Turibius, who was more than conscious of being sandwiched between the civil and ecclesiastical powers—the latter the distinctly weaker of the two—knew how to tread warily. He submitted conciliar provisions to the king, as he was required to do, but also sent him reports regularly, as he did to the pope. Some viceroys were difficult to handle, others understanding and co-operative, and on occasion Philip II would support the archbishop on one or other issue, but the situation was always rendered difficult by the two jurisdictions. In addition, Turibius, for all his conscientiousness, provoked criticism: his absences were irritating to his chapter no less than to the secular authority. What did his journeys in fact achieve? In the course of a few days' visit could he really discover and deal with a latent paganism among the Indian converts? The answer was that he could not. It is true that Turibius tended to take expressions of submission and piety at their face value; not living with the natives as the parish priests did, he failed to see that they could be mendacious. The archbishop may or may not have analyzed the psychology of the Indians, a first-generation conquered people who were converts to Christianity; but in the long term the gesture of love his presence signified was grasped and remembered.

Turibius convoked two other councils at Lima, the fourth and fifth. Though poorly attended by the bishops—many of whom were burdened by age or other problems—and resented by the viceroy, the fourth council went ahead. It was concerned to clarify the relationship between the Ordinary and parish priests who were religious; it also reiterated many of the recommendations of the previous council. There was outright hostility on the part of the viceroy to the idea of a fifth council, but the archbishop insisted that he was obliged to observe the rules of the Church. It met, with nothing like the full complement of bishops, achieved little, and was terminated in a very short time. Philip III did not delay to let the archbishop know of his disapproval: his permission had not been obtained beforehand nor was there a representative of the Crown present.

227

The Third Council of Lima had agreed to the establishment of a seminary, but, for lack of funds and owing to his journey in 1584 Turibius was unable to advance the project. However, he obtained the king's agreement to his handling of funds donated by individuals without interference from the viceroy or his council. These found ways of insinuating themselves: the archbishop had required seminarians and professors to leave their arms outside the building; the viceroy sent soldiers to lay hold of them and went on to forbid any further admissions without his consent. He appointed his own man as steward. The archbishop threatened him with the king's displeasure, but as the viceroy would not yield, Turibius closed the seminary and sent away both students and professors. The king sided with the archbishop, ordering the civil authorities not to interfere in the running of the seminary, which was reopened in 1602. The friction was, all the same, continual. Turibius complained that he was summoned to the council almost always as to a trial of strength; this only served to arouse contempt for the bishops in their subordinates. On his journeys the archbishop got to know first-hand instances of dereliction of duty by the chief magistrates of the Indian villages, who failed to support the hospitals for the Indians or to contribute to the upkeep of the churches from funds received for these purposes. He had to write to the king to obtain a redress of the situation, but in one instance the local authorities of Lima, siding with the chief magistrate, penalized the prelate by freezing his funds.

Turibius also established a home for separated women who had no means of livelihood and, in 1594, a hospital for sick priests. He was concerned also for the quality of religious life, founding in 1605 the Poor Clare convent of Santa Clara, where the strict rule was to be observed.

That year Turibius set out again to visit his archdiocese. After fourteen months on the move he fell ill in Trujillo, but he pushed on as he wished to celebrate Holy Week in Santa Clara. He was obviously dying on his arrival there. When his chaplain told him of his condition he exclaimed, "*Laetatus sum in his quae dicta sunt mihi; in domo Domini ibimus!*" (I rejoiced at what was said to me, Let us go to God's house! Ps. 121:1) On Holy Thursday morning he was taken to the church to receive the *viaticum*, considering it unseemly that the sacrament should be brought to him. He was anointed on his return. The priest was so moved that he was unable to find his place in the ritual; the archbishop found it for him. After renewing his profession of faith, Turibius died peacefully as those around him reached the verse of Psalm 30: "Into your hands I commend my spirit."

He was buried in Santa Clara, but in 1606 the dean and chapter brought his remains to Lima, where he was buried in the then cathedral, awaiting a final resting-place in the new cathedral still being built. He was canonized in 1726 by Pope Benedict XIII and is the patron of Peru.

C. G. Irigoyen, *Santo Toribio: obra escrita con motivo del tercer centenario de la muerte del Santo Arzobispo de Lima* (1906); K. Latourette, *A History of the Expansion of Christianity*,

3, (1947); R. V. Ugarte, *Historia de la Iglesia en Peru, 2* (1959); F. Dussel (ed.), *The Church in Latin America: 1492-1992* (1992). There are modern biographies in Spanish by F. Redondo (1954) and V. Rodríguez Valencia (1957). See also *Bibl.SS.*, 12, 712-5.

Bd Edmund Sykes, *Martyr* (*c.* 1550-87)

Edmund Sykes was born in Leeds in Yorkshire and probably received his early education at the Leeds Grammar School, of which his father was a trustee. He was ordained in Reims in February 1581, returning to work in Yorkshire in June of that year. It was related of him that he "lived a very strict and strait life, wandering as a poor pilgrim, and coming to Leeds did help many with his holy life and doctrine." Four years into his ministry he became ill and fell into the hands of Arthur Webster, a lapsed Catholic, who made it his job to hunt down priests. Edmund Sykes was confined in the prison on Ousebridge in York, where his health deteriorated rapidly in the excessive cold and damp. His weakness made him agree to go to the Protestant church. He was immediately filled with remorse and wished to recant, but his captors refused to listen. He was condemned to perpetual banishment, the more lenient form of punishment.

Set down in Normandy, he begged his way to Douai College in Reims. His health was restored by now, but his lapse gave him no peace. He made a pilgrimage to Rome to do penance for it and beg forgiveness from the pope. While visiting one of the Roman churches he received what he regarded as a divine revelation bidding him return to England to continue his missionary work and there to receive the crown of martyrdom.

He left Reims on 16 June 1586 and once more returned to Leeds, where he resumed his ministry. It is thought that his own brother, who had received him into his house, betrayed him to the authorities. Imprisoned again in York, he consecrated his time to prayer and penance. The old temptation to lapse returned in prison and again during his trial when the judge suggested that he might obtain his freedom as he had done once before, but Edmund was adamant this time: "It was the infirmity of sickness that caused me to go to your service and not for any liking I had of it, the which I have repented and now detest to do it." He was condemned to death as a traitor, "whereat he rejoiced and thanked God." He was kept in solitary confinement until his execution. As he was dragged through the streets he was mocked, pelted with mud, and manhandled but remained unmoved. He was hanged in York on 23 March 1587 and beatified in 1987.

R. Connelly, *No Greater Love: The Martyrs of the Middlesbrough Diocese* (1987); Anstruther, 1, p. 377.

St Joseph Oriol (1650-1702)

José Oriol was born into a poor family in Barcelona, Spain, on 23 November 1650. His father, Juan Oriol, was a silk-weaver who died six months later. After a period of two years his mother, Gertrud Bugugna, contracted a second marriage with Domingo Pujolár, a cobbler, who came to love his stepson as though he had been his own child. Concerned about his education, he confided him to the clergy of his parish church, St Mary's by the Sea. Joseph became a choirboy, was taught music and the catechism, and was probably also given a primary education, without which he could not have gone on to the further studies he later pursued. He was required to undertake the duties of sacristan and in the course of this service gained his great sensitivity to the sacramental presence of Christ. He spent many hours of prayer in the church. His stepfather died when he was about twelve or thirteen, and Gertrud was once again an indigent widow. To lighten her burden, Caterina Brughéra, who had helped to nurse the boy in childhood, took him into her own home, where he remained for thirteen years.

Through the generosity of unknown benefactors Joseph was able to proceed to a university education. Once installed in Caterina Brughéra's home, he gave himself seriously to study and prayer, never leaving the house except to go to school or church. At the age of twenty-three he gained a doctorate in theology from the university of Barcelona and then went on to study moral theology and Hebrew. He was ordained in 1676. Always conscious of his mother's plight, he then took a job as tutor to the sons of Thomas Gasnieri in order to support her. The family was wealthy and lived in a sumptuous house. The tutor moved in, finding himself promoted to a standard of living far removed from the poverty of his childhood. In 1677 an incident at table had a momentous effect on his life. He was about to serve himself from one of the dishes of plentiful and delicious food when he felt his hand held back once, twice, and three times by a hidden but invincible force. He interpreted this strange paralysis as a divine indication that the way of good living was not his to pursue. From that moment he undertook a lifelong fast. Bran bread and water were to be his usual fare; some wild herbs would be added on a feast-day, and a sardine on Easter or Christmas Day. During Lent he would neither eat nor drink except on a Sunday. He remained with the Gasnieri family for nine years, until his mother died in 1686.

Three weeks later he set out on foot to visit the tombs of the apostles in Rome. There he was presented by Pope Innocent XI to a benefice with cure of souls, of the Church of St Mary of the Kings in Barcelona, generally known as Nuestra Señora del Pino. He returned to take up his charge, laying it down only at his death fifteen years later. Exactly a hundred years after Joseph Oriol's induction, Jean Vianney was born in France in 1786. More generally known as the Curé d'Ars (8 Aug.), he is one of the few parish priests in the history of the church to have attained such outstanding sanctity. Joseph Oriol may be considered as remarkable a saint and in many ways a forerunner and a kindred spirit. Both were to subject themselves to a punishing asceticism, both were endowed with special graces, and both were to expend themselves on the pastoral care of those committed to them, spending hours in the confessional.

Joseph rented a narrow attic room from a Dr Padrós, and when the latter died he stayed on with his widow's consent, in fact not leaving until his last illness. The room was remote and quiet and gave him the solitude he needed for his hours of prayer and penance—although the inhabitants of the house could not but be aware of his nightly flagellations. All he possessed was a table, a bench, a crucifix, and a few books. There was no fire to protect him against the cold, nor was there a bed—he never slept for more than two or three hours a night, resting in a sitting position or, if he lay down, using a mat only. He would clean the room himself as a measure of privacy. He wore the same shabby clothes in summer and winter and eschewed a hat against cold or heat. He would not spend anything on himself or on his furnishings, keeping all the money that accrued to him from his benefice for the poor or for Masses for the dead. He had one aim only: to detach himself completely from everything that was not God in order to cling to God with all his might.

Initially he was ridiculed in the streets, bearing it in good part, but that was to change. However far he had to travel, he did so on foot. He spoke rarely but responded courteously and gently to those who addressed him, measuring his words to his hearers' needs. Children would approach to kiss his hand, and he would lead them to church for a catechism lesson; women, who judged they were speaking to an angel rather than a man, had no fear of being repulsed by him. He seemed to have a marked influence over soldiers and prisoners, whom he won over by his gentleness and sympathy. The intelligent and cultured would listen to him respectfully, and even street vendors and tradesmen would rise as he passed. Although grave, he was never morose; on the contrary, he was known as a happy saint. There was an incandescent quality about him that drew others. People sensed that he loved them and they gave him their trust.

He was the first in choir for the office and the last to leave it. He generally confessed before Mass, which he said with deep recollection. His preparation was long, so too his thanksgiving. If he visited a parishioner's house, it was because there was some spiritual need to be met. His conversation there was restricted to the mysteries of the faith; his exhortations concerned the reception of the sacraments and devotion to Our Lady. Above all else there was his ministry in the confessional, to which he gave every spare minute. He had a special gift for direction reinforced by his ability to read his penitents' hearts. At one point he was accused of overseverity and of prescribing penances injurious to health. His critics succeeded in gaining the ear of the bishop, who forbade him to hear any more Confessions. However the bishop died shortly after and his successor restored all Joseph's faculties.

Strangely enough, in the midst of this busy life, he was suddenly seized with an irresistible desire for martyrdom and decided to go to Rome to place himself at the disposal of the Congregation of *Propaganda Fide*. He would brook no appeals against his decision: in vain did the people of Barcelona entreat him to remain; in vain did two older priests urge him to reflect. He started off for Italy but fell ill in Marseilles, where a vision of Our Lady encouraged him to return to Barcelona and spend the rest of his life caring for the sick.

From then on he seemed to grow to perfect holiness, its fruit manifest in the works of compassion he performed for every sort of misery. Experiencing permanent union with God, he was continually rapt out of himself, unseeing and unhearing, unconscious of what he was saying or doing. His body was transfigured as he stood at the altar, and his face, normally pale, became flushed and on fire as he carried the Blessed Sacrament to the sick through the streets, so much so that people stopped to look at him and marvel. The sick, the main recipients of his ministry, felt a flame reach out to them as he laid his hands on them. Every day after Vespers a crowd of them converged on St Mary's from the towns and villages around. He would dip his fingers in holy water and make the sign of the cross or lay his hands on them, bringing about astonishing cures. To relieve the pressure on St Mary's he himself would sometimes go out to neighbouring villages. The only people who were not pleased were the pharmacists, who found themselves losing custom, and those in a state of sin and unbelief. These he recognized and would not heal, hoping that this would bring them to repentance. Joseph retained his humility, marvelling only that God could use such an instrument as he. He firmly believed that all priests could do as much if they wished to use the gifts Christ had given them.

Sensing the time of his death, he requested a room and a bed from a friend and moved in some days before. He was anointed and received the *viaticum*. During the last three days he received the *viaticum* again but had nothing else. When he announced that his death was imminent, those with him were grieved, but he begged them to rejoice with him, promising that he would remember them before God. He remained peaceful, even merry. As death approached he asked for the *Stabat Mater* to be said. During this, with his eyes fixed on the crucifix, he gently breathed his last. It was 23 March 1702, and he was in his fifty-third year. He was canonized in 1909.

Immense crowds collected round his bier and on the day of the funeral the church doors had to be closed to allow the burial to take place.

A.A.S. 1 (1909), pp. 605-22; Masdeu, *Vida del Beato Josef Oriol* (1886); J. Ballester, *Vida de San José Oriol* (1909); Salotti, *Vita di San Giuseppe Oriol (1909)*; E. Anzizu, *Vida de San José Oriol* (Spanish trans. 1910).

Bd Annunziata Cóchetti, *Foundress* (1800-82)

Annunziata Cochetti was born on 9 May 1800 in Rovata, in the diocese of Brescia in Italy, the daughter of landowning parents. She was orphaned when only seven and subsequently brought up by her grandmother. When she was seventeen she opened a school for girls in what had been her parents' home. Conscious of the need to have some professional qualification and legal standing, she obtained a certificate as a qualified teacher, which led to an appointment to the elementary school in Rovato.

After the death of her grandmother, her uncle and guardian wished her to leave Rovato and live with him in Milan. There she stayed for six years, keeping up her contacts in her home town, above all with some aristocratic ladies in and around Brescia who were engaged in social work, especially with the young. Under the inspiration of Don Luca Passi, some of these ladies joined the *Pia Opera di Santa Dorotea,* a movement then gaining strength in Italy.

Don Luca attempted to open a school for country girls in 1821 in Cemmo, but the attempt failed, and the buildings came under the administration of Don Vincenzo Panzerini from Lovere, who tried again to get a school running, putting it in the charge of his niece, Erminia Panzerini. Hearing from the ladies of Brescia that this school needed another teacher, Annunziata offered her services and in 1831 began work in Cemmo. For eleven years she worked together with Erminia and raised the school to a high standard. She was also concerned to further the movement of the *Pia Opera* and set up several branches in Cemmo and the neighbouring parishes.

Meanwhile, during that same year of 1831 Don Luca was in the process of founding an Institute, the Sisters of St Dorothy, to promote the movement of the *Pia Opera.* When Erminia Panzerini died in 1842, Annunziata made a novitiate with these Sisters with the intention of founding her own Institute. She returned, clothed in the religious habit and with two other companions, to Cemmo in October 1842; in 1843 the three took religious vows in the new Institute, the Sisters of St Dorothy of Cemmo. A novitiate was opened in 1853.

Annunziata Cochetti was a woman of immense energy, which she consecrated to the Institute she had founded, but she was also a person of deep prayer, with a great love for Christ and the Holy Eucharist. She sought to implant in both Sisters and pupils a deep sacrificial love of God. In the summer months from 1843 onward she organized retreats for the girls in a special retreat-house. Eventually she herself went to live in the retreat-house and died there on 23 March 1882, at the age of eighty-two.

She was beatified by Pope John Paul II on 21 April 1991. Today the Congregation has houses in England, Argentina, Burundi, and Zaire, with some four hundred members in seventy-two houses.

Bibl.SS., 3, pp. 241-4; F. Holböck, *Die neuen Heligen der katholischen Kirche*, 3 (1994), pp. 221-4.

Bd Rebecca Al-Rayes (1832-1914)

Boutroussieh Al-Rayes was born in the town of Himlaya in the Lebanon; the precise date is unknown, as records were lost when the town was sacked by the Druze in 1860. Her father was Mourad Saber Al-Chabaq Al-Rayes, her mother

Rafqa El-Gemayel, both practising Maronite Christians. Rafqa El-Gemayel died when Boutroussieh was only seven, and her father remarried within two years. The family remained poor, so as soon as she was old enough to take a job, Boutroussieh became a domestic servant with a Christian Lebanese family living in Damascus.

When she was fourteen, she was recalled by her father, who considered that she should now be married, although Boutroussieh herself was not at all disposed to marry. She seems to have remained in Himlaya until she was twenty-one and was known to have repulsed interested young men. Returning one day from drawing water, Boutroussieh overheard her aunt and stepmother having a heated exchange over whom she should marry. Distressed, she decided to leave home and become a religious, so fulfilling a hidden, long-standing desire. She set out in 1853 for the convent of Our Lady of Deliverance at Bikfaya, which belonged to the Mariamette Sisters, an indigenous teaching Congregation recently founded by the Jesuits. On the way she met three other young women and suggested that they go with her. Two agreed and they went on. The three presented themselves to the superior, who accepted Boutroussieh without further ado, asking the others to return another time. The next day, her father and stepmother arrived to take her home, but she begged the superior not to send her to the parlour. She never saw them again.

She was clothed in 1855 and took the name of Anissa (Agnes). A humble and observant novice, she was generally well loved and esteemed. The following year, 1856, found her in Ghazir, where she made her profession. There she was cook for seven years. In her spare time she studied Arabic, writing, and arithmetic and was able to take up teaching in Deir-el-Qamar, where she was sent in 1860. That year the Druze, who had been attacking the Christians from time to time since 1840, launched an attack of such ferocity that almost eight thousand Christians were said to have been killed in the Lebanon in the space of twenty-two days. The streets of Deir-el-Qamar ran with the blood of Maronite men. The Druze did not generally kill women, but to ensure their safety, an Arab hid the Sisters in a stable when the attack began. Sr Agnes could never recall the butchery of those days without weeping.

Two years in Deir-el Qamar were followed by one year in the town of Jbeïl, then a year in Ma'ad. The Mariamettes were then asked by a wealthy Christian benefactor, Antoun Issa, to send a teacher to his village in the same district. Sr Agnes was sent and remained there for seven years, teaching a class of sixty pupils and lodging in the home of Antoun Issa and his wife.

In 1871 a crisis developed in her Congregation. The Jesuits wished to unite the Mariamettes and the Daughters of the Sacred Heart, two Institutes almost identical in their aims, both of which had lost some of their property in the massacres of 1860. The two could not agree on certain points, and the Jesuits decided to suppress them both. Sr Agnes did not wish to return to the world as some Sisters did. Antoun Issa saw her distress and offered to make her his heir if she would stay and continue her teaching. As she was convinced she ought rather to enter a monastery, he offered to pay any expenses and recommended her case to the archbishop. At the age of thirty-nine, on 12 July 1871, Sr Agnes entered the monastery of St Sé'man El-Qarn of the Baladite Order, one of the two monastic Congregations into which the 1695 Maronite Order of Lebanon had split in 1770. She took her mother's name, Rafqa (Rebecca). Her profession took place on 25 August 1873.

Sister Rebecca brought to her monastic round the same qualities of diligence and devotion that had marked her active religious life, coloured now by a feeling of having come home. She had a fine voice and sang the office with all her heart, attentively and joyfully. She was always the first in choir in the morning and frequently visited the church. If she were not to be found at work or in her cell, she would be in church. Her superior considered that her charity toward her sisters had attained a high degree of perfection. If she saw anyone sad, she would try to encourage her; she frequently visited the sick and was prepared to spend her nights beside anyone needing special attention. If anyone were punished, she would beg to be allowed to take on or share that person's penance as a mark of encouragement to the delinquent and to dispel any idea of personal rejection. She sought nothing for herself. She begged never to be given a new habit, preferring to wear a second-hand one. Her only possessions were a cushion, a spindle, and a metal box to hold the skeins for her knitting.

Sr Rebecca, however, still felt there was something in her life not wholly consecrated to God. On Rosary Sunday in October 1885 she went to church and, in her own words, "I realized that my health was good, that never in my life had I been ill, and I prayed then, 'My God, why are you so far away from me? Why do you abandon me? You do not come to me in the experience of illness. Have you then abandoned me?'" That night, she felt a violent pain in her head which extended to her eyes. It was the first sign of the passion that was to last twenty-nine years. Her headaches and eye-aches became almost intolerable, and gradually she lost the sight of her right eye. A visit to a quack doctor resulted in the gouging out of this eye, with a subsequent concentration of pain in the left eye. Her only comfort was that she could sing the offices from memory.

The community could not keep warm at a high altitude without wood fires, the smoke of which exacerbated the pain in Sr Rebecca's eye unendurably, so in 1897 she was sent to another monastery nearer sea level, Saint Joseph at Jrabta. Shortly after her arrival there, she lost her sight completely, and the pains caused by a deteriorating bone structure began. The pain was excruciating and continual. Not only did Rebecca never complain, but she was full of gratitude to Our Lord for the grace to share his sufferings. She would murmur quietly, especially when the pain was intense, "In union with the sufferings of Jesus, with the pains caused by the lance, the crown of thorns. . . ." She was eventually totally confined to bed, able to rest only on one side, unable to move any part of her body except her hands, with which she knitted socks for the community or fingered the rosary. Sr Ursula, her superior, summed up her illness: "She remained seventeen years paralyzed and blind, bearing atrocious pain which only God could measure. . . . In spite of this we never heard her murmur or complain or ask God to free her from her sufferings." Sr Rebecca judged the situation with simple logic: "I asked for this illness of my own accord and with full consent, so I may not complain or murmur. . . . The potter can do what he wants with the clay. Whether he dislocates my bones or breaks them, his will be done." She considered her sufferings as nothing in comparison with those of Christ. "My head is not crowned with thorns; there are no nails in my hands or in my feet. I have sins to expiate, but he, in his love for us, has borne an infinite degree of opprobrium and so much suffering, and we think so little of it."

On two occasions her symptoms were somehow temporarily alleviated. On the feast of Corpus Christi, she conceived an overpowering desire to be present at the Eucharist and prayed earnestly to be allowed this. Suddenly she felt her body slipping from the bed, and her feet dangling to the floor. Soon she was on the floor and dragging herself along to the church. The community was speechless, some weeping with emotion. She remained seated during the Eucharist and asked to sit on for a time afterwards. When it was time to return to her cell she could no longer move. On another occasion her superior asked her if she had no special wish of her own. She replied that she would indeed like to have her sight back just for an hour so that she might see her and the other Sisters. Her sight was immediately restored for the space of an hour and she was able to identify various objects in the room.

Sr Rebecca died on 23 March 1914 at the age of eighty-two and was buried two days later. She was beatified by Pope John Paul II on 17 November 1985. A charming icon of the *beata* in the Syrian tradition was presented to the pope for the occasion.

Joséph Mahfouz: *La Bienheureuse Rafqa (Rebecca) de Himlaya* (2d ed. 1985); *Bibl.SS.,* 11, 66-7.

R.M.

St Fingar (Guigner): see under SS Fingar and Piala, 14 Dec.

St Victorian and Companions, martyrs at Carthage and elsewhere in Africa (484)

St Liberatus, his wife and sons, martyrs in Africa (484)

St Eusebius, bishop of Saint-Paul-Trois-Chateaux, Burgundy (*c.* 600)

St Ethelwald, hermit of Farne (*c.* 700)

St Guibert (orWibert), monk of Gorzes, Lorraine (tenth century)

St Otto, hermit at Ariano in Sannio (*c.* 1120)

24

St Hildelith, *Abbess* (*c.* 712)

St Erkenwald (30 Apr.) was an outstanding bishop of London, revered for his sanctity throughout the Middle Ages. Before he became a bishop, he founded the two monasteries of Chertsey (for men) in Surrey, and Barking (for women) in Essex, about the year 666. He himself ruled the first while the second was entrusted to his sister Ethelburga (11 Oct.), whose holiness Bede extols in his *Ecclesiastical History.*

Bede says nothing of Hildelith being summoned by Erkenwald, whether from Faremoutiers or Chelles, to train Ethelburga and her companions in the monastic life. The tradition derives from later writers and may or may not be reliable. It is certain that on St Ethelburga's death Hildelith was elected abbess in her stead and ruled the monastery for very many years, indeed well into her old age. Bede implies that she possessed a dynamic character, well able to set important schemes in hand and to think of the practical means of ensuring a well-ordered community life. He records that since there was not enough space for a properly laid out cemetery, she had the bones of those buried here and there, men and women, transferred to the church and re-buried in one place. However, her first concern was for the regular observance of the house. She and her nuns must also have had a fair knowledge of Latin, as St Aldhelm (25 May) dedicated his treatise on virginity to them. She was also known to St Boniface (5 June), who esteemed her greatly. In a letter to the abbess of St Mildred's, Thanet, he speaks of a vision Hildelith had had and which she herself had described to him.

The exact date of her death is not known.

AA.SS., Mar., 3, pp. 482-5; Bede, *H.E.*, 4, 10; 5, 18; *O.D.S.*, pp. 160-1; 163-4; 231-2. An Anglo-Saxon drawing of Aldhelm presenting his treatise to St Hildelith still survives.

St Catherine of Vadstena, *Abbess* (1331?-81)

Katerina Ulfsdotter was the fourth of the eight children born to St Bridget (8 Oct.) and her husband, Ulf Gudmarsson. When she was about four or five years of age, her mother was summoned to the service of the king, to whom she was related. Bridget took her young son Gudmar with her, confiding her other children to various religious houses. Catherine and a younger sister, Ingeborg, were sent to the Cistercian monastery of Risaberg, which the latter entered in due course.

Saddened by the death of Gudmar and conscious that the court was becoming more and more worldly and dissipated, Ulf and Bridget decided to leave, using as an excuse their desire to make the pilgrimage to Compostela. Catherine, who showed no inclination to be a Cistercian, was transferred to the Dominican convent at Skenninge, where the younger Cecilia was already staying, until her parents should return. When they did so, it was not to reconstruct the family life for which Catherine was perhaps hankering. Ulf was already a sick man who considered he had won a reprieve from God and must spend his remaining time in a monastery. He was received at Alvastra and died there in 1344, but not before he had arranged a marriage for Catherine with Edgard Kryn.

The marriage was never consummated. Edgard was deeply fond of Catherine and would follow wherever she led. Although not at this time prepared to be a religious, she proposed for them both a way of life that was hardly distinguishable from the religious life. They fasted and prayed, dressed and ate poorly, and slept on the ground. Risaberg may have provided Catherine with a Cistercian structure on which to build her own fancies, but it was her mother Bridget whose influence was paramount. Catherine aspired after the holiness of her mother, whom she deeply loved and admired. In the meantime Bridget herself was being led beyond family concerns into the wider life of the Church. After Ulf's death she gave up many of her possessions and went to the monastery of Alvastra, where she was given a room. Dressed in the habit of a Franciscan tertiary, she adopted an exceedingly austere régime. Guided by her almost daily visions of Our Lord and his mother, her sights were set on Rome, the centre of Christendom, but first she wished to found a monastery in Sweden. The foundation stone was laid in Vadstena in 1346; the Rule was said to have been dictated to her in a vision. After some time at the court, Bridget left for Rome in 1349. Her task was first and foremost to restore the papacy to Rome and then to secure papal approval and confirmation for her own foundation at Vadstena.

Later Catherine was to tell the Sienese Catherine (29 Apr.) that after her mother's departure she forgot how to smile. Now she was consumed with an almost irrational longing to be with her and was only too glad to respond to the pope's call to Christendom to visit Rome for the Jubilee Year of 1350. Edgard was already suffering from the illness from which he was shortly to die, but, always willing to gratify her, he encouraged her to go. Once she had finished the prescribed visits to the basilicas to gain the Jubilee indulgences, Catherine became anxious to return to Sweden. There ensued a period of anguish for the nineteen-year-old as she fought to come to terms with a situation that was by no means as clear to her as it was to her mother. Bridget had received in one of her visions a promise that she would be given a companion to support her in her work. She learned also by the same means that Catherine's husband had died or was soon to die, although the point at which she told her daughter of this cannot be fixed. Catherine may not have known all the facts of the case when her mother asked her to remain with her in Rome. She agreed, but without enthusiasm, as her subsequent wavering between acceptance and refusal was to show. On the one hand there was the tremendous pull of her affection for her mother, the magnetism of Bridget's personality and holiness, on the other the appalling conditions of civil life in Rome, its stifling heat in summer, and perpetual exile from the cool pine forests and clean, clear rivers of Sweden.

The months that preceded the resolution of her problem were not made easier when Bridget forbade her to leave the house for fear of her safety. All the sources agree that Catherine was ravishingly beautiful, and for a long time she would live in fear of abduction; for the moment it seemed she was no more than a prisoner: "I lead a wretched life here, caged like an animal, while the others go and nourish their souls in church. In Sweden my brothers and sisters are able to serve God in peace." One evening Bridget returned to the house after attending Vespers and found Catherine in a rebellious mood. "What's wrong with you?" she asked. Catherine would not answer. Bridget pressed her, but all she would say was, "I can't tell you!" That night Catherine had a dream in which Our Lady is said to have argued with her: "You ask me to help you, but how can I when all you want is to go back to Sweden? You are not being faithful to your promises to our Lord." Catherine immediately promised to do whatever was asked of her. The Virgin replied, "Obey your confessor and your mother." The next day Catherine made her submission to her mother, but Bridget, afraid she might spoil her child, declined to accept her promise of obedience. She was to give that to Peter, their confessor. The struggle still continued for a time, but the day finally came when Catherine felt that she had overcome every reluctance to do what was required of her.

It is not easy to see what specifically was required of Catherine, since her whole existence was to be absorbed in her mother's vocation. Even that lacks clear features. Judging from their activity, their task seemed primarily that of intercession for the return of the pope to Rome. Many hours a day were set aside for visits to the Roman basilicas and shrines, but many hours were spent also in solitary prayer. Contacts with the great families of the city served to bring these back to a sense of Christian morality—of long-term value in preparing the way for the restoration of the Christian character of the city—while succouring the sick poor used up time and resources. There is no evidence for the tradition that Catherine, like her mother, was a Franciscan tertiary, but their personal lives were marked by an extreme poverty and harsh asceticism. They were even forced by their own indigence to beg alms for the support of the household. In addition there was Bridget's correspondence with popes and clerics, prompted by her almost daily visions.

For all her absorption in her mother's activities, Catherine was by no means Bridget's double. Her total self-effacement points to another type of spirituality, almost the opposite of her mother's. They shared the same goal, the same ideals, often enough the same means to the end, but Catherine did not apparently walk the way of visionary familiarity with the supernatural world. She left no revelations, no accounts of supernatural locutions or of ecstasies experienced. She was not told to convey any messages to others. Her way seemed to be that of profound, unfelt faith sustained by assiduous prayer and self-sacrifice. For almost a quarter of a century she stayed at her mother's side, accompanying her everywhere on the daily rounds or on pilgrimage outside Rome. She shared Bridget's short-lived joy at the return to Rome of Pope Urban V. Bridget was granted an interview then and presented her Rule for approbation, which was only partially granted. However, the pope was soon back in Avignon, where he died shortly after. Bridget was not to see Gregory XI in Rome nor to endure the pain of the schism, which she nevertheless predicted. She and Catherine undertook a pilgrimage to the Holy Land, spending some time in Naples on their outward voyage. After their return Bridget fell ill and died in Rome in July 1373.

It fell to Catherine to organize and lead the triumphal return of her mother's remains to Sweden. She waited for several weeks for one of her mother's advisers, Alphonsus de Vadaterra, to return from Avignon before setting out. In the presence of Vadaterra and a large crowd, the coffin was opened. Invaded by the strong perfume that the relics exhaled, Catherine was caught up in a wave of emotion and spoke of her mother as no one had ever heard her speak. Her inspired speeches continued throughout the journey back to Sweden, and she was found advising even prelates about their behaviour—rather as her mother had done. However, Catherine had no other desire for the moment than to withdraw to Vadstena, where she arrived with the relics in June 1374.

She asked to be received as a novice in the community but was acclaimed abbess by common consent. In the few months she spent at Vadstena she attempted to put the community on its feet, materially and spiritually. However, the hierarchy of Sweden sought Bridget's canonization, and they turned to Catherine, asking her to present their petition for this to the Holy Father. She set out once more for Rome in 1375, armed with written testimonies of favours granted through Bridget's intercession. Pope Gregory XI was not yet in Rome, so Catherine went to Naples to collect further testimonies from those who had met Bridget there earlier. The pope arrived in Rome in January 1377, and Catherine had her interview. Her two requests were referred to a commission, which proposed the canonization. Gregory XI died before anything could be done. Urban VI succeeded, but such was his heavy-handedness that a rival pope, Clement VII, was elected. Catherine was granted an interview with the legitimate Urban in full consistory, which she addressed so eloquently that the pope exclaimed, "My child, you have indeed been nourished on your mother's milk!" Urban did much for the community at Vadstena, approving the decision of one of his predecessors that the Rule of St Augustine, modified by

Bridget's own Rule, be observed, and securing many privileges for the community. The canonization was again taken up, but still the pope did not act. It was at this time that Catherine met Catherine of Siena, who, like Bridget, was given the task of bringing the papacy back to Rome. The pope had planned that the two women should go together to Queen Joanna of Naples to divert her from her allegiance to the antipope, Clement VII, but Catherine would not accept what she regarded as a hopeless mission. After five years in Rome, her resources depleted, she decided to return to Sweden. Her mother's cause was completed; the rest was up to the pope, whose inaction due to the state of the papacy was beyond her control.

Catherine returned to Vadstena in July 1380. She was already ill but lived on until March of the following year. She died on 22 March 1381. Boniface IX canonized Bridget on 7 October 1391. St Catherine's name was added to the Roman Martyrology, but it appears that she was never officially canonized. She is depicted in art with a stag beside her, recalling an incident in which she was accosted by a Roman nobleman and saved from his advances by a stag. Sometimes she is portrayed with a hind beneath her cloak; once, when out with a hunting party together with her husband, a hind pursued by the dogs sought refuge beneath her cloak and was saved. Sometimes she is seen adoring the sacred Host, which she was unable to receive on her death-bed because of the nature of her illness.

Ulf Birgersson, a monk of Vadstena, composed a conventional biography of St Catherine some fifty years after her death. It is reproduced in *AA.SS.*, Mar., 3, pp. 501-29, and in a critical edition in *Scriptores rerum Sueciarum*, 3, together with the documents and collections of miracles drawn up for her canonization. These documents were published in full by I. Collijn: *Processus seu Negocium Canonizacionis b. Katerinae de Vadstenis* (1942-6). For a fuller bibliography see the entry for St Bridget, whose biography encompasses that of her daughter.

Bd Diego Joseph (1743-1801)

Diego Joseph was popularly called "the apostle of the Holy Trinity" because of his devotion to the mystery of the Three Divine Persons and the ingenuity with which he contrived to make the dogma of the Blessed Trinity the subject of his eloquent and most fruitful sermons. He was born on 30 March 1743 in the city of Cadiz in Andalusia, Spain. His father was José López Camaño, a native of Túy in Galicia and related to the counts of Villagarcía. His mother, María de Ocaña y García, was from Andalusia; she died when Joseph was nine years old.

The boy was baptized José Francisco Juan María and was said to have preserved his baptismal innocence throughout his life. Attendance at the Capuchin church and the reading of the Lives of Capuchin saints awakened in him a desire to enter the Franciscan Order. He received the habit on 12 November 1757, although he did not begin his year of probation until 31 March 1758, after he had completed his fifteenth year. Diego Joseph, as he was known in religious life, studied philosophy at Écija and then went to Cadiz for his theological training. He lost his fervour over the years and settled into a comfortable existence, but while studying dogmatic theology he had a powerful conversion experience, which led him to take his studies more seriously and intensify his prayer life. He was ordained priest on 24 May 1766 and was sent out to preach.

It was evident from the first that Diego was endowed with gifts of no mean order, for wherever he went his sermons brought about many conversions. His efforts were at first confined to Andalusia, but soon he was travelling throughout Spain, teaching and preaching in remote villages and crowded towns, shrinking from neither fatigue nor hardship. Eschewing the contemporary florid style of homily, he based his sermons more directly on the Gospels. He spoke tenderly of the love of God, of grace, of Christ as the model for every Christian. He described the effects of sin and how to combat vice. He preached about the obligation of all baptized persons to live according to the gospel and fulfil the duties of their state in life. Salvation was a continual process requiring continual effort. He seemed able to establish an immediate rapport with his hearers, so that he won the hearts of the poor and the well-to-do alike, of students and of professors. His work in the confessional complemented his preaching. There he could direct and strengthen those whom his sermons had touched. Any free time during the day was spent visiting prisons and hospitals or in similar works of charity, whilst a great part of the night was given to prayer.

Sometimes the largest churches could not contain the crowds who came to hear him, and he would preach in a square or in the streets to congregations of several thousand. At the close of his sermons he had to be protected from the people who tried to tear pieces from his habit as relics. He shunned all presents and, if obliged to accept them, would immediately distribute them to the poor. Injustice toward the poor was always one of his concerns, and he tried to educate others in their duty to help the oppressed. After he had preached in the town of Antequera the city leaders decided to establish a society to care for the starving poor in prison; on the other hand he was forbidden to preach in Seville for seven years for having spoken against the ecclesiastical system of benefices as this affected the poor.

Fr Diego did not hesitate to attack the government in his defence of the rights of the Church and was consequently imprisoned for three years, but he railed no less against worldliness in the Church. The Pyrenees proved no barrier to the irreligion of the Encyclopedists or the impiety of Voltaire, and he saw it as his mission to alert the faithful to these contemporary dangers.

The posthumously-published correspondence of 1777-84 between Diego and his second spiritual director and much-loved friend, Francis Xavier González, whose cause has since been introduced in Rome, contains a wealth of autobiographical material. It tells that in the midst of Diego's successes as the most popular preacher in eighteenth-century Spain he endured continual dryness of spirit and discouragement and often found himself in the grip of humbling temptations. By temperament he was emotional and indecisive, sensitive and pusillanimous. His saving grace was his obedience. This served him in good stead when Fr González died and Fr Juan José Alcover, a highly-gifted priest but reserved and temperamentally quite different from the affectionate Diego, whom he could not understand, became his third director. By abandoning himself for a period of seventeen years to the firm if authoritarian direction of Fr Alcover, Diego learned to disregard and so master his own sensitivity. On the other hand, Diego's letters of direction to his spiritual daughters show his own warm-heartedness.

He died in Ronda on 24 March 1801. Immediately his death became known, he was popularly acclaimed as a saint. His remains are preserved at the shrine of Our Lady of Peace at Ronda. He was beatified by Pope Leo XIII on 1 April 1894.

His works were published in 5 vols. (Madrid 1796-9) and a bibliography by S. de Asejo (1947); For his biography see D. de Soisey, *Le Bx Diego Joseph de Cadiz* (1902); *C.F.S.*, p. 1; *Dict.Sp.*, 3, 875-8; Sebastián de Ubrique, *Vida del Beato Diego José de Cadiz* (1926); Ambrosio de Valenciana, *El director perfecto y el dirigido santo* (1924); J. B. de Ardales, *La Divina Pastora* (1949); *Bibl.SS.*, 4, 610-12.

R.M.
St Artemon, bishop of Seleucia in Pisidia (second century)
St Timolaeus and Companions, martyrs at Caesarea, Palestine (303)
St Macartan, bishop of Clogher in Ireland (fifth century)
St Caimin, abbot of Cealtra in Ireland (654)
St Bertulf, bishop and martyr at Mondovi in Liguria (*c.* 800)
St Aldemar, abbot of Bocchignano in Abruzzo (eleventh century)
Bd Bertha de Alberti, abbess of Cavriglia in Tuscany (1163)
Bd John "del Bastone" monk at Fabriano in Piceno (1290)

25

THE ANNUNCIATION OF THE LORD

In the Calendar reform of 1969 the title of today's feast was changed from "The Annunciation to the Virgin Mary" to "The Annunciation of the Lord." However, the Annunciation is made to Mary and forms a vital part of her role in the economy of salvation, which is followed in her various feasts retained in the present work. This entry therefore should be read in conjunction with those for the Birthday of Our Lady (8 Sept.), the Visitation (31 May), and the Assumption (15 Aug.).

This celebration would not have occurred in the early centuries when martyrs alone were remembered in the liturgy. However, on the analogy of other feast-days celebrated in the basilicas of the Holy Land, once the empress Helena had built a basilica over the house of Nazareth in the fourth century, a locally-observed feast would have taken root and spread to the rest of the Christian world by returning pilgrims.

In the second century Tertullian reflects the belief that the death of Christ took place on 25 March. St Augustine repeats this, referring to what may have been a commonly accepted pious tradition in Africa that both the conception and death of Christ took place on the same day. There are traces in Spain also of the belief that Christ was conceived on 25 March. However, the celebration of a liturgical feast seems to be dependent on the assignment to 25 December of the feast of the birth of the Lord some time before the middle of the fourth century. Basil of Seleucia and Hesychius of Jerusalem, who both lived in the fifth century, have sermons on the feast, while the seventh-century Sophronius of Jerusalem (11 Mar.) has two, but by the end of that century a liturgical commemoration of the Annunciation on 25 March was widespread, if not uniformly observed due to the reluctance of some bishops to intrude on the liturgy of Lent and Easter. For these, Advent seemed a more propitious time, 18 December being the preferred date. The Advent liturgy has always retained traces of the commemoration of the Annunciation—we have St Bernard's homilies to prove the point—and it still does to this day.

St Bernard protests in one of these homilies that he cannot go beyond the scriptural account: "The prophets speak the Virgin's praise, an angel treats with her, an evangelist recounts what happened. I do not praise her, then, because I dare not. All I can do is devoutly repeat what the Holy Spirit has already brought out by the mouth of the evangelist." Luke's account in fact ranges over the inspired scriptures, using phrases consecrated by centuries of messianic expectation.

Luke wrote his Gospel some seventy to ninety years after the events he narrates, after carefully ascertaining the facts. If Mary divulged those things that she had kept in her heart concerning her son's conception and birth, it would have been to John the apostle, through whom they would have become the common property of the infant Church. As most commentators remark, Luke imposes his own pattern on the material he collected. His account, at once pictorial and profoundly theological, can only be a re-creation of what happened, primarily based on the Virgin's own experience but also on the first disciples' grasp of the mystery of the risen Christ.

Mary is told to rejoice as the recipient of God's special favour. The angel's words, which contain allusions to messianic texts from Isaiah and Zephaniah, are an invitation to messianic joy. The Old Testament frequently personifies the people of Israel as a woman, as the "Daughter of Zion" or the "Virgin daughter of Zion," whether in times of sorrow or in expressions indicative of a joy to come: "Say to the daughter of Zion, Your Saviour is coming!" (Isa. 62:11); "Shout with cries of joy, Daughter of Zion!" (Zeph. 3:14); "Sing and shout for joy, Daughter of Zion, for see I am coming to dwell among you" (Zech. 2:14; 9:9). The joy to which Mary, as daughter of Zion, is invited is founded on the coming of God to his people. She stands in for them now, receiving on their behalf the definitive announcement of the "good news," but even as she represents the old Israel, a change is taking place: Mary is the first member of the new Israel, the first to be favoured in the new era of grace "for the law came through Moses but grace and peace through Jesus Christ" (John 1:17). At the same time, she receives the good news as that individual person, that outstanding member of the Church, who is specifically graced to be the mother of the Messiah. Hers is a new title that supplants that of the Daughter of Zion and is the starting point for Marian theology concerning the Immaculate Conception. St Sophronius (11 Mar.) addresses Our Lady in the second of his sermons: "Conscious of your signal privileges, which surpass those granted to all other creatures, I too cry out in your praise, 'Rejoice, favoured one of God, the Lord is with you.'"

"The Lord is with you" and "have no fear" are phrases used in the Old Testament to encourage and strengthen a person called upon by God to embark on some new course or undertake some action important to the history of the chosen people. Mary is conscious, then, that the angel's address heralds a divine intervention which concerns her, filling her with awe but also with trepidation. In words that almost replicate those of Zephaniah (3:16, 17), the angel responds to her bewilderment: "Do not be afraid . . . you will conceive in your womb." Zephaniah's expression had been addressed to Zion: "The Lord your God is in your womb" (Zeph. 3:17), referring to God's presence in the Temple. Mary is now to be the new temple enshrining God's presence.

The angel continues "and you will bear a son. . . . He shall be great and will be called the Son of the Most High. The Lord God will give him the throne of his father David, he will rule over the house of Jacob and his reign will have no end." This takes up another messianic prophecy concerning the successor to David, promised by God through Nathan the prophet: "The Lord will make you great . . . your House and your sovereignty will always stand secure before me and your throne will be established for ever" (2 Sam. 7:1-17), and "I will be a father to him and he a son to me" (1 Chron. 17:13). The use of these messianic texts leaves no doubt now as to the identity of the son to be born, but Mary is shown as still puzzled, now on her own account. She is engaged though not married to Joseph: she is still a virgin. The angel speaks of a future birth; marriage is presumably likely to follow the engagement and itself could be followed by the predicted birth, yet she does not pursue this obvious line of thought. Luke, however, after the event, knows that Christ was born of a virgin and that Mary remained a virgin; some commentators think that her choice of virginity was subsequent to the birth of Christ and is reflected back into the present scene, providing Luke with the lead into the announcement of the virgin birth.

In his Gospel Matthew quotes Isaiah (7:6): "The Virgin will conceive and give birth to a son, and they will call him Emmanuel, a name which means God-is-with-us," as prophetic of the birth of Christ. John gives us no specific account of the Annunciation, but in his first chapter he may be alluding to the conception of Christ, born "not of human stock nor of the will of the flesh nor of the will of man, but of God," so that salvation might be the work of God alone, using the one human instrument of his choice. Christ is the second Adam, born of a virginal womb as Adam was born of virgin soil; he is a new and sinless creation at the hands of God, not sharing in the solidarity in sin of the original Adamite race. The first Adam was of the earth, earthy, but Christ, who was born of the Holy Spirit, is a life-giving spirit (1 Cor. 15:45). He alone is without sin and so able to atone for sin, for the ideal high priest we needed had to be holy, innocent, uncontaminated, and having no part with sinners (Heb. 7:26).

Joseph is also is to be drawn into the mystery. He is, first of all and as Luke remarks, of the house of David, from which the Messiah was expected. In accepting his role, as Matthew shows that he was prepared to do, he would provide the child with a paternity, extrinsic but legal, to link him with the royal house of David, and he would also protect the Virgin from the charge of immorality, for as St Bernard says, he would not only be a witness to her virginity but would defend her more ably than she could herself. Unmarried and pregnant, she risked being labelled a prostitute and punished accordingly.

The angel explains to Mary how the birth will take place: "The Holy Spirit will come upon you, and the power of the Most High will overshadow you. The child that will be born of you will therefore be holy and will be called the Son of God." The Holy Spirit and the power of the Most High are synonymous terms to describe God's power such as we see it in the account of creation or in the many instances in the Old Testament where the Spirit comes upon certain persons, inciting them to superhuman acts. The same expression refers to the promised descent of the Holy Spirit on the apostles after the ascension. By the use of the word "overshadow" Luke recalls the cloud, sign of the presence of the Lord and his Glory, which settles on the Ark or Tent of Meeting, or the Temple of Solomon at its dedication and the re-housing of the Ark; it is an echo thrown back from the baptism and the transfiguration, when the cloud announced the presence of God and the Father's voice proclaimed Christ as his beloved Son. The one to be born, then, will be holy, set apart as were Samuel and Samson, Jeremiah and Ezekiel, for the service of the Lord, but he will be something more: the Son of God, ultimately to be proclaimed as such through his resurrection from the dead. The birth of John to the barren Elizabeth is the sign that these things will be accomplished, for, as in the case of Sara, nothing is impossible to God. Casting herself in the form of a slave, as her son would do in his Incarnation, Mary expresses her willingness to cooperate with the designs of God, "I am the slave of the Lord," and then exclaims in an ecstatic outburst, "Oh, that it may be done to me as you have said!"

Mary's acceptance signals the moment of Christ's conception. The Council of Chalcedon in 451 declared: "We confess the Holy Virgin to be Mother of God because God the Word was made flesh and became man, and from the very moment of conception united to himself the temple he had taken from her," and in his synodal letter to his fellow-bishops St Sophronius declares his belief: "He was truly made man at the very instant of his conception in the all-holy Virgin."

In Nazareth of Galilee, then, the Glory took up its dwelling within the Virgin Mary when the Holy Spirit came upon her and, like the protective cloud of presence to the front and to the rear of the Israelite armies or the overwhelming presence of the Lord in tent or temple, the power of the Most High overshadowed her. She is the new ark, shelter of the Word conceived within. She is the real ark because she receives the Word not into an inanimate chest but into a living body and clothes that Word in her own humanity. She is the new temple and the Holy of Holies, for she herself becomes the sanctuary of the living God. Nor is she merely a biological instrument; she conceives the Word, as both St Ambrose and St Augustine insist, first in her heart then in her body, fully assenting to the design of God for herself and for the human race. The Word made flesh is henceforth and forever in the image of Mary, and our openness to the unmerited gift of salvation necessarily takes on a Marian tone. This is the work of the Spirit of God.

For Sophronius see *P.G.*, 87, 3; for St Bernard see *P.L.*, 183; *D.A.C.*, 1, 2241-67; 12, 927-9. See also R. Laurentin, *Queen of Heaven* (1956); Raymond E. Brown, *The Virginal Conception & Bodily Resurrection of Jesus* (1973); John McHugh, *The Mother of Jesus in the New Testament* (1975); J Fitzmeyer, *The Gospel according to Luke I-IX*, Anchor Bible, 28 (1981); J. Saward, *Redeemer in the Womb* (1993), and many other commentaries.

A fresco in the second-century catacomb of Priscilla depicts perhaps the scene of the Annunciation, but a fourth-century mosaic in Santa Maria Maggiore certainly does so. Miniatures, mosaics, bas-reliefs, works in ivory, clay, and gold from the first six centuries alone testify to Christian belief in and reverence for this mystery, but increasingly details from the apocryphal gospels appear, mostly in Eastern icons. Mary is shown with a spindle in her hand, recalling a legendary event in the *Protevangelium of James*, or Gabriel appears with a lily, symbol of Mary's virginity. In the fourteenth-century painting by Simone Martini (1333; Florence, Uffizi) the lily takes the central place. In some representations a hand, from which rays extend to the virgin, indicates the act of God communicating the Holy Spirit. Carlo Crivelli's *Annunciation* of 1486 (London, National Gallery) brings in at least three symbolical features: the sealed flask of water, image of Mary's perpetual virginity; the fatal apple; and the peacock of immortality representing the Fall and its reversal. See P. and L. Murray, *The Oxford Companion to Christian Art and Architecture* (1996), pp. 23-4.

St Dismas, the Good Thief (First Century)

Following the traditional belief, as recorded by Tertullian and Augustine, that Christ's death took place on 25 March, the Roman Martyrology assigns to this day the death of the Good Thief: "In Jerusalem the commemoration of the holy thief, who confessed Christ upon the cross and deserved to hear from him the words, 'Today, you shall be with me in paradise!'" It is all that we know of him, although the apocryphal gospels have woven several tales to compensate for the silence of the canonical Gospels.

The two thieves are represented in paintings of the crucifixion at a quite early date, as, for example, in the Syrian Gospel-book illuminated by Rabulas in 586, preserved in the Laurentian Library in Florence. Several early representations of the crucifixion did in fact emerge from Syria, and it is probably in these that the origin of the name *Dismas* lies. Early coins from Syria represent the sun and the moon on their two sides, with the words for east and west inscribed. Sun and moon reappear in the crucifixion scenes over the heads of the two thieves, the words east and west being reproduced also. *Dismas* is close to the Greek word meaning east, and it is significantly in the Eastern Church that the word became a name for the Good Thief: St Dismas. His words are used in the Byzantine Mass at the "great entrance" and again at the Communion.

Echoes of the legend of the Good Thief are found both in the medieval *Cursor Mundi* 11, 16739 ff, in Longfellow's *Golden Legend*, and elsewhere. See also *D.A.C.*, 3, pp. 3065-78; 8, 1403-4.

St Margaret Clitherow, *Martyr* (1586)

Margaret was born around 1553, one of the four children of Jane and Thomas Middleton, Protestant citizens of York. Thomas, a wax-chandler, was a man of means who had held civic posts, including that of sheriff in 1564-5 shortly before his death. Margaret's education was probably pursued at home—St Clement's, the one and only monastery of nuns likely to have provided education for young girls in and around York, had been suppressed in 1536—and was geared mainly to acquiring the housewife's many skills. She was later to show that she had a good mind by her management of her husband's shop and her attempts to master Latin.

Shortly after Thomas Middleton's death in 1567 his widow married Henry May, a man of lesser calibre who does not fare well at the hands of Margaret's biographer. He was to become the mayor of York and to re-appear in the martyr's story. Margaret was fourteen when he became a member of the household and seems to have held him in some affection. Four years later she herself was married.

Her husband, John Clitherow, was a wealthy citizen and probably much older than his bride. He was a grazier and butcher with a well-established wholesale and retail business in the Shambles, the butchers' quarter, which has preserved its medieval character to this day. As with Margaret's father, his wealth brought him civic responsibility in the town, then possible only for Protestants. During the year before his marriage he was appointed bridgemaster, and in 1572 he was elected a chamberlain. Whatever his private opinions or regrets, his religious stance was clear: he conformed to the religious requirements of the State and benefited from that conformity. His brother William, who was a Catholic, was to be ordained in 1582 and to become a Carthusian. In taking a Protestant bride, John underlined the choice he had made for himself. However, though he may have been an opportunist, he was no dogmatist. He was to turn a blind eye to his wife's subsequent Catholicism, paying the fines for her non-attendance at the Protestant service without demur, and to remain kindly, tolerant, and knowingly unknowing throughout their married life.

They had been married about three years when Margaret became a Catholic. Her brother-in-law, William, may have exerted some influence—she was to call one of her own sons William after him—but her biographer, John Mush, merely says that "finding no substance, truth nor Christian comfort in the ministers of the new gospel, nor in their doctrine itself, and hearing also many priests and lay people to suffer for the defence of the ancient Catholic faith" she was led to embrace the old faith. The most striking witness to the Catholic faith at the time must have been that of Thomas Percy, earl of Northumberland, who in 1569 led the rising in the North and was executed in 1572. The witness of the martyrs had even more effect on her than John Mush's few words might suggest. She longed to suffer martyrdom herself and would visit Knavesmire, the Tyburn of York, where five seminary priests were executed in 1582-3, among them her confessor, William Hart. She would pray there during the night hours for as long as her companions would allow her to remain. Her spiritual director observed: "With her it was more necessary to use the bridle than the spur."

The Mass was the source of her joy. She set up a Mass centre in her own home and an alternative centre in a local inn. If it became too dangerous to have Mass in her house, it could be said at the inn, even though she herself might not then be able to attend it daily. She knew the risks she was taking: "I will not be afraid to serve God and do well. This is a war and trial in God's church and therefore if I cannot [do] my duty without peril or dangers, yet by God's grace I will not be slacker for them. If God's priests dare venture themselves to my house, I will never refuse them." To educate her children in the Faith, she secured the services of a young man who had been imprisoned in York Castle. She may have met him there herself, for she visited those in prison for their religion and helped them as she could, spiritually and materially, but she also knew the inside of the prison from having been detained there three times, once spending eighteen months at a stretch, for non-attendance at the Protestant services. Her biographer lists the credits that this relentless recusancy earned: "They persecuted her and she thereby learnt patience; they shut her up into close prison, and she learned thereby to forget and despise the world; they separated her from house, children and husband and she thereby became familiar with God; they sought to terrify her and she thereby increased in most glorious constancy and fortitude, insomuch that her greatest joy was to be assaulted by them. . . ." To Margaret, prison was an opportunity to draw close to God by prayer and penance; it was also an opportunity to read. She learnt the Little Office of Our Lady in Latin by heart and read the Gospels, *The Imitation of Christ*, and Perrin's *Exercises*.

Not only Catholics but many others were drawn to her by her wit and good looks, her gaiety and goodness. Her servants, with whom she could be strict, would never have given her away, while her non-Catholic friends and neighbours would forewarn her of impending danger. Her husband, more than most, recognized her rectitude, her purity, and her utter devotion to himself and their children. He could find only two faults in her: she fasted too much and she would not go to the Protestant church with him. For her part, she could only regret her failure to bring him back to the faith. While she never faltered in loyalty and love for him and was grateful for the freedom to come and go as she pleased, she was not without insight into his mind. Playfully, but perhaps not inaccurately, she said of him with reference to his wealth, "He hath too much; he cannot lift up his head to God for weight of his goods."

It is not at all clear what part John Clitherow played, if any, in their son William's departure for the Continent to complete his education. Margaret may have sent the boy without his father's explicit consent, reasoning that since her husband was kept in ignorance of it, he could not be held responsible and was therefore safe from the sanctions of the law. These she must bear herself, and indeed it was the cause of her arrest. At first she was subjected to house arrest. When the Council of the North had set up a tribunal in York, John Clitherow was summoned to appear on 10 March 1586. This was a ploy to get him out of the way while the house was searched. A priest was in residence, but he was safely hidden in the house next door, of which his room formed a part. Nothing was found until one of the officials reached the schoolroom. A class was in progress and the tutor was taken for a priest. He made his escape, but the officials' suspicion was aroused. One of the children, a half-Dutch, half-English boy of eleven who was staying with the family and was judged to be the most susceptible, was taken aside and stripped while threatened with a cane. Questioned, the terrified child blurted out the information the officials were seeking: Mass was indeed said in the house, and he could show them the entrance to the priest's room. The priest was not found, but vestments, missals, and vessels were discovered. The child was also willing to identify those who attended Mass.

Margaret Clitherow was arrested and led first before the council and then to prison in the castle. John Clitherow was temporarily detained, but it was not intended that he should be brought to trial. Their daughter Anne became a ward of the court. Reassured as to her family's safety, Margaret's usual high spirits took over and, apart from a few hours of anguish, did not forsake her. Her friend Anne Tesh, identified by the child as one of those who attended Mass, was put into the same cell and the two joked and laughed together so much that Margaret exclaimed, "We are so merry together that I fear, unless we be parted, to lose the merit of our imprisonment!"

Margaret appeared, composed and cheerful, before two judges, Mr Clinch and Mr Rhodes, on 14 March, no longer charged with sending a child abroad to be educated but with the more serious crime of harbouring and maintaining priests and attending Mass. She would not plead guilty: "I know no offence whereof I should confess myself guilty." There followed a long tussle of wills as the judges sought to bring her to trial, while Margaret firmly refused a trial. She was assured again and again that she would be leniently dealt with by a jury, since the witness of a child of eleven was hardly enough to incriminate her. However, Margaret had no illusions. The council had long determined on her death and would secure it by whatever means lay at hand. What she wished to circumvent at all costs was precisely a trial by jury in which her children and servants would be called upon to witness either for or against her. In the first case they would perjure themselves; in the second they would have to live with the thought that they had contributed to her death. Few seemed to have understood her motives, and she herself spelled them out only after judgment had been pronounced: "Alas, if I had put myself to the country (*i.e.,* to a jury) evidence must needs have come against me, which I know none could give but only my children and servants. And it would have been more grievous to me than a thousand deaths if I should have seen any of them brought forth before me to give evidence against me. Secondly, I know well that the country must have found me guilty to please the Council, which earnestly seeks my blood; and then they had all been accessory to my death, and damnably offended God. I thought it therefore the way of charity on my part to hinder the country from such a sin; and since it must needs be done, to cause as few to do it as might be; and that was the judge himself."

The first day of the assizes was spent in the fruitless attempt to wear down the prisoner. The next day it was taken up again. Margaret continued to assert, "I will be tried by none but by God and by your own consciences." Mr Clinch was patently unwilling to pronounce against her, the more so as the Puritan minister, who had vainly tried to argue with her the evening before, now pronounced a dire and public warning against the injustice of condemning someone on the evidence of a child. However, Mr Rhodes had had enough and wished to despatch "this naughty, wilful woman." He overrode his squeamish fellow-judge, and the terrible sentence, which English law since 1275 decreed for anyone who would not plead, was pronounced: she was to be pressed to death. She accepted it with the utmost serenity. Once again an appeal was made to her to reconsider. She answered: "God be thanked, all that he shall send me shall be welcome; I am not worthy of so good a death as this." John Clitherow wept when he heard of her condemnation. His wealth seemed then of little moment: "Let them take all I have and save her, for she is the best wife in all England, and the best Catholic also." He was ordered to leave York, while she was imprisoned in a private prison on the Ousebridge.

Even then she was not left in peace but was visited by various people who tried to shake her constancy, among them her stepfather, Henry May, then mayor of York and thought by some to have had an active role in the arrest of his stepdaughter. Seeing that he could not dissuade her, he asked to be given charge of her daughter, Anne, but she would not consent to this. She was never allowed to see her children, and only once did she see her husband, and that in the gaoler's presence. Knowing that the sentence required that she be pressed naked, she sewed herself a linen slip in the hope that she might be allowed to wear it. Two days before, she was told the date of her execution, and for the first time was flooded with anguish, but this passed away as she prayed for strength. The night before her death was spent in prayer. On the morning of 25 March, Friday in Passion Week, the sheriff came at eight in the morning to take her to the toll-booth a few yards from the prison, where she was to die. Crowds had already gathered and were amazed at her radiant expression. She distributed alms as she went, to Sheriff Fawcett's annoyance. "Come away, Mrs Clitherow," he urged. "Good Master Sheriff," she replied cheerily, "Let me deal my poor alms before I go, for my time is but short."

Arriving at the toll-booth, Margaret knelt to pray. The ministers and officials bade her pray with them, which she refused. Ordered to pray for the queen, she composed her own litany: after having prayed for the pope, the cardinals, clergy, Christian princes, and finally for her sovereign, Sheriff Fawcett prompted her: "You must remember and confess that you die for treason." At this she cried aloud, "No, no, Mr Sheriff, I die for the love of my Lord Jesu." She was undressed by some women, who put on her the slip she had prepared. A sharp stone was placed under her back, her hands were tied to stakes so that her body lay in the form of a cross. A heavy door was laid upon her and then charged with a load of some seven or eight hundredweight. As the weight bore down on her, she cried out, "Jesu, Jesu, Jesu, have mercy on me!" Her agony seemed to last for some fifteen minutes, but her body was left in the press for several hours and was buried secretly by the authorities. Six weeks later the place of burial was discovered by some Catholics and the body exhumed. It was found mangled but incorrupt. A second burial took place, but the secret of its location was so well kept that it has been lost to subsequent generations, although one of her hands is preserved in the Bar Convent of York.

Margaret had sent her hat to her husband "in sign of her loving duty to him as to her head" and her shoes and stockings to her daughter Anne to indicate that she should follow in her footsteps—which she did. Anne was at first cruelly deceived by being told, *after* Margaret's death, that she could save her mother's life by attending a Protestant service. She went, but refused to do so ever again when she learned the truth. She spent four years in prison and finally became a nun in Louvain. Two of Margaret's sons became priests.

Margaret Clitherow was canonized in 1970 and is one of the Forty Martyrs of England and Wales commemorated on 25 October.

J. Morris: *Troubles of our Catholic Forefathers*, 3 (1877), gives the biography compiled by John Mush, the martyr's confessor. See also *L.E.M.*, 1, pp. 188-99; J. B. Milburn, *A Martyr of Old York* (1900); M. Munro, *Bd Margaret Clitherow* (1948); and M. Claridge, *Margaret Clitherow* (1966). For a general treatment of the Forty Martyrs of England and Wales, see 25 Oct.

Bd James Bird, *Martyr* (1593)

James Bird was born of good family in Winchester and brought up as a Protestant. While still a young boy he became a Catholic and went to the Continent, where for a time he was a student in Douai College. He returned to England full of zeal for his faith and attracted the attention of the authorities. He was arrested and charged with having converted to Catholicism and for holding the supremacy of the pope. He was convicted of high treason but offered his freedom if he would attend the Protestant church. This he refused to do, even when his father implored him to save his life by complying. The boy replied that he had always been obedient and would be so now if it did not mean offending God. After a long imprisonment he was hanged, drawn, and quartered at Winchester on 25 March 1593, at the age of nineteen.

He suffered courageously and cheerfully. His head was affixed to a pole on one of the city gates and seen by his father, who thought he saw it bowing to him. The distraught man cried, "Oh! my son Jemmy, who not only living wast ever obedient and dutiful, but now also, when dead, payest reverence to thy father! how far from thy heart was all affection or will for treason, or any other wickedness!"

For a fuller treatment of the English Martyrs and for the bibliography, see "BB Martyrs of England and Wales," 4 May.

St Lucy Filippini (1672-1732)

Although the Institute of the *Maestre Pie*, or the *Pontifical Institute of the Religious Teachers Filippini*, is not as well known outside Italy as it deserves to be, it has nevertheless established houses in the United States, Brazil, England, Switzerland, Ethiopia, and India. At its inception, when compulsory education was still undreamed of, it worked wonders both for the religious and social improvement of Italian women. St Lucy was not the foundress of this remarkable organization, but she was perhaps the most zealous, the most influential, and the most holy of all its early promoters.

Lucia Filippini was the last of the five children of Filippo Filippini and Maddalena Picchi, both descendants of noble families. She was born at Corneto-Tarquinia on 13 January 1672 but was not yet a year old when her mother died at the age of twenty-seven; she was just seven years old in 1679, when her father too died. She and her sister Elisabetta went to live with their maternal uncle, Antonio, and his wife, Costanza, and their four children, attending the girls' school run by the Benedictine nuns of Santa Lucia.

In 1687 Cardinal Marcantonio Barbarigo was made bishop of Montefiascone and Corneto. He was a man of great compassion and love, especially for children, to whose welfare he had already dedicated much of his activity, founding schools of Christian doctrine, a girls' school, and an orphanage. On a pastoral visit to Corneto he met and was immediately drawn to the two Filippino orphans, especially Lucy, whom he took with him to Montefiascone. She, for her part, found in him a counsellor and father in God, someone in whom she could confide her deepest aspirations. The cardinal sent her as a boarder to the monastery of Santa Chiara, where, in a prayerful atmosphere, she might be able to discern her vocation.

He continued the oversight of his educational projects. However, he seemed unable to stem the tide of loose living among the young and came to the conclusion that the problem was due to the fact that most young women were uneducated and unformed in the Faith. The solution was to be found in bringing the young girls, the mothers of tomorrow, to a knowledge of Christ, of the tenets of the Faith, and of its moral demands. Hearing of work along these lines initiated by Bd Rose Venerini (7 May) in Viterbo, he invited her to come to Montefiascone to help him launch a girls' school. She stayed at Santa Chiara while working with the bishop, and there she got to know Lucy Filippino. When the time came for her to return to Viterbo, Rose suggested Lucy as someone well able to carry on the work.

Lucy was hesitant but was finally persuaded by the bishop to accept the task. He gave her a religious habit in the cathedral of Montefiascone. Her apostolic and missionary zeal grew as the work took shape and developed. Not only did she look after the school, but she gathered together the women of the town to teach them doctrine and lead them in prayer. Her charity was all-embracing. If she had any preferences, it was always for the neediest and most helpless, and she reaped in return the love and trust of countless women, young and old. Soon it became clear that she could not carry on alone, especially as the bishop had determined to establish schools for girls in all the larger towns of his diocese. A novitiate, under Lucy's direction, was opened by the bishop, who himself undertook to be the confessor of the group. The *maestre* were not to be religious under vows but dedicated women who had made an oblation of themselves to the Lord for a specific mission. Lucy's task was then twofold: the formation and guidance of a new Institute in the Church and the founding and maintaining of girls' schools, together with some peripheral apostolic activity among adult women.

The next twelve years were a time of new ventures, Lucy and the bishop working hand in hand. She handled most of the day-to-day organization, while he sustained the work by moral as well as material support. Each school had to be endowed; generally, vineyards or cellars were purchased by the bishop for this purpose. The impression gained is one of fervent endeavour and prudent administration. Other factors, however, complicated the situation. The monastery of Santa Chiara, where Lucy had spent some time seeking her vocation, had so lost its way that something had to be done to restore discipline. The superior, herself despairing of the future, asked for a transfer to the new Institute of teachers. The bishop attempted a solution to satisfy all parties: Lucy was appointed superior in 1704, the monastery was refurbished and became the motherhouse of the Institute, within which the members of the contemplative community held certain offices. However, no advantage was gained, as jealousy took root the undisciplined refused discipline, while the religious teachers felt constrained by a tight framework unsuited to their task. Lucy resigned her position and returned to her own Institute; the unsatisfactory situation continued, and at that point the bishop died. He had been so generous during his lifetime that there were few resources left. The arrangements he had made for the maintenance of the schools and the remuneration of the teachers were put into the hands of cathedral officials. The new bishop, Sebastiano Bonaventura, confirmed Lucy as superior general and supervisor of all the schools in the diocese. He reinstated Santa Chiara as a strictly contemplative house but ruined the seminary by permitting the imprudent sale of its endowment. He changed the methods in the schools run by Lucy, to Rose Venerini's chagrin. In 1707 Lucy was summoned to Rome to found a school, the first outside her own diocese. There she was quickly dubbed the *Maestre Santa*. This new venture won the support of the Religious Workers, a Congregation of men, whose influence also modified Lucy's methods of teaching. When she left Rome to return to Montefiascone and Rose came to fill her place, the two found themselves on too divergent paths to permit their continued collaboration. Fr Martinelli, the chief inspiration of Rose Venerini's teaching methods, insisted on a break with Lucy, which proved a bruising experience for the latter.

Meanwhile in Montefiascone the clerics entrusted with those funds of the Institute that had been left by Barbarigo for the benefit of the schools were withholding the income. It took Lucy almost three years to reopen or reinstate the schools which had had to be closed and to find new sources of funding. Discovering what they regarded as an irregularity in some of the papers—the fault of a notary—the administrators persuaded the bishop to require Lucy to hand over all the assets of the Institute, even those investments she had herself provided or obtained through the work of the teachers. All the papers pertaining to the accounts were taken, so that future argument or representation would be impossible without access to them. And still there was little revenue coming in.

The plight of the schools and the teachers weighed heavily on the superior, who was already fatally ill. Through highly-placed friends she appealed to the pope to redress the situation. A papal communication to the bishop found its way into the hands of one of the administrators, who dealt with it summarily. It was not until an apostolic visitation had uncovered the deal pertaining to the seminary that the rest came to light; the delinquents were dismissed, but by then Lucy was dead. She died on 25 March 1732, as she had predicted, and was laid to rest in the cathedral of Montefiascone in the presence of enormous crowds. She was beatified in 1926 and canonized in 1930 by Pope Pius XI.

Francesco di Simone, *Della Vita della Serva di Dio Lucia Filippini* (1732); Pascal P. Parente, *Schoolteacher and Saint, A Biography of Lucy Filippini* (1954); Frances Dickinson, *The Light still Shines* (1972); Pietro Bergamaschi, *From the Land of the Etruscans* (1986); *Bibl.SS.*, 8, 257-60.

R.M.
St Dula, martyr, Nicomedia (second/third century)
St Quirinus, martyr, Rome (third century)
St Mona, bishop of Milan (fourth century)
St Humbert, abbot of Marly, Hainault (*c.* 680)
St Hermeland, abbot of Aindre (*c.* 720)
Bd Everard, monk of Schaffhausen, Swabia (1078)
Bd Thomasius, hermit, Costacciaro, Umbria (1337)

26

St Peter of Sebaste, *Bishop* (*c.* 391)

Peter was the youngest of the ten children of St Basil the Elder and St Emmelia, and one of a remarkable family of saints. His grandmother was St Macrina the Elder (14 Jan.), who had been guided in the way of holiness by St Gregory the Wonder-worker (17 Nov.); his eldest sister was St Macrina the Younger (19 June), whose influence, after that of their parents, was paramount in the spiritual formation of the brothers Basil the Great (2 Jan.), Gregory of Nyssa (10 Jan.), and Peter himself.

Basil the Elder died when Peter was a few months old, so that Macrina, the eldest of the family, took complete charge of him. Her only aim was to educate him for eternal life, for which she considered profane studies next to useless. She may have had their brother Basil in mind, the conceited young man who had returned from his university studies bursting with self-importance and whom she had had to redirect in the ways of God. It is true that Basil the theologian never ceased to value his secular studies, especially that of philosophy, but Macrina was nothing if not pragmatic in her approach to the Faith. In due course Peter chose the monastic life and entered the monastery for men founded by his mother and then ruled by his brother Basil.

When Basil was called away by Eusebius of Caesarea in 362 he appointed Peter his successor, and when he was made bishop of Caesarea he ordained him to the priesthood. Peter ruled the monastery for some years and gave proof of his great charity. During a time of famine when the monastery was daily besieged by the destitute, he disposed of all its goods to supply their needs. Both Basil and Macrina died in 379, and a year later Peter was consecrated bishop of Sebaste in succession to the Arian Eustathius, his brother's one-time persecutor. Despite his lack of university education, Peter was a naturally eloquent man. In 381 he attended the general council held at Constantinople. Not only his brother Gregory of Nyssa but also Theodoret and other ancient writers speak of his sanctity, prudence, and zeal.

He died about the year 391. A letter of his to his brother Gregory, entreating him to complete his treatise against Eunomius, is extant.

AA.SS., Jan., 1, pp. 588-91; see *P.G.*, 46, 959-1000, for St Gregory of Nyssa's *Life of Macrina*, the main source of information about St Peter, and *P.G.*, 45, 241-4, for his letter to Gregory.

St Ludger of Münster, *Bishop* (*c.* 742-809)

St Ludger was born around 742. His parents, Thiadgrim and Liafburg, were wealthy Frisians of noble lineage who sent their son for his early education to the abbey school of Utrecht. This was presided over by the gentle and saintly abbot Gregory (25 Aug.), a friend of St Boniface (5 June), whom Ludger may have seen while a pupil there. He describes the apostle as "an old man, white-haired and bent over with age, but full of goodness."

Alubert arrived from York about 767, at a time when Gregory administered both the abbey and its school and the diocese of Utrecht. The abbot himself would not accept ordination to the episcopate, fearing that he would fall victim to worldliness, but he would not refuse to help the diocese, for which no other bishop could be found. Alubert seemed heaven-sent, and Gregory lost no time suggesting that he should have himself ordained bishop and be his co-worker. Alubert countered that he could not ask his own bishop to ordain him just like that. He suggested two companions who might also present themselves as candidates to show they were pursuing a common aim. Sigbold and Ludger were given him, and the three went to York and received orders, Alubert as bishop, Sigbold as priest, and Ludger as deacon. However, Ludger conceived such an affection and admiration for Alcuin, with whom he stayed for a year, that he resolved to return and sit at his feet in York. Gregory reluctantly allowed him to do so, and Ludger spent the next three and a half years in Alcuin's school, returning to Utrecht only when the murder of an earl's son by a Frisian jeopardized the safety of the Frisians living in England. Abbot Gregory died soon after Ludger's return and was succeeded by Alberic, his nephew.

Alberic sent Ludger to Deventer to rebuild the wrecked church over the reputed grave of St Lebuin (12 Nov.). The true site of the grave was made known to Ludger in a dream and the tomb was incorporated in the new building. Once the church was consecrated, Ludger was sent on to evangelize the frontiers of Friesland. He made a number of converts and destroyed several pagan shrines. However, he was still only a deacon, so when Alberic went to Cologne in 778 to be ordained bishop he took Ludger with him and had him ordained priest, then put him in charge of the Ostergau, the five districts at the mouth of the Ems still occupied by heathen tribes. At Dokkum, the place of St Boniface's martyrdom, Ludger built a church, for whose dedication Alcuin sent him a poem he had himself composed. For seven years he worked hard to build up a flourishing community, only to see everything destroyed by a Saxon onslaught under Widukind.

Ludger then went on pilgrimage to Rome with his brother and nephew and then to Monte Cassino, where Ludger himself stayed on for two and a half years. He did not become a Benedictine but studied and observed the Rule because, as his biographer wrote, "he was anxious to build a monastery on his own estate, and this was afterwards done at Werden." In 787 he heard of the conversion of Widukind and returned to rebuild his mission in Friesland; this time his efforts had more lasting results. Moreover, he crossed over into Heligoland, where he preached to the inhabitants and converted many, baptizing them in the fountain in which St Willibrord (7 Nov.) had once baptized three converts. He destroyed the pagan shrines and converted the son of the local chieftain, whom he later ordained a priest. Ludger is said to have cured a blind minstrel named Bernlef. When he was forced to leave the country for a second time due to further unrest, he charged Bernlef with the task of baptizing dying children, a charge diligently executed by his disciple. Ludger returned again to Frisia, but Charlemagne had chosen him for a further task: the evangelization of the recently subjugated province of north-west Saxony, or Westphalia.

Without relinquishing the mission to Friesland, Ludger set out for Saxony, travelling through the country, teaching and preaching, and baptizing his converts himself. His gentleness, persuasiveness, and attractive personality did more to pacify the Saxons than all the emperor's repressive measures. He made his headquarters at Mimigerneford, where he built the monastery from which the town derived its later name of Münster and in which he instituted the Rule of St Chrodegang (6 March) for clergy living in community. At first this untiring missionary hesitated to accept ordination as a bishop—how could he forget the example of Abbot Gregory?—but was finally made bishop in 804. Five years of work remained to him. With the help of his brother Hildegrim he evangelized both Westphalia and Eastphalia and would have gone on to Scandinavia had Charlemagne permitted it.

In spite of all his external activity Ludger allowed nothing to interfere with his devotions. He was so particular about attention at the office, even while travelling, that when one of his clergy once stooped to turn a fire so as to redirect smoke blowing into the bishop's face, he was rebuked at the close of the service. Ludger was accused at one point to Charlemagne of indiscriminate almsgiving and the neglect of the churches in his care—a serious charge in the emperor's estimation—and he was ordered to present himself for an interview. The day after the bishop arrived, a chamberlain came to summon him but found him at prayer. A second messenger was sent and then a third before he was ready. Charlemagne indignantly asked him why he had not obeyed immediately. The bishop replied calmly, "It seemed to me that the service of God should be put before yours or that of any man. Did you not mean this to be so when you appointed me bishop? I thought it unseemly to interrupt the service of God even at the command of your majesty."

Ludger was in much pain toward the end of his life, but he continued working until the last day, Passion Sunday, 26 March 809. That morning he preached at Coesfeld and then hurried to Billerbeck, where he preached again and said Mass. He died peacefully that evening, surrounded by his disciples and in the presence of his sister, Abbess Gerburga. He was buried in his own beloved monastery at Werden. His relics were enshrined in 1175, and on the anniversary of his death in 1984 the shrine was translated to Münster. He is the patron saint of this town and the second patron of the see of Essen.

AA.SS., Mar., 3, pp. 624–63, gives the biography by Ludger's admirer Altfrid. There are biographies in German by Hüsing, Pingsmann, and Krimphove; See *D.C.B.* for an excellent article by Stubbs; W. Levison, *England and the Continent in the Eighth Century* (1946); E. Duckett, *The Wandering Saints* (1960).

The former abbey church of St Ludger, which was founded in 796, possesses the so-called Ludger-chalice, thought to be the oldest chalice in Germany. There are many representations of St Ludger in the diocese of Münster, portraying him as a bishop, with or without insignia, sometimes holding a church. He is seen also with geese, for he was believed to have delivered his diocese from a plague of wild geese.

R.M.

St Castulus, martyr of Rome (fourth century)

St Manuel and Companions, martyrs in Asia minor (third/fourth century)

SS Montanus, priest, and Maxima, his wife, martyrs at Sirmio in Pannonia (304)

St Eutychius, sub-deacon, martyr of Alexandria (356)

St Bercharius, abbot of Hautvilliers, Champagne (685/696)

SS Barontius and Desiderius, hermits of Monte Cavo in Tuscany (eighth century)

St Stephen, abbot of Triglia in Bithynia (815)

St Pontius, abbot of St Andrew's, Avignon (1087)

27

St Rupert, *Bishop* (*c.* 718)

Rupert's first ecclesiastical office was as bishop of Worms, from which he is said to have been expelled, whether by politicians, pagans, or Arians, or a combination of all these. He was then invited by Duke Theodo II of the Bavarians to work in his country. Theodo's territory, comprising present-day Bavaria and parts of Austria, contained residual pockets of Roman Christians, long sustained by ecclesiastical contacts with Aquileia. Such contacts had been cut off by changed frontiers, and the dukes had then looked to the west for a new missionary impulse, in particular to the monastery of Luxeuil.

Rupert has sometimes been considered an Irishman, but this is not altogether evident. Neither can it be asserted that he had once belonged to the monastery of Luxeuil, but it may be significant that he followed the Irish custom of combining the roles of abbot and bishop in his later foundation at Salzburg. He regarded Theodo's invitation as a sign from God and agreed to take up the work of evangelization of the Salzburg region and eastern Tyrol. The duke welcomed him warmly at Regensburg, a one-time Roman camp, where he had his residence and where a Roman community of Christians was assembled around the local church of St George.

Efforts had already been made to evangelize the tribe of the Bajuwares, but much remained to be done to reach the as yet unevangelized and to purify the Christianity of those already converted, which was fused with Arian beliefs and pagan superstition. Rupert set out immediately on a journey along the Danube, preaching in towns and villages as far as Hungary. Returning by land, he came to Lorch, where there was a Roman community also but where he made additional converts. On the nearby Wallersee he built a church dedicated to St Peter, which marked the beginnings of the town of Seekirchen.

When the question of a permanent site arose, Rupert requested Juvavum (Salzburg), once an elegant Roman town but then in ruins. The duke donated the two square miles where the town was sited and enabled the bishop to build the church of St Peter, the first in Salzburg, and a monastery, also dedicated to St Peter, together with a school and other necessary buildings. Rupert also built Nonnberg, a monastery for nuns, which, like the monastery for monks, was to follow the Rule of St Benedict. (Both these monasteries still exist today.) As the conditions were favourable and the work considerable, Rupert sought help from elsewhere—either from his old diocese or from the monastery of Luxeuil—and returned with twelve companions, who were to be the nucleus of the monastery of monks and his missionary helpers. He also brought his niece Ermentrude, whom he installed as abbess of the new community of nuns. Having established a stable base he travelled continuously throughout the land, preaching the Faith and founding many other churches and monasteries. He is said to have developed the salt mines near Salzburg and is depicted, usually on local coins, with a container of salt in his hand.

After a life of strenuous activity he left his helpers to carry on the work and returned to Salzburg, certain that he was about to die. He died on Easter Sunday, probably between 710 and 720. In 716 Duke Theodo petitioned Rome for the erection of a Bavarian ecclesiastical province, which shows that the work of evangelization was deemed to be well advanced. In the event Theodo's death and the subsequent partition of the country in favour of his heirs made this impossible to realize.

The tradition of the abbot-bishop, which Rupert inaugurated in this part of Europe, endured for almost three hundred years until it was suppressed by the twenty-first abbot of St Peter's—although it is not unusual to find abbots in Bavaria still performing episcopal functions. His relics remained in the monastery until 774, when a portion of them was removed to the then cathedral, to be moved again in the seventeenth century to the new cathedral.

AA.SS., Mar. 3, pp. 696-703; *Catholic Encyclopedia,* 13 (1912), p. 229; Jedin-Dolan, 2, pp. 544-9; Fl-Martin, 5, pp. 532-3.

Bd Francis Faà di Bruno, *Founder* (1825-88)

Francesco Faà di Bruno was born at Alessandria in northern Italy on 29 March 1825, the last of twelve children born to Ludovico Faà di Bruno and Carolina Sappa, both from aristocratic families. He died in 1888, so his life spans one of the more turbulent eras in Italian history, when the forces of liberalism and secularism, deriving ultimately from the Enlightenment and the French Revolution, were pitted against the papacy and its temporal power, against the Church's dominance of education and its medieval panoply of clerical privilege, at times against the very concept of religion. No one, least of all a Piedmontese, could be immune to the anguish attendant on the birth-pangs of the modern State, many aspects of which were welcomed initially by Pius IX, though he turned against the *risorgimento* when its anti-religious and anti-Catholic elements gained the upper hand. Francis was a man of thirty-six when, in 1861, Italy was declared a unified State.

Francis trained as an officer at the military academy of Turin. King Victor Emmanuel II was so impressed by his fine character and breadth of learning that he appointed him tutor to his two sons. To prepare himself, Francesco went to Paris to further his studies. In 1852 he returned to Turin to take up his post, only to find that the king's advisers had quashed the appointment. Victor Emmanuel II had ascended the throne of Piedmont subject to conditions set by the liberal members of the Chamber of Deputies. He was required to swear loyalty to the Constitution of 1848 and was left in no uncertainty about his future should he challenge the will of the Chamber. In the same year that the Constitution was promulgated the deputies had passed a law restricting the role of the Church in education, handing over to the State control of the curriculum as well as the appointment of teachers. The deputies would hardly have been in a mood to tolerate a man known for his ardent Catholicism as tutor to the princes.

The following year Francis left the army and returned to Paris to obtain a doctorate in mathematics and in astronomy. He published his dissertation in 1856 and other papers as well on music, religion, and the ascetic life. In 1857 he returned to Alessandria; he was nominated candidate for the Catholic Conservative Party but was defeated in the final ballot. He then took up an academic career, lecturing at the university of Turin. He was appointed professor of topography and trigonometry in 1859 and of geodesy in 1864.

Although a committed scholar, Francis found time for extensive charitable work. He founded the Society of St Zita for maids and domestic servants, later adding branches for female apprentices, teacher-trainer students, and unmarried mothers. Hostels were set up for the elderly, the poor, sick women, and priests. In 1867 he had a church built in Turin to the memory of those soldiers who had had to pay with their lives for the unification of Italy. On the advice of St John Bosco (31 Jan.) he decided to become a priest to extend the scope of his ministry to the needy. This was opposed by the archbishop of Turin, but Pius IX's intervention on behalf of late vocations overruled the archbishop's objections, and Francis was ordained in Rome at the age of fifty-one. He continued to lecture and was given the professorial chair for higher geometry and mathematics, which he held until his death.

Francis spent his inheritance, his income, and his whole self on his works of charity. In 1877 he added a hostel for prostitutes to those he had already established. In 1881, together with Agostina Gonella, he founded the Congregation of the *Suore minime di Nostra Signora del Suffragio* to carry on his work.

The love of God, constantly nurtured through prayer, was the moving principle of all his activity. He used to say: "Giving oneself to God means surrendering oneself to a higher activity, which carries one along to God like a torrent in spate." He died in Turin on 27 March 1888 and was beatified a hundred years later, in 1988.

E. E. Y. Hales, *Pio Nono* (1954); F. Holböck, *Die neuen Heiliger der katholischen Kirche*, 3 (1994), pp. 69-72; *A.A.S.* 15-16 (Nov. 1955), pp. 750-2.

R.M.

St Paul, bishop of Corinth in Achaia (tenth century)

St Gelasius, bishop of Armagh (1174)

Bd Frovinus, abbot of Engelburg, Switzerland (1178)

Bd Peregrinus, priest of San Severino in Piceno (1232)

Bd Panacea de Muzzi, martyr of Novare in Piedmont (1383)

28

St Hesychius of Jerusalem (*c.* 450)

Hesychius, priest of Jerusalem, has been described as an "almost anonymous witness to Christian tradition," such was his diffidence and modesty. By the accidents of history, moreover, only a portion of his work has come down to us.

A tenth-century menology says he was born and educated in Jerusalem, became a monk and hermit, and was later ordained by the bishop of Jerusalem. Cyril of Scythopolis' Life of St Euthymius (20 Jan.) records that Hesychius was one of the group that came from Jerusalem in 429 to be present at the dedication of the monastic church of the *laura* established by that saint. He is described as an erudite priest and teacher of the Church of Jerusalem. He was, therefore, well known to his contemporaries, for whom it would have been natural to see him in the bishop's entourage. He lived under three bishops, John, Praylius, and Juvenal, and he would have met Jerome (30 Sept.), Cyril of Alexandria (9 Feb.), Melania the Younger (31 Dec.), and Peter the Iberian. By contrast with them, however, there is very little trace of the polemical in his own writings. John, bishop of Jerusalem, who seems to have been a fair-minded person, reluctant to condemn a heretic before hearing what he had to say in his own defence, invited Pelagius to Jerusalem, but there is no echo of this in the writings of Hesychius, nor of the Arian controversies that tore apart the Churches in the period between the councils of Nicaea and Constantinople.

Like Cyril of Jerusalem (18 Mar.), Hesychius directed his attention to the scriptures, but within the framework of the liturgy, which allowed him to develop its themes and furnished him with his vocabulary. He avoids exegetical minutiae or personal digressions. For him the scriptures are "perfect wisdom, the point of departure and the point of arrival, to which the whole of our existence should be conformed." His Easter homilies were probably delivered in the *Martyrium*, the open space within the Constantinian basilica thought to be the place of the crucifixion; they fittingly exalt the cross, the instrument of victory of the risen Christ, whose resurrection is a guarantee of our own. He makes interesting references to the paschal candle, to Christ the light set on the lampstand of the cross. Christ is also the trumpet of the resurrection, in which he is revealed as both God and man.

St Basil tells us that Hesychius wrote a commentary on the whole Bible, but only the commentaries on Leviticus and the Psalms are now extant. In addition to these he has left meditations on Job, a few sermons on the Presentation of the Lord, some fragments on the prophets, and some sermons on Our Lady, whose perpetual virginity and perfect purity he exalts: "You have guarded the integrity of the temple [of your body]; you have kept your tabernacle free from all sin, so the Father becomes your guest, the Holy Spirit overshadows you and the Only Begotten Son incarnate is born of you." These works open up for us a unified view of scripture, which tends toward and finds its culmination in the person of Christ: "The mystery of the Incarnation enters from the start into the perspectives of the first creation."

His Eucharistic doctrine, like that of Cyril of Jerusalem, is strongly realist: "A person may, through ignorance, perceive the mystery yet be unaware of its power and awesomeness, not discerning that it is truly the body and blood [of Christ]." The Eucharist is a sacrifice, identical with that of the cross: "He was immolated beforehand by his own hands at the mystic meal when he took the bread and broke it, and subsequently on the cross when he was nailed to the wood"; all the same, "unless it had been placed on the cross, we should never have perceived the mystic body of Christ." Not only do we eat the body of Christ, but we eat the very "memorial of his passion," which calls for an identification of ourselves with that passion. Christ is present in order to transform us through our inner absorption of his whole being, divine Word and immolated Lamb. The whole of the Christian life indeed is nothing but the grace of God eliciting our personal adherence: "Keep yourselves free from sin so that every day you may share in the mystic meal; by doing so our bodies become the body of Christ."

St Hesychius may have lived to see the Council of Chalcedon but probably died around the middle of the fifth century.

M. Aubineau, *Homélies Pascales, S.C.*, 187; H. Savon, *Les Homélies festales d'Hésychius de Jérusalem* (1980); *Dict.Sp.*, 7, 399-407. *P.G.*, 93; 55; 79. C. Renoux and C. Mercier (eds.), *Hésychius de Jérusalem, Homélies sur Job* (1983); T. P. Halton and R. D. Sider, *A Decade of Patristic Scholarship 1970-1979* (1982-3); *O.D.C.C.* (1997), pp. 764-5. Hesychius' authorship of the *Centuries on Temperance and Virtue* has been questioned by some scholars, who attribute the collection to the monastery of Batos on Mount Sinai and ultimately to St John Climacus (30 Mar.).

Bd Christopher Wharton, *Martyr* (1600)

Christopher Wharton was born at Middleton in Yorkshire. A fellow of Trinity College, Oxford, he gained his M.A. there. He was ordained in Reims in 1584 and left for the English mission in 1586. He was arrested, probably in 1599, and imprisoned in York Castle.

He was tried in 1600 and charged with being a seminary priest, unlawfully resident in the realm according to the Elizabethan statute. Fr Wharton attempted to counter the charge by claiming that his ordination predated the statute, which was consequently void in his case. The judge stated that he himself had known the accused in Oxford after the promulgation of the statute and that he was not then known to be a priest. He recommended a guilty verdict to the jury, and Christopher Wharton was condemned on the charge of high treason. He was executed at York on 28 March 1600 and beatified in 1987.

Anstruther, 1, p. 377.

Bd Renée-Marie Feillatreau, *Martyr* (1751-94)

Renée-Marie Feillatreau was born in Angers on 8 February 1751 and condemned in that same town by the revolutionaries on trumped-up charges. She was accused of having been involved with Catholic "brigands," of having encouraged the fanaticism of non-conforming priests, of having robbed the Republic, of having shouted out "Long live the King!" and of having conspired against the sovereignty of the French people. What she had done, in fact, was to join the Vendeans when they came to Angers and shout with them, "Long live religion! Long live the King!" She hid the vestments and sacred vessels used for Mass from the revolutionaries and in so doing robbed the Republic of what its officials considered rightly belonged to it.

Her real guilt consisted in her devotion to her Catholic faith. She declared before her judges that she would rather die than renounce it, that she did indeed visit and protect priests faithful to the Roman Catholic Church and had attended their Masses. Furthermore, she would have nothing to do with those priests who had taken the oath. She was guillotined on 28 March 1794 and beatified in 1984.

For a general treatment of the Martyrs of this period in France, see "Martyrs of the French Revolution," 2 Jan.

R.M.

St Castor, martyr at Tarsus in Cilicia (*n.d.*)

St Cyril, deacon and martyr at Heliopolis in Phenicia (*c.* 362)

St Mark, bishop of Arethusa in Syria (364)

St Proterius, patriarch of Alexandria (454)

St Gontran, king, at Chalons in Burgundy (593)

St Hilarion, abbot of Mount Olympus in Bithynia (eighth century)

St Eustratius the Faster, martyr of Kiev in Ukraine (*c.* 1096)

St Stephen Harding, abbot (1134)—see "SS Alberic, Robert, and Stephen Harding," 26 Jan.

Bd Conon, hermit of Nesi in Sicily (1236)

Bd Antonius Patrizi, priest, Siena, Tuscany (*c.* 1311)

Bd Joan de Maillé, widow of Tours—see 6 Nov.

29

SS Jonas and Barachisius, *Martyrs* (326/7)

While Christians in the Roman Empire found peace at last under Constantine, those in Persia were exposed to a bitter persecution. Eighteen thousand were said to have perished in the main cities after excruciating tortures. Constantine himself wrote to King Sapor II—though to no avail—asking that clemency be shown to the Christians. The extant account of the passion and martyrdom of these two saints was written down by Isaiah, a knight in the service of the king and an eyewitness of the events he relates.

Persecution was unleashed against the Christians in the eighteenth year of King Sapor's reign. Orders were given to destroy churches and monasteries and to require believers to sacrifice to the gods. The compliant were to be honoured, the stubborn tortured without mercy. Jonas and Barachisius, two Christians monks in the hamlet of Iasa, heard of the persecution and set out for Bardiaboc, where some Christians were being held. They found nine of them already under sentence of death and encouraged them to persevere to the end.

The nine were martyred, and Jonas and Barachisius were delated to the same chief judges who had condemned the others: they would not sacrifice nor would they worship the sun, fire, or water; above all they had encouraged their fellow-Christians to disobey the king. These judges had the two brought before them and asked them whether they were prepared to obey the king and adore the elements. They replied: "As princes and judges appointed by the king of the Persians, it is only reasonable that you should give us a hearing. You are supposed to judge justly. Ought you not to reverence the one who gave you wisdom and understanding rather than an earthly king? Ought you not to acknowledge the God who is ruler of heaven and earth and of all beings that exist, who established the changing seasons, governs all things and has endowed you with that prudence which enables you to judge men of flesh like yourselves? We adjure you then to tell us truly and sincerely which God ought we to deny, the God of heaven or a god on earth, the eternal God or a mortal god? We believe in the God who made heaven and earth and not in mortal man. Nor is it right that we should believe in one who lives a short span, dies and is buried just like the rest of us."

This served only to enrage the judges, who ordered rods and whips to be brought, but first they separated the two and stood Jonas before them. He was promised promotion if he did what he was told, severe torture if he did not. Jonas answered, "Never shall I deny my Lord Jesus Christ who lives for ever. . . ." He was made to lie face downward with a sharp stake under his middle while he was mercilessly flogged. He prayed quietly all the while and finally roared a challenge at the judges: "I believe in the Father, the Son and the Holy Spirit, the true and triune God, who sustains the whole world, who made all things, including your gods, whom you imagine you can make us adore by force." He was then bound and thrown out of doors to remain there all night in the winter cold and frost.

Barachisius was then summoned, given the same choice, and told that Jonas had apostatized. He said calmly that this was a lie and then spoke so eloquently and courageously of God as the source of all created things that the judges were taken aback and even feared that such intense conviction might convert others. They decided to try him that night when no one was about to hear his impassioned speeches. Angry that they could not prevail, the judges had him cruelly tortured with hot pitch and sent him back to prison, where he was to be suspended all night by one foot.

The next morning Jonas was brought in and asked how he had weathered the cold and frost. "I have never had a more peaceful night . . . ," was the reply. "I drew comfort from the cross to which my Lord Jesus Christ was nailed." Told that Barachisius had renounced the Faith, he interrupted the judges: "He renounced the devil and his angels long ago, I know, and has since held fast with all his heart to our Lord Jesus Christ." They asked him, "Is it not better for you to give up your God and save yourself?" He retorted, "If corn is hoarded, it diminishes not multiplies. If a person loses his life in this world for the sake of Christ, believing in him and doing his will, he will be renewed in light imperishable when the Lord comes again to make all things new." His fingers and toes were cut off and flung away with the taunt that he would have them back at harvest time. He was then thrown into a vessel of burning pitch, and finally a press was called for on which he was crushed and his bones broken.

Barachisius was now exhorted to have a care for his own limbs. "I did not make them nor shall I suffer their loss. God who made me will remake me by his power. . . ." He was first impaled on stakes then put into the same press and had his bones broken. Finally, burning pitch was poured down his throat.

Upon receiving news of their death, an old friend bought what was recoverable of the bodies of all eleven martyrs, promising never to divulge the sale.

AA.SS., Mar 3, pp. 767-70, which is based on the Greek text, translated into Latin by Petrus Franciscus Zinum. The Syriac text is to be found in S. E. Assemani, *Acta Sanctorum Martyrum Orientalium*, 1. For the Greek, see Delehaye in *Anal. Boll. 22* (1903), pp. 395-407, and *Patrologia Orientalis*, 2, pp. 421-39.

SS Gundleus and Gwladys (Sixth Century)

Gundleus, the Latin form of Gwynllyw (corrupted to Woolo), was the name of a chieftan of south-east Wales. The story goes that he kidnapped Gwladys, one of the children of Brychan of Brecknock, and made her his wife. Cadoc (25

Sept.), one of the most outstanding of Welsh saints, was their first child. He was baptized by St Tatheus, to whom he had been entrusted for his education, and became a monk and a much-travelled founder of monasteries.

Cadoc brought about his parents' conversion and prevailed upon them to leave the world. They led an austere life close to each other on what is now Stow Hill at Newport in Monmouthshire, where the ancient St Woolo's church stands. However, he wished them to separate altogether, so Gwladys went to Pencarnau in Bassaleg, where the present Catholic church is dedicated to her. They both lived in solitude until they died. Their memory is preserved in several place names and church dedications in the country.

AA.SS., Mar., 3., pp. 780-1; A. W. Wade-Evans, *Vitae Sanctorum Britanniae* (1944); S. Baring-Gould and J. Fisher, *Lives of the British Saints* (1907-13), 3, pp. 202-4, 234.

St Berthold, *Founder* (*c*. 1195)

St Berthold is often regarded as the founder of the Carmelite Order, but compared to other founders he remains a shadowy figure. The date of his birth and his early life are unknown, and late accounts stating that he was born in Limoges and educated in Paris are now accepted as untrustworthy.

The beginnings of a liturgical cult of the prophet Elijah by Christians is first mentioned in 1163 by a Jewish rabbi, Benjamin de Tudela, who speaks of a church on Mount Carmel; the existence of this church is confirmed by other writers as well. A hermitage in the same place, with which he himself was associated, is mentioned in the life of Aymeric, patriarch of Antioch, who was a relative of Berthold. It is said that he visited Berthold and helped him to establish a community of hermits and even took some of them with him to Antioch in 1160 to found two other convents.

John Phocas, a Greek monk who visited Mount Carmel in 1185, bears witness also to the hermitage there. He relates that he had met there a Western monk who had gathered round him a group of hermits in a small monastery close to the supposed cave of the prophet Elijah.

The first Carmelite Rule was composed not by Berthold but early in the thirteenth century by Albert de Vercelli, patriarch of Jerusalem, who relied heavily on the Rule of St Augustine. Fifteen daughter communities were founded in Palestine, but in 1238 most of the friars were obliged to emigrate on account of the Saracen invasions. They went to Cyprus, Sicily, Marseilles, and Valenciennes. The monastery on Mount Carmel remained until 1291, when its inmates were massacred and the buildings set on fire.

Carmelite friars arrived in England in the middle of the thirteenth century and a few years later were established also in Charenton near Paris. The Order spread slowly throughout Europe but was widespread by the end of the thirteenth and the beginning of the fourteenth century.

AA.SS., Mar., 3; *Catholic Encyclopedia*, 3 (1908); Melchoir de Sainte-Marie, "Carmel," *D.H.G.E.* 11, pp. 1070-1104; Jean le Solitaire, *Aux sources de la tradition du Carmel* (1953).

St Ludolph, *Bishop* (1250)

Ludolph was a canon regular of the Premonstratensian Order, elected bishop of Ratzeburg in 1236. He gave to the chapter of his cathedral the Rule of St Norbert, which he himself continued to observe, and built and endowed the Benedictine monastery for women at Rehna.

He came into conflict several times with Duke Albert of Sachsen Lauenburg over the question of the alienation of church property. The duke imprisoned, ill treated, and finally banished him. Duke John the Theologian received him at Wismar, where he died in 1250 as a result of his ill treatment, for which he has sometimes been regarded as a martyr. He was canonized in the fourteenth century.

AA.SS., Mar., 3, pp. 789-91.

R.M.
St Eustace, bishop of Naples (third century)
Bd William Tempier, bishop of Poitiers (1197)

30

St John Climacus, *Abbot* (Seventh Century)

The treatise *Ladder (Klimax) to Paradise* has had an immense influence, especially on the Eastern Church, and won for its author, John the Scholar, the name *Climacus*, by which he is now universally known.

His origin is obscure. He is known to have joined the monks settled on Mount Sinai at the age of sixteen and first to have led a semi-eremitical life with Abba Martyrios, who gave him the monastic tonsure three years later. On the death of his guide, when he himself was about thirty-five, he became a complete solitary in Thole, where he remained for forty years. At some point he visited a monastery in Egypt and was struck by the profoundly spiritual life of the monks there and by its remarkable *abba*. He was himself much sought after as a spiritual guide, indeed, so much so that he was stigmatized by the other monks as a chatterbox. John took this as a reprimand and a caution and declined to receive any visitors for about a year, when his critics themselves suggested that he take up counselling once more and not deprive others of his gift for spiritual direction. He was elected *igumen* of the cenobite community of Mount Sinai when he must have been about seventy-five and ruled it for four years. He then retired once more to his hermitage, where he died, perhaps during the second half of the seventh century.

John had had some experience then of three forms of monastic life, so that when he was asked in his latter years by *abba* John of Raithou to write a treatise on the spiritual life he brought to it a wide experience, a mature and comprehensive grasp of its demands, a shrewd understanding of human nature, compassion, humour, and a learning not often found among the hermit population. He had read Evagrius (Ponticus; 11 Feb.) and, while dependent on him, did not always agree with him; he knew Origen's writings—of which he disapproved—and followed the theological controversies of the time, coming down squarely on the side of orthodoxy. Gifted with a strong will and a clear and independent mind, he must also have been very approachable and a man of charm, as his own career and the ease with which he interviews the Egyptian monks suggest.

The *Ladder*, which is read every Lent in Orthodox monasteries, repays careful study. A first impression may induce a sense of discouragement because so much of it is given over to a study of the vices, but John is well aware that when one consecrates one's life to the pursuit of union with God, one's own fallen nature becomes an omnipresent hurdle. As he says, "Get rid of sin, and tears will become superfluous. Adam did not shed tears before the fall and after the resurrection there will be no more." The description he gives of the monastic prison he visited in Egypt might now seem the most shocking part of his treatise. He himself passes no judgment on the system but unquestionably admires the invincible faith with which these repentant monks endure years of frightful penance to atone for their lapses.

In his other work, *To the Shepherd*, addressed to the father of a monastery, John tells him that he should teach not from books but from what he has learned through experience. John himself writes from the fullness of his own. He is not interested in the outer forms of the monastic life but in its inwardness. What is important in the monastic scheme of things is not the practice of asceticism but the seeking after humility and purity of heart. In a dense passage John looks beyond the discipline of the way to the aspirations that set a person on a course distancing him from ordinary human life: "To live in exile means to lead a disciplined life; no one will trumpet our store of wisdom, no one will suspect our treasure of knowledge. It is a hidden life and its ideals are hidden. None will even know that we pray. It is for humility that we strive in this exile, poverty that we desire, the divine for which we yearn. It is a life of love outpoured—a rejection therefore of pride—it is to make one's home in the depths of silence." John does not hesitate to call the monastery "heaven on earth," so a monk must attune his heart to discipline and, like the angels, serve the Lord. There may be mourning, but "God does not expect us to mourn from motives of sorrow" but rather "to rejoice for love of him with the laughter of the soul."

To free the soul for the spiritual life by a régime of unremitting physical hardship was undoubtedly an accepted axiom in the early centuries of Christianity, which were dominated by Neoplatonism, but these monastic teachers also had a canny grasp of the psychosomatic. Body and soul could so interweave their demands that, without disciplining both, one might get nowhere in the drive to acquire the virtues. Yet the body is not an enemy; we are simply fallen creatures: "How can I hate [my body] when my nature requires me to love it? How can I run away from it when it will be my companion at the resurrection? It is my helper and my enemy, my friend and my opponent, a protector and a traitor." The monk's aim is not to destroy this ambivalent yoke-fellow but to arrive at "a body made holy." Asceticism and obedience are the two indispensable tools of the spiritual craft, although these are useless without faith, hope, and love, which "bind and secure the unity of the whole...." Love "never falls, never tarries on its way, never permits the one wounded by its blessed rapture to take his ease." The treatise begins with the explanation that it is concerned with the imitation of Christ insofar as that is possible for mortal beings, it closes with the joyful certainty that one can indeed attain to a resemblance to God: "Love of its nature is a likeness to God insofar as it is humanly possible to attain it."

The idea of the ladder as a device for the elaboration of the spiritual ascent to God had already been used by Origen, Gregory of Nazianzen (2 Jan.), John Chrysostom (13 Sept.), and Theodoret of Cyrus, but the work of Climacus, while reflecting his own personal experience, also presents a synthesis of three centuries of monastic experience. The treatise was drawn on for the propagation of the method of Hesychasm, which concentrates on the use of the *Jesus Prayer*. The invocation of the name of Jesus goes back to Macarius the Egyptian and is known to Diadochus of Photike, Barsanuphius, and John the Prophet. Climacus is the first person we know of to speak of linking the invocation to the rhythmical movement of breathing. He writes, "Let the remembrance of Jesus be present with your every breath, and you will then understand the value of stillness (*hesychia*)," thereby merely emphasizing the necessity of continual prayer. The *Centuries of Hesychius*, thought to have been the work of Hesychius of Jerusalem (28 Mar.) but probably originating in the monastery of Batos, also on Mount Sinai, takes this up, as do other authors. However, it was not until the fourteenth century that the "remembrance of Jesus" was refined by the monks of Mount Athos into a technique such as is described in the nineteenth-century *Way of a Pilgrim*.

The *Ladder* was soon translated into other languages: into Syriac in the seventh century, Arabic, Georgian, Armenian, and Slavonic in the tenth century, and Rumanian in the seventeenth century. Monastic renaissance in fifteenth-century Russia owes much to the *Ladder*. A complete translation into Latin was first made by the Franciscans in the fourteenth century, and the work is reputed to have occasioned Angélique Arnaud's conversion in the seventeenth century.

The short treatise *To the Shepherd* was also written at the request of John of Raithou. In it Climacus spells out his conception of spiritual fatherhood. An *abba*, who is responsible for the spiritual welfare of others, is a teacher: "What we need above all is power from above so that those whom we have begun to introduce into the Holy of Holies, to whom we strive to reveal Christ hidden on the mystic table, whom like infants we draw away from multiplicity . . . may come to abide in the house of the Lord." The *abba* is even more a physician who is prepared to take on himself all the sicknesses and trials, the anguish and weaknesses of his disciples, who "surrenders his life for the other." He is the captain of the ship, who, if he foresees a tempest and fails to alert the crew and an accident follows, will be held responsible for the shipwreck. He is a shepherd who will pray earnestly for the sheep he sees in difficulties. A lion is not best fitted to look after sheep, so he himself will be meek and humble of heart. In fact, "what constitutes the shepherd is the very same love which put the Shepherd on the cross." Finally, he has the best task in all the world: "God could not have given us a greater blessing than to have the opportunity to offer him these repentant souls. The whole world is not worth so much as a single soul; it will pass away, but the soul is immortal and eternal." In art John is always represented with a ladder.

There is an ancient but unreliable Life of St John Climacus by Daniel, a monk of Raithu. Any of the manuals of patrology can be consulted, but see L. Bouyer *et al.*, *The Spirituality of the Middle Ages* (1968); D. Chitty, *The Desert a City* (1966); in the series C.W.S. see J. Climacus, *The Ladder of Divine Ascent*, which has an excellent preface and introduction by K. Ware (1982); *P.G.*, 88; *Dict.Sp.*, 8, 369-89, 575-650, 1126-50; 7, 381-99; I. Hausherr, *La Théologie du Monachisme chez St Jean Climaque* (1961); J. Martin, *The Illustration of the Heavenly Ladder of St John Climacus* (1954).

St Osberg, *Abbess* (? Seventh Century)

Nothing is known of the life of St Osberg, although her existence is not disputed. Unfortunately, research has been arrested by the antiquarian Leland's statements that Cnut founded the monastery of women in Coventry and placed Osberg at its head. Dugdale in his *Monasticon* had already voiced his reservations concerning Leland's statements. Cnut does not appear on the scene until about 1014. It is certainly difficult to accept that he, a Dane, founded a monastery in Mercia during the two years he was devastating the country before becoming king in 1016, the year the monastery was destroyed, supposedly by Danes.

Local memory of a figure more distant in time must be reflected in the choice of this saintly abbess as one of the patrons of the new monastery of monks built on the site of the nuns' convent in 1043. Had Osberg been abbess as recently as the early eleventh century she could hardly have been so speedily exalted to become a patron saint of another monastery some twenty years later. Sam Timmins, a historian of Warwickshire, suggests that Osberg was a seventh-century abbess and that the town of Coventry owes its name to her monastery. He offers no manuscript or archaeological evidence for this suggestion, but placing the saint earlier allows events in Mercia during the second decade of the eleventh century to fall into place.

The Danish invasions were a consequence of Ethelred's slaughter of the Danes in his service, known as the "Massacre of St Brice's Day," Sweyn and Cnut launching their savage attacks on the English in revenge. In Mercia Edric of Streona led his own forces, which destroyed not only the nunnery of Coventry in 1016 but other towns and villages in Warwickshire. Cnut was initially impressed by Edric and appointed him earl of Mercia, but a year later he had him executed.

Leofric, a knight of an ancient and noble family of Mercia, was appointed earl in 1017 in place of Edric. This Leofric, with his wife, Godiva, founded the monastery for men on the site of Osberg's monastery. Four charters concerning its foundation are extant. Leofric's own charter, committing himself to the foundation, specifically names Osberg as one of the patron saints. The monastery continued until its suppression by Henry VIII except for a short break, when secular canons were temporarily installed. Osberg's tomb within the monastic church remained the focus of a local cult. So many miracles were reported that in the year 1410 the clergy and people of Coventry petitioned their bishop for a celebration in her honour. The petition was granted in October 1410—the rescript, in addition to Leofric's charter, providing further written evidence of her cult—and the feast was observed throughout the archdeaconry of Coventry.

The first church to be built by Archbishop Ullathorne in Coventry during the nineteenth-century revival of Catholicism was dedicated to St Osberg. It was consecrated by Cardinal Wiseman on 9 Sept. 1845, and this date, which would obviate the difficulty of a Lenten commemoration, has been suggested for her feast (optional memorial) in the diocesan calendar.

J. Leland, *Collectanea* (1770), 1, p. 50; 3, p. 72; Dugdale, *History of Warwickshire* (1656), p. 85; *Monasticon* 3, pp. 177, 182 (new ed. 1846); Sam Timmins, *A History of Warwickshire* (1889); R. Stanton, *A Menology of England and Wales* (1892), p. 137.

St Peter Regalado (1390-1456)

Peter Regalado was born in Valladolid in Spain to a noble family of Jewish extraction. He was still an infant when his father died and only in his thirteenth year when he obtained his mother's permission to enter the Franciscan friary in his native town.

He had no other ambition than to lead a life of prayer and penance. He even regarded his mother's visits as too much of a distraction and prayed that they might cease. His prayers were heard more thoroughly than he might have expected. Peter of Villacreces, who was engaged in restoring the primitive observance of the Rule of St Francis in Spain, passed through Valladolid and fired the young man with his ideals. Peter went with him in 1404 to the hermitage of La Aguilera and there found the solitude, prayer, and poverty that he desired. Lope de Salinas y Salazar, another young man also recruited by Villacreces, joined the friary at the same time and became the reformer's companion on his journeys. He and Peter were to fall out eventually over the foundation of new hermitages, Peter being unwilling to exceed the twenty-five hermits Villacreces had always considered a desirable maximum. Lope was to accept the nomination of vicar to Juan de Santa Ana, provincial of Castile, with full jurisdiction over the friaries of Burgos and was to go on to establish some sixteen other hermitages before his death.

In 1414 Peter of Villacreces left for the Council of Constance to obtain approval of the Constitutions of his reform and left Regalado temporarily in charge at La Aguilera. Both Peters were present in 1422 at the provincial chapter of Conventuals at Peñafiel, where Villacreces died. Peter Regalado was called upon to succeed his mentor in the government of the hermitage of La Aguilera. In 1426 he went to Burgos to entreat Lope not to abandon the Villacrecian reforms. In fact Lope was not to do so in essentials, as his *Testamento* confirms.

Peter Regalado was neither a founder nor a reformer, nor a man of ideas. He was an ascetic and a contemplative, content to have found in the Villacrecian reform all that corresponded to his desire for holiness. His penances and poverty were extreme, but his care for the brethren and his love and generosity to the poor were proverbial. His affectionate nature expressed itself in the so-called gift of tears, while his burning love for God was manifested even outwardly. It was said of him, without any malice, that he accomplished little apart from the miracles he worked on the banks of the Duero.

In 1427 he was present at the *Concordia* of Medina del Campo, a meeting at which the followers of Villacreces decided to remain associated with the Conventuals. In 1442 he was elected vicar of the Villacrecians, the third successor of the founder. After his death the movement lost some of its dynamism, though it was to surface again at the end of the century. Indeed, the general chapters held in the sixteenth century and up to the first half of the seventeenth consistently attempted to conserve the current of fervour that the Villacrecian movement had set in motion. By 1642 one house of recollection had become obligatory for every province. In Spain it reached its high point in the Alcantarine reform, which in its turn was to produce its own group of friaries within the larger Franciscan family.

Some of the writings issuing from the Villacrecian reform have been attributed to Peter Regalado but could equally well have been the work of Villacreces himself or of Lope Salinas. The Prologue only to Vilacreces' *Memoriale religionis* —some fifteen lines—is said to be certainly by Peter Regalado; some of his letters survive.

Probably sensing that he had not long to live, Regalado left for Fresneda in Burgos in 1456 to ask Lope to accept the vicariate of the Villacrecians, but he failed to win his acceptance. Regalado died at La Aguilera on 30 March 1456 in his sixty-sixth year. As so many miracles were reported after his death it was decided to transfer his relics to the church. This was done thirty-six years later, when his body was found to be incorrupt. He was canonized by Benedict XIV in 1746. He appears in Spanish and Italian paintings distributing bread to the poor while directing their attention to a crucifix.

AA.SS., Mar., 3, pp. 850-70; Léon, 2, pp. 150-9; *Dict.Sp.*, 3, 542-3; 12, 1657-8; *Bibl.SS.*, 10, 861-4. On the Alcantarine reform, see St Peter of Alcántara, 19 Oct.

Bd Amadeus of Savoy (1435-72)

Amadeus was born at Thonon in 1435, the son of Duke Louis I of Savoy and Anne of Cyprus and the grandson of the antipope Felix V, also known as Amadeus of Savoy. While still an infant he was engaged to Yolande, daughter of Charles I of France. He grew up to be a handsome man but subject to fits of epilepsy. These he accepted as a corrective to the inevitable subservience of his father's courtiers and an opportunity to live close to God. Daily Mass and the time spent in prayer were his source of strength.

His marriage took place in 1452, and the couple retired to the comparative quiet of the province of Brescia, the portion assigned to him together with the governorship of Piedmont. His brother Philip so resented this that he was prepared to take up arms against him and was imprisoned by their father. On the latter's death, Amadeus immediately procured Philip's release, arranging for his marriage to Margaret, daughter of Charles, duke of Bourbon. He made over the territory of Brescia to him as well and in the end won him over by kindness.

Amadeus had been provoked by the Sforzas of Milan also. When Duke Francis of Milan died and his son, Galeazzo, who was in France at the time, tried to pass incognito through Savoy in order to return to Italy and was arrested, Amadeus immediately had him released and provided with an escort. Galeazzo was not grateful for the favour; he even insolently broke the treaty his father had agreed with Amadeus. Philip was all for going to war with him, but Amadeus found another solution: he gave him his sister Bona in marriage.

When it came to defending Christendom against the Turkish threat, Amadeus acted without hesitation, conscripting an army for the defence of the Peloponnese. He was one of the first to respond to Pius II's invitation to an assembly of princes to deal with the danger and pledged soldiers, arms, and money. However, his immediate concerns were always for the poor at hand. When an ambassador boasted of the packs of hounds and different breeds of dogs kept by his master, the duke led him to a terrace outside the palace furnished with tables at which the poor of the city were fed. "These are my packs and my hunting-dogs. It is with the help of these poor people that I chase after virtue and hunt for the kingdom of heaven." The ambassador wondered how many of them were vicious and undeserving, idlers and hypocrites. Amadeus answered, "I will not judge them too severely in case God should judge me severely."

Although his generosity was unlimited, the exchequer was never strained. Through careful administration he had in fact liquidated the debts incurred by his predecessors. His own life was extremely austere. Far from allowing himself any relaxations on account of his poor health, he let it be known that he was obliged to fast on account of it. As his weakness increased, he handed over the administration of the duchy to his wife, Yolande, in 1469, but his subjects rose in revolt, and he himself was imprisoned until his brother-in-law, Louis IX of France, obtained his freedom.

When he realized that he was near death he confided the care of his children to his wife and uttered a last admonition in their presence and that of his ministers, "Be just. Love the poor and the Lord will grant peace to the whole length of the land." He died on 30 March 1472 and was beatified in 1677.

AA.SS., Mar., 3, pp. 871-91; J. F. Gonthier, *Oeuvres historiques*, 3 (n.d.), pp. 95-121; E. Fedelini, *Les Bienheureux de la Maison de Savoie* (1925).

St Antony Daveluy and Companions, *Martyrs* (1866)

Antoine Daveluy was born on 16 March 1818 in Amiens. He joined the *Missions Etrangères de Paris* in 1843 and arrived in Macao in 1844. Bishop Ferréol persuaded him to accompany him and another Korean priest to Korea. Two years later Antony began pastoral work there, and in 1856 Bishop Berneux (8 Mar.), successor to Bishop Ferréol, appointed him coadjutor bishop. In addition to his pastoral work he compiled a Korean-French dictionary and wrote the history of Catholicism in Korea. After the martyrdom of Bishop Berneux, Bishop Daveluy succeeded him as the fifth vicar apostolic of Korea but was to remain such only for a period of twenty-three days. Bishop Daveluy and his assistant Luke Hwang Sok-tu were arrested on 11 March 1866. The two were imprisoned together with another priest, Peter Aumaître, tortured, and interrogated.

Pierre Aumaître was born on 8 April 1837 in Angoulême. He entered the seminary of the *Missions Etrangères de Paris* in 1857 and was ordained in 1862. He arrived in Korea in 1863 and, after learning the language, worked in Naep'o, where he was much loved by the Catholic population. As the persecution broke he encouraged his people to bear public witness to the faith. He himself went to the village where Bishop Daveluy lived and gave himself up to the police. After severe torture he died at the age of twenty-nine.

Martin Luc Huin was born in Guyonville on 20 October 1836. He was ordained priest in his own diocese but joined the *Missions Etrangères de Paris* in 1863. He arrived in Korea in 1865, together with Simon de Bretennières, Bernard Beaulieu, and Pierre Dorie (8 Mar.), but went on to his own mission field in Sekori, Haptok. Before his martyrdom he lamented, "I am sorry to die, not because I am still young nor because it will be a horrible death, but because I have done nothing for the salvation of my beloved Koreans." He was thirty.

Joseph Tjyang Tjyon Keni was born in 1802 of a rich family in Suwon. When he was twenty-six, he and his family were baptized by Fr Pacificus Yu Pang-je, a Chinese priest. In recognition of his fidelity he was appointed a catechist. When the question of a seminary in Paeron was mooted, Joseph offered his own house for the purpose and himself performed the duties of caretaker for eleven years. He was arrested with the missionaries in March 1866, but Fr Pourthié, the rector, obtained his release. The catechist returned to Paeron disconsolate. Five days later the police arrested him and sent him to the governor of Chech'on. Joseph said that he was indeed the owner of the seminary building. The governor would have liked to spare him and tried to persuade him to apostasize, but Joseph remained firm. He was sent to Seoul and tortured. He was sixty-four.

Luke Hoang Syek-tou was born at Yonp'ung in 1811, the only son of a wealthy noble family. On his way to Seoul to sit his final exams he met a Catholic who spoke to him about the faith. The boy was touched and took some Catholic books away to read. He immediately returned home and told his father that he had already passed the exam, for which he was severely whipped. However, he and his wife became Catholics. His father threatened him with death, so Luke pretended to be dumb for over two years. Worn down by his mute resistance, the family decided to investigate the Catholic faith and were converted. On his father's death he was nevertheless dispossessed. He was appointed a catechist and also taught Chinese literature. He co-authored books with Bishop Berneux and was later assistant also to Bishop Daveluy, with whom he was arrested. He was martyred at the age of fifty-four.

These five martyrs were beheaded, at their own request, on Good Friday, 30 March 1866. They were beatified in 1968 and canonized among the 103 Martyrs of Korea by Pope John Paul II in Seoul in 1984.

M.S.K. See 20 Sept. for a general treatment of the martyrs of Korea.

St Leonard Murialdo, *Founder* (1828-1900)

It is remarkable that SS John Bosco (31 Jan.) and Leonard Murialdo, so very alike in their pastoral approach, should have lived in the same town of Turin at roughly the same period of time and devoted themselves to similar work among the neglected young boys of the town.

Leonardo Murialdo was born in Turin in 1828, of a well-to-do family. His father died while he was still young. His mother, conscious of the gap this would leave in the boy's life, promised to make it up to him by the strength of her own affection. And indeed his happy family life may have been the inspiration for his pastoral work among boys, to whom he would be both father and mother, providing them with the love and security and the religious upbringing that he himself had known.

He was educated at home and with the Scolopians at Savona. A sermon on hell led him to decide to become a priest. He studied at the university of Turin, obtaining a doctorate in 1850, and was ordained in 1851. He immediately gave himself to pastoral work while keeping in touch with Don Cafasso (St Joseph; 23 June), who had firmly guided Don Bosco away from missionary work to the apostolate of the young, and with Don Bosco himself. His first "case" was a chimney-sweep, whom he brought home to his attic, soon to become a dormitory for his new family. His real family was commandeered to deal with the linen! Don Bosco asked him to take over the Oratory of San Luigi in Turin, which he agreed to do. He kept an open door. One day a widower arrived and told him that he was unemployed and could no longer feed his two sons, whom he handed over to the priest. A mother with a terminal illness went to him and left her children in his care. "I shall soon be dead," she told him, "and only you will save these children."

In 1865 he went to France to spend a year at the seminary of Saint-Sulpice in Paris, then went on to visit the Netherlands. At this time he was deeply concerned for young workers, whom he found everywhere required to do heavy work beyond their strength. On his return to Turin he took up the directorship of the *Collegio Artigianelli*, a school set up to provide a general Christian education as well as proficiency in some trade, and this made it possible for him to work directly and on a long-term basis for the good of young workers. He held the post for thirty-four years, facing enormous difficulties to provide for the Christian and technical formation of the young in the many workshops he had set up. He envisaged the needs of the family as a whole, so he established schools, residential houses for the young, workshops, farms, agricultural colleges, and other enterprises.

Murialdo was a pioneer of education specially designed for young workers. Very early on he had worked out educational, professional, community, and legislative programmes to instruct, prepare, and impart to the new industrial populace a feeling of solidarity, which modern society would later incorporate in its own agenda. He wished to make the unorganized, poor, and defenceless masses, already incited by the revolutionary voices of contemporary class conflict, into a new people aware of its rights, taking a stand freely and responsibly, as required by any modern democratic organization, on the progressive development of social justice. In Turin his labour exchange was the first to offer jobs to the unemployed, and already in 1869 he was petitioning the government of the day to enact protective legislation for women and children working in factories. He was the first to try to organize the workers and to establish Catholic unions (1871). He belonged to the *Opera dei Congressi*, which worked for the re-Christianization of society and the freedom of the Church. At its sixth Congress (1883) he achieved a national federation of companies to raise the standard of the press and launched the monthly *La Buona Stampa*.

The Society of St Joseph, later the Congregation of St Joseph (Giuseppini del Murialdo), was established in 1873 to carry on the educational work he had begun: it was intended "to educate young people without means, orphans, abandoned children, or those in need of rehabilitation, through religious practice, general and technical schooling." It soon spread to Venice, Oderzo, Vicenza, Modena, and elsewhere. At present there are about 850 members, half of them priests, in about a hundred houses throughout Italy and the world. The Murialdine Sisters, who work with them, are volunteers dedicated to the different tasks of ministry but especially to helping and educating the children of the working-class poor.

There was nothing in the life of St Leonard that expressed outwardly his intense inner life, nor in his seemingly ordinary though dedicated life any extraordinary happenings that would have marked him out as an especially charismatic type of the man of God. Rather, he brought his whole power of mind and heart to bear on the needs of the poor and on the means he might employ for an amelioration of their condition in the present and in the future through the development, under grace, of their human potential.

Illness in 1877 threatened to bring everything to an end, but Don Bosco visited Fr Murialdo at the time and told him that he had more years of work before him. He died on 30 March 1900 and was canonized by Pope Paul VI on 3 May 1970. His Congregation commemorates him on 18 May.

There is nothing available in English, but see *N.C.E.*, 10, p. 83. In Italian: G. Vercellono, *Vita e Spiritu del Servo di Dio Teologo L. Murialdo* (1941); F. Bea, *Beato L. Murialdo* (1963); J. Cottino, *Il beato L. Murialdo* (1963); A. Marengo, *Contributi per uno Studio su L. Murialdo Educatore* (1964); E. Reffo, *Il Teologo L. Murialdo* (1964); *N.S.B.* 1, pp. 33-5.

Bd Restituta Kafka, *Martyr* (1894-1943)

Helene Kafka was born on 1 May 1894 in Brno in Moravia (then part of the Austro-Hungarian Empire, now in the Czech Republic). She was the sixth of seven children born to Anton Kafka, a Czech shoemaker, and his wife, Marie. Both came from Catholic families; Anton had met his wife, who was also Czech, while a guest-worker in Vienna. They were married in St Leopold's Church in Vienna in 1887 but in 1892 returned to Brno, and Helene was baptized in the Church of the Assumption there on 13 May 1894.

Two years later the family emigrated permanently to Vienna and settled in the working-class Brigittenau district, where thousands of Czech immigrants lived. Helene was an average pupil at the local primary school, made her First Communion at St Brigitta's at the age of eleven, then moved to the three-year middle school for girls, known as The Guardian Angel School because it had a large statue of a guardian angel above the entrance. She was cured of a bad stutter by the drastic treatment of being forbidden by the headmistress to say a word for three months.

She left school at the age of fifteen and took various jobs as a maid; she later recalled that at about this time she decided to join a nursing Order "to help those who are suffering and desperately in need of help." In 1913 a new hospital was opened in the Lainz district of Vienna, and the Hartmann Sisters, or Sisters of Christian Charity, founded in Vienna in 1857 (they have no official name in English), were asked to provide the nursing staff. Helene started work as an unskilled general assistant at the new hospital and so could observe the nursing Sisters at close hand.

When she came home one evening she asked her parents for their permission to join the Order. For some reason, they refused. Her mother was the more vehemently opposed and tried to persuade her to change her mind, but when Helene was nineteen and still a minor she ran away from home to the Hartmann motherhouse. Not long after this her parents accepted the situation and gave their consent to her joining the Order. They were, however, unable to provide the required dowry, so the sister superior applied to the archdiocese for a bequest. Helene became a novice on 23 October 1915, taking the names Maria Restituta, after St Restituta of Sora (formerly 27 May), who was beheaded for her faith under Emperor Aurelian (270-5) in about 272 and originally buried in the catacombs.

She was still a novice when World War I broke out in 1914. With casualties pouring in from the front lines, she soon started work in the operating theatre. After the war, in May 1919, a request for a theatre sister came from the district hospital in Mödling, a market town to the south of Vienna. The surgeon there, though skilled, was known to be nervous, moody, and difficult to work with. Sr Restituta volunteered for the post and was soon in charge of the operating theatre there, becoming a first-class theatre Sister and anaesthetist.

She soon became known as Sr "Resoluta" because, small and round as she was—she weighed all of fourteen stone (196 lbs or 90 kgs) in peace time—it was not wise to contradict her once her mind was made up. But she was also lovable and caring, with a great sense of humour. After a heavy day's work she would go round to her local hostelry and order "a goulash and a pint of my usual"—her favourite brand of beer.

Soon after the *Anschluss* of 1938 all religious activity in hospital wards was forbidden, but Sr Restituta continued to pray with the dying and, whenever possible, ensured that they received the last rites in secret. Knowing that he could not carry on without her, the surgeon, Dr Lambert Stumfohl, though a fanatical Nazi, dared not report this. But when she put up crucifixes in each of the rooms of a new ward and was found making copies of an anti-Nazi ditty, he called the *Gestapo*. A group of *SS* stormtroopers came for her on 18 February 1942, Ash Wednesday. After over a year in prison, where she gave most of her scant rations to to others who needed them more, saving the life of a pregnant woman and her baby by doing so, she was sentenced to death on the orders of Hitler's secretary, Martin Bormann, who insisted on making an example of her. On 30 March 1943, weighing half what she had, she was sent to the guillotine, her hands tied behind her back and wearing only a paper shirt. The prison chaplain, Fr Ivanek, C.Ss.R., who was allowed to accompany her to the door of the death chamber and whom she asked to make the sign of the cross on her forehead as she walked to her death, heard a "dull thud" as the blade fell.

Sr Restituta was the only nun in the German territories of the Third Reich to be beheaded by the Nazis. For fear that she would be revered as a martyr, the Nazis refused to release her body, which was thrown into a mass grave. For many years there was opposition to her beatification in Austria, but it was finally possible to start the process, and her story became widely known. At the beatification ceremony, which took place in Vienna on 20 June 1998, a small piece of her habit, instead of the customary relics, lay in the glass reliquary presented to Pope John Paul II. It was all that could be found of her earthly remains.

Today the Mödling district hospital in which she worked has a large maternity ward. In 1995 the street on which the hospital stands was re-named "Sr Restituta Street," so all babies born in the hospital carry her name on their birth certificates.

The principal sources are Hilda Daurer, S.F.C.C., and Edith Beinhauer, S.F.C.C. (the promoter of her cause), *Schwester Maria Restituta Kafka. Märtyrin aus dem Widerstand. Dokumentation* (1998), with a preface by Cardinal Christoph Schönborn of Vienna; Antonio Sagardoy, O.C.D., *Gelegen und Ungelegen. Die Lebenshingabe von Sr Restituta* (1996). There have been several exhibitions devoted to her in Vienna museums.

   The Hartmann Sisters (S.F.C.C., from their Latin name, *Sorores Francescanae a Caritate Christiana*) have three houses in Austria and also five in Argentina, one in Paraguay, and one in Brazil. In German their full title is *Kongregation der Barmherzigen Schwestern vom des 3ten Orden des Heiligen Franziskus, gennant "von der christlichen Liebe."*

R.M.

St Rieul, bishop of Senlis (? fourth century)
St Zosimus, bishop of Syracuse (seventh century)

31

St Stephen of Mar Saba (794)

The semi-eremitical *laura* of Mar Saba was the most famous of all the monasteries in Palestine, according to Cyril of Scythopolis. Founded by St Sabas (5 Dec.) in the fifth century, it was first and foremost a place of prayer and penance, but it also had an important role to play in the theological controversies of the day. In the time of Stephen many of the fiercer controversies had been left behind, but that of the legitimacy of sacred images preoccupied the mind of his uncle, St John Damascene (4 Dec.). However, no breath of controversy stirs the pages of the Life of St Stephen as set down by his disciple Leontius, nor is there the slightest hint of the excellence in many branches of learning and hymnography that characterized the monastery in his time.

John had abandoned his career in Damascus and entered Mar Saba in 735, accompanied by his adopted brother, Cosmas, and his nephew, Stephen, who was ten years old at the time. Given the general reluctance of Palestinian hermits to admit those whom they referred to as the unbearded, it is strange that Stephen was received at so early an age, but since he spent fifteen years under his uncle's tutelage the arrangement may have been a special one. John was one of the most learned men of his day and would have given his nephew a thorough grounding in scripture, the writings of the Fathers, and monastic principles. Leontius, Stephen's biographer, describes him in his turn generously dispensing his accumulated wisdom to all those who came to see him. John died in 749, and Stephen, then twenty-four, began an eight-year period of service to the community. He was guestmaster, cantor, dispenser, and special guestmaster to those received in the *igumen's* quarters.

However, Stephen desired the eremitical life. He approached the *igumen* Martyrios and told him that for eight years he had wanted to cut himself off completely but that till then God had not clearly responded to this desire. He begged Martyrios to tell him in the grace of the Holy Spirit whether or not he should become a hermit. Martyrios hesitated, suggesting a compromise: Stephen might lead an eremitical life, but he should also be available to those who needed counsel; he added prophetically that there might not be any outstanding hermits after him. Did he foresee that twenty of the community would be massacred by the Arabs two years after Stephen's death (Martyrs of Mar Saba, 19 Mar.)? In any case Stephen accepted Martyrios' decision with complete equanimity. Martyrios himself died, greatly mourned by the monks, who saw no one left to equal him in stature. To combat this very natural reaction, providence seemed to wish to point a finger in Stephen's direction. When a certain monk was lamenting that Stephen could not be compared with Martyrios, he saw Stephen's cell flooded with light. Since no fire was found, the phenomenon was taken to indicate divine approval.

Although Leontius gives no dates or details, he tells us that Stephen had been ordained a priest. He goes on to relate that the holy monk Christopher was eager to have Stephen celebrate the liturgy in his cell. The sequence of events is not clear, but we may assume that it was Christopher who witnessed Stephen's transfiguration during a celebration on the feast of the Exaltation of the Holy Cross.

> As he lifted up the consecrated elements, proclaiming, "Holy things to the holy," the grace of the Lord shone out from him and the Holy Spirit descended on him, filling the whole oratory with an infinite splendour. Stephen's whole body radiated light so that he felt himself rendered wondrously pure and undefiled, the heavens and the whole world becoming like the splendour of the sun. As the light persisted and he was transformed into something different with no sign of his previous self, he was seized with fear. . . . He humbled himself in spirit, remembering that he had been fashioned from the dust of the earth. . . . The holy man was afraid, I think, of the danger of vainglory, especially if he should be more highly regarded than others. However, divine providence did not permit this to happen. God's gifts are without recall; while he increases good-will in a person and gives him wings that he may fly, like a good master concerned for that person's salvation, he wills him to experience feelings of dread also. Seized then with great awe, the blessed man prayed earnestly and at length to be spared: "Lord, do not be angry with me but restrain the flood of your grace as it exceeds my strength. Mercifully grant me only this: when I pray for my fellow-men, heal them and build them up. . . . Hold back your many gifts and bestow them rather in the blessed life to come. Give me only what is needful here at the moment of the the offering of the Mysteries." From then on whatever he asked between the offering and the showing of the Mysteries was immediately granted, whether a revelation of something hidden, an interior inspiration, a vision, or knowledge of the future. These he would speak of when it was fitting or necessary to do so.

From the age of thirty-two to thirty-seven, Stephen spent some years of relative eremitism, as perhaps envisaged by Martyrios, Monday to Friday being given to solitary prayer, while Saturdays and Sundays were free for seeing others. Leontius notes the very human touch: Stephen pinned a notice on his cell-door, "Forgive me, Fathers, in the name of the Lord, but please do not disturb me except on Saturdays or Sundays." At the age of thirty-seven he went into total solitude for some fifteen years, three times going out into the desert around the Dead Sea to observe Lent. When he was fifty-two he returned to a more relative form of eremitism and accepted disciples. This may be the period during which he earned the epithet of *Wonder-worker*. He had an infinite compassion for his fellow-men and a seemingly preternatural gift for saving others in difficulty, whether spiritual or material. He knew of those lost in the desert, of nuns pursued by rapists, of runaway and fallen monks. He was aware of what was going on in the Great *Laura*, as he was of the unworthy ambitions of the monk Theodore and his friend, Basil. He cured some sick from afar and some at the celebration of the liturgy. His admirer, Christopher, was obsessed by an irrational desire to go and see the patriarch, who had been taken captive to Persia, and he consulted Stephen. The hermit told him that he would be better advised to remain in his cell and warned him that should he insist on going, he would never in fact return, for death would overtake him in Persia, as indeed it did.

Stephen's warm-hearted love became especially apparent in his relationship with his disciples. Leontius, who was one of these during the last four years of the hermit's life, was well placed to witness to his Christ-like willingness to suffer in place of others. Leontius himself had been buffeted by temptations of every sort, so much so that in his despair he had thought of taking his own life. All his penances and tears had failed to bring him relief. He had gone to Stephen but, overcome with shame, could not even talk about his problems. The hermit offered to keep vigil for him that same night, and Leontius afterwards confessed that he could not even remember what the terrible temptations had been.

Stephen received many: monks of the Great *Laura* as well as those from other monasteries, his own disciples, and laity from all parts. He cured sicknesses of the body and sicknesses of the soul. His mere presence was an instrument of grace and repentance, but he would have no praise of himself: "I am no more than a dead, dry stick, sterile and full of bitterness." He spoke out of his familiarity with the scriptures and the Fathers but also from his own infused knowledge. His whole life might be summed up in his words: "To know the Lord is the principle of good. Abide in this knowledge and you will draw close to God. There is nothing of value in life except the soul's gain, but the soul's gain is to be found only in the love of God."

Stephen's compassion was not restricted to his fellow-men. With his own hand he fed the starlings, ravens, doves, and gazelles. The birds alighted on his shoulders, his hands, his knees. He would offer them food, let them fight over it, and then, when they had had their fill, bid them be off. He was particularly concerned about the black worms to be found on the ground of the hermitage. He would painstakingly collect them and put them in a safe place. "He often argued with us," says Leontius, "forbidding us to kill the worms by carelessly walking on them outside the hermitage in the dark. 'Do you not realize that if a person acts without compassion toward irrational nature, he will do the same toward his neighbour?'" Stephen spent Holy Week and the Triduum of 794 apparently in good health, but when asked in the middle of the week whether he would be celebrating the liturgy he told the inquiring Brother that it would be his last. Three days before Low Sunday he fell ill. As he lay dying, the Brothers came to receive his last blessing. Some stayed to accompany him to his final moments, some went away happy to be blessed by him, some he dismissed with uncompromising sternness: "Your life is evil even though it may not appear so outwardly." He died on the Monday of Low Week, 30 March. At the end of his biography Leontius returns to the traits he most valued in the old man: "Whatever help, spiritual or material he was asked to give, he gave. He received and honoured all with the same kindness, even unbelievers. He possessed nothing and lacked nothing. In total poverty he possessed all things."

Translations above from the Latin Life in *AA.SS.*, July, 3, pp. 497-584; *Eastern Churches Review*, 2, 4; *Bibl.SS.*, 12, 14-15. See *Anal.Boll.* 77 (1959), pp. 332-69, for an early Life in Arabic.

St Secundus, *Martyr* (? 119)

The late Acts of Secundus make him a deeply religious man, well known in Asti in the Piedmontese region of Italy, but they associate him with figures of dubious historicity. So they tell that he learned about the Christian faith from St Calocerus, whom he used to visit in prison. Hearing that Sapricius, whom the emperor Hadrian had sent to replace the prefect Antiochus, had arrived in Asti, he went to see him and asked for what crime Calocerus had been imprisoned. Sapricius explained that he persuaded people to despise the gods, adding moreover that he had learned that there was one Marcianus, a Christian, in Tortona and he wished to go there. Secundus asked to accompany him, and Sapricius agreed. When Calocerus heard this he predicted that Secundus would receive Baptism and return to Asti, where he would be martyred. On arriving at Tortona, Secundus was met by Martinianus, the bishop, who said the same thing.

Leaving Sapricius in Tortona, Secundus went to Milan, where he met SS Faustinus and Jovita. Faustinus baptized him and gave him the body of the Lord to consume and also to take with him to Marcianus and Calocerus as a sign that he had indeed been baptized. On his return to Tortona Secundus sought out Marcianus in prison and gave him the sacrament, begging prayers for himself. The next day Marcianus was summoned to appear before Sapricius and commanded to sacrifice to the gods or be killed by the sword. He refused, was taken out of the city, and was beheaded.

To his surprise, Sapricius learned that Secundus had buried the body of Marcianus. He summoned Secundus, who declined to see him, saying that the prefect had the blood of a just and innocent man on his hands. Three times Sapricius sent for him and three times Secundus refused. Finally Secundus was put in prison, but the next day he was obliged to appear before the prefect; he firmly acknowledged that he was a Christian. Sapricius pleaded with him but to no avail, had him tortured, and sent him back to jail. The story then takes off into the realm of the marvellous, saying that the next day the prison was found to be still shut but there was no sign of Secundus. Angry now, Sapricius gave orders to return to Asti. He would take it out on Calocerus, whom he knew he had in his hands. When his servants went to the prison to summon Calocerus, they were delighted to find Secundus with him. Both refused to sacrifice; Calocerus was beaten and sent back to prison, but Secundus was immediately taken outside the city walls and beheaded.

St Secundus is the patron saint of the town of Asti, where his relics are kept.

AA.SS., Mar., 3, pp. 792-807. The *acta* of St Secundus, collated by the Bollandists from four codices, may be a late composition, but there is no doubt that St Secundus suffered for the Faith and was venerated in Asti from earliest times.

St Guy of Pomposa, *Abbot* (1046)

Guy, or Guido (also called Guion, Wido, Witen, and Wit), was born near Ravenna. His parents, Alberto and Merocia, doted on their first-born. They dressed him in fine clothes, gave him the best education available, and when he reached young manhood selected a bride for him. Respectful as he was toward his parents, Guy, however, had other ideas. He put his dilemma to his father, asking him to be the judge: Faced with two women, one of whom he must take as his wife, which should he choose—the more beautiful but more demanding woman for whose intimacy he must pay a high price or the less beautiful woman whose intimacies were readily available to ensnare and entangle him? When his father told him to choose the better and more beautiful of the two, Guy took this as a command to follow the gospel. He sold his expensive clothes and gave the money to the poor, then set out for Rome, dressed in rags. There he received the tonsure and planned to go on to Jerusalem but was inspired to return to Ravenna and submit to the guidance of Martin the hermit, who lived on a little island in the Po. They remained for three years together, and then Martin sent him to the abbey of Pomposa, near Ferrara, to learn the discipline of community life. After Guy had held many posts, Martin put him in charge of the abbey of St Severus, but when the abbot of Pomposa left to take up the eremitical life and John, his successor, died, Martin wished Guy to succeed John as abbot of Pomposa.

There was such an influx of vocations, among whom were his father and brother, that Guy had the monastery enlarged. He delegated to others responsibility for the practical aspects of life, while he concentrated on the spiritual direction of the community. It was at his request that St Peter Damian (23 Feb.) spent two years at Pomposa teaching sacred scripture. Damian's *De perfectione monachorum* was dedicated to Guy. From time to time Guy himself withdrew to a cell about three miles from the abbey where he fasted and prayed.

Despite his blameless life Guy was not in favour with Heribert, the archbishop of Ravenna, who determined to destroy the monastery. Warned of an impending attack, he and the community fasted and prayed for three days. When Heribert arrived at the monastery gates with his soldiers, Guy greeted him courteously and led him into the church. Heribert was so touched by the abbot's humility and deference that he begged his pardon for the harm he had planned to inflict and promised him his protection for the future.

Another secular figure caused as much turmoil by his esteem for Guy. The emperor Henry III, having arrived in Italy, wished to consult the abbot of whose sanctity he had heard so much. Guy, who had by then retired to a hermitage, obeyed with great reluctance. He took leave of the community, telling them he would see them no more, and set off. He fell ill on arriving at Borgo San Donnino near Parma and died three days later. The emperor had the body taken to the church of St John the Evangelist at Speyer.

AA.SS., Mar., 3, pp. 905-13.

Bd Bonaventure of Forli (1491)

Bonaventure Tornielli was born at Forli of a good family. He entered the Order of Servites when he was thirty-seven, his extraordinary fervour making up for the late start. After his ordination he spent a year in solitude in order to prepare for an apostolic life and then began to preach with eloquence and success. Pope Sixtus IV commissioned him to undertake a mission throughout the Papal States, and his sermons brought many back to a practice of the Faith.

He was elected vicar general of his Order in 1488 and showed both charity and administrative ability in this office. He continued his missionary work and had just finished a Lenten retreat in Udine when he died, worn out by work. Eventually his relics were taken to Venice, where his cult flourished.

F. Cornelius, *Ecclesiae Venetae*, 2, pp. 34-51, and *A.A.S.* 3 (1911), pp. 659-60, for the confirmation of his cult in 1911.

R.M.

St Benjamin, deacon, martyr at Argos in Persia (*c.* 420)

St Abdas and companions, martyrs in Persia (*c.* 420)

St Agilulf, bishop of Cologne (752)

St Blaise, abbot in Constantinople (911)

Bd Jane of Toulouse, anchoress (thirteenth/fourteenth century)

(Names are listed for those saints and blessed who have entries in the main body of the text. Those listed in the RM paragraph at the end of each day are omitted.)

Consultant Editors

DAVID HUGH FARMER. Former Reader in history at the University of Reading. Author of *St Hugh of Lincoln* and other biographical studies of saints. Author of *The Oxford Dictionary of Saints*. General consultant editor.

REV. PHILIP CARAMAN, S.J. Author of numerous biographies of saints and chief promoter of the cause of the Forty English Martyrs (canonized in 1970). Consultant on English Martyrs.

JOHN HARWOOD. Librarian of the Missionary Institute in London and course lecturer on the Orthodox churches. Consultant on Eastern and Orthodox saints.

DOM ERIC HOLLAS, O.S.B. Monk of St John's Abbey, Collegeville, Minnesota, and director of the Hill Monastic Manuscript Library in Collegeville, where he also teaches theology at St John's University. General consultant, U.S.A.

PROF. KATHLEEN JONES. Emeritus Professor of Social Policy at the University of York. Author of many books and articles on social policy and mental illness. Honorary Fellow of the Royal College of Psychiatrists. Translator of *The Poems of St John of the Cross* (1993). Consultant on social history and abnormal behaviour.

DOM DANIEL REES, O.S.B. Monk of Downside Abbey and librarian of the monastery library. Bibliographical consultant.

DR RICHARD SHARPE. Reader in diplomatic history at the University of Oxford. Author of *Medieval Irish Saints' Lives* (1991), *Adomnán of Iona. Life of St Columba* (1995), and numerous articles on Celtic saints. Consultant on this subject.

REV. AYLWARD SHORTER, W.F. Long experience of African Missions and author of many books on the subject. Former President of Missionary Institute, London, now Principal of Tangaza College, Nairobi. Consultant on missionary saints.

DOM ALBERIC STACPOOLE, O.S.B. Monk of Ampleforth Abbey. Fellow of the Royal Historical Society. Secretary of the Ecumenical Society of Our Lady. Editor of several works, including *Vatican II by Those Who Were There* (1985). Engaged on a study of St Anslem. Consultant on feasts of Our Lady.

DOM HENRY WANSBROUGH, O.S.B. Monk of Ampleforth Abbey, currently Master of St Benet's Hall, Oxford. Member of the Pontifical Biblical Commission. Author of numerous works on scripture and Editor of the *New Jerusalem Bible* (1985). Consultant on New Testament saints.

SR BENEDICTA WARD. Anglican religious. Lecturer at Oxford Institute of Medieval History. Author of numerous works on hagiography, spirituality, and mysticism. Consultant on Middle Ages and age of Bede.